Taming Your Dragon

Addressing Your Technical Debt

Dr. Andrew Richard Brown

apress®

Taming Your Dragon: Addressing Your Technical Debt

Dr. Andrew Richard Brown
England, UK

ISBN-13 (pbk): 979-8-8688-0263-8 ISBN-13 (electronic): 979-8-8688-0264-5
https://doi.org/10.1007/979-8-8688-0264-5

Copyright © 2024 by Dr. Andrew Richard Brown

This work is subject to copyright. All rights are reserved by the Publisher, whether the whole or part of the material is concerned, specifically the rights of translation, reprinting, reuse of illustrations, recitation, broadcasting, reproduction on microfilms or in any other physical way, and transmission or information storage and retrieval, electronic adaptation, computer software, or by similar or dissimilar methodology now known or hereafter developed.

Trademarked names, logos, and images may appear in this book. Rather than use a trademark symbol with every occurrence of a trademarked name, logo, or image we use the names, logos, and images only in an editorial fashion and to the benefit of the trademark owner, with no intention of infringement of the trademark.

The use in this publication of trade names, trademarks, service marks, and similar terms, even if they are not identified as such, is not to be taken as an expression of opinion as to whether or not they are subject to proprietary rights.

While the advice and information in this book are believed to be true and accurate at the date of publication, neither the authors nor the editors nor the publisher can accept any legal responsibility for any errors or omissions that may be made. The publisher makes no warranty, express or implied, with respect to the material contained herein.

Managing Director, Apress Media LLC: Welmoed Spahr
Acquisitions Editor: Shiva Ramachandran
Development Editor: James Markham
Coordinating Editor: Jessica Vakili

Cover image designed by eStudioCalamar

Distributed to the book trade worldwide by Apress Media, LLC, 1 New York Plaza, New York, NY 10004, U.S.A. Phone 1-800-SPRINGER, fax (201) 348-4505, e-mail orders-ny@springer-sbm.com, or visit www.springeronline.com. Apress Media, LLC is a California LLC and the sole member (owner) is Springer Science + Business Media Finance Inc (SSBM Finance Inc). SSBM Finance Inc is a **Delaware** corporation.

For information on translations, please e-mail booktranslations@springernature.com; for reprint, paperback, or audio rights, please e-mail bookpermissions@springernature.com.

Apress titles may be purchased in bulk for academic, corporate, or promotional use. eBook versions and licenses are also available for most titles. For more information, reference our Print and eBook Bulk Sales web page at http://www.apress.com/bulk-sales.

Any source code or other supplementary material referenced by the author in this book is available to readers on GitHub (https://github.com/Apress). For more detailed information, please visit https://www.apress.com/gp/services/source-code.

If disposing of this product, please recycle the paper

For Kumi, 和田久美

Table of Contents

About the Author xvii

Foreword by Dorothy Graham xix

Acknowledgments xxi

Introduction xxiii

Part I: Exploring Technical Debt 1

Chapter 1: What Is Technical Debt? 3
    Defining Technical Debt 3
        Technical Debt Is Not a Technical Problem 3
        Technical Debt Is a Trade-Off Problem 4
        Technical Debt Is Also a Systems Problem 4
        Technical Debt Is an Economic Problem 5
        Technical Debt Is a Wicked Problem 5
        Technical Debt Is a Broken Analogy 5
    The Technical Debt Onion Model 6
        Technical Layer 7
        Trade-Off Layer 7
        Systems Layer 8
        Economics/Games Theory Layer 8
        Wicked Problems Layer 8
    Is All Technical Debt the Same? 8
        The Technical Debt Quadrant 9
        Interest Rate 10
        Level: Architecture/Code/Other 11

TABLE OF CONTENTS

    Where in the SDLC Was the Debt Created? 11
    What Was the Debt a Trade-Off for? 12

Further Reading 13
Summary 13

Chapter 2: Why You Need to Address Technical Debt 15

Is Technical Debt Really a Problem? 15
How NASA Engineers Designed the Space Shuttle 16
How Technical Debt Killed Netscape Navigator 17
A Tale of Technical Debt at HMV 18
    Additional Cost to Every Software Project 20
    Slows Down Tempo and Delivery 20
    Technical Debt Makes Project Delivery Less Predictable 21
    Estimations, Schedules, and Projections Become Unrealistic 21
    Technical Debt Can Even Prevent a Project Occurring 21
    A Spiral Into Debt: Self-Reinforcing Loops 22

Further Reading 22
Summary 22

Chapter 3: Why Has Technical Debt Proved So Resistant to Solutions? 23

Technical Debt Is Misunderstood 23
We Deal with Technical Debt at the Wrong Place 24
Proximate Causes and Ultimate Causes 25
Technical Debt Is Rarely Urgent 27
Technical Debt Is Not Sexy 28
There Are No Silver Bullets for Technical Debt 28
We *Desperately Want* Technical Debt to Be a Technical Problem 29
Reducing Technical Debt Requires Change Management 29
Further Reading 30
Summary 31

TABLE OF CONTENTS

Part II: Understanding the Technical Debt Problem 33

Chapter 4: The Broken Analogy 35

Johannes Had a Problem 35
Why We Use Analogies 36
The Power of a Good Analogy 37
Characteristics of a Good Analogy 39
Analogy Familiarity/Accuracy Quadrant 40
Analogy Suitability Analysis Tool 41
Ways That Analogies Go Wrong 41
Rethinking Our Technical Debt Analogy 42
Alternative Analogies 44
    The Obesity Problem 44
    Environmental Pollution 46
    Addiction 47
    Friction 50
Other Analogies 51
Analogy Quadrant Analysis 51
Analogy Suitability Analysis Tool 52
Further Reading 53
Summary 54

Chapter 5: Technical Debt As a Trade-Off Problem 55

The Origin of Our Decision-Making Capability 56
Conditions of Our Ancestral Past 57
Decision-Making Occurs in Our Subconscious 57
The Affect Heuristic 58
When Heuristics Fail 59
The Technical Debt Trade-Off Decision 60
Why Smoking Prevention Programs Initially Failed and then Succeeded 62

TABLE OF CONTENTS

Appeal to Emotions Through a Story 65
Precision and Valence 67
    Precision, Valence, and the Challenger Launch Decision 70
Ulysses Contracts 72
Simultaneous Versus Sequential Decisions 73
Other Factors That Influence Decisions 74
    Overdue Projects and Crazy Risk-Taking 74
    Effect of Time Constraints 75
    Hyperbolic Discounting 76
Further Reading 77
Summary 78

Chapter 6: Technical Debt As a Systems Problem 79

The Unhappy CTO 82
What Is a System? 83
The Organization As a System 84
    Crucial Difference Between IT Systems and Social Systems 85
    Conflict Between the Placenta and Y Chromosome 86
Introducing Change: The Prohibition Problem 89
Basics of Systems Dynamics 90
    Stocks and Flows 90
    Variables and Causal Links 91
    Feedback Loop 91
Common Dynamic System Behaviors 91
    Exponential Growth 92
    Balancing Behavior 92
    Growth, then Leveling Off 93
    Overshoot and Collapse 94
Systems, Individuals, and Technical Debt 95
    Individuals Constrained by Role 95
    Overdue Projects and Schedule Recovery 98
    Project Underestimation 99

    Overshoot and Collapse 100

    Policy Resistance 104

Further Reading 105

Summary 106

Chapter 7: Technical Debt As an Economics Problem 109

Benefits of an Economics Point of View 110

Principal-Agent Problem 113

    Potential Solutions 114

Project Phases When the Principal-Agent Problem Leads to Technical Debt 115

    Requirements and Design 115

    Overdue and Behind Schedule Projects 116

The Tragedy of the Commons 117

    Potential Solutions 118

Externalities 118

    "That's Not My Problem!" 119

    Externalities Driven by Organizational Structure 120

    Can Externalities Be Good? The Coase Theorem 120

    Potential Solutions 121

Short-Termism 121

    Short-Termism in Nature 122

    Short-Termism and Technical Debt 122

    Potential Solutions 123

The Tyranny of Small Decisions 123

    Potential Solutions 125

Creeping Normality 125

    Potential Solutions 126

Price of Anarchy 126

    Potential Solutions 128

Moral Hazard 128

    A Technical Debt Register Increases Technical Debt 129

    Potential Solutions 130

TABLE OF CONTENTS

Additional Things You Can Do 130

Further Reading 131

Summary 132

Chapter 8: Technical Debt As a Wicked Problem 133

Wanted: One-Handed Economist! 134

"It's Always a People Problem" 134

Why Study Wicked Problems? 135

Example Wicked Problems 136

Wicked and Tame Problems 137

Characteristics of a Wicked Problem 138

 1. You Cannot Understand the Problem Until *After* You Have Found a Solution 139

 2. Stakeholders Have Radically Different Worldviews 140

 3. How You Understand the Problem Determines What Solution You Try 140

 4. Solutions Are Not True or False, but Better or Worse 141

 5. You Do Not Have a Test of Your Solution 142

 6. Every Solution Is a "One-Shot Attempt" 143

 7. Wicked Problems Are Interconnected with Other Wicked Problems 144

 8. You Have No Way of Knowing When to Stop 145

Social Complexity and Fragmentation 145

Dichotomy of Design 147

Trade-Offs, Systems, Economics, and Wicked Problems 150

Addressing Technical Debt As a Wicked Problem 151

Further Reading 153

Summary 153

Chapter 9: Common Technical Debt Anti-patterns 155

There's a Hole in My Bucket! 155

How Exploring Anti-patterns Helps Us 156

Causal Loop Diagrams 157

List of Anti-patterns 159

Estimation Trap 160

  From Project Overrun to a Short-Term Focus 161
  From Short-Term Focus to Technical Debt Levels 162
  From Level of Technical Debt to Estimation Errors 163
  Estimation Errors: A Complete Picture 164
 Last Race of the Day 165
 Moral Credential Effect 168
 Broken Windows Theory and Learned Helplessness 169
 Goal Culture 170
 Social Loafing 171
 OKRs and the Surrogation Effect 173
  PS General Slocum 174
  OKRs and the Social Contract 175
 Descent into Firefighting 176
 Limited Environments 178
 Prototype into Debt 179
 Further Reading 180
 Summary 181

Chapter 10: Modeling Technical Debt with System Modeling Tools 183
 What You Gain from Dynamic Models 184
 Modeling Tools 185
 Getting Started 186
 Software Projects 189
  Main Workflow 190
 Modeling Technical Debt Creation 192
  Workforce View 194
  Quality and Productivity View 195
  Dashboard View 195
 Run a Simulation 197
 Findings from the Model 199
  Why the Project Was Underestimated 203

TABLE OF CONTENTS

    Effect of Technical Debt on Current Project 204

    Effect of Technical Debt on Subsequent Projects 205

Friction 207

Implications for Projects 208

Social Loafing 210

Considerations when Developing a Simulation Model 212

Further Reading 212

Resources 213

Summary 213

Part III: Tackling Technical Debt 217

Chapter 11: Safely Convincing Everyone 219

Dr Semmelweis 220

Lessons from Dr Semmelweis 223

The True Lesson from Dr Semmelweis 224

What Could Dr Semmelweis Have Done Differently? 225

    Avoid Alienating Colleagues 226

    Better Communications 227

    Recognize the Sensitivity of Gentlemen Doctors 228

    Build a Coalition of Supporters 228

    Wait for an Opportune Moment 229

    Engage a Different Community 229

First Seek to Understand, Then to Be Understood 229

The Problem of Externalities 230

It's a People Problem: Involve Everybody 230

Begin by Understanding One Person at a Time 231

Develop a Shared Commitment Among Stakeholders 232

What If Your Organization Won't Change? 233

Safely Convincing Everyone Checklist 234

Further Reading 235

Summary 235

Chapter 12: A Program to Address Technical Debt 237

Technical Debt Reduction Program Framework 237
Preliminary Information Gathering 238
Workshops for Problem Understanding 238
Additional Information Gathering 239
Workshops for Solution Development 239
Pilot Solutions 239
Rollout and Stabilization 239
A More Complete Framework 240
Summary 241

Chapter 13: Preliminary Information Gathering 243

The Corporate Marshmallow Test 243
Understand Where You Are Now 245
    How Much Technical Debt Do We Have? 245
    How and Why Did We Acquire It? 246
    Where Is Your Organization Feeling Pain? 246
    What Code-Related Technical Debt Is Out There? 247
    What Architecture-Related Technical Debt Is There? 247
    Are We Firefighting Our Way into Debt? 248
    Inadvertent Descent into Firefighting 249
    Questionnaires for Anti-patterns 250
Determine How to Go Forward 250
    Understand Your Trade-Offs 251
    Understand Your System 251
    Understand Your Potential Leverage Points 252
Prepare Individuals for Change 253
Software Simulation Models 253
Further Reading 253
Resources 253
Summary 254

Chapter 14: Workshop for Problem Understanding 255

Agenda 256

PowerPoint Slide Deck 258

Workshop Details 260

    Introduction 260

    Understanding Trade-Off Decisions 260

    Understanding Systems Effects 262

    Anti-patterns 264

    Technical Debt from an Economics PoV 265

    Wicked Problems, Social Complexity, and Fragmentation 266

    Putting It All Together 267

Workshop Preparation 269

    Understand Your Workshop Goal 269

    Decide Who to Invite 270

    Room and Setup 271

    Preparing Your Attendees 272

    Prepare Your Material 272

    Dry Run Your Material 273

    After the Session 273

Further Reading 273

Resources 274

Summary 275

Chapter 15: Additional Information Gathering and Sensemaking 277

Recap 278

Understanding the Political Landscape 278

Addressing Missing Information 280

Sensemaking: What Does It All Mean? 280

Shaping Potential Solutions 283

Preparation for Your Next Workshop 285

Dynamic Simulation Models 286

Further Reading 286

Summary 287

Chapter 16: Workshops for Solution Development 289

Workshop Purpose 290

Agenda 290

PowerPoint Slide Deck 291

Workshop Details 292

    Recap and Update 292

    Explore First Candidate Intervention 295

    Explore Second and Third Interventions 298

    Summary and Next Steps 298

Useful Workshop Techniques 299

    Wicked Questions 299

    TRIZ 300

    PMI, Plus, Minus, Interesting 302

    Chesterton's Fence 302

    Imagining an Alternative 304

    9 Whys 305

    Dialogue Mapping/Argument Mapping 305

Workshop Preparation 306

After the Session 306

Outputs 307

Further Reading 307

Summary 307

Chapter 17: Pilot Solutions 309

Dangers of Pilot Projects 310

Must We Run a Pilot Project? 312

Using Past Project Data 312

Agree Goals and Plan Intervention and Metrics 314

Select Your Pilot Project 315

TABLE OF CONTENTS

 Set Timeline 316

 Run Pilot and Gather Information 316

 Analyze Results and Create Report 317

 Capture Lessons Learned and Identify Next Steps 317

 Further Reading 317

 Summary 318

Chapter 18: Rollout and Stabilization 319

 The Perils of Change 319

 Change Management Models 321

 Kotter's Eight-Step Transformation Process 322

  Establish a Sense of Urgency 323

  Form a Powerful Guiding Coalition 324

  Create a Vision 324

  Communicate the Vision 325

  Empower Others to Act on the Vision 327

  Create Short-Term Wins 328

  Consolidate Improvements 328

  Institutionalize New Approaches 328

 Critical Success Factors 329

 Further Reading 329

 Summary 330

Chapter 19: Conclusion 331

Afterword by Mark Stringer 335

Appendix 337

References 349

Index 357

About the Author

Dr. Andrew Richard Brown has worked in the software industry since 1999, where he started as an SAP programmer fixing Y2K bugs, although sometimes he inadvertently replaced them with Y-2050 bugs.

Several years later, he realized that the biggest problems in software development were not technical ones but, instead, were very human problems. What's more, he realized that while many others also recognized this, no one had yet figured out what to do about it, or even if they could do anything!

Since then, he has looked for ways to help teams improve their performance through understanding how human problems and the organizational systems those teams exist within combine to drive the suboptimal behavior that results in so many of the software development problems we see today.

He coaches organizations on quality engineering issues, organizational systems issues, and issues driven by human biases. He is particularly active in researching long-standing issues in software development, such as technical debt, risk in complex systems, and project estimation errors.

He runs a research program that explores how software development problems are driven by cognitive biases. He also investigates how to address these problems using behavioral science techniques. His research has proven highly fruitful, leading to new and counterintuitive insights into the true causes of software development problems, as well as fresh approaches to solving them. This research has raised considerable interest in the software development community and has led to many requests from international software conferences, where he is now a regular speaker on the conference circuit. He has a growing YouTube channel dedicated to understanding software development problems caused by human factors.

Foreword by Dorothy Graham

I have heard Andrew speak at a number of software testing conferences over the years and have always been fascinated by his insights into the interaction of human beings and the software industry.

In this tour de force, Andrew brings his psychological expertise to the seemingly intractable problem of technical debt. In this book, he takes the issue apart, turns over the component pieces, and investigates the causes of technical debt to see exactly how it works. He explains why it is so damaging to organizations and why it is so difficult to conquer. His explanations of famous disasters and the descriptions of true experiences in the workplace (of his own and others) bring the lessons vividly to life. The book concludes with extensive practical advice and additional material to help make lasting changes to conquer this problem.

So what is technical debt? It is not a technical problem; it is a trade-off problem. We are more likely to choose a short-term suboptimal solution which brings us immediate relief, even though it would be better for the organization to "bite the bullet" and address the underlying but more difficult long-term solution. We trade off a small gain now by making potentially larger problems for the future. How and why do we do this? Andrew explains how we really make decisions, using the "affect heuristic," based on emotions rather than logic – this is rather different to the way we think we make decisions! This impacts not just technical debt but many other aspects within organizations.

The most familiar analogy for technical debt is financial debt, and this is useful to some extent, but has serious shortcomings. Financial debt is straightforward: you know what you owe, what the interest rate is, and when it will be paid back with regular payments. With technical debt, you don't know what the consequences (if any) are until much later, how long you have before they become critical, or whether the costs may then be too high to recover from disaster. The book also includes analogies from other areas, from economics to social interactions. We see how various factors can influence decisions that often result in unexpected and undesirable effects. A number of technical debt anti-patterns help to illustrate the points as well. An onion diagram takes us through different levels, giving insights relating to technical issues, trade-offs, systems issues, economics and games theory, and characteristics of "wicked problems," complex and almost impossible to solve.

FOREWORD BY DOROTHY GRAHAM

I remember encountering technical debt long ago (though I didn't know the term then). One of the programs that needed updating was very poorly organized and very difficult to change correctly. I thought I could write a much better one starting from scratch. But would I be allowed to take the time to do it? If this book was available then, it would have given us the knowledge and tools to make that decision with much greater confidence. I did rewrite it, which took a week, and every change to it afterward was much quicker and much less error-prone, saving far more time than I had invested.

More recently, I see another common area of technical debt – in test automation. Building a lasting and effective set of automated tests is software development and is subject to the same pressures that cause technical debt in software. This leads to test automation testware with high maintenance costs, flaky tests, zombie tests, and worthless tests. This book is also a great resource to help you in dealing with test automation technical debt.

But this book is not just about the problems – it offers solutions with practical support.

Chapter 10 of the book takes us through the use of a simulation tool which can help us to visualize the longer-term consequences of decisions made on the current project. For example, it shows how excessive deadline pressure can actually make late projects even later. Andrew shares models he has devised for technical debt which you can use to help explain and demonstrate to your colleagues the complexity of these issues.

However, Andrew understands better than most people that just having a good solution is not enough. The book explains why change is so hard within organizations and what we need to do about it in order to make changes that stick. He gives useful advice about each stage of a change management initiative. As well as numerous helpful checklists and the additional models for the tool, he even gives you a link to a PowerPoint presentation that you can adapt.

This book is well-organized with clear explanations and the evocative use of stories. It will change the way you look at not just technical debt, but human behavior in other areas of work and life. Even if you are not specifically looking at technical debt, I recommend this book to you. But if you do want to tackle your own technical debt, this book is essential and can help you achieve your own goals to reduce and eliminate it.

Dorothy Graham, software testing and test automation consultant and author
April 2024

Acknowledgments

First, I would like to thank Mark Stringer, who has performed a fantastic job as editor of the initial drafts. He has challenged many of my vaguely formed ideas, helping me to sharpen up some of them into clearer concepts, plus discard others that could not be sharpened or were faulty in other ways.

I would like to thank James Markham, my development editor at Apress, who honed the manuscript into a publishable form, as well as kept me from straying too far from my subject matter, a perennial danger for myself. I would also like to thank Shonmirin P.A. and other members of the editorial team at Apress for helping navigate me through my first book.

I would also like to thank Rohan Nzenwa-Jasons, who made suggestions that eventually led to the concept of the technical debt onion.

I would like to thank Steve Forbes for sharing with me his ideas on technical credit.

Also, a special thanks to Keith Yorkstone, whose example and encouragement helped give me the self-belief to develop my ideas into a book proposal and send it to his publisher, Apress.

I would like to thank Rakhee Shah for our many conversations around human biases and their influence upon software development.

A big thank you to Edith Rose, for her encouragement to write this book, plus for sharing her experiences of the book publication process.

I would like to thank Antonia Seager, for suggesting that we needed to turn technical debt into a sexy cowboy.

I am particularly grateful to Dorothy Graham, Isabel Evans, Iflaah Salman, Iris Pinkster, and Richard Egren, who read and reviewed my manuscript for a previous book on software development. Although this manuscript never found a publisher, it did give me experience in writing a book-length work and also indirectly led to many of the ideas that have surfaced in this book.

I would like to thank the many software-testing conferences I have attended and spoken at. I find these events an invaluable source of ideas, encouragement, and inspiration, and I believe that we all have much to learn from the ideas freely exchanged at conferences and meetings. The conferences I would particularly like to thank include

ACKNOWLEDGMENTS

EuroSTAR in various cities throughout Europe; **HUSTEF** in Budapest, Hungary; the **Romanian Test Conference** in Cluj; **Scottish Testing Group** in Edinburgh; **TestCon** in Vilnius, Lithuania; **ExpoQA** in Madrid; **Testbash** in cities throughout Europe; and the **Test Managers' Forum** in London.

I would like to thank the many people I have met at those conferences and other places, with whom I have had many stimulating and thought-provoking conversations. In particular, I would like to thank Chris Ambler, Chris Armstrong, Sue Atkins, Emna Ayadi, Francis Balfe, Abby Bangster, Manjit Bharaj, Michael Bolton, Richard Bradshaw, Tony Bruce, Fiona Charles, Andrei Contan, Alex Cusmaru, Wim Decoutere, Anders Dinsen, Sakaya Doss, Atilla Fekete, Graham Freeburn, Paul Gerrard, Peter Gfader, Martin Goossens, Claire Goss, Janet Gregory, Paul Holland, Chloë Hutchings-Hay, Mike Jarred, Bryan Jones, John Kent, Csilla Kohl, Ilya Kozhevnikov, Ard Kramer, Sophie Kuester, Gustav Kuhn, Michael Kutz, Rhian Lewis, Emma Lilliestam, Ben Linders, Mike Lyles, Rik Marselis, Adam Matłacz, Hugh McCamphill, Gaspar Nagy, Antti Niittyviita, Declan O'Riodan, Stuart Pates, Moses Ponnippas, Drew Pontikis, Simon Prior, Maaret Pyhäjärvi, Sowmya Ramesh, Dave Rigler, Jeroen Rosink, Phil Royston, Hanna Schlander, Huib Schoots, Szilard Szell, Roy Thomas, Neil Thompson, Rick Tracy, René Tuinhout, Santhosh Tuppad, Sanne Visser, and Steve Watson. If I have missed out any names of individuals that have sparked good ideas in me, I'm sorry but my memory is no longer what it once was.

By way of a backhanded compliment, I would like to thank my bout of sciatica, which regularly woke me up at approximately 1:30 a.m. each night over a six-week period. As I paced around the house in the middle of the night, trying to work off my sciatica pains, I read through the rough drafts for the critical chapters, Chapters 4–8, improving them substantially, if somewhat painfully.

I would particularly like to thank the ambulance crew, Kayla and Mel, plus the professionalism of the staff of the Cardiac and Stroke Receiving Unit of Wycombe Hospital, without whom this book may not have been completed.

Finally, I would like to thank my wife, Kumi, and my daughters, Sasha and Sakurako, for their encouragement, patience, and support.

Introduction

Imagine the following. You are scheduled for an operation to relieve a chronic migraine pain within your head. The surgeon has you scheduled for an operation later that day, which will involve drilling a series of small holes into your skull.

However, the holes are not being drilled into your skull to insert a medical implant, drain fluid, or relieve pressure. Instead, within your world, chronic migraines are believed to be caused by evil spirits that have become trapped within your head. Therefore, the holes are intended to allow this evil spirit residing inside your head to escape.

How would you feel about the likely success of your forthcoming operation?

Today, we know that it is an obvious nonsense to drill holes into people's skulls to allow evil spirits to escape. However, it is not so long ago that we performed this, plus many similar operations. We carried out these operations not because of incompetence or malice, but because of an inappropriate set of beliefs about the causes of the problem. Although it was an ineffective technique, it was a rational thing to do within the belief systems that existed at that time.

Today, we address technical debt and many other problems that exist within organizations with solutions that are reminiscent of drilling holes into skulls to allow evil spirits to escape. We hire consultants. We fire consultants. We hire and fire staff, outsource them, then bring the work back in-house to some new staff, before reorganizing everything, introducing a new technology or a new methodology.

Few, if any, of our actions have proven effective in allowing the evil spirits within our organization to escape. We carry out these actions not because of our incompetence or malice, but because of an inappropriate set of beliefs about the causes of our problems. Although our actions are no more effective than the skull-drilling, they are a rational thing to do within our current belief system.

As you work your way through this book, I hope to change your beliefs about the causes of technical debt and other long-standing problems within your organization.

INTRODUCTION

Why Is Technical Debt Important?

Most organizations recognize they have a problem with technical debt. Organizations complain that they have too much technical debt, while at the same time they are running projects that will *increase* their technical debt levels. And most organizations fail to see the irony of this situation, or if they do, they are at a loss for how to address it.

One reason technical debt remains such a big problem is that most people fundamentally misunderstand the problem itself. Because we misunderstand technical debt, many of our current approaches for dealing with this problem are ineffective or even counterproductive. This book aims to clear up our misunderstandings about what technical debt is and then show us how we can manage it and so tame the dragon of technical debt.

Who This Book Is For

This book is aimed at **people in software teams**, both those on projects, who are sometimes making decisions that result in technical debt, as well as those in support of DevOps, who must deal with the consequences of that debt.

However, the book is not intended to be used to address that debt directly. Such an approach will not lead to any lasting change. Instead, this book will help you understand technical debt's underlying causes and then enable you to advocate to stakeholders how you can address those causes in a planned intervention aimed at producing lasting improvement.

This book is also aimed at **managers and business stakeholders**, who wish to understand why software development takes so long and costs so much. This book will help you understand how you end up with high levels of technical debt that slow down every software project. It will also help you devise a program to reduce your technical debt to manageable levels and then keep it manageable.

This book is also aimed at **consultants** who have traced an organization's problems to its high level of technical debt. This book will show you how to implement a technical debt management program.

What Can You Achieve with This Book?

This book will help you build within your organization the conditions and change of mindset required to commence addressing your technical debt problem.

Once you have established these conditions and your organization is ready for change, this book then provides you with a step-by-step guide to creating a change program to reduce and then manage your technical debt.

How This Book Is Organized

In **Part 1**, Exploring Technical Debt, we look at what technical debt is, why we should address it, plus why it has proved so resistant to solutions.

Part 2, Understanding the Technical Debt Problem, is the heart of this book, where we dive deep into understanding the different facets of the technical debt problem.

We start in **Chapter 4**, where we explore the analogy to financial debt. We look at the ways this analogy has helped our understanding, plus the ways that it has hindered us. We then look at alternate analogies and explore how each analogy can offer us a fresh perspective of the technical debt problem.

In **Chapter 5**, we look at how technical debt is the result of making trade-off decisions. We explore how we make trade-offs, plus why technical debt fares so badly in those trade-offs. We finish by exploring techniques we can use to make better trade-off decisions around technical debt.

Our decisions are influenced by the organization within which we work. In **Chapter 6**, we look at technical debt as a systems problem. We explore how our role in the organization often constrains us into making decisions that are not in the best long-term interests of our organization. We then look at how we can address this, so that we make better decisions within that organizational setting.

We in software are not alone in making trade-off decisions while part of a larger organization. In **Chapter 7**, we explore some extensively studied economic problems that illuminate some rarely considered aspects of the technical debt problem.

Technical debt is not a problem that we can solve, like a chess or crossword problem that has an identifiable solution. However, we can and should manage the problem toward a better outcome. In **Chapter 8**, we learn about the differences between wicked problems, like technical debt, and tame problems, like chess. We learn why technical debt is a wicked problem, plus how this should change our approach to addressing the problem.

INTRODUCTION

In **Chapter 9**, we briefly look at some common technical debt anti-patterns.

In **Chapter 10**, we introduce you to system modeling software and then explore how you can use it to model the problems that technical debt causes. You can then use the results from your models to strengthen your case for a technical debt initiative.

In **Part 3**, Tackling Technical Debt, we look at how you can build an intervention program to tackle your organization's technical debt.

In **Chapter 11**, we look at how you can gain the support of others by convincing them of the importance and urgency of your technical debt problem. Support from senior stakeholders is critical to success, so unless you have the backing of senior stakeholders, any strategic changes are likely to fail, and you should limit yourself to tactical improvements.

In **Chapters 12–18**, we work through the stages of an intervention to reduce and then manage technical debt. This initiative begins with information gathering and moves into workshops for problem understanding and then solution development, finishing with developing a pilot solution, then rollout, and stabilization.

In **Chapter 19**, we finish with a conclusion and summarize our new understanding of the technical debt problem.

In the appendix, you will find details of the questionnaires, games, and exercises you will find useful for the workshops of your successful intervention.

Reducing your organization's level of technical debt is not easy. However, the benefits in terms of improved capability to deliver the change your organization needs make it an ultimately worthwhile and rewarding journey.

I wish you the best of luck with your journey!

PART I

Exploring Technical Debt

CHAPTER 1

What Is Technical Debt?

In this chapter we begin by learning what technical debt really is. We'll learn that it is not a technical problem, but rather it is the consequence of trade-off decisions we make, where we take on technical debt in exchange for a benefit, like an additional feature or earlier delivery.

We'll also learn that technical debt is influenced by factors like the organizational structure we make those decisions within or whether the project is on schedule or late.

We'll construct a new model to describe the technical debt problem, the onion model. We then use this model to understand why previous attempts to address technical debt have been largely ineffective.

Most of us are already familiar with the technical debt quadrant as a model to characterize technical debt. We look at several other models, including an interest rate model.

Defining Technical Debt

Before we can address technical debt, we first need to understand what it is. In the following sections, we'll debunk some common myths around technical debt and explore what it really is.

Technical Debt Is Not a Technical Problem

The technical debt analogy was first coined by Ward Cunningham in 1992. A widely accepted definition is:

> *Technical debt is the implied cost of future reworking required when choosing an easy but limited solution instead of a better approach that could take more time.*
>
> —Technopedia

If we examine this definition, we come to a surprising conclusion: *Technical debt is not primarily a technical problem*.

So, if technical debt is not really a technical problem, what kind of problem is it?

Technical Debt Is a Trade-Off Problem

Technical debt is primarily a *trade-off problem*. It is a problem about how individuals make decisions about trade-offs. We don't create technical debt just for the fun of it. Instead, we decide to take on technical debt in exchange for a benefit, such as additional features or earlier delivery.

The technical debt problem is about trading current benefits and future costs. It is the classic vice versus virtue dilemma – the same dilemma we find ourselves in every time we pass a complimentary cake display on the vendor stand at the software conference.

Therefore, to understand our technical debt problem, we must first understand how we make trade-off decisions. Once we understand that, we can then look to understand why technical debt comes off so badly in that trade-off.

In Chapter 5, we explore how we make decisions, which is by using a heuristic known as the **affect heuristic**. This heuristic is tremendously powerful, enabling us to make rapid, effective decisions with only limited, poor-quality, or even contradictory information. However, when we make decisions about technical debt using this heuristic, it leads us to pile up too much of the stuff.

We then look at other factors that influence our decision-making on technical debt. One of the most relevant is project pressure. We see how a project becoming behind schedule causes us to change our decision-making, particularly our appetite for risk and our willingness to accept technical debt.

We also explore how factors like time constraints, hyperbolic discounting, and uncertainty drive us toward decisions that build up too much technical debt.

Technical Debt Is Also a Systems Problem

When we make decisions involving technical debt, we rarely do so as an isolated individual. Instead, we make decisions while fulfilling a role as part of a team within an organization. Often, we know that our choice will likely lead to a longer-term problem and would prefer to make a decision that does not lead to technical debt.

However, we are often constrained in our choice by the situation or system we are working within. Thus, we end up making a decision that solves an immediate problem but results in an increase in technical debt.

In *Chapter* 6 we examine how technical debt can build up simply because we make decisions as part of a team within a larger organization. We learn how organizations are often structured in ways that create unintended effects, like reinforcing feedback loops, which drive undesirable consequences, including high levels of technical debt.

Technical Debt Is an Economic Problem

Once we recognize that technical debt is a problem about individuals making trade-off decisions while working within a system, we can introduce fresh ways of thinking to this problem. We can also call upon a vast cornucopia of tools that we would not otherwise have imagined using if we had limited ourselves to thinking of this as a purely technical problem.

We in the software community are not alone in facing the challenge of making trade-off decisions within the constraints of a larger system. Indeed, economists study little else. In *Chapter* 7, we borrow ideas from the economics and the games theory communities and then use them to interpret the technical debt problem from the viewpoint of some well-understood economic and games theory problems.

Technical Debt Is a Wicked Problem

The technical debt problem has existed ever since the first days of software development. Why has it remained unsolved, when our community has solved so many other complex and challenging problems?

It remains unsolved because technical debt is a wicked problem. In *Chapter* 8, we learn about wicked problems and tame problems. We learn that technical debt is always a wicked problem and why this is important to us, plus how this knowledge should cause us to change our approach to tackling technical debt.

Technical Debt Is a Broken Analogy

Although the analogy to financial debt helps us understand the problem and allows non-technical people understand its challenge, the analogy does have significant limitations.

In *Chapter* 4, we explore this analogy in more depth. We look at ways in which it is helpful, plus other ways in which it is harmful. We then explore several alternate analogies, each of which offers us a fresh insight to a different facet of the problem.

The Technical Debt Onion Model

As you learn more about technical debt, you will discover it to be a far more complex beast than you originally thought. To tackle the problem effectively, you need a better model. For this, I developed the technical debt onion model, shown in Figure 1-1. You have probably seen similar models for concepts like the agile onion or planning onion, to help understand the concepts of agile or planning.

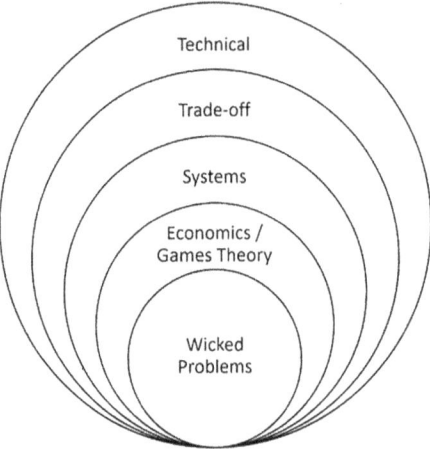

Figure 1-1. *The technical debt onion model*

This model consists of multiple layers, with each layer representing a different facet of the problem. To address the technical debt problem, we must address all layers. If we don't, and we typically only address the top layer, then the layers underneath will soon undo any work we have done.

Technical Layer

At the uppermost surface of this model is the **technical** layer. This is the layer we encounter most of the time, and it is what usually springs into our minds at the mention of technical debt. Unfortunately, many people within the software industry, including some who have spent considerable effort addressing technical debt, go no deeper than thinking of technical debt as a technical problem.

If we think of technical debt purely as a technical problem, then when we try to address the problem, we will limit our approach to tackling existing items of known technical debt. We draw up a list of problems to be tackled and then work on them, typically in between other pieces of work. Later, we become puzzled and frustrated when our levels of technical debt do not reduce.

We cannot address technical debt in this way, at least not permanently. Technical debt is not static, but rather it is continually created and destroyed. (Usually more is created than is destroyed.) This means that if we attempt to address technical debt by working through a list of known technical debt items then, no matter how effective we are, technical debt will eventually revert to the same level it was at before our intervention.

Technical debt is a system that exists in homeostasis.

Having a technical-focused initiative to clear up technical debt is like a city parks' department having an initiative to clear up litter in the parks. If the department does not also address the problem of how the litter is added to and removed from the parks, then no matter how pristine the parks may be immediately after a cleanup initiative, within a short while they will have returned to their previous state.

To address technical debt on a sustainable basis, we need to address all the layers.

Trade-Off Layer

The layer beneath the technical layer is the **trade-off** layer. This layer represents how we as individuals make trade-off decisions. We do so by using our gut feel, also known as the affect heuristic. To address this layer, we must understand how this affect heuristic works, how we use it to make our trade-off decisions, and why we select trade-offs that we later regret, plus how we can make a different selection.

We also need to understand how certain environmental factors cause our affect heuristic to modify its decision. For example, if the project is behind schedule, then we make very different trade-off decisions than if the project is on schedule.

Systems Layer

Beneath the trade-off layer lies the **systems** layer. This layer represents how we change our decision-making when we become part of a system. When we work within an organization, we have a role, our goals, plus some tasks or activities to achieve those goals. An ideal organization would be integrated, so that all our goals are aligned with the organizational goals. However, most of us do not work in an ideal organization. (At least, I can never recall working in one.)

In this layer, we explore what it is about the system or organizational structure we work in that may cause us to make decisions that result in higher levels of technical debt than the organization would prefer.

Economics/Games Theory Layer

Beneath the systems layer is the **economics/games theory** layer. Strictly speaking, we could integrate everything we say in this layer into the trade-off and systems layers. However, the economists' models add so much clarity and value to our understanding that it is worthwhile including this as a separate layer.

Wicked Problems Layer

The final layer is the **wicked problem** layer. It is important you recognize that at the very heart of the technical debt problem is a wicked problem. Wicked problems are very different from tame problems, and if you attempt to tackle a wicked problem as if it were tame, you will fail and rapidly become disillusioned with your lack of progress. This wicked problem aspect is so important, and wicked problems are so little understood that we devote a whole chapter to exploring them.

Is All Technical Debt the Same?

Of course not! In the same way that all code is different – the SQL statements we use to access a database are very different from the JavaScript code we use to make the UI more interactive – so is all debt different.

Here is a more comprehensive definition of technical debt:

In software intensive systems, technical debt consists of design or implementation constructs that are expedient in the short term but that set up the technical context that can make a future change more costly or impossible. Technical debt is a contingent liability whose impact is limited to internal system qualities – primarily but not only, maintainability and evolvability.

—Managing Technical Debt

Looking at this definition, we can see that technical debt will take many different forms, from architecture, to code, to documentation.

The Technical Debt Quadrant

Let us start by looking at one of the first attempts to characterize different types of technical debt – the technical debt quadrant by Martin Fowler, shown in Figure 1-2.

	Reckless	Prudent
Deliberate	"We don't have time for design"	"We must ship now and deal with the consequences"
Inadvertent	"What's layering?"	"Now we know how we should have done it"

Figure 1-2. The technical debt quadrant

The technical debt quadrant characterizes debt along two dimensions: reckless/prudent and deliberate/inadvertent. As we look at the above quadrant, we can imagine situations where a team may create reckless or prudent debt, or debt that was deliberate or inadvertent. This model is useful, as it forces us to think of debt beyond a simple list of items.

However, while useful, it is only one way of characterizing technical debt. As we learn in the later chapter on technical debt as a broken analogy, if our only tool is a hammer, then every problem looks like a nail. Therefore, we should look for other ways to characterize technical debt.

In what other ways can we characterize technical debt? There are plenty.

However, first a caveat – one of the biggest problems of technical debt is that it is *not* a technical problem, but we treat it as if it was one. As we explore different ways of characterizing technical debt, we should keep this in mind and avoid disappearing down the rabbit hole of constructing an enormous taxonomy of technical debt types. Instead, we want to explore just enough to give us a better understanding of technical debt, plus, as always, we want to open our minds to alternative ways of thinking about debt.

One way we can characterize debt is by its interest rate.

Interest Rate

We readily understand that different types of financial debt may attract different types of interest rate. For example, a house mortgage will have a lower interest rate than a credit card debt. Extending the analogy from financial debt to technical debt, we should expect that different types of technical debt will have different interest rates.

For clarity, we will define interest rate as the rate at which the cost to fix the debt increases as we delay addressing it.

For simplicity, plus avoidance of that rabbit hole, let us limit ourselves to three levels of interest rate: high, low, and zero.

In an area of a high interest rate level, we understand that if we do not pay down the technical debt when it occurs, it rapidly becomes far more expensive to address. This situation is likely to occur in areas of the application where there is a high level of change, plus those changes build upon one another. Just like a payday loan or credit card with an extortionate interest rate, we are best off paying down any technical debt that attracts a high interest rate.

In an area of low interest rate, changes are likely to be less frequent, the code less complex, or with fewer interdependencies. Here, the consequences of not addressing debt are less severe, so we may choose to focus our efforts elsewhere, unless we are already making a change in that area and can opportunistically pay down the debt.

CHAPTER 1　WHAT IS TECHNICAL DEBT?

An area of zero interest rate would imply no changes, both within that area plus in other parts of the code base that rely upon that area. You should avoid expending resource on fixing debt that has a zero interest rate.

Level: Architecture/Code/Other

Another approach is to characterize technical debt according to whether it sits in architecture, code, or elsewhere. We could draw up categories such as

- Architecture
- Code
- Test
- Documentation
- Technology shift (The technology world has moved on.)

This approach is useful on a couple of levels. Firstly, it would suggest where the most expensive debt is. Your most expensive debt is almost certainly going to be architecture debt, as problems here often require a major rewrite.

Secondly, it also indicates who is best placed to fix that debt. Okay, it may seem self-evident that the architects are best placed to fix the architecture debt, but unless the issue is labeled as such, that may not be immediately obvious.

Where in the SDLC Was the Debt Created?

Knowing when a debt was created may not be directly useful in understanding that debt itself. However, if you are planning a technical debt management program, knowing at what stage in the software development lifecycle, SDLC, a debt was created, plus the conditions existing on that project or team at the time, could provide you with key insights.

To use an analogy to smoking, most smoking prevention programs seek to identify situations in which the patient normally smokes and then aim to avoid the patient placing themselves in those situations. For example, if you only smoke while drinking with friends, a prevention program would aim to avoid putting you in a pub with your 20-a-day mates from the Gauloises unfiltered appreciation society. Obesity reduction programs have similar approaches.

Therefore, if you are building an initiative to reduce the buildup of technical debt (as opposed to simply paying it down), then understanding the conditions under which debt items have been created is likely to be a key part of your analysis.

The ways you can characterize debt by creation period include

- On schedule/behind schedule
- Early stage/late stage of project
- Project/maintenance

By characterizing your debt in this way, you will find many useful insights. For example, you are likely to find that a disproportionate amount of your coding debt is generated on projects that are behind schedule. Similarly, you would expect that most architecture debts would occur in the early stages of the project, when architecture decisions tend to be made.

To characterize debt in this way, you will probably need to interview different members of the organization and interpret their responses, rather than simply relying upon data entries in a technical debt register.

This is because the date an item is entered into the register is unlikely to be the same as the date that it was created. Also, different decision-makers become aware of any schedule slippage at different dates. Typically, stakeholders and those tasked with ensuring work progress become aware of schedule slippage later than those who do the work.

Collecting this data and characterizing it also provides you with evidence in support of advocating changes to how software development projects are run.

What Was the Debt a Trade-Off for?

In the same way that understanding where in the SDLC that technical debt was created, understanding what the trade-off was for provides you with useful information for a future debt management program. Note, often you will not be able to pinpoint exactly what the trade-off was for, although project conditions will give you a general indication.

The two most common trade-offs are

- Additional functionality
- Schedule recovery

By discovering what trade-offs are being made, you can gain insights into why debt is accumulating, thus suggesting a way toward a potential solution.

For example, if a large portion of the debt is due to trade-offs to gain additional functionality, is there an issue of overly dominant product managers? Conversely, if most debt is acquired to try and recover schedule, are your organization's estimations overly optimistic?

Further Reading

For the original article on technical debt, read Ward Cunningham's blog on *The Wycash Portfolio Management System*.

The original article on the technical debt quadrant can be found on Martin Fowler's web page.

If you want to explore the more technical side of the debt problem, then try *Managing Technical Debt* by Kruchten, Nord, and Ozkaya.

Summary

In this chapter, we learned the following about technical debt:

- Technical debt is not a technical problem.
- Technical debt is a problem about trade-off decisions.
- We make our decisions when working inside an organization. The structure of the organization strongly influences the decisions we make.
- The onion model is useful for understanding the complexities and different facets of technical debt. To address technical debt successfully, we must address all layers.
- As well as the technical debt quadrant, we can use alternative characterizations such as interest rate, architecture/code, SDLC stage, and trade-off reason.

CHAPTER 1 WHAT IS TECHNICAL DEBT?

Before we charge into understanding technical debt and addressing its problems, we should first check that technical debt really is the big problem we think it is. In the next chapter, we will examine the problems and consequences of technical debt.

CHAPTER 2

Why You Need to Address Technical Debt

In this chapter, we look at why we need to address technical debt better than we currently do. We learn that certain types of debt are inevitable, plus some debts are even good for us. However, we also learn that some debts are avoidable and should be avoided, especially since much of this debt is around for far longer than we ever anticipate.

We also learn the role that technical debt played in the death of Netscape Navigator, plus how debt affected us during my time at HMV.

Is Technical Debt Really a Problem?

Let us use the analogy to financial debt, a topic we return to in Chapter 4. Many of the major things we do in our lives, such as buying a house to live in, would be impossible without incurring financial debt. Furthermore, many of those debts are not intrinsically bad for us. For example, most of us are better off choosing to take out a mortgage debt that we eventually pay off, rather than spending years or decades renting a house that we will never own. Similarly, if we need a car to get to work, then we would normally be better off taking out a car loan than being unemployed.

So, when does financial debt become a problem to us?

Financial debt can become a problem in three circumstances:

1. When we are unable to service the debt.
2. When we have a better alternative, such as using our own money or not incurring the expense in the first place.
3. When we use the wrong type of financing. For example, we don't take out a mortgage to buy an ice cream, nor do we buy a house on our credit card.

Is technical debt similar to financial debt?

In many ways, yes. Incurring technical debt can be good, if it allows an organization to do things that it would not otherwise be able to do.

Similarly, if an organization is uncertain about the best direction to go, then it may be better to build a prototype or temporary solution and get feedback on that, before building anything permanent. If you're thinking of buying a holiday cottage in the Lake District but you're not sure if you can stand all the rain, then renting before you buy is probably a good idea.

However, a lot of technical debt does not match these criteria.

And the thing about technical debt is that it can be around for an awful long time.

How NASA Engineers Designed the Space Shuttle

If you look at a photograph of the space shuttle sitting on the launchpad, you will notice two large booster rockets attached to the side of the main fuel tank. These are the solid rocket boosters, made by Thiokol in their factory in Utah.

Now, the engineers would have liked to have made these boosters larger, but they had a problem. These boosters had to be shipped by train through a tunnel in the mountains, so they had to fit through that tunnel.

The railway tunnel was built wide enough to accommodate the US standard gauge track of 4 feet 8.5 inches. That's an odd number, so why did the US railroad engineers choose that dimension? Well, they based it upon the dimensions of the railroads in England, which was the world leader in railways at that time and is still the world leader in striking railroad workers.

So, why did the English engineers use this odd dimension? The answer is they based it upon their tramways, which used this dimension, which in turn was based upon the standard size for building horse carriages. So, why did English horse carriages have their wheels spaced at this odd dimension?

The answer is that many English roads had a pair of ruts built into the road, spaced at this dimension. These ruts guided the carriage wheels, for better performance and reduced wear and tear. So, who decided the spacing of these ruts?

The Imperial Roman Empire. They built a network of roads throughout their empire, along which they ran their chariots. The Romans worked out that if they built their chariots to a standard dimension and built appropriately sized ruts into their roads, they could transport their armies throughout the Empire. So why did the Romans choose this dimension?

It was based on the width of a horse's rear end.

More correctly, it was based on the width of two horses' rear ends, as the Romans drove their chariots with a pair of horses side-by-side.

So, the dimension of a horse's rear end in Roman times influenced the design of the space shuttle, approximately 2000 years later.

Now, your code that has that technical debt within it is unlikely to leave a legacy as long as that horse's rear end. But it may be around for a whole lot longer than you originally thought.

How Technical Debt Killed Netscape Navigator

Technical debt is important not just because it is around for a long time (although perhaps not as long as that horse's rear end). If you get it badly wrong, technical debt can even kill off your organization. This is what happened to Netscape.

Remember Netscape Navigator? If you are of a certain vintage, like me, you will probably have fond memories of Netscape Navigator as your very first Internet browser. I can still recall the first time I saw Netscape Navigator, on a 15-inch monitor in my client's lab in downtown Tokyo, where I was working in 1995. And yes, the guy was trying to surf porn sites. Very little changes.

Netscape Navigator was the first successful browser, right at the start of the Internet age. In those early days, it dominated the market, having close to 80% of market share at its peak.

However, trouble was in store. The web was evolving very rapidly. There were a lot of new technologies coming in, things like cookies, CSS, and JavaScript, which Netscape struggled to keep up with. Meanwhile, Microsoft was using its enormous resources to play catch up, with its Internet Explorer product.

As the rate of change increased, the code quality in Netscape Navigator plummeted, as technical debt built up. After the release of Netscape Navigator 4.0, Netscape took a decision which, with the benefit of hindsight, appears disastrous.

They chose to rewrite the entire product from the ground up. This is the technical debt equivalent of declaring bankruptcy and starting afresh – it may clear your debts, but it will be some time before you are free of your bankruptcy. For Netscape, it was 3 years. That was the time between the release of Navigator 4.0 and Navigator 6.0 (there wasn't really a 5.0).

Three years is a long time in a new and rapidly changing industry. During that time, Internet Explorer caught up and far surpassed Navigator, both technically and with market share.

Nobody can say with certainty that it was the high technical debt and subsequent decision to do a complete rewrite that sealed Netscape's fate. Microsoft was a formidable and deep-pocketed competitor. However, at the point before the rewrite – at Navigator 4.0 – Netscape was a credible competitor to Microsoft's Internet Explorer, but by the time Navigator 6.0 was released Netscape was no longer a credible competitor.

I have a similar and more personal experience of technical debt, through my days at HMV, a company that was once the world's largest music store.

A Tale of Technical Debt at HMV

When I ran the testing at HMV, technical debt was an endemic problem.

Most software projects were strongly impacted by technical debt and needed to factor it into their project plans. If you examined closely the items on any software project plan, it would be quite usual to find up to a third of the software development was focused upon addressing technical debt items.

But these were just the identified debts we knew about and had a plan for. A bigger problem came when we got hit by unexpected technical debt. Addressing this threw the project off schedule. Or rather it threw the project further off schedule, as most of our projects were underestimated. (Of course, we didn't always know the project was off schedule at that point, because not everything was accurately, or truthfully, reported.)

Another problem with this unexpected debt was that we usually encountered it in the middle of coding, not design. This meant that we were searching for a solution with our coding hats on, not our design hats. The result was that most times we encountered unexpected technical debt we put in a workaround fix, rather than spend time developing the best long-term solution.

In the analogy to financial debt, we were making an interest payment, rather than paying down any principal. In fact, we were often *adding* to that principal.

Once we became aware that our project was behind schedule, things became much worse, technical debt wise. In Chapter 5, we learn more about how our mental state changes when our project becomes overdue. For now, it is enough to know that slipping behind schedule caused us to pile up even more technical debt, as we struggled to try and recover that lost schedule.

The net result was that each project generally finished up leaving the HMV IT estate with more technical debt than when it started, even though a significant portion of all project resources had been allocated to addressing technical debt items.

Sometimes, we devoted a whole project entirely to repaying technical debt, although, thankfully, not on the same scale as Netscape Navigator.

In the early 2000s, we developed a product known as the HMV Jukebox. Think of something like Spotify, but a decade before it existed. A short time earlier, Apple's iTunes had entered the scene, disrupting the music market, so you can understand the HMV senior stakeholders wanting to address this threat, and quickly.

These stakeholders wanted to move fast, to use fresh, original ideas, plus not to be held back by interference from vested interests or turf wars within the HMV. Therefore, the directors outsourced the entire project to an external consultancy that specialized in ecommerce and new media. This consultancy then developed a solution largely independent of the HMV IT team. This consultancy was Microsoft focused, which meant that they developed the solution in C#.

The problem was that, like many other retailers, HMV was an IBM shop. Pretty much anything you touched within HMV, from tills to X-series mainframes, were IBM. The HMV ecommerce website was built in Java using IBM technology.

The result was that you had support developers trying to maintain two entirely different technology stacks. You also had the problem of maintaining a system where an ecommerce customer could build up a mixed basket of purchases, with some fulfilled in an IBM – Java system – while other items had to go off to a Microsoft, C# system. And everything from that Microsoft system needed to come back into an IBM system, as the accounting systems were IBM.

Unsurprisingly, a couple of years later, the biggest project we embarked upon that year was to convert the Jukebox from the Microsoft – C# technology stack into an IBM – Java one.

Some conspiracy theorists in HMV wondered if Steve Jobs had managed to insert a secret agent into senior HMV ranks and get the decision to go the way it did, just to be absolutely sure that iTunes won. However, few believed this, as nobody could imagine Steve Jobs finding it within himself to recommend a Microsoft technology stack.

As well as marching up and down different technology hills, like the Grand Old Duke of York, we also experienced the inefficiency of having otherwise attractive projects that were never started, simply because we discovered that the costs of paying down the technical debt to enable the project made it uneconomic.

Just like Netscape, technical debt was not the biggest problem that HMV faced. It was suffering new ecommerce competition from the likes of Amazon, a newly created digital download market dominated by iTunes, plus supermarkets competing by selling the top charts albums in with your weekly grocery shop. However, the high level of technical debt that HMV experienced did hinder its efforts to compete.

Some lessons I can share from an organization experiencing high levels of technical debt are discussed in the following sections.

Additional Cost to Every Software Project

Technical debt imposes an additional cost onto every software project. This cost is driven in two ways.

Firstly, the project may incur costs in paying down debt that must be addressed to complete the project. This is equivalent of repaying the principal of the loan.

Secondly, the project may not actually pay the debt down, but nevertheless incurs costs in working around that debt, for example, by more convoluted programming. This is the equivalent of interest repayments.

Whenever we encountered unexpected technical debt at HMV, it was far more likely to be addressed by working around that debt, that is, paying interest but not paying off the principal.

Slows Down Tempo and Delivery

Technical debt slows down the tempo of the project, since time spent addressing or working around the debt is time that cannot be spent on creating project deliverables.

In HMV, this slowdown of the tempo was particularly troublesome, due to the short window during which our development could be delivered.

The Christmas period is important to most retailers, but it was particularly important for HMV, as many of its sales were gift purchases. Up to a quarter of HMV's annual sales revenue was made in the 4 weeks before Christmas. For this reason, there was a hard code freeze at the beginning of November.

Similarly, because so much of its sales were in the Christmas period, the company could never decide its IT budget until the Christmas sales figures were calculated, which meant that IT projects began in early April.

This gave a window of approximately 6 ½ months to do all software development for the year. Therefore, a slowdown of tempo due to technical debt had a disproportionate effect upon software project delivery.

Technical Debt Makes Project Delivery Less Predictable

Organizations with a lot of technical debt often do not have a clear idea what they will encounter when they embark upon a project. Since they are not aware of the details of this debt, it is difficult to make allowance for it during project estimation, thus making project delivery less predictable.

Estimations, Schedules, and Projections Become Unrealistic

Because projects were unpredictable, the estimates, schedules, and projections that are created become unreliable. This is often compounded by a refusal to set realistic confidence limits on any estimation.

At HMV, for example, I was often asked to estimate the length of time required for the testing phase of a project. Frequently, I was prevented from including a +/- confidence limit with the estimate. The project manager wanted an exact number.

Incidentally, one of the things I did notice was that the further a person was from the technical side of things, the more demanding they were for exact numbers, while at the same time the less worried they were about adding technical debt. If you meet someone who demands an exact number in estimation, they are likely to be pretty blasé about adding technical debt to the organization's estate.

Combining an unreliable estimate with a zero-width confidence limit makes for unrealistic estimations.

Technical Debt Can Even Prevent a Project Occurring

If technical debt levels are sufficiently high, then the cost of paying down that technical debt may cause otherwise attractive projects to be rendered economically unviable.

Every year at HMV, we would experience at least one occasion when stakeholders were keen to embark upon a specific project, but during project discovery we uncovered sufficiently high levels of technical debt that the stakeholders reluctantly decided to forego the project.

A Spiral Into Debt: Self-Reinforcing Loops

If you are unfortunate enough to suffer high levels of financial debt, it can become difficult or impossible to escape a debt trap, as you will find most of your finances become committed to simply servicing the existing debt, plus the interest rates become increasingly high. You end up trapped in a self-reinforcing loop.

In a similar way, organizations with high levels of technical debt can become trapped in a technical debt trap, where high levels of technical debt lead to projects overrunning, which in turn lead to those projects piling up more technical debt, as they attempt to recover schedule.

Once you have descended into a debt spiral deep enough, additional self-reinforcing effects may occur. In Chapter 9, we discuss the *broken window theory*, whereby team members observe the high level of technical debt that already exists and become desensitized to it, adding further debt unnecessarily. You may also experience *non-linearities*, whereby an increase in debt does not lead to a linear increase in cost or delay. Finally, your system may reach a *tipping point*, beyond which you switch from an efficient mode of working into an inefficient firefighting mode.

Further Reading

For further insights on the Netscape debacle, read Joel Spolsky's book *Joel on Software*.

Summary

In this chapter we learned that many things, including technical debt and horses' rear ends, hang around for a lot longer than we expect. We learned that technical debt can be critical – it can even kill off a whole company. We also learned about the effects of technical debt within an organization that was mired in it, like HMV in the early 2000s.

In the next chapter, we will explore the reasons why technical debt has proved so resistant to our attempts to resolve it.

CHAPTER 3

Why Has Technical Debt Proved So Resistant to Solutions?

Many have attempted to address technical debt, with varying degrees of success. In this chapter, we look at why the technical debt problem remains with us, despite our many attempts to solve it.

There are quite a few reasons why technical debt has proved so resistant, with many of these reasons interconnected. We'll start with the most fundamental one – most of us do not fully understand what technical debt is.

Technical Debt Is Misunderstood

We think of technical debt as a technical problem, caused by those technical people (of course, who else?). We believe that the technical debt exists because we didn't apply the correct solution at the time, so we must now go back and fix it, provided we have the time and provided we deem it important enough to fix.

Because we think of technical debt as a technical problem, rather than something else, like a trade-off problem, we end up looking in the wrong place for a solution. It is like the joke about the drunk searching for his lost keys beneath the light of the lamppost. He lost his keys in a different place, in the darkness, but it's so much easier to search beneath the lamppost.

Our misunderstanding is compounded by our tendency to be overconfident, a tendency all humans have. This is a cognitive bias – the **overconfidence effect**. Often, this bias is a good thing. Humans would never have expanded out from Africa, sailed the oceans to inhabit new lands, or developed the technology to put a person on the moon or put a pop tart in a toaster without some of our ancestors being a bit too cocky and reaching beyond what was currently possible.

However, this overconfidence also means that we believe we understand things better than we really do. We use a financial debt analogy to help us understand the essence of the problem, even if we don't understand many of the details.

However, because we understand financial debt so well, we mistakenly believe that we also enjoy a similar level of understanding of technical debt. This mistaken belief prevents us from exploring the problem further – after all, we know what the problem is. It also causes us to implement solutions that don't fully address the problem, but we are confident will work.

We Deal with Technical Debt at the Wrong Place

Figure 3-1 shows an illustration of what we often think of as the technical debt life cycle.

Figure 3-1. *Technical debt life cycle, starting from when it is created*

We start at the point where the technical debt is created. We may be aware that we are creating debt – this is the intentional debt in Martin Fowler's technical debt quadrant – or we may be unaware we are doing so.

Often, the next time we come across the debt is when we are doing other work and stumble across this debt. Usually, we'll put in a workaround, rather than fully address this debt, the equivalent of paying interest on a financial debt.

There are several reasons why we may do this. The new work may be small, relative to this debt, and we don't have the time and resources to address it. Alternately, we may not fully understand why it was written in this way, so we're reluctant to change something we don't fully understand. This is generally a good principle, which we'll come back to in the workshop chapters, under the topic of Chesterton's fence.

Later still, we may come across this debt, but now we'll pay it down. We do this either because we have to as part of a needed change, it is expedient because we are changing code there anyway, or it is part of a technical debt reduction program.

This represents what most of us think of as the technical debt life cycle.

However, if we restrict ourselves to only considering debt from the moment it is created, then we are missing the first half of the life cycle. Figure 3-2 is a more complete illustration of the technical debt life cycle.

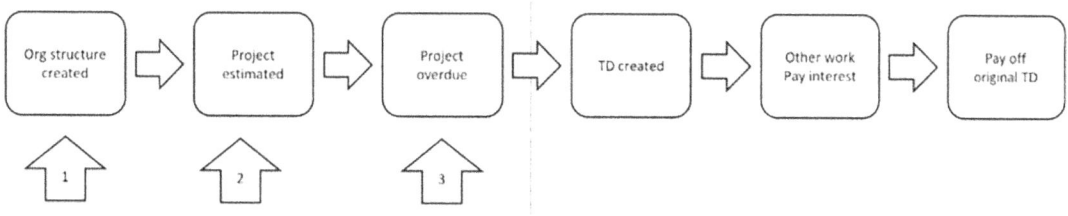

Figure 3-2. *Technical debt life cycle, beginning with events that led to its creation*

The technical debt life cycle really begins when we create an organizational structure, indicated by Arrow 1. It is here that we put into place the structures that later drive us to make decisions that favor creating technical debt, rather than avoiding it.

The next stage of the technical debt life cycle, indicated by Arrow 2, is when we estimate the project. We usually end up underestimating the project, causing it to be under-resourced and with insufficient time. This sets up our conditions for the project to become overdue, at Arrow 3.

When our project becomes overdue, our mindset changes, leading us to make decisions that result in technical debt being created.

Technical debt will always remain a problem for us until we address those root causes, including our organizational structures, project estimation practices, and how an organization responds to an overdue project.

Our blindness to half of the technical debt life cycle is partly due to our tendency to confuse proximate causes and ultimate causes, our next topic.

Proximate Causes and Ultimate Causes

When we try to understand why an event happens, we need to distinguish between the immediate, proximate cause of that event and its ultimate cause.

For example, if we are trying to understand why someone has died, we may learn that they died because their heart stopped. This is not particularly enlightening. Indeed, cessation of heartbeat could be considered a *definition* of death.

We may then learn that their heart stopped because of a traumatic loss of blood. This gets us closer to an ultimate cause, but still leaves the question – why did they suffer that traumatic blood loss?

Perhaps we learn that they suffered a traumatic blood loss following a traffic accident. Finally, we learn that a driver was distracted, or perhaps had been drinking, which led to the traffic accident.

In the example of a road traffic victim, there is a clear causal chain, so we are unlikely to conflate the proximate cause of heart stoppage with the ultimate cause of drink-driving.

However, in the case of technical debt that is incurred through software development, the causal chain leading to that technical debt is often unclear, leading us to conflate proximate causes with ultimate causes.

For example, the technical debt may have occurred because the developer elected to implement the code in a certain way. However, this is merely the proximate cause. If we stop here, then we learn little that can help us reduce our technical debt.

Instead, we must dig deeper and ask why the developer elected to implement the code in this way. We then need to ask "Why?" to that response, and then repeat this until we reach the ultimate cause. This is the heart of the five whys technique, commonly used in root cause analysis.

Was it because the developer was unaware of the limitations of their chosen approach? If so, why was that? Alternately, were they unaware of planned future development that would be hampered by this implementation? If so, why were they unaware?

Perhaps, most likely, the developer was under significant schedule pressure, and this solution offered a way to quickly deal with this coding problem and then move onto the next pressing problem on their list. If so, your chain of subsequent questions will likely lead you in a very different direction from the one you originally anticipated.

In accident investigations, it was previously normal to stop at the proximate cause of an accident, which was usually identified as the operator in charge at the time of the accident. This often suited the parties conducting the investigation – they had a cause, a person to blame (who was not themselves), and they could show they had conducted an investigation. This approach also allowed the organization to avoid any painful self-examination.

The major downside was that the investigation was ineffectual, little was learned, and a repeat accident often ensued.

The accident investigation community has moved on from this naive approach, with the result that far more is learned from accidents, which has led to significant safety improvements in many industries, especially in aviation and medicine.

Organizations trying to reduce their technical debt are frequently handicapped by focusing upon the proximate causes of that debt, while ignoring the ultimate causes. They may even be unaware that ultimate causes exist.

This focus upon proximate causes occurs for similar reasons to those in the accident and safety investigations. Firstly, the causal chain to the proximate cause is clear and distinct, whereas ultimate causes are usually hidden and diffuse. Secondly, there is a desire to get to a clear-cut ending, which a proximate cause provides. Finally, identifying the code or an operator as the cause avoids any painful self-examination by the organization.

Any organization that wishes to be successful in dealing with technical debt must go beyond looking for the proximate causes of that debt, and instead it must seek out that debt's ultimate causes.

Technical Debt Is Rarely Urgent

I have two kinds of problems: the urgent and the important. The urgent are not important, and the important are never urgent.

—President Eisenhower

Currently, I am writing this book. It is important to me, as well as to the publisher. However, my deadline for submitting a manuscript is a whole 9 months away, so I can hardly describe this task as urgent. I am also writing a proposal for a paper at a software conference. This task is considerably less important than writing this book. However, the deadline is only 3 weeks away, so while this second task is less important, it is more urgent.

Finally, I need to create some slides for a client meeting in a few days. This task is the least important one, at least to me. However, it is my most urgent task, so I know that I will prioritize working on those unimportant slides.

Technical debt is like the writing of this book – it is important, but rarely urgent. Therefore, it often lies low in our hierarchy of priorities.

The problem of balancing the needs of the urgent and the important is made more difficult by the tendency of many organizations to overload employees, so that they always have many more things to do than they can sensibly accomplish. The result is that tasks are prioritized by urgency, not importance, and employees never look at important but non-urgent tasks until their level of urgency becomes higher than competing demands.

Technical Debt Is Not Sexy

If you succeed in addressing your technical debt, then you will have fixed a great many problems that will now never happen. Unfortunately, as Nelson Repenning (2001) states, "Nobody ever gets credit for fixing problems that never happened."

You'll never impress your boss, nor get noticed by senior management, for a successful technical debt reduction program.

The benefits of technical debt reduction are neither immediate, nor are they usually concentrated around one area that stakeholders care deeply about. Instead, those benefits are spread over many areas and projects, plus they are experienced in ways that are not clearly attributable to a technical debt reduction program.

What's more, those benefiting parties, like the project team and stakeholders, are often unaware of the extent to which they benefited from the technical debt reduction. And even if they are aware, they're often unlikely to acknowledge it. Instead, they prefer to claim credit for themselves and their own efforts.

Hence, reducing technical debt is not sexy, but rather it is unloved.

There Are No Silver Bullets for Technical Debt

In *The Mythical Man Month*, Fred Brooks predicted that the software industry would not discover a silver bullet that would slay the werewolf of low productivity. Today, almost five decades later, Fred Brooks has continued to be proven largely right.

Technical debt reduction is not a silver bullet, one that with minimal effort will yield large and immediate productivity improvements. Technical debt requires upfront effort and investment, plus a willingness to forego an immediate payoff.

The central question of technical debt is not, "Do you want to reduce your technical debt burden?" but rather, "What are you prepared to sacrifice today in return for reducing your technical debt burden tomorrow?"

Any technical debt reduction initiative competes for resources against rival initiatives. If those rival initiatives appear to offer a silver bullet, then the technical debt initiative will be passed over in favor of an apparently more attractive alternative.

We *Desperately Want* Technical Debt to Be a Technical Problem

Managers and executives *desperately want* technical debt to be a technical problem. That way, they can get on with all the exciting stuff, like starting new initiatives, without being constrained by technical debt considerations.

Most executives don't want to discover that technical debt was caused by a decision to allow scope creep, which the development team resolved by short-cutting some development and leaving behind a swath of technical debt.

Nor do those executives want to discover that technical debt was caused by underestimation, which left the project under-resourced for the mission allocated, nor to discover that it was driven by frequent changes in requirements, or not providing an adequate test environment.

Nor are we techies entirely innocent in this respect. We too want technical debt to be a technical problem. That way, we can park those problems until later, rather than admit they are part of trade-off decisions we are making today. Also, if technical debt is a technical problem, then we get to play with lots of new toys, like SonarQube.

While we continue to think of technical debt as primarily a technical problem, then those business decisions that trade off additional functionality or early delivery for debt will continue to be made in ways that lead to high levels of technical debt.

Reducing Technical Debt Requires Change Management

Most technical debt reduction initiatives are resisted. Some are undermined. Almost all end up achieving less than originally hoped for. A major reason for this is that reducing technical debt requires many individuals to change what they do. And we all resist change.

If you want to make a significant, long-lasting difference to your technical debt problem, you cannot avoid making big changes. Sure, you can get some improvements by making small tactical changes. These changes may stick, but these alone will not make a big, permanent difference.

If you want to enjoy big improvements, you need to focus on what is causing that technical debt to be created, rather focusing on how you fix it afterward. You'll need to address why your organizational structure creates technical debt through systems effects and why technical debt does so badly in your trade-off decisions, plus why your projects end up being underestimated.

There are many individuals in your organization who will resist the required changes, particularly those who are doing well under the current setup. If you do not prepare by putting in place a change management process to overcome this resistance, then your technical debt reduction initiative will fail to achieve its full potential.

If your organization were putting in any other new process that involved significant change, like a new sales process, it would invest considerable effort in thinking how to make that change successful. A technical debt reduction initiative should do the same.

In a later chapter, we'll look at how to use a change management approach to embed the change necessary for a successful technical debt reduction initiative.

Further Reading

If you have not yet read *The Mythical Man Month,* you should do so. Even though it is half a century old, the ideas it contains are just as valid today.

For an understanding of how proximate causes can be traced back to ultimate causes in accidents, try reading works by Sidney Decker or James Reason.

Biologists, especially evolutionary biologists, are also a good source of examples of tracing proximate cause to its ultimate cause. For an interesting read on tracing the evolutionary causes of sickness, try *Why We Get Sick* by Randolph Nesse.

We'll cover books on change management in a later chapter.

Summary

In this chapter, we explored why technical debt has proven so resistant to a solution. We learned that technical debt is misunderstood, we try to deal with it in the wrong place, and we confuse proximate and ultimate causes. We also learned that technical debt is neither urgent nor sexy, plus we have no silver bullets for it. Also, we desperately want technical debt to be a technical problem.

Finally, it has proved resistant to solutions because we rarely treat our initiative as a change management initiative, something we must do if we wish to successfully tackle technical debt.

We now move from exploring technical debt to trying to understand the technical debt problem. We begin in the next chapter, where we explore why the technical debt analogy is a broken analogy.

PART II

Understanding the Technical Debt Problem

CHAPTER 4

The Broken Analogy

In this chapter, we look at why we use analogies and the benefits they provide, plus why they sometimes go wrong. We then look at the benefits and difficulties of using the technical debt analogy. We finish by looking at how alternative analogies could help us better understand and communicate different aspects of the technical debt problem.

Johannes Had a Problem

The research group Johannes was a member of had built a model to account for the movements of a collection of objects within a system. His task was to make some small corrections to the calculations for one of the objects in that model, since observations showed occasional small perturbations from what the model predicted. Johannes' task was expected to take a couple of weeks.

That was 3 years ago, and Johannes was less than halfway through completing his task, although it was probably fortunate that he was unaware of this.

Fortunately for Johannes, as well as the rest of the world, his boss had never read a book on project management, and his research group had never heard of OKRs. So, he was allowed to continue for another 4 years and complete his 2-week task.

However, by the end of his task, Johannes had not simply made a few small corrections to the predicted motion of this object. Instead, he had built an entirely new model that swept away over 2,000 years of theory.

His name was Johannes Kepler, the problem he had been trying to calculate was the orbit of Mars, and his new theory was the laws of planetary motion.

One difficulty Johannes Kepler faced was that the existing model for planetary motion was based on an incorrect analogy – that of an astronomical clock, with the stars and planets running on a clockwork-like perpetual motion. Clockwork runs like, well, clockwork. It doesn't slow down, speed up, and then slow down again, all in a predictable manner. But the planets did.

CHAPTER 4   THE BROKEN ANALOGY

Kepler knew that planets orbited around the sun, although the Catholic Church had needed to burn a few heretics at the stake before abandoning their geocentric worldview and accepting a heliocentric version.

However, Kepler also knew that the planets did not move in perfect circles but instead moved in an elliptical orbit. Also, planets closer to the sun orbited faster. Why was this?

The current model, or analogy, was that each planet contained a spirit within itself that was responsible for the motion. This model assumed that planets closer to the sun were, for some reason, filled with a stronger spirit and hence orbited it faster.

Kepler was dissatisfied with this answer and searched for alternatives. However, he was so far beyond the boundaries of previous thoughts, even those of the burned heretics, that there were no obvious models. Kepler turned to analogies.

Kepler first used an analogy to heat and smells, which are known to dissipate as they get further from their source. This meant that a planet further from the sun would receive less moving power. However, these analogies presented difficulties, as heat and smell can be detected along their path.

Kepler tried an analogy to light, which emanates from the sun and is received on the earth but is not detectable in between. However, planets do not stop moving during an eclipse, so this analogy had problems too.

Kepler used a vast cornucopia of analogies, from magnetism to a boat in a whirlpool. Each time he became stuck, he unfurled a new analogy and then interrogated it mercilessly, looking for flaws and inconsistencies, then refining his theory.

Kepler compensated for his lack of definitive knowledge of this planetary moving force through his extensive use of analogies. Had it not been for his use of analogies, Kepler may never have developed his laws of planetary motion, a work that provided the foundations for Isaac Newton's theory of gravitation.

Why We Use Analogies

We use analogies for the same reason that Kepler used them – to **help make sense** of a problem or situation. Sometimes the analogy is to help our own understanding. At other times, the analogy is to help others understand.

We also use analogies to **establish a common reference point** with others, to **stimulate thinking** around an idea, or to **encourage discussion** around a complex or unfamiliar subject.

We use analogies and metaphors all the time, including in software development. Think of "brittle software," the analogy we used to indicate code that is easily broken by a minor change. Obviously, code is not brittle in the same way that a China dinner plate would smash if dropped onto a stone floor. Nevertheless, the analogy is useful, as we can easily conjure up an image of a plate smashing into pieces when handled thoughtlessly. We can then use that image to understand code "breaking" or failing to work following an ill-considered change.

Similarly, agile and waterfall processes, code smells, software engineering, and software factories (or "software craftsmanship," when our sales rep is trying to raise the client day rate) are all analogies. They are useful to the extent that they help us understand a situation or communicate our understanding to others.

But are we using our technical debt analogy like Kepler used his analogies? Are we "ruthlessly interrogating" our analogy to financial debt for flaws, then discarding it in favor of a better analogy? Later, we'll see that the analogy does have some serious flaws, and since we haven't discarded it, we cannot be acting like Kepler. This partly explains why our technical debt problem is so enduring. We have based too much of our understanding upon a single, flawed analogy.

Later, we'll see that we have prioritized helping business people and others gain an understanding of technical debt, over developing a more complete and accurate understanding of technical debt.

The Power of a Good Analogy

You can use a good analogy to help find a solution that you would not otherwise have discovered. This was demonstrated in experiments by Karl Duncker and then repeated by others. An example of the problem is below:

> Suppose you are a doctor faced with a patient who has a malignant tumor in his stomach. It is impossible to operate on the patient, but unless the tumor is destroyed, the patient will die. There is a kind of ray that can be used to destroy the tumor. If the rays reach the tumor all at once at a sufficiently high intensity, the tumor will be destroyed. Unfortunately, at this intensity, healthy tissue that the rays pass through on the way to the tumor will also be destroyed. At lower intensities, the rays are harmless to healthy tissue, but they will not affect the tumor either. What type of

CHAPTER 4　THE BROKEN ANALOGY

procedure might be used to destroy the tumor with the rays, while at the same time avoid destroying the healthy tissue?

Can you think of a solution?

If not, don't worry, as only 10% of people managed to solve it initially. However, when people are then given the following story, the percentage who solve it increases.

> A general wishes to capture a fortress located in the center of a country. There are many roads radiating outward from the fortress. All have been mined, so that while small groups of men can pass over the roads safely, any large force will detonate the mines. A full-scale direct attack is therefore impossible.
>
> The general's solution, as shown in Figure 4-1, is to divide his army into small groups, send each group to the head of a different road, and have the groups converge simultaneously upon the fortress.

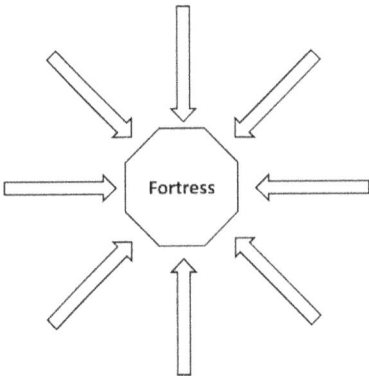

Figure 4-1. *The general's army approached the fortress from multiple directions*

The fortress problem drew people's attention to the analogy of dispersing the force and approaching from multiple directions, thus enabling sufficient concentration of force at the critical point, without overloading any of the routes.

The analogy worked. Of those who heard the fortress analogy, 30% solved the radiation problem. Of those who heard two similar analogies and were specifically directed to use those analogies, 80% solved the problem.

Duncker's problem is useful to us at two levels. Firstly, it demonstrates the power of using analogies to offer a fresh viewpoint in the search for a solution. Secondly, the idea of converging on a problem from multiple directions is directly helpful to us in tackling our technical debt problem. Our problem has multiple dimensions – it is a trade-off problem, a systems problem, a wicked problem, and so on. To solve technical debt, we need to converge upon a solution from multiple directions.

Clearly, a good analogy can help us make sense of situations and solve problems, so we should apply it to our technical debt problem.

But what are the characteristics of a good analogy?

Characteristics of a Good Analogy

An analogy is essentially a compromise between two conflicting goals: **familiarity** and **representativeness**.

A good analogy is familiar. It expresses a complex, abstract, or unfamiliar idea in terms of something that is familiar to us. We have all experienced breaking chinaware through careless handling, so the concept is familiar to us (some of us more than others). We can then extend that understanding to breaking software code.

Therefore, a good analogy is one that is expressed in terms of an idea that we already understand deeply. It is important that the idea is familiar to the person whom you want to gain the understanding. This is why the technical debt analogy to financial debt is so useful when we try to communicate the problems of excessive technical debt to the business; they are familiar with financial concepts, including the benefits that can be gained through acquiring debt, plus the consequences of acquiring excessive amounts.

A good analogy should also **spark your curiosity,** encouraging you to think in new ways about the situation, perhaps to explore in depth an aspect that you had previously paid little attention to.

A good analogy also needs to **offer an accurate representation**, at least in the relevant dimension. The analogy of brittle code to fine but brittle chinaware is reasonably accurate, in the sense that the analogy leads us to understand the need to be far more mindful and cautious when making changes to software considered to be brittle.

CHAPTER 4   THE BROKEN ANALOGY

A good analogy has both explanatory and predictive power; it should enable you to explain things you could not previously explain and predict things that you could not otherwise have predicted. It should extend your understanding of a situation, providing you with knowledge that is both more complete and more accurate. If the analogy leads to your understanding becoming less accurate in some way, then it has not served you well, even if it has made a previously unfamiliar concept appear familiar.

Later, we'll see that while the analogy to financial debt is accurate in some ways, it is not in others. A major problem is that the financial analogy is very familiar to senior stakeholders, who are often highly literate, financially speaking. This leads to individuals who are financially literate but technically illiterate extending the analogy until it is broken and no longer representative of the technical debt problem.

These individuals sometimes then propose solutions that are unrealistic or potentially harmful.

Analogy Familiarity/Accuracy Quadrant

We can combine these two dimensions of familiarity and accuracy into a quadrant, like the technical debt quadrant, as shown in Figure 4-2.

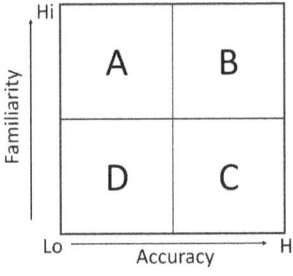

Figure 4-2. *The analogy familiarity/accuracy quadrant*

Analogies in **quadrant A** are familiar to us but have low accuracy. You should use an analogy from this quadrant when you need to impart *some sort of understanding* to individuals who lack any familiarity with the field and where those individuals cannot or will not engage with a more accurate but less familiar or less easily understood analogy. Later, we'll see that our technical debt analogy to financial debt falls into this quadrant.

Analogies in **quadrant B** are both familiar and have high accuracy. This is the ideal analogy, if you can find one.

Analogies in **quadrant C** are accurate but not familiar. When you are trying to understand a novel or unfamiliar problem, you will spend a lot of time searching out analogies in this quadrant. Some of Kepler's analogies fell into this quadrant.

Analogies in **quadrant D** are neither accurate nor familiar. Therefore, you should avoid using them when you are trying to help others understand a novel concept. However, when you are exploring a novel problem, you will likely come across many analogies like this during your analogy search.

Analogy Suitability Analysis Tool

Another useful tool is the analogy suitability analysis tool, which can be found later in this chapter plus in the *Red Team Handbook*. It contains four key questions we should ask whenever we are presented with an analogy:

1. Is the analogy valid? (Are there enough similarities?)
2. Is the analogy relevant? (Is the context applicable to the current situation?)
3. How is the analogy useful?
4. How is the analogy dangerous or misleading?

As we go through alternate analogies for technical debt, you should keep these four questions in your mind, plus ask whether the analogy is familiar, representative, and sparks our curiosity.

Later, we'll use a variation on this tool, plus the analogy quadrant, to evaluate alternate analogies to technical debt.

Ways That Analogies Go Wrong

Not all analogies prove useful. In a variation of the radiation problem, Mary Gick found that when people were presented with a different analogy, one which did not offer a useful insight, the percentage of people who found a solution fell.

Returning to our chinaware analogy, if you drop a plate and it smashes, you cannot easily reverse the process and return to an un-smashed state. Sure, you can try gluing it back together, and, if the damage is merely a chipped edge, you may end up with a reasonable result. However, the damage cannot be reversed, and you still have a damaged plate.

This is not necessarily true with brittle software. Often, you could reverse the changes, to leave the software in its original state. If you followed the analogy of brittle software too closely, you may not recognize that you could reverse your way out of the broken software problem. In this case, the analogy would have been harmful.

Similarly, if you drop a plate and it smashes, then it is immediately apparent that it is broken, and you need to replace it. (Or, if you're a small kid, you could try carefully placing the pieces at the bottom of the plate stack, so it doesn't get used for ages, then acting all surprised and innocent when the breakage is finally discovered. That sometimes works.)

In contrast, breakages to brittle software only become apparent when the broken part of the code is executed.

We can see that even with a relatively simple analogy, like brittle software, it is not a totally accurate representation. Hence, whenever we encounter an analogy being used to explain a concept, we should always be mindful of its limitations and check whether someone has extended the analogy beyond its breaking point.

Rethinking Our Technical Debt Analogy

Firstly, we should acknowledge the tremendous value that the technical debt analogy has provided us. It has enabled technical people to engage with business stakeholders, who often have limited technical knowledge, and enabled those stakeholders to understand a complex, abstract issue sufficiently well to make mostly reasoned decisions about it.

The financial debt analogy is effective at engaging stakeholders for two reasons. Firstly, finance is the lingua franca of the business world, and all inhabitants must speak it if they wish to be understood by others. Sales may have its beloved pipelines, marketing its market segments, and DevOps its pipelines (different pipelines, but equally beloved by developers). However, we all talk to each other in dollars, pounds, and euros. The financial analogy helps non-IT people understand technical debt and its importance, and it does this by speaking through this common language.

Secondly, almost everyone has personally experienced financial debt. Most of us have experienced the worry of a large debt, such as a property mortgage or an urgent repayment. Hence, we can easily relate to the analogy.

The ways in which the analogy to financial debt is valid and relevant include

- Repayment is usually required.
- Its cost grows with time.
- Its existence may prevent you doing other things you want to do.
- High levels of debt may impose a serious burden.
- When trying to manage debt, your focus is on the monies coming in and out, not the mechanics of the Swift banking system or how to write a check.

However, the technical debt analogy does have issues because, like the brittle software analogy, it's not a perfect match.

Why do we have these issues? Because *we've prioritized understandability over accuracy*. Those wanting to communicate the problems of technical debt to the business deemed it more important to engage the business with an easily understood but flawed analogy, than to seek an accurate analogy that the business may not even engage with.

This is understandable. Business is the reason that most IT exists, not the other way round. Technical debt cannot be addressed without business agreement. In turn, this means that business must understand the problem and its importance sufficiently well to prioritize resources toward it.

Our problem is not that the analogy is wrong – all analogies are wrong. Our problem is that after gaining engagement with the business, by using a useful but flawed analogy, we have not moved on and explored other analogies to allow both technical and business people to understand where this analogy is valid and useful, plus areas where it breaks down to become unhelpful, dangerous, and misleading.

Here is a closer analogy to what technical debt is like.

Suppose to get a job in the next city, you need a car, so you need to take out a loan. All good so far. However, suppose that with this loan, you don't really know how much you owe at any point. Nor do you know when you will need to repay that loan. In fact, you may be lucky and never need to repay it. (However, don't count on it.)

You don't know in advance how much your interest rate is, which can be very different for various parts of the loan. There is a lack of liquidity, so you cannot always pay down debt when you choose to. The repayment schedule is controlled by external events, of which you have limited advance warning. The debt is owned by an organization that is indifferent to your needs and outside the control of the financial regulating authority.

CHAPTER 4   THE BROKEN ANALOGY

Finally, the loan company has handed out to your relatives some free credit cards linked to the loan account, including one to your spendthrift teenage daughter, where her card is awaiting collection at her favorite Jimmy Choo shoes store.

Suddenly, that debt has become a lot scarier! (And I say this as a parent, with a daughter who once owned 35 pairs of shoes.)

Like, Kepler, having interrogated our analogy of finance and found it flawed, we should search out other analogies that may work more effectively. Why should we search out several analogies, instead of just one? Because all analogies are wrong, but they each tend to be wrong in diverse ways. Taken together, these analogies can enhance our understanding of the problem.

This is especially valid, as technical debt is a multilayered problem, with different layers of our technical debt onion representing distinct aspects of the problem. Therefore, different analogies offer fresh understandings of the different layers of the problem.

Alternative Analogies

Kepler used analogies to great effect in his research, trying and then discarding each in turn. We'll do similar, although we'll keep the analogies, while acknowledging their limitations.

In analogies, we are limited only by our imagination. We can compare the technical debt problem to obesity, environmental pollution, addiction, friction, and incurable disease, to name a few. One exercise you could try is to generate as many analogies as you can for the technical debt problem.

The first analogy we'll look at is the obesity problem.

The Obesity Problem

Obesity is abnormal or excessive fat accumulation that presents a risk to health (World Health Authority). It is a growing problem, and in many countries today, being obese kills more people than being underweight.

The obesity problem analogy is useful to understanding technical debt in two distinct ways. Firstly, there are parallels between the effect of obesity on a body and the effect of technical debt on an organization. Secondly, important aspects of both obesity and technical debt have been profoundly misunderstood. In both cases, this has led to inappropriate countermeasures being taken.

Effect of Obesity on an Individual

Obesity leads to increased risk of many serious and debilitating diseases, including diabetes, heart disease, and some cancers. Some pathways are direct, such as the mechanical stress of carrying additional weight. Others are indirect, involving complex changes in hormones, metabolism, and the ability to exercise. Extreme obesity can become self-reinforcing, as highly obese individuals become less able to exercise, and hence reduce their obesity. Also, tackling obesity often involves managing conflicting goals. While individuals may desire to reduce their obesity, they may also desire, or even crave, food items or other lifestyle choices that prevent them achieving obesity reduction.

We can see obvious parallels. High levels of technical debt can lead to serious and debilitating conditions. Those pathways can be direct, such as additional work to correct the debt, or indirect, such as a project rendered uneconomic by high levels of debt. Also, high levels of technical debt can become self-reinforcing. Finally, organizations often face conflicting goals that hinder or prevent them successfully addressing technical debt.

Hence, the analogy to obesity is valid, relevant, and useful.

Obesity Has Been Profoundly Misunderstood

Obesity started to become a significant problem in many countries around the 1970s. At the time, it was commonly believed that high levels of dietary fat were the primary driver of obesity. Consequently, government health authorities looked to reduce fats, particularly saturated fats, from their nations' diets.

However, despite significant reductions in dietary fat, obesity levels have continued to rise alarmingly. The primary reason is that at the same time as the food industry was reducing fat levels in food products, it was busy replacing those fats with sugars, particularly high-fructose corn syrup (HFCS).

This led to many problems. Firstly, our liver finds it problematic to break down fructose, leading to metabolism problems. Secondly, ingesting sugar, unlike fat, does not trigger satiation, so we continue to feel hungry and consume food well past what we need. Thirdly, sugar is addictive.

Again, we have a useful parallel between technical debt and the obesity problem. If we continue to believe that the drivers of technical debt are primarily technical, then, like the sugar/fat replacement, we'll be vigilant about monitoring certain drivers of debt, while being lax about other factors that are also driving the high levels of technical debt. We can also see parallels between technical debt and addiction.

Other Lessons from the Obesity Analogy

We can draw several other useful lessons from our obesity analogy.

When you've been good at your dieting, and not eaten all day, don't you feel you deserve a reward? Of course, you do, which is one reason why we subsequently binge on a sugar or chocolate-laden snack. This is like the *moral credential effect*, whereby we feel that a previous good deed excuses our later bad behavior. In the chapter on anti-patterns, we'll see a similar effect when teams address unexpected technical debt, leading them to feel justified in leaving behind our own technical debt.

Another useful lesson from exploring an obesity analogy is that it leads us to a useful tool for tackling technical debt – **systems mapping**.

The UK government, like many governments, has become increasingly concerned about rising levels of obesity within its population. One tool it has employed is to produce a systems map of the UK obesity problem. However, it is much more than a simple map – it is more of a system atlas, which attempts to map out the problem from multiple directions.

This atlas leads to an important insight – what happens if we create similar maps for distinct aspects of technical debt? You will encounter these maps later in the chapter on anti-patterns.

Environmental Pollution

Pollution is the introduction of harmful materials into the environment. Pollutants could be natural, like volcanic ash, or created by human activity, like pesticides.

The most useful insight from this analogy is that it is *the polluter who both decides to create the pollution, plus who benefits from the actions that result in pollution*. In contrast, those who suffer the consequences of that pollution often have little or no say in the decision that leads to its creation.

Technical debt is similar. Those who make a decision that results in the creation of technical debt, invariably do so to receive some benefit they personally value, like additional features, early delivery, or schedule recovery. In contrast, those who suffer the consequences of that debt, that is, incur costs to address or work around it, generally have little say in its creation. This is an important insight, one which we'll return to in the chapter on economics and game theory, where we explore externalities.

Another useful lesson from the environmental pollution analogy is that prevention is often cheaper than a subsequent cleanup, so that addressing an issue before it becomes technical debt usually works out cheaper for the organization. However, we learn in the section on externalities that while it may be better for the organization overall, the decision-makers may find it personally better for the organization to take on that debt and impose a higher overall cost on itself.

Addiction

Whenever we hear mention of addiction, our minds immediately fly to drugs like heroin, cocaine, or perhaps alcoholism. This gets people's sensitivities up, and everybody is ready to be highly defensive. Therefore, you need to tread carefully around this topic.

However, the subject of addiction is far wider than illegal drugs, alcohol, or the nicotine in tobacco or vaping. We also become addicted to everyday items, like caffeine, sugar, or even eating itself. We can even become addicted to exercise, or rather the endorphins produced through exercise. (I can honestly say this is an addiction I am unlikely to ever suffer.)

If we define addiction as a dependency on a behavior, activity, or substance to obtain a result, then addiction also covers many areas we would not normally associate with the topic. For example, at times in our recent past we have become addicted to the use of pesticides in agriculture. What has caused this?

Agriculture has increased the growth of single crops, with their attendant benefits of greater yields and higher quality. This has enabled us to feed a far larger population. However, we encounter a problem with single crops, when a pest specializing in eating that crop becomes prevalent. Nevertheless, we can address that problem using pesticides, which is an easy, quick, and cheap solution.

An alternative is to change farming practices, which is hard and expensive, plus we risk growing crops that people don't particularly want to eat. So, our farmers respond to what we, the consumer, want and use pesticides. However, the pest eventually develops resistance to the pesticide. This results in farmers using ever-increasing levels of pesticides for diminishing results, becoming locked into an addiction cycle.

In a similar way, various industries have become addicted to industry subsidies. Those subsidies were generally introduced as a temporary solution to address a short-term problem, but, as with all addictions, once the subject becomes accustomed to it, it is very difficult to wean them off.

CHAPTER 4   THE BROKEN ANALOGY

More recently, many countries in Europe had become addicted to cheap energy from a supplier that turned out to be, in the long run, against the strategic interests of those countries.

A common theme running through addiction is that it causes us to do things that make us feel good, at least temporarily, but those things have subsequent negative repercussions. However, we find it difficult or impossible to stop doing those things.

Using this wider term for addiction, we can now ask – are we addicted to technical debt?

Now, strictly speaking, we're not addicted to technical debt itself. Technical debt is merely a consequence of other things that we are addicted to.

Remember, I'm not suggesting we *enjoy* technical debt, in the way that an addict enjoys the high from their drug. Instead, I'm suggesting we have become *dependent* upon using technical debt to solve a problem, in the same way that many farmers were once dependent upon using ever-increasing levels of pesticides to solve a pest problem.

For example, we use technical debt to allow rapid or late changes, enabling us to satisfy a senior stakeholder who demands their desired functionality within a short timeframe.

We also use technical debt to meet project deadlines, especially after we encounter unexpected technical debt or some other obstacle. Consider the project represented in Figure 4-3.

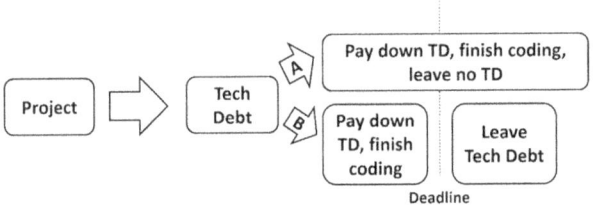

Figure 4-3. *Project encounters unexpected technical debt*

Everything is going smoothly, or as smoothly as projects ever go, when the project encounters unexpected technical debt. This debt is significant and must be paid down to complete the project. It will cause the project to be late. Or rather, it will cause the project to be even later, because the project was already underestimated, and hence under-resourced, before it ever started.

The project has two choices:

A. Pay down the technical debt, and then finish coding as intended, leaving no more technical debt than before.

B. Pay down the minimum it can get away with, and then cut as many corners as possible in the coding, to finish not too far from the deadline.

Most of us recognize that the best decision for the organization is Option A. However, we also recognize that this is probably not the option that will be chosen by the project. To understand why, we need to think of the incentives facing the project team for choosing each of these options.

If the team chooses Option A, then at the very least they will be criticized for delivering late. They may also miss out on bonuses or promotions. At the very worst, the project may be canned, and they get fired.

Now consider Option B. By doing the minimum, they can get away with and cutting corners, they may well finish late, but nowhere near as late as Option A. They are less likely to be criticized or fired. Hence, Option B looks attractive.

But what about all that technical debt? Surely, creating debt will count against the project team?

Firstly, most organizations care more about achieving a deadline than any technical debt left behind. Secondly, project teams do not leave behind technical debt, but rather they *bury* that technical debt. And often they bury it so deep and so well that nobody knows about it, until the next project comes along and stumbles across it, at which time it becomes somebody else's problem.

The difficulty is that subsequent projects now encounter more technical debt, as shown in Figure 4-4.

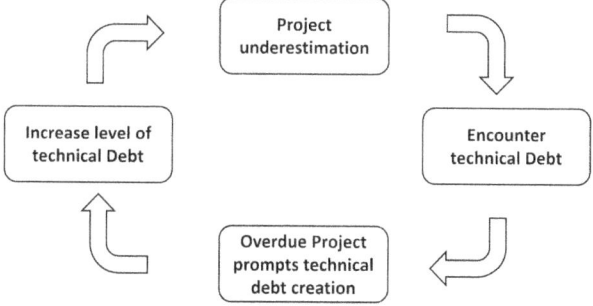

Figure 4-4. *Self-reinforcing loop of project underestimation, followed by technical debt creation*

Organizations can become stuck in a self-reinforcing loop as follows. Projects are underestimated, so when they encounter unexpected technical debt or another obstacle, their common response is to cut corners and create technical debt, thus increasing the level of debt in the organization. Project estimation errors are caused in part by the presence of technical debt, so when debt increases, estimation errors also increase, thus creating a self-reinforcing loop.

This happened to us at HMV, where projects, which were already underestimated, encountered unexpected technical debt that put them at risk. We discuss this cycle more in the chapter on anti-patterns.

Friction

In his classic book, *On War*, Carl von Clausewitz develops an analogy to friction, using it to describe the myriad of difficulties that accumulate in war and prevent even the simplest of tasks from being accomplished.

> *Everything is very simple in war, but simple is not the same as easy, and the simplest thing is difficult. These difficulties accumulate and produce a friction, which no man can imagine exactly who has not seen war.*
>
> —Carl von Clausewitz

The effect of technical debt on a project progress is very much like the friction described by von Clausewitz. High levels of technical debt often mean that even the simplest of coding tasks becomes difficult, requiring additional work to address or circumvent the debt, causing other tasks to be completed late, initiatives to fall short of their goal, plus leaving behind a legacy of additional debt to cause increased future friction.

Von Clausewitz elaborates further, saying that friction will always be present, and we should make allowance for it. That we can never eliminate it, but we should always make every effort to reduce it to a minimum. In the chapter on wicked problems, we'll learn that, like friction, technical debt will always be present, and we can never eliminate it. However, we should try to manage it and keep it to a minimum.

The analogy to the friction described by von Clausewitz is valid and relevant. It also provides us with terrific insights in how von Clausewitz advocates addressing friction in war.

In a later chapter, we use simulation models to explore how project pressures and decisions lead to the buildup of technical debt. In these models, technical debt accumulated from earlier projects causes friction within later projects, slowing them down.

Other Analogies

We could easily develop a whole host of other analogies. We'll briefly touch on two.

We can make an analogy to an **incurable disease or illness**. Just like an incurable disease, you cannot cure technical debt. However, just as you can and should manage an incurable disease to achieve a better outcome for the patient, so you should manage technical debt to achieve a better outcome for the organization. Also, some diseases prove fatal if not managed, like the fate of Netscape and its technical debt.

In addition, a delay in treatment may not only increase the costs and complexity of that treatment, but it may also change its nature, with a delay resulting in certain treatments becoming no longer viable.

Finally, we could use an analogy to a **leaking pipe**. Firstly, the best approach is to fix the leaking pipework, rather than collecting the leak in a bucket and then boiling it off. Secondly, the leak may occur only during substantial overpressure – if we reduce pressure in the system, the leak may stop itself naturally.

Analogy Quadrant Analysis

In Figure 4-5, we apply the analogy quadrant tool to the analogies we have created.

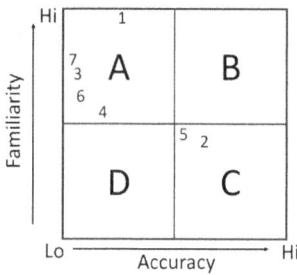

Figure 4-5. *Analogy quadrant tool applied to our analogies. (1) Financial debt, (2) obesity, (3) environmental pollution, (4) addiction, (5) friction, (6) incurable disease, (7) leaking pipe*

CHAPTER 4   THE BROKEN ANALOGY

1. The **financial debt** analogy is highly familiar to us. However, financial debt and technical debt differ in the details of their behavior, and this difference misleads us.

2. The **obesity** analogy is less familiar, particularly in the myriad of causal mechanisms that lead to obesity. However, the close study of these mechanisms leads to some remarkable insights.

3. The **environmental pollution** analogy is familiar, but its accuracy is limited to insights over passing on of costs, plus prevention is cheaper than remediation.

4. The **addiction** analogy is familiar, but its accuracy is limited to insights over becoming locked within addictive behavior. Nevertheless, this one insight is essential to any resolution of the technical debt problem.

5. The **friction** analogy of von Clausewitz is not familiar to most people. However, the similarities between friction in war and the friction imposed by technical debt are highly useful.

6. The **incurable disease** analogy is familiar, but its usefulness is limited to a couple of similarities.

7. The **leaking pipe** analogy is familiar but of limited usefulness.

None of the analogies offer us a perfect match. However, we can see that the obesity and friction analogies are, in some ways, better than the financial debt analogy.

Analogy Suitability Analysis Tool

In Table 4-1, we see the results of applying a variation of the analogy suitability analysis tool to the technical debt problem.

CHAPTER 4 THE BROKEN ANALOGY

Table 4-1. *Suitability of each analogy, based upon applying a variation of the analogy suitability analysis tool. H=high, M=medium, L=low*

Analogy	Valid	Relevant	Useful and *unhelpful* insights
1. Financial debt	M	M	• Enables business engagement • *Extended until broken, then misapplied*
2. Obesity	H	H	• Multiple routes to condition • Consequences of misunderstanding the cause of a problem • Use of systems mapping
3. Pollution	L	L	• Benefits accrue to decision-maker, costs to another party • Prevention cheaper than remediation
4. Addiction	M	M	• Concept of becoming locked in undesirable cycles and anti-patterns
5. Friction	M	M	• Effect of current decisions on future capabilities • Problem should be managed
6. Incurable disease	L	L	• Problem should be managed
7. Leaking pipe	L	L	• Problem occurs under conditions of high pressure

We see that no single analogy provides us with a perfect match to technical debt. However, each analogy offers us a different insight into the problem, and combining the analogies together into a table offers both an understanding of the different facets of the technical debt problem, plus it shows why we should explore multiple analogies.

Further Reading

For a good understanding of how Johannes Kepler used analogies, plus an excellent discussion of how analogies work, try reading the papers of Dedre Gentner.

If you are interested in the UK government obesity map, it is freely available on the UK government website. A URL is given in the references under "Obesity systems map." For an in-depth understanding of how our misunderstanding of the role of sugar and fat in obesity has led to severe problems, see *Sugar, the Bitter Truth*, by Robert Lustig.

For a discussion of friction in war, read Von Clausewitz's book *On War*.

CHAPTER 4   THE BROKEN ANALOGY

For a discussion of Karl Duncker's radiation problem, see his paper. Alternately, look up the paper by Gick and Holyoak.

For a discussion of addiction within systems, plus many other systems problems, *Thinking in Systems* by Donella Meadows is a highly readable book.

Summary

Our use of the technical debt analogy is partly responsible for both our success in engaging with the business, plus our lack of progress in further managing of the technical debt problem.

The analogy of technical debt to financial debt is a useful but incomplete and flawed analogy. Its greatest benefit is that its familiarity enables non-technical people to understand the challenge posed by technical debt. However, it is not a comprehensive representation of the problem, and it fails to fully explain all the challenges. Moreover, by presenting the technical debt challenge as like financial debt, it misleads stakeholders into believing that they understand the problem more fully than they do.

Through Kepler, we learned that we should not restrict ourselves to a single analogy, but instead we should explore a multiplicity of analogies, each of which may reveal a fresh insight into our problem.

We also learned to use the analogy quadrant and the analogy suitability tool to assess the suitability and limitations of any analogy. We then applied these tools on the analogies we had created.

In the next chapter, we start to look at the layers in our technical debt onion. We begin with a puzzle that is central to our whole technical debt problem – how on earth do we make decisions, and why does technical debt do so badly in that process?

CHAPTER 5

Technical Debt As a Trade-Off Problem

You recall the technical debt onion model, from Chapter 1? In this chapter, we focus on the trade-off layer of that onion.

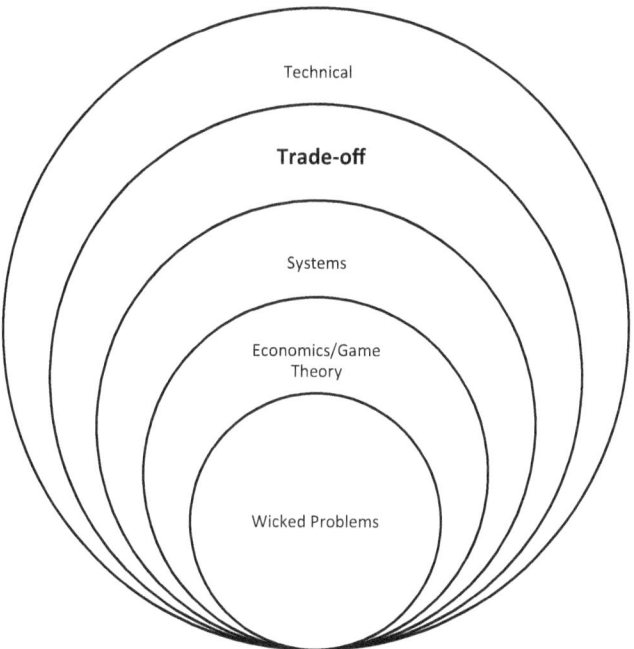

Figure 5-1. *The technical debt onion model*

In this chapter, we'll explore a subject that is central to understanding why we have such high levels of technical debt – how we make decisions, especially trade-off decisions. We make these decisions by using a heuristic, known as the affect heuristic.

CHAPTER 5   TECHNICAL DEBT AS A TRADE-OFF PROBLEM

We look at how this heuristic drives our decision-making, plus why it leads to higher levels of technical debt than we would otherwise wish. We then examine techniques you can use to nudge your affect heuristic toward decisions that avoid technical debt.

But first, let's explore why we ever developed a decision-making capability.

The Origin of Our Decision-Making Capability

It's important we understand where our decision-making capability came from, because it offers us important clues, both to the nature of our decision-making, plus the conditions under which it will go wrong.

Nature is parsimonious. This means that nothing ever evolves without a good reason. Even something as apparently superfluous as the peacock's tail evolved to attract peahens, and hence enhance their evolutionary fitness.

Our ancestors evolved the ability to make decisions because it enhanced their evolutionary fitness. Stated simply, intelligent creatures are more likely to survive and pass on their genes than stupid creatures. The wily fox left more descendants than the foolish one.

This statement is so simple that it appears trite. However, it contains a hugely important implication – if decision-making has evolved to enhance our evolutionary fitness, then we will be good at the sort of decisions that enhanced that fitness, and *not necessarily good at decisions irrelevant to that fitness.*

This is why you come back from Las Vegas having lost all that money. Your ancestors' survival was not linked to how well they understood the odds in poker, but rather how well they understood the odds of facing up against a saber-toothed tiger or hunting down a mammoth.

Also, we'll be good at making decisions *within the environment our ancestors lived in*, which is obviously very different from our environment today.

Therefore, to make good trade-off decisions around technical debt, we're relying on an ability developed for an entirely different purpose and intended to work within a very different environment. It is therefore not entirely surprising that our decisions around technical debt are sometimes less than ideal.

Conditions of Our Ancestral Past

What were conditions like in our past? We can obtain some idea from archaeological finds, plus from studying people, like the Yanomami, many of whom live under similar conditions to those faced by our ancestors (Barrett).

Things were pretty tough. Our ancestors faced constant danger from threats like predators, natural events, disease, uncertainty of food supply, and other humans. Threats were mostly immediate, with some longer-term dangers, like reduced food availability during winter. Decision aids were limited to simple items, like reduced daylight hours and temperature indicating the onset of winter.

Given the above, we can identify some requirements for a successful decision-making system. It would need to be:

1. **Fast**: It must be fast enough to respond effectively to the threats it faced, which could materialize extremely rapidly.

2. **Function well, even with poor-quality information**: Information was limited to what our ancestors could observe or, after language developed, what they were told by people whom they already knew. Much of this information would have been incomplete, ambiguous, conflicting, or even part of a deception attempt by a predator, prey, or rival. Nevertheless, their lives depended upon making good decisions based on this information.

3. **Impose a low cognitive load**: When facing a threat, you want all your cognitive facilities available for monitoring and responding to that threat, rather than engaged in deep analysis.

Decision-Making Occurs in Our Subconscious

The most important implication of the above requirements is that most of our decision-making *must occur within our subconscious*. There are three reasons why:

1. Our *conscious reasoning is simply too slow* to function in the few hundred milliseconds of time available between perceiving a threat, say from a predator, and that threat materializing.

2. Our *conscious, logical reasoning works badly when supplied with poor-quality information*.

3. Our alternative, of conscious reasoning, *imposes a very high cognitive load upon us*. Think of when you were immersed in deep thought, only to be surprised by something you were not paying attention to. Imagine that something was an ambush predator.

If we don't use conscious reasoning, how do we make our decisions?

The Affect Heuristic

We make decisions using the same approach that we do for many other mental activities – we use a heuristic. This is a mental shortcut, involving a simplification, that focuses on the most relevant aspects of the problem, which enables us to solve it well enough most of the time.

For example, when we catch a ball, we do not attempt to calculate its trajectory, but rather we fixate our gaze onto the ball, then move our position until the ball appears to remain motionless in our gaze. This is the **gaze heuristic**. Bats and birds use it to catch their prey. They fly toward their prey, and then keep it within sight and in the same relative position. This means that no matter what evasive maneuvers their prey attempts, they remain on an intercept path with it.

You are already aware of the heuristic that you use to make decisions. *You make your decisions using your gut feel*, in other words your emotions. Psychologists have labeled this process the **affect heuristic**, but you know when your gut feel is talking to you.

You use this heuristic more than you realize. Have you ever walked into a room full of people and immediately sensed that something was wrong? Or been in two minds about a decision that seems to tick all the right boxes, but nevertheless still doesn't feel quite right? You may not have been able to define exactly what was wrong, but your affect heuristic, or gut feel, was warning you that something was amiss.

This heuristic takes your current emotion, or *affective impression*, and then uses it to *guide* your decision. It is extremely fast; functions well, even with poor-quality information; and does not impose a high load onto you. It ticks all the boxes you needed for an effective decision-making mechanism in the environment of your ancestral past.

Table 5-1 shows some relevant characteristics of your affective decision-making system, compared with your rational system. You can see they are very different.

Table 5-1. *Characteristics of affective and rational decision-making systems (Adapted from Epstein 1994)*

Characteristic	Affective system	Rational system
Mechanism:	Emotions	Analysis
Behavior mediated by:	Mediate through "feel"	Conscious appraisal
Rapidity:	Fast	Slow
Ability to change:	Resistant to change. Changes only through experience	Can be changed through reason
Accessible to conscious evaluation:	No. Pre-conscious only	Yes. Is a conscious process

Two important points about the affect heuristic are firstly that we cannot easily change the emotion that guides any decision-making – we can only do so through new and different experiences. Secondly, it is not accessible to our conscious evaluation, which means that even if we were able to change it, we would not be aware of what it is thinking, or how it should change, anyway.

Hence, even when we believe we're making rational decisions, those decisions have usually already been made by our affective system, so all we are really doing is indulging in *post-decision rationalization*.

Next, let's look at what happens when heuristics fail.

When Heuristics Fail

Have you watched any of those amusing videos, where baseball fielders run into each other or the stadium fencing, because they become fixated on the ball and not where they are running? They have taken the gaze heuristic and then applied it to a different context.

Similarly, we have taken the affect heuristic and are now using it for an entirely different purpose – making decisions within a business and IT context. It is unsurprising we sometimes get suboptimal results.

The affect heuristic lets us down in another way. Recall that in our ancestral past, life was dangerous but simple. Threats were mostly immediate and obvious, and decisions were about relatively simple matters.

This means that we have not evolved to be good at making complex decisions that involve multiple assessment criteria. This is a problem since technical debt decisions are always such decisions, very different from the relatively simple decisions our ancestors made, for which our emotion-based decision-making mechanism evolved to support.

Does this mean we are forever locked into following decisions made by a system that is impenetrable to our conscious mind?

Not necessarily. Richard Thaler won a Nobel Prize for showing how individuals, organizations, and governments can improve their decisions, using carefully engineered cognitive "nudges."

However, to make good decisions, we need to understand how different criteria influence the affect heuristic. If some influence it too much or too little, then we need to adjust that influence. If we cannot do this, we will make poor decisions.

Let's look at those criteria, and whether we can influence them.

The Technical Debt Trade-Off Decision

Imagine you are a product owner in a meeting that is trying to decide whether to take on a major new feature. However, there is a problem. This feature is so big that you can only complete it if you take some shortcuts, adding a large amount of technical debt in the process. The feature is important to you. But so is having a low level of technical debt.

You decide whether to take on this feature plus the debt by using your affect heuristic, even though you would prefer to use your rational logic, and even though you are not even aware of this heuristic.

What are the characteristics of the new feature and its associated technical debt, plus how will each influence your affective system, and hence your decision?

If you choose to develop that new feature, then, as a product owner, you will receive a benefit that has the following characteristics:

- **Immediate**: You get to enjoy the feature just as soon as the code is delivered.
- **Certain**: You know what you are getting, or believe you know, as you have a specification, screenshot, or mock-up of it.
- **Concrete**: Or rather, as concrete as anything ever gets in software.

- **Experienced by us**: You get to enjoy the feature or enjoy the credit for delivering that feature to end users.

- **Emotional**: You *want* the feature, as it will do good things for you and your end users.

You see that each of these characteristics appeals to your emotions, creating a strong affective impression. *Consequently, the benefits of the new feature will strongly influence our affective system*, as it makes that trade-off decision on your behalf.

Note if the trade-off is for early delivery, instead of additional features, the characteristics are similar – immediate, concrete, emotional, and experienced by us.

In contrast, if you choose *not* to develop that new feature, and hence not take on that technical debt, then the benefit of avoiding that debt has very different characteristics:

- **Future**: Any debt repayment will affect you in the future.

- **Uncertain***: As we discussed in the chapter on broken analogies, you don't know when you'll have to repay this debt, how much you'll have to repay, or indeed if you ever do need to repay it. This is a key difference between ordinary debt and technical debt.

- **Intangible***: At this point you're not entirely sure what the future repayment would consist of. It might be a major rework, or it may be a few minor changes.

- **Experienced by others**: This future work is likely to be picked up by another person. If you count your future self as a different person, and many psychologists believe we do, then this debt will definitely be experienced by others.

- **Rational**: Avoiding this technical debt is a bit like saving for your pension. You know it's a good idea, but it appeals to your rational sense, not your emotions.

(*Later, in the precision and valence section, we'll see how uncertainty and intangibility cause a lack of precision, leading us to undervalue the benefit of avoiding technical debt.)

None of these characteristics appeal to your emotions, although they do appeal to your rational system.

Hence, *the consequences of adding technical debt will barely influence your affective system* as it makes your trade-off decision, even though your rational system will acknowledge the value of avoiding that debt.

All of this is extremely bad news for technical debt. Your decision-making mechanism is trying to make a trade-off decision between a new feature and technical debt, but the technical debt half of that trade-off barely registers in your mechanism.

Is there anything we can do to weigh those technical debt characteristics more, so that they adequately influence our affective system?

Yes, there is. To understand how, we'll look at how governments addressed a very similar problem in their smoking prevention programs.

Why Smoking Prevention Programs Initially Failed and then Succeeded

Logically, nobody today should begin smoking. The disadvantages are well-known and significant, whereas its benefits are minimal. You could also extend this argument back 50 years, to the 1970s, when the disadvantages were also known and widely publicized.

However, unlike today, in the 1970s, many people did begin smoking. Exploring why people made different choices in the 1970s and today provides us with crucial insights into how we make decisions. Later, we'll use these insights to help us create conditions for better decisions around technical debt.

Most people who start smoking do so as a teenager. Therefore, to understand the problem, you need to understand the perceived benefits and disadvantages from a teenager's point of view.

For many teenagers, the biggest perceived benefit of smoking is social acceptance. It's "cool" to smoke. All the bigger kids and cooler kids are doing it. Smoking is a route to that social acceptance.

The perceived benefits of smoking have the following characteristics:

- **Immediate**: We get the benefit now.
- **Certain**: We will definitely feel the effect of the nicotine, plus, we hope, the social acceptance or "coolness."
- **Concrete**: That benefit is real.
- **Experienced by us**: We get the nicotine, plus the coolness.
- **Emotional**: We yearn for that coolness.

These characteristics will strongly influence our affective system. Therefore, on an emotional level, smoking will appeal strongly to many teenagers.

But what about the disadvantages? Well, the primary disadvantage is that smoking is a potential hazard to our future health, causing a variety of diseases, including lung cancer, heart disease, and emphysema.

Okay, that doesn't sound too good. But let's drill down into the characteristics of those disadvantages:

- **In the future**, decades from now.

- **Uncertain**: You may get cancer. Or you may not.

- **Intangible**: Most teenagers don't know or care what emphysema is. Heart disease can be anything from very mild to extremely serious.

- **Experienced by others**: Provided we consider our future self as another person, which, to all intents and purposes, is true for most teenagers.

- **Rational**: The disadvantages involve future risks and probabilities. It's difficult enough to get software managers to think about future risks and probabilities, never mind horny, hormone-laden teenagers.

These characteristics barely influence our affective system, although they will resonate strongly with our rational system. Therefore, it is understandable why many teenagers take up smoking.

By the 1970s, governments had become acutely aware of the dangers (and costs to the taxpayer) of smoking. Therefore, many governments introduced mandatory health warnings on cigarette packets and advertising. The warning below is from an American cigarette packet:

SURGEON GENERAL'S WARNING: Smoking Causes Lung Cancer, Heart Disease, Emphysema, and May Complicate Pregnancy.

However, if you study this warning, you'll see that it's aimed at people's *rational* thinking. If you were considering whether to start smoking as a rational decision-making process, this warning may deter you. However, your decision is primarily emotional, not rational, so this health warning has little impact on you.

Meanwhile, on that same cigarette packet you would see images from the tobacco manufacturer. Images of rugged cowboys, or well-to-do socialites. The tobacco manufacturer was not aiming at consumers' rational system. (How many of us have a realistic chance of becoming a cowboy?) Instead, the image was aimed squarely at smokers' emotional system.

The tobacco manufacturers bet hundreds of millions of dollars that their message to a smokers' emotional system would beat the message from health authorities. And they were right. Tobacco manufacturers never once lost that bet; in the battle of rational message versus emotional message, *whoever controlled the emotional message always won.*

However, the health authorities eventually won the battle to prevent teenagers commencing smoking. And they did this by changing who controlled that emotional message.

If you look at a packet of cigarettes in many countries today, you will see a generic, unbranded carton. Governments have stripped away the ability of tobacco manufacturers to send a message to teenagers' emotional systems.

The rational health warning message is still there. But the cigarette carton is now dominated by a graphic, visceral image of a human body part severely damaged through tobacco smoking, an image that induces strong emotions of revulsion.

Although this is not the only difference, this change from a logical health message to an emotional one has played an important part in the success of smoking prevention programs.

The implication for technical debt is clear. In our trade-off, the characteristics of acquiring a new feature match the characteristics of a teenager commencing smoking, while the characteristics of avoiding technical debt match those of the health benefits of avoiding smoking. Hence, if we wish to be successful in our appeal to reduce technical debt, we need to learn the smoking prevention lessons of our governments and health authorities.

> *If you want to shift decisions toward avoiding technical debt, then you must shift those technical debt arguments away from logic and toward emotion.*

If you can also steer those arguments for additional features or earlier delivery away from emotion and into logic, so much the better.

You need to take the rugged cowboy off the software development carton and replace him with those nicotine-damaged body parts.

How can you do this? One way is to paint a vivid picture laden with affective images.

Appeal to Emotions Through a Story

One death is a tragedy. One million deaths are a statistic.

—Joseph Stalin

Most historians agree that Joseph Stalin was a monster. However, hidden within his callous and cynical quotation is an important truth – if you wish to engage with people, don't begin with facts and numbers, which will connect to people rationally but leave them unmoved emotionally. Instead, engage them on an emotional level with a story about an individual or event. Then you can give them the facts and figures.

You need a good story. Look through your technical debt register for one. If you don't have a register, talk to your development team about their war stories – they'll have plenty of those.

You want a story that fits the following criteria:

- The issue could not be addressed at the time (typically due to project pressures).
- The business stakeholders assured everyone the issue would be fixed in the future.
- Repeated opportunities to fix it were passed over.
- Not fixing the issue became painful.

You are looking to tell a story of a debt growing in cost, complexity, and raising the level of organizational "friction."

Here is an example from HMV, my former employer. Our music data was originally structured to belong in a single genre. That made sense at the time, since a customer searching for a Mozart concerto did not want to be bothered by Snoop Dog from Hip-Hop popping up.

However, the business needs changed, and the business wanted to display the same product within multiple genres (although Snoop Dog is still not welcome in the Mozart concerto section). The correct solution was to redesign the database, but this entailed major changes to the database architecture.

Now, HMV, like many retailers, made much of its profits at Christmas. We therefore had a strict Christmas code freeze, to stop anybody breaking the live site, just as half the population of England were scrambling to buy the last available copy of *Now That's What I Call Music!* CD for auntie Doris's Christmas stocking.

The database redesign could not be completed before the Christmas code freeze. This gave business a difficult choice – delay a major project until after Christmas or look for a temporary workaround.

We looked for a temporary workaround. We found that if we created a series of duplicate tables, we could display any product in one additional genre. (Some bright spark worked out that with triplicate tables, we could display a product in two additional genres. And with quadruplicate tables …. However, we kept quiet about that idea and its stairway to lunacy.)

This was obviously a temporary solution. It was messy, plus there was an ongoing cost to manually ingest a weekly data feed.

The business stakeholders decided to go ahead with the workaround. They also committed to fixing it in the very first project after the Christmas code freeze.

Christmas came and went. Winter passed, and the code freeze thawed.

The business did genuinely intend to address the problem. However, when we began our first project in April, we discovered numerous Christmas code fixes based upon that workaround had gone into live. This made addressing the issue far more problematic than anyone anticipated. The project stakeholders decided not to pay off the debt in their project, although they kept the additional funding allocated to them for that purpose.

Each subsequent project avoided addressing the workaround, until it was all but forgotten about and became part of the legacy code.

You want a story like this, one that your stakeholders can emotionally engage with. Highlight the pain the business is suffering, the foregone opportunities, and the continual costs of ongoing maintenance, plus growing costs of any rectification.

By beginning with a story that engages people's emotions, you avoid the mistake of the health authorities, who spent years trying to engage teenage potential smokers with messages of facts and figures, while the tobacco companies wooed them with emotion-laden messages.

However, to influence the trade-off, you must be able to attach emotional weight to any technical debt characteristic you intend to use. This is a problem, because, as we mentioned earlier, the downsides of technical debt tend to be uncertain and intangible, like those future health risks associated with smoking. In other words, they lack **precision**.

An important factor in determining just how much weight any characteristic carries with the affect heuristic is its precision. In the next section, we'll explore how precision and valence influence our decisions.

Precision and Valence

Imagine you are a music student. You are studious, so, in addition to all your required textbooks, you wish to purchase a music dictionary. However, you are not a particularly wealthy student, so you need to purchase it from one of the many secondhand bookstores in your university town.

You wander into your favorite secondhand bookstore, replete with textbooks from last year's graduates. This bookstore has two music dictionaries. You pull them off the shelf and compare them, side-by-side, as shown in Figure 5-2.

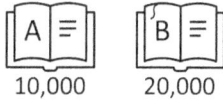

Figure 5-2. You see two dictionaries, side-by-side. Joint evaluation

Both dictionaries were published in the same year and have a similar depth of coverage for each entry.

- Dictionary A has 10,000 entries. It is in perfect condition, as if it were new.

- Dictionary B has 20,000 entries. The front cover is torn, but otherwise it is like new.

Which dictionary would you prefer to buy?

Your reasoning will probably go as follows. As a music student, you are most concerned with the contents, which you will frequently refer to during your studies. This isn't a coffee table book that you show off to your friends. After a few months of usage, both dictionaries will have a similar, well-thumbed appearance. Hence, you don't really care about the torn front cover. Therefore, you prefer dictionary B, which has twice as many entries.

After consideration, you are prepared to pay **$19** for dictionary A, and **$27** for dictionary B, that is, you are prepared to pay $8 more for dictionary B.

Most people would think like you. In an experiment, Christopher Hsee (1996) found that when people compared the dictionaries side-by-side, they were prepared to pay those amounts.

However, what would have happened if you had found only one dictionary in the bookstore, as shown in Figure 5-3?

CHAPTER 5   TECHNICAL DEBT AS A TRADE-OFF PROBLEM

Figure 5-3.   You only ever see one dictionary. Separate evaluation

Now things become interesting, because the outcome is reversed.

When you see *only* dictionary A, with its intact cover, and you cannot compare it with dictionary B, you are willing to pay *more* for it. Your offer increases, from **$19** to **$24**, an increase of **$5**.

In contrast, when you see *only* dictionary B, and you cannot compare it with dictionary A, you expect to pay *less* for it. Your offer decreases, from **$27** to **$20**, a decrease of **$7**.

Now, instead of being willing to pay $8 more for dictionary B, instead you are willing to pay $4 more for dictionary A, a clearly inferior dictionary when you compare them side-by-side.

This is *preference reversal under conditions of joint and separate evaluation*.

It is important you understand why we reverse our preferences like this, because this preference reversal lies at the heart of why we do not prioritize technical debt as highly as logic would suggest we should do.

To understand why we reverse our preferences, we need to understand two terms from psychology: **valence** and **precision**.

Valence is the intrinsic goodness or badness of an event, object, or situation. It's how good or bad we think something is.

Precision is the exactness, accuracy, or lack of variation in something.

Recall that our *affective impression* is how much we like or dislike something, or an aspect or dimension of that thing. This affective impression can vary in both valence and precision.

In the music dictionary example, the dictionaries had two dimensions, which together formed our judgment about its value.

The first dimension was whether the dictionary was free from defects. Dictionary A was defect-free, so it scored high on valence. Dictionary B had a torn front cover, so it scored much lower.

But what about the precision of this defect-free dimension? This precision is high, as we can easily determine that one dictionary is defect-free, whereas the other has a very obvious defect. What's more, we can give this dimension a precise valuation, even in the absence of the other dictionary for comparison. We don't need to see an undamaged item to understand that we dislike a damaged one.

This means that, for both dictionaries, *we can always put a very precise valuation on the defect dimension, irrespective of whether we observe the dictionaries separately or jointly.*

What about the second dimension – the number of dictionary entries?

Dictionary A had 10,000 entries and dictionary B had 20,000 entries. But how do we know if these numbers are good, bad, or indifferent? We need a way to translate each number onto some sort of goodness/badness scale. Without it, we simply don't know how good or bad either number is. This dimension *lacks intrinsic precision*, so we cannot easily evaluate it.

Thus, when we view each dictionary separately, we do not have a second dictionary we can compare the number against, so we cannot determine whether this number is good, bad, or indifferent.

In contrast, when we view the two dictionaries side-by-side we can briefly glance at the two dictionaries and immediately know that 20,000 entries are much better than 10,000 entries.

When we come to evaluate each dictionary separately, we can precisely evaluate the defect dimension. However, we cannot evaluate the number of entries dimension with any precision.

Consequently, when we evaluate each dictionary separately, we value dictionary A more than dictionary B, even though dictionary B is far superior on the dimension we care about most, the number of dictionary entries.

This concept becomes important when we try to evaluate the technical debt trade-off, which has several dimensions, and where we cannot evaluate all those dimensions with equal precision.

> **If the dimension we care most about cannot be measured with precision, then your attempts at evaluation may not help you. They may even hinder you.**

Considerations of valence and precision are extremely relevant to technical debt. As you recall, technical debt is a trade-off, typically between new features/earlier schedule and acquiring technical debt. This debt will eventually equate to fewer new features or a delay in the schedule at some future date.

Now, we can determine the benefits of a new feature or earlier schedule to a reasonably high degree of precision. We know what that extra button will give us, and we can count saved schedule days exactly. Therefore, the features/schedule side of the trade-off has a high degree of precision.

But what about the technical debt side?

Technical debt usually lacks any degree of precision. Remember those characteristics of uncertainty and intangibility. We don't know when we'll have to repay that technical debt, if indeed we ever do. We don't know what we must do to repay it, or the events or circumstances that may require us to pay it off. Often, we are not even entirely sure what that debt is.

This lack of precision means that the technical debt side of our trade-off lacks weight when we are making our decision. So, just like the music student who only ever saw one music dictionary, we cannot accurately evaluate our debt and whether we should avoid incurring it. We may later regret our decision, but that regret is in the future, and it is a permanent regret.

As Humphrey Bogart told Ingrid Bergman in that parting scene in *Casablanca*, "If that plane leaves and you're not with him, you'll regret it. Maybe not today, maybe not tomorrow, but soon, and for the rest of your life."

How can we address the problem of lack of precision?

We'll explore this question further in the workshop chapters. However, we have already mentioned about appealing to emotions through telling a story. In that story, we can add precision, by making those details specific and telling a vivid story. The more precision we can get into our story, the more weight that story will carry in a trade-off.

Also, when we calculate the cost of repaying a particular debt, precise numbers will be more influential than round numbers.

A lack of precision affects far more than just our judgment around technical debt. An absence of precision was instrumental in the launch decision that led to the Challenger space shuttle disaster.

Precision, Valence, and the Challenger Launch Decision

The launch decision that resulted in the Challenger space shuttle disaster was caused in part by a failure to properly consider an observation that was important, extremely bad (a low valence), but which lacked sufficient precision to even be presented to the decision-makers.

The observation was damage to the O-ring seals on the solid rocket boosters, which had occurred during two previous launches in cold weather conditions. This damage was caused by O-ring failure and subsequent blow-by, or unwanted leakage, of ignited gases. The information available to the decision-makers was that there had been two O-ring failure and blow-by's, one at 75F (degrees Fahrenheit) and one at 53F.

What the decision-makers did not appreciate was that the blow-by at 75F had been only minor. Photographs showed a thin streak of soot that extended beyond only a small area of the O-ring, before it sealed. In contrast, the blow-by at 53F had been severe – a thick streak of jet-black soot spread across a large area.

The air temperature at the time of the launch decision was a frigid 36F, far below any previous launch, and barely above freezing. We now know that at low temperatures, the rubber of the O-rings lost much of its elasticity and hence its ability to seal. Hence, the lower the launch temperature, the greater the risk of O-ring failure and subsequent blow-by of ignited gases.

Because this blow-by damage information was not made available to decision-makers in a way that lent it any precision, it carried little weight in the eventual decision to launch the Challenger space shuttle.

One reason that concerns were not raised more forcefully by engineers from the Thiokol rocket subcontractor was of the culture within NASA. Hung upon a wall within NASA was a large prominent sign displaying the following message:

In God we trust. All others must bring data.

Imagine if you were a subcontractor engineer with a hunch that your photograph of the blow-by damage was important, but you couldn't quantify it. There is every chance that NASA's sign and the culture behind it would intimidate you enough to hold back from voicing your strong but unquantified hunch.

If this can happen at NASA, think of how likely something similar may happen at your own organization. Perhaps, a developer or other technical person is concerned about a particular piece of technical debt. They want to raise their concern but cannot easily point to how the debt item will lead to a big problem in the future. If the culture of your organization is to trust only God, with all others having to bring data, will that person raise their concern?

As well as changing the precision of a characteristic, there are other ways you can guide decision-making toward a more balanced outcome. One of these is through a Ulysses contract.

CHAPTER 5   TECHNICAL DEBT AS A TRADE-OFF PROBLEM

Ulysses Contracts

Ulysses, also known as Odysseus, is a legendary character in Greek mythology. He was one of the Greek champions during the Trojan War, but on his journey home after the war, he encountered so many adventures that he took 20 years to return. His adventures even included an interlude when he was washed ashore on the island of Ogygia, and then Calypso compelled him to remain as her lover for 7 years. No doubt, Ulysses' wife had something to say to him about that interlude.

In one adventure during his journey home, he needed to sail close to the Land of the Sirens. These are humanlike beings with alluring voices. The sirens' singing is so beautiful that they drive men mad with desire, luring them toward the sirens' island, where they are shipwrecked upon the rocks and drowned.

Ulysses wanted to hear the sirens. However, he didn't want to drown. So, he devised a plan. He filled his crew's ears with wax, so that they could not hear the sirens' songs. He then got his crew to tie him to the mast and instructed them to sail close to the island, but not to deviate from their path, no matter what happened. (The order of events may be somewhat different – he may have given his crew the instructions first, before filling their ears with wax.)

Ulysses was thus able to enjoy listening to the songs of the sirens. He was driven almost mad by desire and begged his crew to sail closer to the island. However, he was tied to the mast, his crew was deaf to his pleadings, so he was unable to break his previous commitment.

This is the essence of a Ulysses contract. It is where we enter a commitment that is designed to bind ourselves in the future, under certain prescribed circumstances. Ulysses contracts are common in medicine, especially advance directives, where they are known as living wills.

One use of a Ulysses contract within software development is to address technical debt. An organization may agree that a project is allowed to create a piece of technical debt, to solve a tactical project problem. However, the organization has a mechanism for reserving time and funds to subsequently pay off that technical debt.

A Ulysses contract can help you step aside from the immediate pressures of a situation, and, under the right conditions, it can form part of a technical debt strategy.

For example, when you use an agile process with retrospectives, like Scrum, you could include into your retrospective some time to discuss the technical debt that has been created during that sprint. If that level of debt created during the sprint has risen above a certain threshold, this could trigger a Ulysses contract-type clause, requiring the team to take into a subsequent sprint a given number of stories/story points that are recognized as technical debt backlog, rather than feature backlog.

Another way you can nudge the decision-making toward a more balanced outcome is by making several decisions simultaneously, rather than sequentially.

Simultaneous Versus Sequential Decisions

Suppose you work at the office of a large corporation, which has a staff canteen. The canteen food is good. Actually, it is too good, because you have been putting on a bit of weight recently. So, you have decided that on some days you will eat a bit healthier, say a salad. How will that work out?

On Monday, you turn up at the canteen. The weekend is over, and you face a full week of hard slog, so you need a bit of comfort. No salad today.

Tuesday is curry day, so no salad today. Wednesday is the middle of the week, so you need some comfort food. Thursday is burger day, and Friday is fish and chips day. Next week, you repeat the same.

Despite your very best intentions, you finish each week without ever having seen a single salad, never mind eating one. This is because you made a series of *sequential* decisions. You made your week's five decisions one-by-one, and each time you did, you stood in front of the canteen food offering and were faced with a more tempting alternative.

If instead of making your lunchtime food decisions one day at a time, you had bundled up all your week's decisions into a single decision session, preferably away from the canteen and when you were not feeling hungry, then you would have looked at your five days of unhealthy meal choices and substituted in a healthy option for one or two of those days.

You would have made healthier meal choices because you leveraged a bias, known as **diversification bias.** Read (2001) identified that people tend to include more variety when choosing several items simultaneously, rather than when choosing them sequentially.

We can use this finding to make better decisions regarding technical debt, provided those decisions do not need to be made immediately, but instead can be bundled up so that several decisions are made simultaneously.

For example, when you use an agile process, sprint planning sessions provide you with a good opportunity to diversify your choices. These sessions are usually dominated by stories that add additional features to the product. Some of these features will also add technical debt (although you may not know all the debt at the time of sprint planning).

When you add stories to the Sprint backlog, you can explicitly consider to what extent they are feature stories, feature stories that increase debt, or stories that pay down the debt. If you discover that many stories are feature stories that increase debt, you can now substitute some technical debt "salad" for some of your additional feature "burgers."

Note, during this sprint planning, you must explicitly consider the debt dimension of each story – it is not enough simply to bundle all your decisions together. In the analogy of healthy eating, if you simply made up your weekly lunchtime meal list without explicitly considering of your healthy eating goals, it would make no difference whether you made decisions sequentially or simultaneously.

Other Factors That Influence Decisions

Technical debt is a trade-off decision, one that is driven primarily by the affect heuristic. However, other factors also influence you.

One important factor is that technical debt decisions are normally made within a project. Whether that project is on track or, more commonly, behind schedule, has a profound effect upon those technical debt decisions.

Overdue Projects and Crazy Risk-Taking

How do our decisions change when a project goes from being on track to being behind schedule? We can get the answer from Nobel Prize winner Daniel Kahneman and his Prospect Theory paper, in which he describes how we make decisions under conditions of uncertainty.

In the classic book, *Thinking, Fast and Slow*, Kahneman poses a problem where people need to decide whether to follow a risky course of action, but one that may save more lives, or follow a more certain course of action that will result in fewer lives saved, but a more certain outcome.

When the problem is framed in terms of a gain, people choose the risk-adverse option, but when it is framed in terms of a loss, people choose the riskier option that offered the opportunity to save more lives but with a lower probability of success. This problem indicates how we make decisions on projects.

When a project is on track, we make decisions that are risk-adverse.

When the project is behind schedule, we make decisions that are risk-seeking.

Now, risk-adverse does not mean that we will not take a risk. Rather, it means that we only take a risk when the net gains, adjusted for probability, are greater than the net losses. We only take risks when it makes sense.

When a project changes from being on track to one that is behind schedule, our perception changes, from one of gains to one of losses. This in turn causes us to switch our risk appetite, from being risk-adverse to being risk-seeking.

When we are risk-seeking, we will take risks**, even when it is not in our rational interest to do so**. Most of us can recall being on an overdue project that ended up taking some completely crazy risks.

We'll also engage in other acts that economists would describe as "irrational behavior." One way we do this is to focus upon short-term goals. This is the overdue project behavior most responsible for the buildup of technical debt.

We desperately want to get our project back on track. And in this air of desperation, we make some extremely poor trade-offs, piling up large future technical debt problems, simply to try and edge our project a little closer to being back on schedule.

When you realize that many projects spend more time behind schedule, in crisis mode, than they spend on schedule, you recognize that a significant proportion of technical debt within an organization was created by projects behind schedule desperately trying to recover.

One approach to reduce your organization's level of technical debt is to improve project estimation, so that fewer projects end up behind schedule. Another approach is to get rid of schedules by using continuous delivery and integration.

Effect of Time Constraints

The affect heuristic is fast. It can make a decision in a few tens of milliseconds. In contrast, decision-making by our rational system is slow, as it must work by conscious appraisal.

Therefore, the less time you have available for a decision, the less opportunity you have available to apply conscious appraisal through your rational system. In any trade-off decision on technical debt, the more you need to rely upon your affective system, the more that trade-off decision will be biased toward increasing the level of technical debt.

This is a further reason individuals on overdue projects, which are usually under considerable time pressure, tend to make decisions that pile up the technical debt.

One possible solution is to try and slow down your decision. If you can stop and reflect, then you have a greater opportunity to apply conscious appraisal.

Hyperbolic Discounting

What do we really mean when we say that we have too much technical debt?

Do we mean that today we are unhappy with a trade-off decision that we made yesterday? If so, why would we be unhappy? There are three possibilities:

1. We weighted the benefits and disadvantages in our trade-off decision wrongly. This is our affect heuristic getting things wrong.

2. Conditions at the time of decision-making led us to make a suboptimal decision. This is an overdue project distorting our decision-making.

3. We judge past, current, and future decisions differently. This is hyperbolic discounting, which we discuss next.

Hyperbolic discounting is the tendency to have a stronger preference for more immediate payoffs, relative to later payoffs. It leads to choices that are inconsistent over time. We make choices today that our future selves would prefer we had made differently, despite using the same reasoning on both occasions. This certainly sounds like our technical debt problem.

In one study, Richard Thaler (1981) showed that subjects had an equal preference for $15 today, $30 after 3 months, $60 after 1 year, or $100 after 3 years. These are equivalent to interest rates of 277%, 139%, and 63%.

The technical debt part of any trade-off decision is always in the future, so hyperbolic discounting effects are relevant. When we make the trade-off decision in our minds, we heavily discount those future costs of debt. Later, our future selves will regret that we didn't make that trade-off decision differently. Humphrey Bogart was warning Ingrid Bergman against hyperbolic discounting; only he said it a bit better.

While hyperbolic discounting does play a part in decisions that lead to technical debt, the affect heuristic, plus the influence from the lack of precision and overdue projects, is more important, so we shall note hyperbolic discounting, but not explore it further.

Further Reading

If you want to learn in more depth about how evolution and our ancestral environment have influenced how you think, behave, and decide, try one of the evolutionary psychology textbooks from Barrett, or Buss, or Gaulin, listed in the references. Alternately, for an easier and more entertaining read, try *Behave* by Robert Sapolsky.

An alternative explanation as to why we humans evolved our highly advanced intelligence is given by Geoffrey Miller in *The Mating Mind*, who advocates that our intelligence evolved as a form of sexual selection, like the peacock's tail.

If you are interested in learning more about how your mind makes decisions, then *Descartes' Error* is a useful read, although somewhat difficult to digest.

If you are interested in learning more about the affect heuristic, try the paper by Epstein (1994). Alternatively, try the paper by Slovic (2007).

For an understanding of Daniel Kahneman's Prospect Theory, plus his other work, try *Thinking, Fast and Slow*. Alternatively, try reading his original paper.

If you want to know more about how you can influence yourself and others to make better decisions, try *Nudge* by Richard Thaler.

If you are interested in how the decisions around the launch of the Challenger space shuttle were made, *Truth, Lies, and O-Rings: Inside the Space Shuttle Challenger Disaster* is written by Alan McDonald, who worked at Thiokol, the makers of the solid rocket boosters. Alternately, try *The Challenger Launch Decision – Risky Technology, Culture, and Deviance at NASA* by Diane Vaughan.

Summary

In this chapter, we explored a topic at the center of understanding technical debt and how to manage it – how our mind makes decisions, including those all-important trade-off decisions that result in technical debt.

We explored the origin of our decision-making capability, which came from our ancestral past, when we needed to make rapid decisions based on poor-quality information under a variety of conditions, and always ensuring we avoided making a disastrous life-ending choice.

We learned that our default decision-making mechanism is the affect heuristic, which we know as our gut feel, with our rationality coming a poor second. This heuristic is biased toward accumulating too much technical debt. However, we can alter this, and we saw how governments used it to influence teenagers to avoid taking up smoking, plus how we can use it to steer our decisions toward taking on less debt, including by engaging stakeholders with a story, rather than facts and figures.

We also learned about precision and valence, why we may choose the wrong music dictionary in a secondhand bookstore, plus why a lack of precision in our trade-off leads us to favor taking on too much technical debt.

We learned that we could reduce our vulnerability to making poor decisions around technical debt, by using techniques such as Ulysses contracts, or making several decisions simultaneously rather than sequentially.

We also learned why overdue projects take crazy risks and pile up technical debt, why we will add more technical debt if we are making a decision in a hurry, plus why hyperbolic discounting will cause us to favor piling up technical debt for next year.

Later, in the workshop chapters, we'll pull these ideas together to suggest some practical steps toward changing our behavior and reducing our vulnerability to taking on technical debt.

However, when we make our decisions about technical debt, we rarely do so alone. Rather, we make decisions within a role that is part of a system or organization. When we do this, the characteristics and constraints of that system cause us to make very different decisions than we would make if we were acting alone.

In our next chapter, we'll explore how and why the decisions we make change dramatically when we make them not as an independent individual, but rather as someone constrained by the system we work within.

CHAPTER 6

Technical Debt As a Systems Problem

In this chapter, we focus on the systems layer of the technical debt onion model.

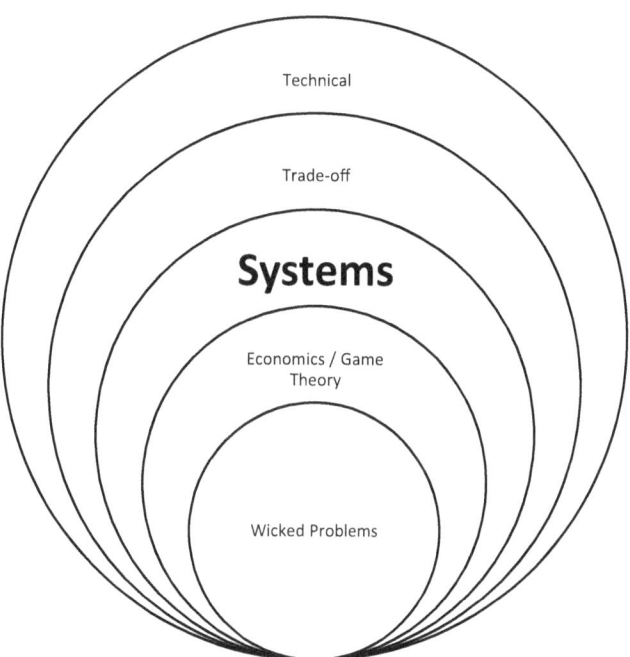

Figure 6-1. *The technical debt onion model*

CHAPTER 6   TECHNICAL DEBT AS A SYSTEMS PROBLEM

We have a lot of mysteries within software development. Many are mysterious only because we fail to explore them from a systems point of view.

In the previous chapter, we learned that we make decisions using the affect heuristic. We also learned that when we use this heuristic to make decisions about technical debt, we often end up with too much of the stuff. The good news is that we can make better decisions by applying techniques like Ulysses contracts, adding in precision, or bundling decisions together to make them simultaneously.

However, even if we applied all these techniques to our project, we would still create too much technical debt. This is because we make decisions about technical debt not as an isolated individual, but as a person *acting out a role* within a system. And that role changes the decisions we make. To address our technical debt problems, we must understand how systems work. We must then change our system, so that it behaves in ways that do not create excessive levels of technical debt.

In this chapter, we'll look at how the system our organization has created influences us to make decisions that are often not in the best long-term interests of that organization. We also look at how thinking about our organization as a system, with us making decisions while occupying roles within that system, offers us a fresh understanding of our technical debt problem.

In a later chapter, we'll extend our use of systems thinking to build dynamic models of systems using modeling software. Running these models reveals important patterns about the behavior of systems. These are patterns that are not visible if we consider systems as simply static entities.

As you read through this chapter, you may feel overwhelmed with the many diverse ideas that we explore on the journey to our destination. Don't worry, as most of these ideas are fairly simple. Keeping them together in your mind is a bit more of a challenge, so for clarity I'll summarize the main ideas we'll go through:

1. Organizations and software projects can both be seen as systems.
2. The behavior of any system is primarily determined by its structure.
3. Systems are composed of multiple interconnected components.
4. Those components often have different goals - they want different things.

5. The result is that when they're combined in new ways, or when a change is made, we get unexpected results.

6. In a social system, these goals and wants reside within the individuals, but the ways the system behaves is attributable to the system, not the individual.

7. Projects tend to be underestimated.

8. When they are, individuals, who have personal goals, place the system under pressure to become more productive.

9. This pressure causes other individuals to **stop doing some auxiliary activities** that allow the project to remain productive, maintain the software development environment, and thus keep that system safe.

10. Stopping auxiliary activities causes an initial improvement in apparent productivity, but this improvement is eventually reversed. It also **creates a danger of system collapse through a degraded environment**.

11. To address technical debt, plus many other problems, we must structure our systems so that individuals within them are not motivated to behave in ways that are detrimental to our overall goals or that risk system collapse.

This is a long list, which means that we won't encounter the most important chapter lessons until we approach the bottom of that list. Therefore, to avoid you wondering where on earth we're heading as we go through this chapter, I'll give you a brief summary of that most important lesson. That way, as we go along, you'll know where we're heading.

The most important idea to grasp is that most technical debt is a consequence of a system condition called **overshoot and collapse**.

Overshoot and collapse: Overshoot occurs when population growth exceeds the carrying capacity of the environment. Population decline and collapse soon follow, due to insufficient capacity to sustain the population. This collapse is often exacerbated by a further reduction in capacity, due to environment degradation.

Overshoot and collapse is caused by degrading your environment to a point beyond which it can no longer recover. Organizations with high levels of technical debt are usually also organizations that are also in a condition of collapse. The two are related, which is something we'll look at in the chapter on wicked problems. Strategies for avoiding overshoot and collapse will also allow you to avoid technical debt.

Let's begin by looking at some individuals behaving in a system that is placed under considerable pressure.

The Unhappy CTO

It was Thursday morning, and the CTO was not happy. The bank was scheduled to go live with its very first Internet site on Monday. The marketing and PR campaign had been running for weeks. The financial press packs had just been delivered by the printers. And in anticipation of customers transferring their branch accounts to the Internet, the bank had even begun drawing up a list of branch employees they'd like to fire.

The only problem was that the Internet site was nowhere near ready. It was now time for the CTO to earn his money and inject a bit of "can-do" attitude into the team, to encourage them across the line.

The entire project team, of over 60 people, were ordered into the assembly hall. Contractors were directed to sit on the left and employees on the right. As the team filed in, the CTO watched from behind a curtain on the stage. He could see that the audience was becoming increasingly nervous. Good. Once the CTO had judged the tension was sufficiently high, he strode out onto the stage.

"We have a go-live on Monday to get to!" The CTO bellowed, glaring at the audience. "And I'm not letting anyone of you rabble break that promise." He pointed to his right, and the audience's left, where the contractors had been directed to sit.

"You lot," he said, jabbing his finger at several audience members. "If we're not live on Monday, you're all fired. And don't bother asking for a reference, as I'll make sure you never get a job in a bank ever again."

He turned toward his left, where his own employees were sitting. "And you lot, if we're not live on Monday, your contracts will be canceled and don't bother sending me your bill!"

In addition to confirming to the audience what they had long suspected – that their CTO really didn't know his left from his right – he instilled the importance of hitting the go-live date, *no matter what*.

On Saturday evening, they were still writing new code. That's right, not fixing code, but rather writing code for functions *that did not yet exist*.

The bank's Internet site did go live on Monday. And stayed live for approximately 90 minutes before problems forced the bank to pull the plug on it.

The above horror story may sound unlikely but did in fact happen to a UK bank, where a contractor friend of mine was working. It is an extreme example of what can happen within a system when the individuals within it are placed under considerable pressure. Also, if you're ever planning on a dramatic gesture while on stage, just make sure you haven't mixed up your left and your right.

Later, we'll see that the behavior of the CTO and others in the story was driven by their acting out their roles within the system.

But what is a system? Next, let's look at what we mean by a system.

What Is a System?

Donella Meadows offers the following definition of a system:

> *A system is a set of elements or parts that is coherently organised and interconnected in a pattern or structure that produces a characteristic set of behaviours, often classified as its 'function' or 'purpose.'*

Therefore, for something to be a system, it must have the following characteristics:

1. **Parts**: Something that has only one part, such as a ball, is not a system.

2. **Interconnected parts**: A lead weight and a piece of string are not a system. But if you connect the lead weight to the string and suspend it from the ceiling, then you have a pendulum system.

3. **The structure of the interconnections produces a characteristic set of behaviors or patterns**: For example, the pendulum produces a regular, periodic motion, where the length of the string determines the period of the motion.

The third point is important to us. Although systems are influenced by external factors, the patterns of behavior they produce are driven by *their internal structure*. It is the length of string that determines the period of the pendulum. You cannot alter that period with an external stimulus, such as giving the weight a push.

Later, we'll consider our organization as a system within which software development resides. We'll show that the patterns it produces, *including the patterns of technical debt generation and removal*, are driven by internal factors, that is, the structure of that system. Therefore, if you wish to produce a lasting change within your levels of technical debt, you must change the organization of that system.

The Organization As a System

Thinking about things as systems is hardly a novel concept in IT. If you were implementing an Enterprise Resource Planning (ERP) system, your project team would include someone whose role encompassed thinking about the components as a system, as shown in Figure 6-2.

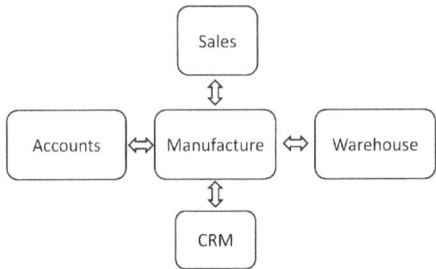

Figure 6-2. *A high-level diagram of an ERP system*

However, what we often forget when implementing that ERP system is that there exists another system that is also important. It consists of the project team, plus wider parts of the organization involved in building that ERP system, as shown in Figure 6-3.

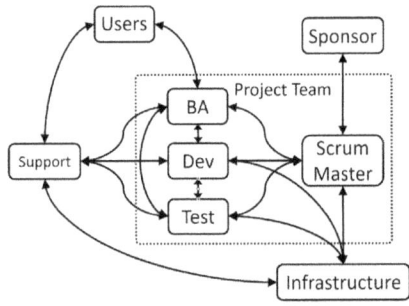

Figure 6-3. *The wider team implementing the ERP system*

How that project team is structured, plus the relationships within the team and stakeholders, has important ramifications for what is built and how long it takes, plus what technical debt is left behind afterward. For example, if the sponsor is autocratic and responds to setbacks by exerting pressure to remain on schedule, then issues are likely to be resolved by creating technical debt.

When we build software, we rarely give much thought to how the structure and behavior of that organization *as a system* influences the software we are building. Yet, that organizational system is central to what is built. Our failure to analyze the project team and stakeholders as a system lies at the heart of many unresolved software development problems, including excessive technical debt.

Crucial Difference Between IT Systems and Social Systems

There exists a crucial difference between IT systems and social or biological systems. The components or subsystems within an IT system generally *lack the ability to pursue their own goals.*

This is not true with biological or social systems, where subsystems can pursue their own goals. These goals are often in conflict with one another.

What do we mean by "pursue their own goals"? Obviously, we do not mean that one fine day a certain subsystem, say your innermost toes, woke up and decided that life would be a whole lot finer if they were bigger than all the other toes, so they set about doing this.

What we mean is that there was some natural variation in the sizes of your ancestors' innermost toes, and that at some point in our past, perhaps when apes descended from the trees and began running away from predators, ancestors with bigger toes had an advantage and left more descendants. This process of natural selection would have continued, with the bigger toed individuals leaving more descendants each time, until all species' members were endowed with bigger inner toes than their ancestors.

Now, it would be incorrect to say that your inner toe pursued its own goal, of getting bigger than all the other toes. However, while it is incorrect to say this, we are employing a literary conceit, since it is more convenient and far shorter to talk about subsystems determining or pursuing their own goals.

In the next section, we'll talk about a Y chromosome and a placenta having conflicting goals, with the Y chromosome "wanting" more nutrients but the placenta "wanting" something different. Obviously, neither the Y chromosome nor the placenta "wants" anything, at least in the sense that we think of wanting something. However, Y chromosomes that were configured in a way to get more nutrients to their host's body were likely to result in a host that was more successful and left more descendants than Y chromosomes that did not "want," or manipulate the situation, to obtain more nutrients for their host. Y chromosomes and placentas do not "want" anything, but it's an awful lot easier to follow the logic if we pretend that they do.

Conflict Between the Placenta and Y Chromosome

Parent-offspring conflict is common within biology (Barrett, 2002). The goals of parent and offspring are similar, but not identical. For example, a mother's goal is often best served by weaning her offspring as early as possible, to continue reproducing, whereas her offspring's goal is to receive nutrients for as long as possible.

Conflicts also exist between subsystems within a body, where each subsystem pursues its own optimal strategy. Usually, these conflicting effects balance out, but there can be unexpected results if one effect is absent. Let's look at a conflict between the Y chromosome and placenta in two strains of mice; *Peromyscus polionatus*, where the females are monogamous, so they only mate with one partner, and *Peromyscus maniculatus*, where the females are promiscuous, mating with any available male.

Now, the babies from both strains are born normal, as you would expect. However, can you predict what will happen if you cross a male from one strain with the female from another strain? It's not obvious, is it? Let's see what happens.

If you cross a female from the monogamous strain with a male from the promiscuous strain, the babies are born giant sized. In contrast, if the mother is from the promiscuous strain and the father from the monogamous strain, the babies are born tiny.

To understand why this occurs, you need to look at the problem from both the Y chromosome's point of view, plus the placenta's point of view. (Remember, this is just a literary conceit.) Let's consider the promiscuous strain first, as shown in Figure 6-4.

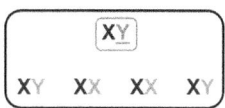

Figure 6-4. Y chromosome in the womb, with unrelated DNA, as indicated by the color and underlining

The Y chromosome always comes from the male, so it probably shares the womb with unrelated DNA. Therefore, it has every incentive to manipulate the situation to benefit itself at the expense of the mother and unrelated DNA, as shown in Figure 6-5.

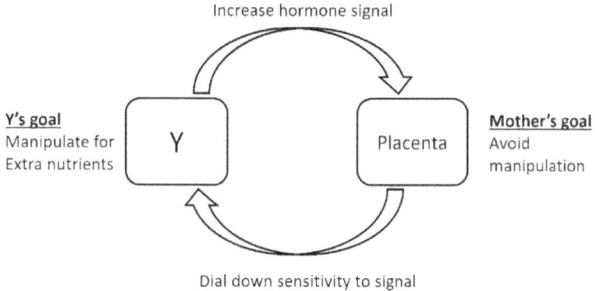

Figure 6-5. Manipulation attempt by Y chromosome, plus counteraction by placenta

The Y chromosome attempts get extra nutrients for itself by sending additional hormone signals to the placenta. However, this is not in the mother's best interests, so she dials down her sensitivity to that signal. The manipulation and its countermeasure balance out, creating normal-sized babies.

The case of the monogamous strain is shown in Figure 6-6.

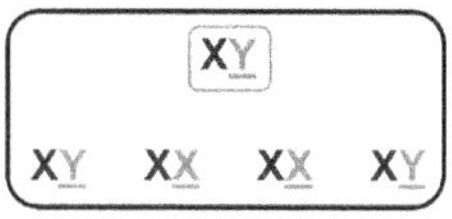

Figure 6-6. Y chromosome in the womb with related DNA

Here, the Y chromosome shares the womb with related DNA, so it has far less incentive to benefit itself. Therefore, it does not attempt to get extra nutrients, and the mother does not counteract this by dialing down her sensitivity.

However, when only the father is from the promiscuous strain, the chromosome still attempts to manipulate the mother into giving extra nutrients, but this mother lacks a countermeasure. Consequently, she provides massive amounts of nutrients, so the babies are born giant sized.

In contrast, when only the mother is from the promiscuous strain, she reacts with a countermeasure that is not needed. Consequently, she provides inadequate amounts of nutrients, and the babies are born tiny.

The most important lesson from this is to recognize that we could not predict the outcome, *until we had examined the situation from a systems point of view.*

This is highly relevant to our technical debt problem, plus many other systems problems within software development. As we stated at the start of this chapter, *many of the biggest mysteries within software development are mysterious only because we have failed to explore them from a systems point of view.*

Moreover, we can see a direct analogy between the mouse problem and our problem of software development.

There are two competing "wants" in the mouse system. Firstly, there is the "want" of the baby mouse to be born in the most advantageous state possible, by receiving plenty of nutrients. In other words, baby mouse wants a successful delivery of some functionality. Secondly, there is the "want" of the mother to keep herself alive and well nourished, so that she can continue to reproduce. In other words, momma mouse wants to maintain her system, so that it can continue to deliver functionality in the future.

In a software development system, there are also two competing "wants." Firstly, there is the "want" of the project, to deliver functionality. This is analogous to the baby mouse. Like the baby mouse, it wishes to be born in the most advantageous state possible. It can do by getting as many organizational nutrients as it possibly can, plus disposing of its unwanted waste products into the environment, as technical debt. Secondly, there is the "want" of whoever is keeping the software development system alive, so that it can deliver future functionality. This is analogous to the momma mouse.

So, if we want to reduce our technical debt, can we just dial down the demand for functionality and dial up the demand for stability? Unfortunately, it's not that simple, as it's not just within strains of mice that introducing change leads to unexpected results. In the next example, we see how the United States experienced an unpleasant surprise when it introduced alcohol prohibition.

Introducing Change: The Prohibition Problem

What happens when we make a change within a system? An IT system is deterministic, in the sense that all the states and values within it are potentially available to us for inspection. Therefore, systems that don't have conscious actors in them can often be thought of as predictable, provided we did enough calculation.

However, in a social system, actors have self-awareness and their own subgoals, which we are largely unaware of. (Let's face it, we struggle even to understand our own goals, never mind other people's goals.) Once a change occurs, actors respond by optimizing for their own subgoals. Hence, making a change sometimes often leads to entirely unexpected results, as the legislators who introduced prohibition in the United States discovered.

In the early twentieth century, many industrialized countries experienced rising levels of alcohol consumption. This caused many problems, such as increased violence, crime, and antisocial behavior. The US government attempted to address these issues through prohibition – banning the sale of alcohol. Unfortunately, they did not fully understand the system of alcohol creation and consumption, nor did they think through what might happen after alcohol was prohibited.

Before prohibition, alcohol sales were controlled through a licensing system. After prohibition, there was no more alcohol to buy, and the bars disappeared. However, consumers still existed and wanted alcohol.

Now, economics 101 tells you that if you have a demand but no supply, an entrepreneur will step in and create a supply. Of course, that was illegal, but that did not deter individuals who were already engaged in illegal activities.

The licensing system that previously controlled the drinks industry had been removed, so illegal bars sprung up everywhere, opened whenever they wished, and served alcohol to whoever they pleased, irrespective of age or state of intoxication. Consequently, alcohol consumption increased. Also, quality plummeted, and cases of poisoning increased.

The criminals running the now illegal drinks industry became immensely wealthy, powerful, and extremely violent, as they protected their interests. Crucially, they also became more *organized*, since before prohibition, organized crime had been only a minor part of criminal activities.

Consequently, the biggest long-term effect of prohibition in the United States was not the elimination of alcohol consumption, but instead was an effect that was entirely unintended – the growth of organized crime.

Arguably, the mistakes of prohibition could have been avoided if those intending to implement it had thought through the problem from a systems point of view. They may have then recognized that so long as demand for alcohol existed, removing its legal supply would likely result in replacement by illegal means.

Before we dive any further into thinking about technical debt in terms of systems, we need to cover a few basics of systems dynamics.

Basics of Systems Dynamics

System dynamics is the study of the non-linear behavior of complex systems over time using stocks, flows, feedback loops, and time delays. We'll be using parts of it in this and later chapters to understand how the structures of our organizations drive behavior that leads to technical debt. But first, we need to learn some basic principles of systems dynamics, beginning with stocks and flows.

Stocks and Flows

The most basic stock and flow diagram is shown in Figure 6-7.

Figure 6-7. *A simple stock and flow diagram*

The stock is represented by the box labeled "A." Stock is the most central part of any system. Stocks are items you can see, touch, or count. It may be something obviously physical, such as automobiles in a parking lot, or water in a bathtub. It could also be something less concrete, such as your supply of goodwill or patience with a person.

Stocks change over time through flows. In Figure 6-7, the pipe marked "inflow" represents a flow into the stock, while the pipe labeled "outflow" represents flow out of the stock. If the stock A represented automobiles in a parking lot, then the pipe marked "inflow" would represent automobiles entering the parking lot, while "outflow" would represent automobiles leaving. The cloud at the outside end of each pipe represents the external environment, which we are not concerned about here.

The convention is that stocks are represented by a capitalized word surrounded by a box, whereas flows are represented by a lowercase word linked to a pipe.

CHAPTER 6   TECHNICAL DEBT AS A SYSTEMS PROBLEM

Variables and Causal Links

Figure 6-8 shows two variables connected by a causal link.

A ⟶⁺ B

Figure 6-8. *Two variables, A and B, and a causal link*

A variable is something that influences another variable or flow. For example, in a population growth model, the variable "birthrate" influences the number of births.

Variables influence other variables and flows through causal links, shown as arrows. The direction of the arrow indicates the direction of causation: A causes B. The positive sign indicates a positive relationship, so an increase in A results in an increase in B.

Feedback Loop

Figure 6-9 shows a feedback loop.

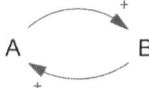

Figure 6-9. *A feedback loop*

A causes B, and B causes A. Both causal linkages are positive, so this is a positive or reinforcement feedback loop. Reinforcement loops can lead to runaway system effects. Negative or balancing feedback loops tend to introduce stability to a system. You can work out if a feedback loop is a reinforcement or a balancing loop by counting the number of negatives in the loop. An odd number of negatives indicates a balancing loop, whereas an even number indicates a reinforcing loop.

Common Dynamic System Behaviors

You recall Donella Meadows' definition of a system, "A set of elements… coherently organised and interconnected… *that produces a characteristic set of behaviours*…." Therefore, the most important thing to understand about any system is the *patterns of behavior* it produces. This means that to fully understand a system, you must observe it behaving dynamically. Examining its static structure is not enough.

CHAPTER 6   TECHNICAL DEBT AS A SYSTEMS PROBLEM

Next, we examine some dynamic behaviors of systems, beginning with exponential growth.

Exponential Growth

Figure 6-10 shows exponential growth, sometimes known as the runaway system effect.

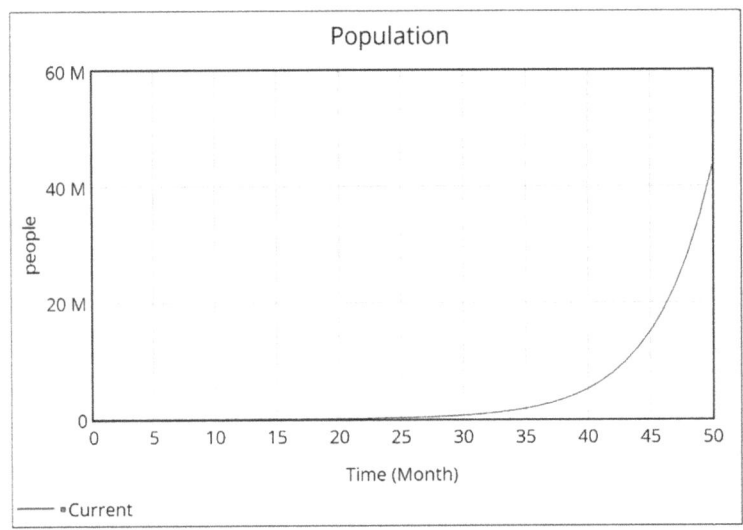

Figure 6-10. Exponential growth, or runaway system effect

This behavior occurs when there is a reinforcing, or positive feedback, loop present and conditions are such that the reinforcing loop dominates the system behavior. One example is the unpleasant effect of acoustic feedback when you hold a microphone too close to a loudspeaker. When you move the microphone away, the reinforcing loop no longer dominates, and the sound dies down.

Balancing Behavior

Figure 6-11 shows the balancing behavior exhibited by the temperature of a room controlled by a thermostat.

CHAPTER 6 TECHNICAL DEBT AS A SYSTEMS PROBLEM

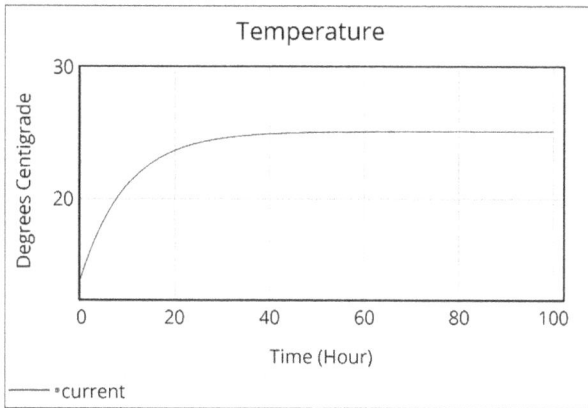

Figure 6-11. *Temperature of room controlled by a thermostat set to 25C*

Balancing behavior is typically caused by the presence of a balancing, or negative feedback, loop, where that balancing loop is dominating system behavior. When this behavior is intentionally built into a system, it is known as goal-seeking. A thermostat is a system that displays goal-seeking behavior, where the goal is to maintain the room at the desired temperature.

Balancing loops often bring stability to a system.

Growth, then Leveling Off

Figure 6-12 shows growth, then leveling off.

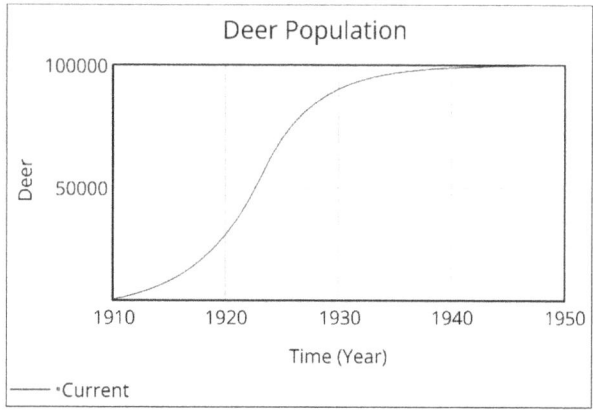

Figure 6-12. *Population growth, followed by leveling off*

93

No physical system can grow infinitely, so all systems approach a limit. Therefore, a common behavior of systems is an initial period of rapid exponential growth, followed by tapering off to a stable level.

This growth and then leveling behavior generally indicates that the *system contains two feedback loops*, one reinforcing and one balancing. At low population levels, the reinforcing loop is dominant, so the population experiences rapid growth. Later, as the population increases, factors cause the balancing loop to become dominant, causing growth to taper off to a stable level.

Examples of this behavior include an animal population that grows until it is limited by food availability, or a consumer market that experiences rapid growth, followed by market saturation.

Overshoot and Collapse

Figure 6-13 shows an example of overshoot, followed by collapse.

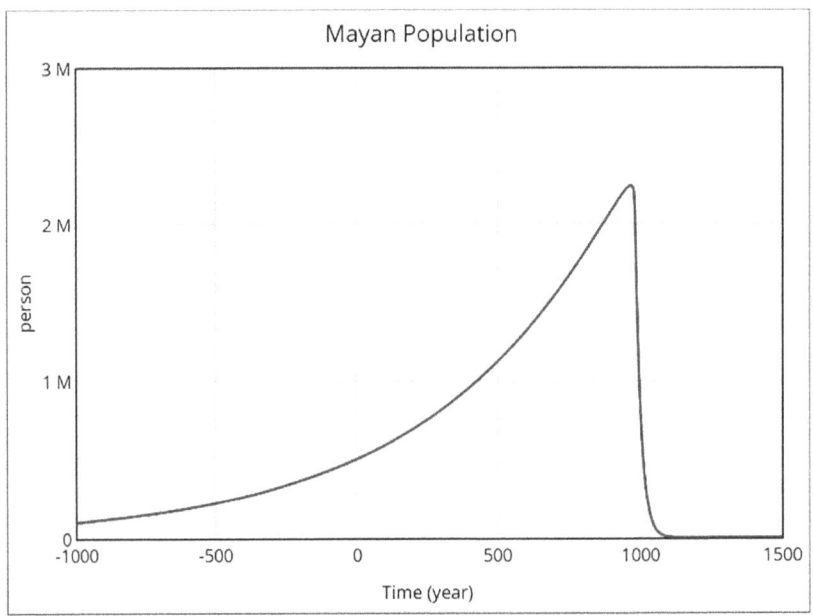

Figure 6-13. *Mayan population: 1,000 BC–1500 AD, showing overshoot and collapse*

Overshoot and collapse typically occurs in systems where there is a renewable stock or resource and that resource is harvested beyond a sustainable rate, so that the resource is depleted beyond the point from which it can recover.

Many ancient civilizations have experienced overshoot and collapse, usually driven by environmental damage to food sources (Diamond). A recent example of overshoot and collapse is overfishing within the commercial fishing industry (Meadows).

Next, we look at some effects of individuals working within systems.

Systems, Individuals, and Technical Debt

Recall that a critical difference between social and IT systems is that individuals within social systems determine and pursue their own goals. This can lead to entirely unexpected results, as the US government learned in the Prohibition problem.

We'll now look at some ways in which individuals pursuing their own goals while working within a system can drive technical debt:

1. Individuals constrained by role
2. Overdue projects and schedule recovery
3. Project underestimation
4. Overshoot and collapse
5. Policy resistance

Individuals Constrained by Role

All the world's a stage,

And all the men and women merely players

—William Shakespeare

Shakespeare drew the audience's attention to the way that all human beings are players, who merely play their assigned role every day. If somebody is a soldier, then they will play that role. When the war is over and they return to their role as a baker or butcher, they no longer play that role of soldier.

People make decisions on software projects not as independent individuals, but as a person playing a role. Often, individuals making those decisions, whether it is about technical debt or something else, recognize that their selected option is not in the best long-term interests of the organization. However, they are *constrained by their role* into making a decision that is congruent with that role, even though it's against the organization's best long-term interests. Those few individuals who step outside of their role and try to work for what they believe are the best long-term organizational interests are often sidelined, not promoted, or pushed out.

What the Hell Is Water?

Although the system plays a central part in what we do, most of the time, we are unaware of the system we are embedded within and just how much it influences us. We are like the two young fish in David Foster Wallace's parable, who swimming along meet an older fish swimming the other way. The older fish nods at them and says "Morning, boys. How's the water?" Afterward, one fish looks over at the other and asks, "What the hell is water?"

Just like these two young fish, we are often unaware of working within a system and the profound effect it has upon what we do. This leads to a bias, known as the fundamental attribution error.

Fundamental Attribution Error

Often, we fail to recognize that a person's behavior within a situation is constrained by their position or role. For example, you may feel that a given service charge on your hotel bill is unfair and you ask for its removal. The hotel receptionist may empathize with you and wish to waive it. However, if they've been given specific instructions otherwise, they are unable to do so. You may feel frustrated and attribute the receptionist's unhelpful behavior to their intransigent personality. If so, you are falling for the **fundamental attribution error**, where you attribute people's behavior to their personality, rather than their role or situation.

Like the hotel receptionist, many of us on projects are constrained by roles that require us to deliver something or adhere to certain guidelines. This may lead others to feel frustration with us. Similarly, we may feel frustration at what we see as unhelpful behavior by others but is often merely an individual constrained by *their* role. Both our frustration of others and others' frustration with us are simply examples of the fundamental attribution error.

Consequences of Individuals Constrained by Role

One example of individuals acting out their roles leading to a compromised outcome is the estimation process. Here, a proposal has been sent by an evaluation team to several contractors to bid upon. We'll cover this more in the section on project underestimation. This process generally results in the project being underestimated, sometimes significantly so.

We'll see that the reason it is underestimated is that all actors within the system – the evaluation team, stakeholders, developers, project managers, IT partners, and so on – are each making decisions not in isolation, but as part of a system. However, when each actor makes a decision, they optimize it from the *point of view of their role, not the system as a whole.*

This is analogous to the Y chromosome and placenta problem in those mice. The chromosome has evolved to pursue a strategy optimal for the unborn mouse, while the placenta pursues a strategy optimal for the mother. These conflicting strategies end in a good result for both the mouse and mother, but only because mice have had thousands of generations to eradicate any bad solutions. As soon as you make a change, like cross-breeding the monogamous and promiscuous strains, you get a huge problem.

In software development, we do not have the luxury of thousands of generations in which to trial and error solutions and eradicate the bad ones. This is one reason why changes to software development processes so often end badly.

In a later section on overshoot and collapse, we'll see individual fishing boat captains making decisions that benefit their immediate interests, despite their collective decisions being against the best long-term interests of themselves, their industry, and the environment.

If you are a business owner, you may feel frustrated by individuals acting in this way. However, to expect different is merely wishful thinking. *If you want to change how an individual behaves in a role, then you need to change the system structure, so that the role behaves differently.*

One solution is to avoid creating roles that will be in conflict with each other, or at least try to minimize that conflict. This is easier said than done, particularly in situations where you have limited control over whatever restructuring you can do.

Also, you could try to avoid recruiting or promoting the types of individuals that place their own personal goals far ahead of the organizational goals. Again, this is easier said than done, as such people are often very good in interviews.

Next, we look at how overdue projects drive increased technical debt.

CHAPTER 6　TECHNICAL DEBT AS A SYSTEMS PROBLEM

Overdue Projects and Schedule Recovery

In the previous chapter, we learned that when our project falls behind schedule, we switch our risk appetite, from risk-adverse to risk-seeking. We also learned that hyperbolic discounting causes us to undervalue the future costs of any technical debt. Also, a lack of precision in technical debt items causes that debt to have limited influence on the affect heuristic in a trade-off decision. In the chapter following this, we learn about externalities and how our trade-off decisions change when one part of the trade-off becomes somebody else's problem.

However, what we're looking at here is something different. It is that we make a decision we know is going to be bad for the organization, not because of those heuristics, biases, or shortcomings, but rather because *we make our decision based upon our role we occupy within the organization.*

Consider the CTO in the earlier story, who mixed up his left and his right onstage in front of an audience of 60 people. As he stood behind that curtain on the stage, he probably knew that going live on Monday was a bad idea for the organization. So why did he decide to follow his highly theatrical approach to forcing the team to stick to the original deadline?

In his role as CTO, he believed that his interests were best served by getting the project to go live on the agreed date, a date he had repeatedly assured his fellow directors was achievable.

Similarly, the project manager also knew that there would be big problems if they went live as scheduled. However, after the CTO's speech, he also knew that pointing this out would simply lead to him exiting the organization. On the other hand, if they went live, they may get lucky and not get hit by a showstopping problem. (Remember everyone's risk appetite has switched into risk-seeking mode.)

Those developers cutting code on Saturday evening also had a pretty good idea of the disaster awaiting them on Monday morning. However, they wanted to get paid, so they didn't want to put any unnecessary hurdles to payment in place of that.

People on overdue projects trying to recover schedule generally know that recovering schedule at the expense of increasing technical debt is probably not in the organization's best long-term interests. What's more, most project managers do care sufficiently that they would very much like to do that trade-off differently. However, like the hotel receptionist who cannot waive that item on your bill, people are locked into their role within a project.

Possible solutions include as follows:

1. Avoid estimation errors, a common source of overdue projects.

2. Allow schedule recovery without comprising technical debt, by using approaches like Ulysses contracts, as discussed in the previous chapter.

3. Adopt a development method, such as agile, that is less vulnerable to estimation errors.

Projects become overdue due for a reason, most commonly poor project estimation. We briefly look at this topic next.

Project Underestimation

Project underestimation is endemic within software development – almost every estimate is wrong, and almost always in the direction of underestimation. A common reason for underestimation is the structure of the bid process, as shown in Figure 6-14.

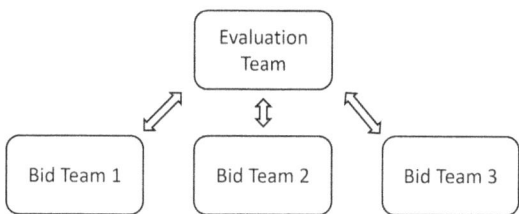

Figure 6-14. Elements within the bid process

The evaluation team want the bid to be as low as possible, as they want the best deal for their organization. However, there is another reason they want a low bid. They know that their organization cannot fund all possible projects. Therefore, if their estimate is too high, then a rival project may be funded instead. Note that of these two reasons, only the first one is always in the best interests of the organization.

Meanwhile, each bidding team wishes to win, and they are acutely aware that the winning bid is generally the lowest one. Hence, each team has an incentive to provide the lowest bid. It is preferable to bid too low, win the business, and then deal with that problem, rather than submit an accurate bid that does not win.

Why might a team bid too low? There are several possible reasons. They could be using the bid as a loss leader for additional work. Alternatively, they could be lowballing, where a subcontractor puts in an unprofitable bid that they anticipate will become profitable, either through skimping on quality or through charging high prices for changes.

But what if the lowest bid is too low, so that the winning contractor cannot fulfill it? Under these circumstances, it is not in the organization's best interests to accept a bid for a project that is never completed.

However, the evaluation team may still accept that bid, even if they know it is unfeasibly low. They know their project is in competition with other projects, so if their bid is too high, other projects may win their funding. Remember, people in evaluation teams often have a vested interest in seeing their evaluation accepted. Therefore, given the choice between accepting an accurate but higher bid that will lose out to a rival, or accepting an inaccurate, low bid that will win but cause problems later, they will choose the inaccurate bid.

Underestimation causes two problems on those subsequent projects. Firstly, it causes the project to become behind schedule. This causes all the difficulties outlined in the preceding section.

Secondly, project underestimation creates a fiction. Almost everybody on the project knows the estimate is wrong, and therefore everything based upon it must also be wrong. However, nobody wishes to be the one who calls it out. Therefore, a fiction is created. Every piece of information that is created, managed, or digested, plus every decision made, is distorted by the existence of this fiction *and the need to maintain it*.

The continued maintenance of this fiction means that important issues are often not addressed until they become impossible to ignore, by which time, they have become arduous and expensive to address.

A possible solution is to avoid setting up organizations in ways that provide parties with an incentive either to create or accept an underestimate. The most effective way to do this is to somehow avoid combining your estimation process with your bid/selection process.

Overshoot and Collapse

In *Collapse*, Jared Diamond explores civilizations that collapsed, like the Anasazi, Mayan, and Easter Island civilizations. He also explores civilizations that faced similar conditions but did not collapse, like those in the New Guinea highlands, Tikopia, and Tokugawa Shogunate of Japan.

A common factor in many collapsed civilizations was a degradation of the environment, particularly the environment's ability to sustain the population through crops or food resource. Sometimes, this degradation was caused, at least in part, by climate or environmental change. For example, both the Anasazi and Mayan civilizations both collapsed following prolonged droughts.

However, in most cases this environment degradation was caused or exacerbated by human intervention. For example, the Mayan agricultural practice of forest clearing, followed by several crop cycles and then abandonment after soil depletion, led to an initial increase in food production but subsequent decreased food availability. Unfortunately, this reduced food availability occurred at the same time as the population was increasing.

More recent examples of overshoot and collapse can be found within the modern commercial fishing industry. In *Thinking in Systems*, Donella Meadows explores three scenarios that result in (a) small overshoot and reduced but sustained harvest, (b) overshoot and oscillation, and (c) overshoot and collapse.

In the collapse scenario, efficiencies are introduced, such as sonar, that increase a fishing boat's efficiency and lead to higher profits and hence greater investment. This leads to an unsustainably high harvest rate and a reduced catch. However, fishing continues, as efficiencies from sonar still allow fish to be caught, plus reduced supply leads to higher market prices and hence maintained profitability.

When each fishing boat captain makes a decision, they do so while trapped within their role inside the fishing industry. Many of them can see their own catch dwindling, plus they know from talk on the quayside that other fishing boats are suffering the same reduced catches. But they have a bank loan on their fishing boat and tackle, employees to pay, and a family to support. And even though the catch size is going down, the price of fish is going up, so they can still make a living, even though shoals of fish are becoming ever smaller and harder to find.

When collapse does finally occur, it is far more permanent, because the harvest and depletion continued well beyond the point where non-sonar-equipped fishing vessels would have been forced to abandon activity. Now, the fishing stocks are so low it can no longer recover.

A common factor in both civilization collapse and the collapse of commercial fishing industries is this sustained degradation of the environment due to *multiple interventions aimed at increasing current production*. Each intervention enables a temporary boost to current production but comes at the cost of degrading future production.

Overshoot and collapse also occurs within software development. It is more common than we realize, mainly because within software development, we often do not recognize our problem as one of overshoot and collapse. Our overshoot is not in the number of fish caught or crops produced, but rather it is an overshoot in the completion rate of tasks. This rate is increased beyond a sustainable level, followed by collapse. The process occurs as follows.

Projects run most efficiently if they carry out certain auxiliary activities to a high standard. The activities include things like producing good requirements, collaboration between team members, effective testing, and avoiding excessive technical debt. However, while these activities allow a project to run more effectively and efficiently, *few of these activities are essential to the completion of the tasks that people are measured by*.

When a project comes under pressure, these auxiliary activities are either abandoned or only done to a minimal standard. This allows the project to concentrate on activities that are deemed required. The result is an apparent improvement in progress, as project team members, now freed from auxiliary activities, spend more time on required tasks, as shown in Figure 6-15.

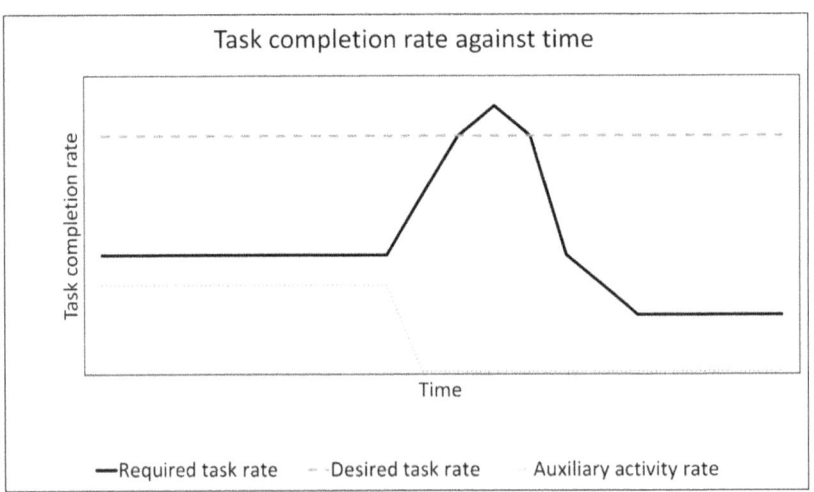

Figure 6-15. *Completion rate of required tasks and auxiliary activities. Note: only the required tasks are directly relevant to the current deliveries*

However, any improvement is only temporary, and, like the Mayan food production or commercial fishing catch, it is followed by a collapse, whereby the project's rate of progress falls below its previous level. This collapse begins when project team members commence tasks that rely upon auxiliary activities that have not been done.

These tasks now take considerably longer to complete and are likely done to a lower standard, impacting follow-on tasks. This collapse often becomes self-reinforcing, as the project slips into an increasingly inefficient firefighting mode.

Overshoot and collapse is often compounded by a failure to recognize that those auxiliary tasks are not being done, as this may have been concealed. This leaves decision-makers unaware that the additional project pressure has resulted in auxiliary activities being abandoned.

Once collapse has occurred, recovery is difficult and largely beyond the control of those involved. The European fishing fleet cannot pull the North Sea cod stock out of its collapsed state – even if all fishing ceased, stocks may still not recover. Similarly, a project team mired in firefighting cannot pull itself out of that condition – even if it somehow managed to stop creating more technical debt, all the debt from previous firefighting would still remain.

Like the collapse of commercial fishing industries, collapse in software development is exacerbated by interventions that allow a temporary boost to current production, but at a cost of continued degradation of future capacity.

Overshoot and collapse usually creates a problem of technical debt. This is because a lot of problems in a firefighting project are solved by creating technical debt items.

If we look at overshoot and collapse from the point of view of different actors within the system, we can better understand how the problem develops.

For the stakeholders and project managers, they want the application or functionality to be delivered. They are also aware that some project team members have other priorities. Therefore, it makes sense from their point of view to ensure that their stuff is prioritized by applying enough pressure.

For those under pressure – the BAs, developers, and so on – it makes sense to prioritize the tasks they are pressured to complete, at the expense of auxiliary activities. They are aware of the consequences on those auxiliary activities but will nevertheless neglect them for one of two reasons.

Firstly, if the auxiliary activity benefits another individual, like a business analyst producing a good requirement for a developer to work from, then they are not personally affected if that activity is done badly. We'll return to this later in the chapter on economics, where we talk about the externality problem. Secondly, if the task benefits their future self, they will underrate its importance due to hyperbolic discounting.

CHAPTER 6   TECHNICAL DEBT AS A SYSTEMS PROBLEM

The best solution is to avoid overshoot and collapse occurring, or to address it at a stage before complete collapse. This is just as true in software teams collapsing into firefighting mode as it is in the collapse of fishing stocks or in climate change.

To avoid collapse, you must avoid setting up structures and organizations where parties have an incentive to degrade their environment, whether that environment involves the North Sea cod stock or an organization's code base and infrastructure.

Once collapse has occurred, recovery is very difficult and probably cannot be achieved using only the resources available to the project. The most obvious route to recovery is to begin carrying out the auxiliary activities to a high standard, which should eventually allow the project to return to an efficient mode of working. However, by this stage, the project is mired deep in firefighting, and it has neither the time nor resources for this.

A further complication to recovery by this route is that recovery is not immediate. Things will appear to get worse before they get better. This often prevents the project team making decisions that lead to recovery. We explore this problem later, firstly in the chapter on economics, where we look at the tyranny of small decisions, and then secondly in the chapter on wicked problems.

Next, we look at the problem of policy resistance.

Policy Resistance

Policy resistance is where actors within a system find ways to work around the rules or policy, or otherwise behave in ways that negate the benefits intended by a policy change.

One example is governments that improve highways to relieve traffic congestion. However, any relief is only temporary, as those highway improvements result in additional travel and hence congestion.

Behavior that results in the negation of a policy change sounds suspiciously like the effect from a balancing loop, which is exactly what it is. At the heart of any policy resistance, you'll find a balancing loop. In the case of highway construction, there are several balancing loops – if you improve highways, people make additional discretionary trips, take longer journeys, increase their car ownership, and reduce their public transport usage.

An example of policy resistance in the context of projects is as follows. The UK government has recognized the problem of systematic project underestimation, which leads to budget overruns. Hence, it has mandated a policy that an allowance of 20% must be added to each project estimation.

The first policy resistance to this is that the estimation value that would previously have been given is now reduced by approximately 20%, and then an additional 20% will be added on to that reduced estimate, leaving the estimate submitted pretty much the same as before.

However, this 20% allowance now takes on a life of its own and introduces a further problem. This is the second part of this policy resistance. The project team members and stakeholders are aware of the government mandate. They mistakenly believe that the project has 20% "slack" within it somewhere, so they whittle away at this fictitious slack through adding additional features, a problem known as scope creep. This leaves the project even more overbudget and behind schedule than if the 20% allowance had never been mandated.

Later, we look at an example of policy resistance in technical debt, where we explore the counterintuitive finding that establishing and maintaining a technical debt register leads to an increase in technical debt, rather than a reduction.

Further Reading

For an introduction to systems thinking, start with *Thinking in Systems: A Primer* by Donella Meadows. It is a little dated now, but it does a good job of explaining the ideas of systems thinking.

If you are ready for a deeper dive into systems thinking, particularly system dynamics, try *Business Dynamics* by John Sterman. It gives you a thorough grounding in system dynamics, but be prepared for a heavy read.

If you want to understand the dynamics of how an organization can descend into firefighting, then the paper by Repenning (2001) models this effect occurring within new product development.

If you are interested in how civilizations can collapse, then *Collapse: How Societies Choose to Fail or Succeed* by Jared Diamond is a fascinating read into how various human societies have collapsed, plus others that survived and prospered.

If you wish to understand conflict within biology, particularly evolutionary biology, try one of the textbooks (e.g., Barrett) suggested in the further reading section of the previous chapter.

If you found the Y chromosome–placenta battle interesting, try *The Red Queen* or *Genome*, by Matt Ridley.

If you wish to learn more about prohibition and its effects, try *Last Call: The Rise and Fall of Prohibition* by Daniel Okrent. Alternatively, break out the popcorn and watch *The Untouchables* again.

If you wish to learn more about how the UK government estimates large public infrastructure projects and other government tomfoolery, try following the Google links for "UK Government Treasury Green Book," or use the link in the references.

Summary

In this chapter, we explored technical debt as a systems problem, beginning with some systems basics, looking at what a system is, and then looking at the organization as a system.

We learned that a crucial difference between IT systems and social systems is that IT subsystems do not pursue their own goals, whereas pursuing personal goals is the norm for individuals within social systems. We saw how these differences in goals lead to conflict.

We saw that when we institute a change within a social system, we sometimes get entirely unexpected results, like prohibition in the United States leading to the growth of organized crime.

We looked at some basic system dynamics, like stocks and flows, causal links, and feedback loops. We then looked at some common system effects, like runaway behavior, balancing behavior, and overshoot and collapse.

We explored how systems effects within an organization can lead to undesirable levels of technical debt. We then learned that systems effects cause many individuals to make decisions that do not serve the best long-term interests of the organization. However, those individuals feel little alternative option, given the constraints within which their role places them.

The most important lesson that you can take away from this chapter is the **lesson of collapse**. Many stable systems are finely balanced. Think of the Y chromosome-placenta system, or the Prohibition problem. When we introduce a disturbance, we often experience results that are both unintended and wide-ranging. These disturbances often lead to irreversible change, as in the collapse of North Sea fishing stocks or the Mayan civilization. This collapse can occur *even when nobody within that system desires that outcome.* None of those fishing boat captains desired the fishing stocks upon which their livelihoods depended to collapse. Yet, they were trapped within their system and, as individuals, were powerless to act in any way other than one that contributed to their own demise.

Many of us in software development are in a similar position to those fishing boat captains. Our software development systems are finely balanced. When we introduce a disturbance, we often experience results that are unintended, wide-ranging, and irreversible, like collapse. Nobody working within a software development system wants their system to collapse. Yet, just like those fishing boat captains, we each contribute to that collapse, often doing so in the full knowledge of the likely consequences of our decisions. We do this because, like those fishing boat captains, we are trapped within our system and, as individuals, are often powerless to act in any other way.

To address high levels of technical debt within your organization, you must address the limitations and perverse incentives caused by your organizational structure that drive it toward system collapse. It is most important that you address these issues in good time. Once collapse occurs, recovery is difficult, if not impossible.

We have just spent two chapters studying how our mind makes decisions, plus how these decisions become distorted when we make them while acting out a role within a system. In the next chapter, we'll pull these ideas together, as we explore technical debt as an economics problem.

Or rather, we'll explore a series of problems previously studied by economists that shed light on our technical debt problem. (Yep, we're too late for that Nobel Prize in economics.)

CHAPTER 7

Technical Debt As an Economics Problem

In this chapter, we focus on the economics layer of the technical debt onion model.

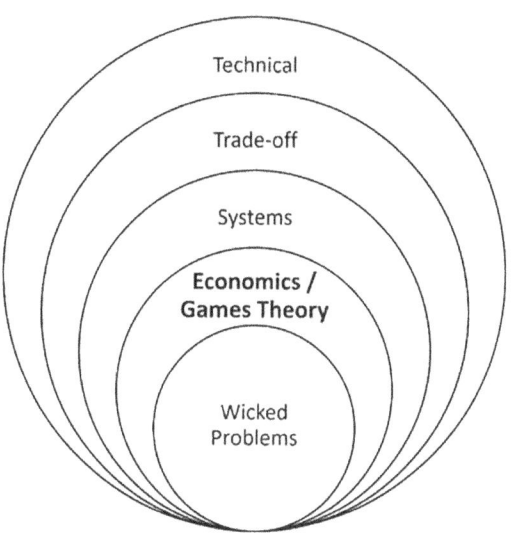

Figure 7-1. The technical debt onion model

Economics is a way of looking at problems involving agents acting for their own self-interest within a system. This sounds a lot like what is going on within a software development project. It also sounds like what we've just been exploring in the previous two chapters.

In this chapter we'll look at eight economic problems that are particularly pertinent to technical debt and then use them to gain fresh insights into our technical debt problem.

At the end of this chapter, we're not going to have a neat collection of how-to steps that we can apply to our technical debt problem. Instead, we'll have gained fresh insights from economics that we can use to change how we think about our technical debt problem. We can also use these insights to change how we think about *every* problem we encounter within software development.

Let's start by looking at what benefits we'll get from studying software problems from an economics point of view.

Benefits of an Economics Point of View

The benefits of exploring technical debt from an economics point of view are threefold:

1. Fresh perspectives offer new insights, plus potential solutions.
2. Economics offers many fruitful lessons.
3. Economics offers us a common language.

Let's now look at each of these in turn.

Economics offers us a fresh perspective on our technical debt problem. Technical debt is a difficult, long-standing problem that has proven highly resistant to solutions. This means that our current ways of looking at technical debt are not working. Therefore, we need fresh ways of looking.

Economics offers many fruitful lessons for us. Adam Smith published *Wealth of Nations* in 1776, the same year that America published its declaration of independence from Great Britain. Since then, thousands of economists have studied a vast array of problems, producing an enormous storehouse of readily available knowledge that has been applied in almost every field. The problems we face in software development are not unique to us. Rather, many in other fields have faced similar problems. Some may even have succeeded in solving their problems. We should take advantage of this cornucopia of knowledge to solve our problems rather than trying, and failing, to reinvent the wheel.

Economics offers us a common, authoritative language. In the earlier chapter on technical debt as a broken analogy, we identified that the financial debt analogy was useful because senior stakeholders, whom we must influence, were already familiar with the concept. It gave us a common language.

Similarly, exploring technical debt through the lens of economics offers us a similar common lexicon with which to speak to senior stakeholders. Importantly, this language has gravitas. Later we'll see the expression "monkey on your back," a term used for a problem that has been passed on to you.

While this colloquial expression is convenient, highly visual, and somewhat amusing, it suffers a distinct disadvantage. It never generates positive change. If you talk in these terms, people are not motivated to improve the system. They may even be motivated to pass their problems onto others, including you.

However, if you speak of the problem of externalities, then describe the conditions under which it arises, and the consequences of excessive levels of externalities, plus how to mitigate its effects, then people are more motivated to address the problem.

Although we'll examine several example economic problems, they tend to revolve around a recurring theme – an organization is a construction and so lacks an intelligence of its own. However, it needs to act intelligently. It must therefore rely upon others, or **agents**, to evaluate information and make decisions. Those agents may not always act in the best long-term interests of the organization. This can occur for several possible reasons:

1. The agent may not have available all relevant information or may lack the ability to process it. This is **bounded rationality**, which we covered in our chapter on trade-off problems.

2. The agent's role may direct them to act in a way that is optimal for that role or team but is suboptimal for the whole organization. This was covered in our chapter on **systems effects**.

3. The agent's best interest may not be aligned with the organization's best interest, so the agent follows their own best interest. This is the **principal-agent problem**, which we'll examine in the next section.

CHAPTER 7   TECHNICAL DEBT AS AN ECONOMICS PROBLEM

The economic problems we'll examine in this chapter are

- **Principal-agent problem**: The people who do the work and the people who want work done have different objectives, leading to a conflict of interests.

- **Tragedy of the commons**: It's rational to take as much as you can from a common resource if you don't pay the consequences of that extraction. This leads to resource destruction, despite nobody wanting that to occur.

- **Externalities**: This is where one party can impose costs upon another without the other party having a say in the matter.

- **Short-termism**: What is in an agent's short-term interests is different from their long-term interests.

- **Tyranny of small decisions**: Lots of small decisions add up to a larger, bad decision, one that we probably wouldn't have made.

- **Creeping normality**: A major change can be accepted as normal, provided it happens gradually through small increments.

- **Price of anarchy**: There is often a substantial price to pay for allowing multiple agents to act in their own self-interest.

- **Moral hazard**: When people who benefit from taking a risk are divorced from the consequences of their actions, risk-taking increases and bad things happen.

Each problem can cause organizations to accumulate more technical debt than they would otherwise wish.

Many of these problems fall into the category of a **social trap** or **social dilemma**. This is where a perverse incentive causes individuals to seek a short-term personal gain, but which eventually leads to an adverse outcome for all parties.

Let's begin by looking at the principal-agent problem.

Principal-Agent Problem

The principal-agent problem is a conflict in interests and priorities that arises when one party, the agent, carries out actions on behalf of another party, the principal.

—Eisenhardt, K. (1989)

The principal-agent problem is probably the most important of the economics problems that we explore in this chapter. For the principal-agent problem to occur, at least one of the following factors must be present:

1. A **discrepancy of interests** exists between the principal and agent.

2. **Asymmetric information**, with the agent possessing information that the principal lacks.

3. The principal **lacks the means to reward**, punish, or otherwise influence the agent.

The greater the discrepancy of interests and information asymmetry, plus the fewer means the principal has to influence the agent, the greater the principal-agent problem is likely to be.

Discrepancy of interests. The principal-agent problem is more common in activities that are useful to the principal but costly to the agent. This is relevant to much of technical debt, because writing debt-free code, or other activities to produce functionality that is debt-free, is useful to the principal (stakeholders), but is costly to the agent (development team members), who must expend the additional effort and resources to produce that debt-free code.

Asymmetric information. The principal-agent problem is also more common in activities that are costly or difficult for the principal to observe. Again, this is highly relevant to technical debt, since most stakeholders, and indeed many project leads, lack the technical skills or relevant technical experience to be able to make an informed observation.

Lacks the means to reward. This factor is generally less true – the principal can usually fire the agent. However, difficulties in replacing scarce technical resource may lead a principal to be reluctant to follow this route.

With two out of three factors normally present, the problem of technical debt is likely to be a fertile breeding ground for the principal-agent problem.

So far, we have only considered the situation where there is one principal. Things become considerably more complex when there are two or more principals. Having multiple principals is common in software development projects. Think of matrix management, or projects where the stakeholders include representatives from several business areas, plus the project, support and maintenance, operations, and an architecture team.

When the agent, or project team, needs to act on behalf of several principals, those principals need to agree with the agent's objectives. If they cannot do so, they face a **collective action problem** in the governance of the project.

> *A collective action problem is a situation in which all individuals would be better off cooperating but fail to do so because of conflicting interests between individuals that discourage joint action.*
>
> —Brown (2018)

A collective action problem can lead to one or more principals petitioning the agent(s) to act in their best interests, rather than the collective best interests of all. Different agents may be petitioned by different principals, leading to conflicting and incompatible goals. Does this sound familiar to you?

An example would be a project where accounts, production, and sales each want their module finished first. The product owner is petitioned to add stories for each, when a better approach would be to focus on one module at the time.

Potential Solutions

Game theory suggests changing the rules, so that the principal-agent interests are more closely aligned. One possibility is the eat-your-own-dogfood approach. This is where executives at a pet food manufacturer should sample their own product. This approach will entail software project team members supporting and maintaining the product, beyond the usual go-live hyper-care period.

However, most software development projects ramp up and down with external resource. Therefore, project team members are often aware that they will not be responsible for maintaining their code after the project ends. An organizational structure that extends a team beyond the project lifetime would create very different incentives around technical debt.

To be effective, team members must know *in advance* that they will be maintaining this code. Given many organizations' reliance upon external resource for projects, this would require a major change for those organizations.

An alternative solution is to reduce your reliance upon external resource for software projects, plus have a policy of rotating individuals between development and support. However, rotating personnel presents two challenges. One is the relatively short time spent in an organization. Many technical people now switch jobs after less than 2 years, leaving little time for rotations. The second challenge is that many individuals have a clear preference for a specific role, so they may be unhappy and possibly leave if forced into a role that is not their preference.

Project Phases When the Principal-Agent Problem Leads to Technical Debt

There are two phases where projects are particularly vulnerable to the principal-agent problem creating technical debt: requirements and design and projects behind schedule.

Requirements and Design

During requirements and design, important architectural decisions that impact the organization's technical debt may be taken without consulting the architectural team.

We previously discussed the HMV Jukebox project, where an external consultancy developed a solution that was entirely incompatible with the HMV IT architecture.

This was an almost textbook perfect example of the principal-agent problem. There was a discrepancy of interests between the principal and agent. The principal needed a solution compatible with their existing IT estate, which meant a solution coded in the IBM – Java technology stack. The agent specialized in the Microsoft–C# stack, so it wanted to use that.

Also, because the HMV directors had excluded their own IT team from the project, they had created a situation of asymmetric information. The employees who knew that selecting a Microsoft–C# technology stack would cause problems were excluded and hence could not point out this problem.

The agent followed their own best interests and designed a solution in C#. This led to considerable technical debt, until it was paid down.

It is also an example of a collective action problem, where multiple principals – the business and the IT support team – have divergent goals, and one principal, the business, petitions the agent to act in their best interests, rather than the collective best interests of all the principals.

Potential Solutions

The most obvious solution is to involve your architecture team in the early design, especially if you are using an external consultancy to develop that design.

Next, we look at how projects behind schedule influence the principal-agent problem.

Overdue and Behind Schedule Projects

We saw earlier that when a project becomes behind schedule, our mental state changes, so that we behave irrationally and don't make the best of decisions.

However, the decisions made on a behind schedule project are often also distorted because of the principal-agent and collective action problems.

The project stakeholders are keen to get the project finished in some shape or form. After all, they have stumped up their money and want to see something for it. From their viewpoint, getting even a flawed, buggy solution into live is preferable to getting the whole project canned. Therefore, in any kill-the-project/technical debt trade-off decision, they will vote to keep the project alive, at the cost of piling up the technical debt.

The development team are also mostly behind any decision to pile up technical debt. Their bonuses, promotions, and perhaps even continued employment may be resting on a (partially) successful project completion.

The stakeholders least keen to accept increased technical debt are the architecture team and the support team, who will have to nurse and support this code for the rest of its life.

In this way, overdue projects see the principal-agent problem influence their decisions, leading to increased technical debt.

Potential Solutions

To address the problem, you must ensure better alignment of principal-agent interests. For the development team, this could include extended periods in support, beyond the usual hyper-care period. It could also mean increasing your ratio of permanent employees. To change the project stakeholders' behavior, you may need to look at making organizational structure changes.

The Tragedy of the Commons

The tragedy of the commons refers to the overuse of common land or resource. Lloyd (1833) developed this concept using an example of cattle herders sharing common land.

Each herder wished to avoid overgrazing through having too many cattle on the land. However, for each additional animal a herder put on the land, they would receive all the benefits from that animal, while the damage to the commons was shared by everyone. This meant that if all herders made the decision to add an additional animal, a rational choice when made individually, the common land would be depleted or destroyed. This was to the detriment of everyone, including themselves. We saw a similar situation in the previous chapter, with the example of overfishing.

This is the essence of the tragedy of the commons. If independent individuals enjoy unrestricted access to a finite resource that is degraded through overuse or misuse, they will each tend to overuse it, resulting in its damage or destruction. If any individual exercises restraint, other individuals will take further advantage. This means that restraint is not a rational choice.

If we consider the technical estate to represent our commons, then organizations face the dilemma of the tragedy of the commons as follows.

Each actor within the organization values having a high-quality, debt-free (or minimal debt) technical estate. This is the equivalent having a commons in good condition. However, most actors can gain more value from an action that is the equivalent of putting an extra head of cattle on the land. That action could be a product owner squeezing an extra feature in at the expense of reduced testing, or a developer cutting and pasting a block of code, rather than re-factoring the original block.

The software development process itself can also exacerbate the tragedy of the commons effect. This is through a strategic factor known as **simultaneous versus sequential decisions**, which is the order in which people harvest from the commons. If individuals harvest from a limited resource pool and those harvests take place sequentially, then those that come first take more than subsequent individuals.

This is most relevant to waterfall projects, where processes typically occur sequentially. In this case, the early activities, like analysis, design, and coding will tend to take more of any common resources available. This will leave later activities, such as testing, with less resources. The result is that later resources have little alternative but to shortcut their activities, often by adding to the level of technical debt.

Potential Solutions

The essence of the tragedy of the commons is that it is, well, a commons. In the original example of grazing commons, there was not an owner who had the interests of the land in mind. If the land had been owned, then the owner would have had an obvious incentive to prevent overgrazing and thus maintain the quality of their land.

One possible solution is to ensure better and clearer ownership of all technical assets. This solution can be improved further by combining it with Ulysses contracts.

Another observation is that people take less from the common pool in public situations than anonymous ones. Therefore, if sources of technical debt are publicly known, this may lead to some restraint. However, there are obvious risks and downsides to such an approach.

Another solution is suggested by research on cooperation in commons dilemmas, which indicates that individuals are more likely to cooperate and find a suitable solution if the organization has an appropriate culture and social norms (Kopelman 2002). You can help develop this culture and norms by using tools described in the workshop and appendix sections of this book.

Externalities

An externality is a cost or benefit that one party is able to impose upon another party, without the other party being able to do anything about it.

The most commonly cited example of an externality is pollution. For example, motor vehicles produce a pollution cost, with city residents paying through health hazards. Similarly, a factory or farm can impose external costs on others through pollution of land and waterways. Until recently, those suffering the consequences of pollution had little redress.

At HMV, imposing an externality was commonly referred to as "passing the monkey," where the "monkey on your back" was an annoyance or unpleasant task that you wished to pass on to others. Related expressions include "passing the buck" and "somebody else's problem."

"That's Not My Problem!"

The above comment was the favorite response from one of the HMV project managers, whenever his project imposed some inconvenience or cost on another party within the organization. (When I say favorite response, obviously I mean it was *his* favorite response. Everybody else found it profoundly irritating. And while it was this project manager's favorite response, he was definitely not our favorite project manager.)

The message that this manager was trying to convey, albeit in a clumsy and self-centered manner, was twofold. Firstly, he was indicating that he was able to impose an externality upon another party, with the other party powerless to stop him.

Secondly, he was demonstrating that our organization was sufficiently dysfunctional that an externality was not regarded as a shameful act to be hidden away. Rather, it was an accepted way of getting things done, as well as reminding everyone who was more important than whom in the grand scheme of things.

The term "externality" originated from the meaning "external to the market." This origin indicates a problem contained within externalities – they are generally not efficient. A market brings efficiency. Therefore, something external to a market is inefficient.

Specifically, externalities are not Pareto efficient. A Pareto-efficient outcome is one where there is no other allocation available that makes one party better off without making another worse off. The existence of an externality undermines the justification for using a market economy mechanism and private property rights.

Note that we are back to the concept of property rights. In other words, we are back to someone "owning" the asset that contains the technical debt. This is an additional reason for not treating your IT estate as a common good.

Note that externalities caused by temporal or time differences will be covered in the later section on short-termism.

Externalities Driven by Organizational Structure

For externalities to exist within an organization, they must somehow be permitted. This usually means that the organization is structured in a way that permits one party to impose an externality upon another party.

In the earlier example of the HMV project to display products in multiple genres, we saw how the solution – creating a set of duplicate tables – led to technical debt. The decision to create duplicate tables is also an example of an externality driven by the organization's structure, as shown in Figure 7-2.

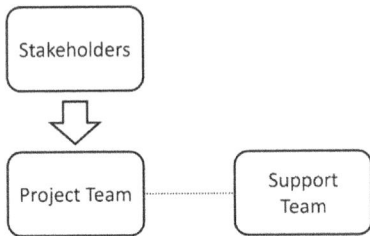

Figure 7-2. Organizational structure, driving imposition of externalities on support, by the project team

The stakeholders were able to impose their preferred solution upon the project team. They did this so that they could complete their project before the Christmas code freeze.

However, by doing so they also imposed an ongoing external cost onto the support team. This was the cost of the developer's time to do the weekly data ingest. This cost was borne entirely by the support team, who were unable to do anything about the decision.

Can Externalities Be Good? The Coase Theorem

Could there be situations when the ability of one party to impose external costs on another is good? The Economist Ronald Coase (1960) believed so. He argued that an efficient outcome could be achieved, provided the following conditions held true:

1. Property rights are well-defined.
2. People act rationally.
3. Transaction costs are minimal.
4. Complete information is available.

However, in most circumstances relating to technical debt, at least one of these conditions will not be true. First, the property rights of the technical estate are rarely well-defined. While someone may "own" the estate, they rarely have rights of redress for any debt imposed upon them. This is like owning a woodland area but having no legal redress against fly-tippers.

Second, the assumption that people act rationally is rarely true, as shown in the chapter on technical debt as a trade-off problem.

Finally, on the fourth point of complete information, much of what happens on a project occurs within a world where many things are unknown and unknowable. In any case, much of what we believe we know turns out to be a fiction.

Therefore, the Coase theorem generally does not hold true for us, so we have no reason to think that parties imposing externalities on others is a good way of resolving decisions about technical debt.

Potential Solutions

So long as individuals can pass on costs to others, many will do so. The best solution is to define better property rights around the technical estate where that debt is piling up. Additionally, you can raise awareness of what an externality is, plus how it impacts our technical debt problem.

Short-Termism

> *Short-termism: A way of thinking or planning that only considers the advantages or profits you could have now, rather than the effects in the future.*
>
> —Oxford Learner's Dictionary

Short-termism is distinct from externalities. Within an externality, the one imposing the cost and the one suffering the cost are different parties. Within short-termism, it is the same party, just at different times.

Short-termism is highly relevant to technical debt, as repayment of that debt is always in the future, while the benefits are generally now. In addition, while the timescale of costs associated with a piece of technical debt is generally uncertain, that timescale often extends beyond the project horizon. Costs that are incurred only after the end of the project risk being ignored by decision-makers, especially when those decision-makers are from an external organization.

Short-Termism in Nature

Short-termism also occurs within the natural world. One example is infanticide within lions. This occurs when the males replace other males in the lion pride, they will usually kill all the lion cubs. This happens because male lions typically only have a 2-year window in which they rule a lion pride and hence are able to pass on their genes. By killing the existing lion cubs on dynasty change, the male lions cause the nursing females to ovulate, become available for pregnancy, and hence sire infants. If the male lions did not do this, there is a good chance they would not leave any surviving offspring from their dynasty (Pusey, 1994).

Short-Termism and Technical Debt

The timeline for the cost/benefit of repaying a technical debt item is indicated in Figure 7-3.

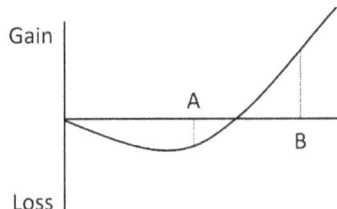

Figure 7-3. The cost/benefit of repaying a technical debt item against time

If the project has a short time horizon, finishing at point A, then the curve remains negative at that point. This means that it is not worthwhile for the project to pay that debt off (although it may be worthwhile from the organization's point of view). It is only when the project has a longer time horizon, point B, that it becomes worthwhile for the project to pay that debt off.

In addition, there is the problem of hyperbolic discounting that we discussed earlier, which will tend to devalue those future benefits.

The above argument assumes that parties are making rational choices, which they may not be. When the project becomes behind schedule, parties are much less likely to act rationally and will consider a much shorter time horizon, thus exaggerating the short-termism problem.

Potential Solutions

Many individuals in software development are embedded within a software project. They have limited visibility of what will occur to them beyond that project horizon. If the individual is from an external organization, it is highly uncertain whether they will even remain within their host organization beyond the project horizon.

It is unrealistic to expect individuals to care about a time horizon that is beyond their own personal time horizon.

Therefore, if you want to address short-termism, you focus on addressing three areas:

1. Signal to project decision-makers that the organization intends their horizon to extend beyond the current project. Note the signal must be credible.

2. Shift decision-making toward making those technical debt trade-off decisions by employees, rather than external parties.

3. Involve the architecture team more.

The following three problems – tyranny of small decisions, creeping normality, and the price of anarchy – are similar and overlap somewhat. However, there are two reasons for exploring all the problems. Firstly, there are subtle differences – tyranny of small decisions is about unrelated individuals making individual small decisions, whereas creeping normality is more about a gradual deviance, often due to cultural issues. Secondly, remember that we're looking for fresh perspectives. The more tools you have, the more likely you will gain an insight from a fresh perspective.

The Tyranny of Small Decisions

Tyranny of small decisions: A phenomenon where a myriad of decisions that are individually small and inconsequential result in an outcome that is neither optimal nor desired.

—Alfred E. Kahn (1966)

The term "tyranny of small decisions" is attributed to Alfred E. Khan, although the earliest references to the idea go back to Thucydides and Aristotle.

Khan illustrated the point using the withdrawal of a railway service in Ithaca, New York. This railway was the only reliable way to get in and out of Ithaca. It provided services in high season and off season, plus in all weather conditions. Airline and bus companies provided service during high demand and good weather, leaving the railway to provide service at less attractive times.

The rail service was eventually withdrawn, in part because of the myriad of small decisions made by potential passengers to use a non-railway service, thus making the service uneconomic to the railway. Many individuals were severely inconvenienced by the closure, as they had no way of traveling during periods of low demand and poor weather.

The *tragedy of the commons* we examined earlier is an example of the tyranny of small decisions, made by the cattle herders. Other examples include environmental degradation, where many small decisions are individually not obviously harmful, but collectively lead to destruction of environment and habitat (Odum, 1982).

When organizations descend into firefighting or collapse, they often do so not as a result of a single disastrous decision, but rather as a result of a series of small decisions, each optimized to best respond to the tactical situation of the moment.

Ideally, major decisions should be made through a series of nested levels of decision-making. Higher decision-making levels are carried out first and set the desired direction. From there, progressively lower levels of decisions are made.

Unfortunately, important decisions are often made using an entirely different approach. A series of small, apparently innocuous decisions are made, often by practitioners while they are doing the work. The result is that a major decision is made as a post hoc accumulation of these small decisions. The central problem is never addressed by the high-level decision-makers, and the process rarely delivers an optimal result for the organization.

The tyranny of small decisions is most relevant within coding. Developers make a huge number of small decisions each time they create or modify code. What's more, they make most of these decisions alone. Many of those decisions are tiny, but collectively they can add up to great significance.

Potential Solutions

One suggested approach that environmental projects use is to develop and safeguard the upper levels of decision-making. For software development, this would mean that higher decision-making levels occur first to set the desired direction and then clearly communicate that direction to all. However, you should be careful, as this approach risks descending into a growth of bureaucracy and politics.

Another approach within a software development context is to develop and safeguard your organization's technical architecture capability while ideally avoiding those problems of bureaucracy and politics.

An additional safeguard is to include within your code review sessions a period to examine whether a series of small decisions have resulted in an unintended major decision.

Creeping Normality

> *Creeping normality: The phenomenon whereby a major change or deviance goes unnoticed because it happens gradually through small incremental change.*

This phenomenon goes by many names, including gradualism, boiling a frog, camel's nose, salami tactics, and slippery slope.

Creeping normality has been offered as an explanation for the Volkswagen emissions scandal, where groups of engineers made multiple small tweaks to the car software, so that it reduced emissions under certain circumstances, such as formal emissions tests.

In *The Challenger Launch Decision*, Diane Vaughan described this behavior as the **normalization of deviance**, whereby we create and progressively adjust rationales to justify ever-increasing risk-taking. The space shuttle went through nine successful launches in ever lower temperatures. After each launch, the engineers noted the deviance and decided it was not so different from before to cause a problem. This approach was successful until on a particularly cold morning in 1986 the O-rings failed catastrophically.

In his book, *Collapse*, Jared Diamond attributes the collapse of the civilization on Easter Island to creeping normality causing the population to become accustomed to the gradual degradation of the island's environment. Explaining why the Easter Islanders would, apparently irrationally, have chopped down the last tree: "... Disaster happened not with a bang but with a whimper.... The forest the islanders depended on for rollers and rope didn't simply disappear one day – it vanished slowly over decades."

Within our technical debt context, creeping normality can occur through the gradual introduction of behaviors, often during an "emergency" issue. However, when the emergency is gone, the behavior does not revert to pre-emergency, but instead it remains and becomes the new normality.

Potential Solutions

An effective, long-term solution is difficult. After all, NASA and Volkswagen are both excellent organizations. If they are vulnerable to creeping normality, then preventing its occurrence must be difficult.

Normalization of deviance is also an issue within healthcare delivery (Banja 2010). Recommended solutions include as follows:

1. Pay attention to weak signals.
2. Resist the urge to be unreasonably optimistic.
3. System operators need to feel safe in speaking up.
4. Realize that oversight and monitoring are never-ending.

Perhaps, the most effective way of defending against creeping normality is paying attention to the organization's culture, to ensure everything can be challenged without fear.

Other potential solutions include as follows:

1. Never use past success to redefine acceptable performance, as occurred in the Challenger launch decisions.
2. Avoid groupthink.
3. Keep safety and quality programs independent from the activities they evaluate.

Price of Anarchy

Price of anarchy: A measure of how the efficiency of a system degrades due to the self-interested behavior of the agents within it.

Imagine a road transport system for a city, with many agents trying to get from a start point to a destination. We define efficiency as the average travel time for an agent. In a centralized system, the route for each agent is set by a central authority. In the decentralized system, each agent is free to choose its own route. The price of anarchy measures the ratio between the average time of the two cases.

$$PoA = \frac{Td}{Tc}$$

PoA = Price of anarchy

Tc = Average time in centralized system

Td = Average time in decentralized system

This price of anarchy is generally higher than the value 1. This means that the average journey time *increases* when agents are free to choose their own route. It increases for the following logic. Some agents can reduce their journey time by choosing an alternative route. However, by doing so they will increase other agents' time by more than their gain. In turn, these other agents may be able to decrease their journey time, but at others' expense. And so it goes on until all agents have minimized their journey times, but their average time is now greater.

If you wish to go deeper into this area, you can try picking up a text in game theory. However, I feel it's only fair to warn you that it won't be long before you start spouting terms like "Nash equilibria" or "Bayesian-Nash incentive-compatibility (BNIC)" to all and sundry, at which point all your friends will disappear, to be replaced with algorithms. You have been warned.

The relevance to technical debt is that whenever an individual makes a decision that impacts technical debt, they will generally behave like the agent in the decentralized system, maximizing their own benefit but leaving behind debt that is the equivalent of an increased journey time for others.

In extreme cases, the ultimate price of anarchy will be system collapse.

Potential Solutions

Centralize decisions that have a high price of anarchy. One such type of decisions is those that impose externalities.

Another approach to reducing the price of anarchy is for centralized policies, such as coding standards, a technical design authority, or a policy for code reviews.

Moral Hazard

> *Moral hazard: A situation where a person will take more risks because they do not bear the full costs of that risk.*

An example of a moral hazard is a homeowner who takes out home fire insurance and then becomes more careless in extinguishing the open fire at night.

The original meaning of the term moral hazard dates back to the seventeenth century and was related to insurance companies. This meaning has become extended beyond its original definition, particularly within the financial area. Economist Paul Krugman described moral hazard as "any situation in which one person makes the decision about how much risk to take, while someone else bears the cost if things go badly."

More generally, we can interpret moral hazard as individuals changing their behavior, particularly into a less social way, when they become aware that they will no longer bear the costs of their behavior change.

In *Predictably Irrational*, Dan Ariely describes a situation in a child day care center. The teachers were frustrated with parents, who sometimes were late to collect their children. This forced the teachers to remain until the children were collected, inconveniencing them. To solve the problem, that day care center imposed a fine on parents who arrived late, intending it as a deterrent. However, it had the opposite effect to what was intended. After the fine system was imposed, the incidence of late collection *increased*.

The reason was that, before the fine system, parents had a *social contract* with the teachers. If they were late and inconvenienced the teacher, they felt guilty. Therefore, they avoided being late.

However, the introduction of a fine system removed the social contract and replaced it with a transactional one. Parents no longer felt guilty and were now prepared to be late and simply pay the fine. They found payment of a small fine far preferable to feeling guilty.

There was a further twist to this story. Once it became obvious that the fine system did not work, it was removed. However, the incidence of parents being late to collect the children did not return to the previous level, but instead remained at the new, higher level.

This is an important lesson – if you institute a policy that replaces a social norm with a market transaction or rule, *that social norm is now destroyed and will not return*, even if the policy is reversed. This is characteristic of a wicked problem, which we'll discuss in the next chapter.

The relevance to our technical debt problem is as follows. In many organizations, technical debt is kept at a reasonable level by pro-social activities that are based upon social norms. If you disturb those norms, you may end up in a permanently worse situation.

The likelihood of moral hazard increases if agents are being pressured to achieve a goal, which they can work toward by trading off against less social behavior. For example, many of those parents at the child day care center would have been collecting their child after completing work. If they had not been under pressure at work, they are more likely to have been punctual. Similarly, in software development, the presence of pressure to achieve a goal will increase the likelihood of moral hazard and the destruction of social norms.

Before exploring solutions, we'll look at the moral hazard of introducing a technical debt register.

A Technical Debt Register Increases Technical Debt

Yes, that's right. If you keep a technical debt register, you are likely to find that the technical debt level within your organization *increases*, rather than decreases. Why is this?

Part of the reason can be explained by **survivorship bias** – the error of concentrating on items that pass a selection process, while overlooking those that did not. If we create a technical debt register, then we notice a whole lot of technical debt that we otherwise would have overlooked.

However, the larger part of the reason lies within the tardiness problem at the child day care center, and how those parents reacted once they were released from their social contract with the teachers.

Once you have created a technical debt register, you have legitimized debt creation. Now, all manner of things that a project would have previously addressed (okay, maybe sometimes would have secretly buried) are instead placed upon the register. And because they are on the register, they become, at least partly, the problem of whatever poor sucker owns that register.

This problem of legitimizing the creation of technical debt by entering it into a register becomes particularly acute once projects become overdue or significantly behind schedule. People on overdue projects become risk seeking, suffer from short-termism, and are generally behaving irrationally, so that debt register looks like an inviting option.

Moreover, the more active you are in addressing items on the technical debt register, for example, with a "technical debt team," the greater the temptation for some people to add just one more item to that register. After all, somebody's doing something about it, so one more item won't hurt.

Potential Solutions

Before you make any changes to your software development processes, think about the extent to which those processes depend upon the existence of a social contract. Then, think about how that, possibly fragile, social contract may be damaged by your proposed change.

We've looked at eight economics problems related to technical debt. Let's now look briefly at what additional things we can do with our newfound way of thinking about software development problems.

Additional Things You Can Do

What can you do with your newfound paradigm, of considering debt as an economics problem? Here are three courses of action you can follow.

Firstly, you can **try out some of the suggested solutions** offered for each of the problems. Not every solution will be appropriate for everybody in every situation, but there definitely will be *some* solutions that are applicable to you and your situation.

Secondly, you should **change your arguments and language**. Use terms and concepts commonly used by economists. If you are trying to raise awareness of the problems caused by allowing a culture of externalities, then talking about people "passing the monkey on their back" will likely be met with commiserations or indifference. At worst, you may have inspired somebody to game the system and get the monkey off their own back, possibly onto yours. Language of monkeys and backs is unlikely to inspire a team to change in a constructive way.

However, talk about the problem of externalities and you change people's mindset. Instead of feelings of helplessness, tactical solutions, or self-interest, people start thinking about the true causes of the problem, plus how to develop an effective, lasting solution. This is particularly true when you combine it with ideas from the next chapter – Wicked Problems.

Thirdly, you can **explore further economic puzzles** for solutions to technical debt and other software development problems. The economic literature is vast and spans from popular economics like *Freakonomics*, through more serious works like *The Wealth of Nations*, to specialist economic papers on subjects like Prospect Theory.

Many of our long-term problems in software development remain unresolved because we have not yet found a way of looking at them that offers a solution. Economists have studied many of our most intractable problems and may have solutions to many of them.

Further Reading

If you wish to explore a little deeper into economics problems, there are many interesting and useful books aimed at the non-specialist. Start simple. Popular economics books aimed at the non-specialist reader are both highly entertaining, as well as thought-provoking. Try *The Armchair Economist*, *Freakonomics*, *The Economic Naturalist*, or *The Price of Fish*.

If you want to learn more about the tragedy of the commons, then try the 1968 paper by Hardin or the original 1833 work by Lloyd.

If you want to learn more about how creeping normality can lead to tragedy, then try *Challenger Launch Decision*, by Diane Vaughan; *Truth, Lies, and O-Rings: Inside the Space Shuttle Challenger Disaster*, by Allan McDonald; or *Collapse*, by Jared Diamond.

If you are interested in learning more about game theory, then *Game Theory 101* is a good starting point.

If you are interested in learning more about the benefits and disadvantages of centralization/decentralization, which is related to the price of anarchy, then try reading *The Starfish and the Spider*.

CHAPTER 7   TECHNICAL DEBT AS AN ECONOMICS PROBLEM

Summary

In this chapter, we explored eight economics problems that are highly relevant to technical debt. Those problems were as follows: principal-agent problem, tragedy of the commons, externalities, short-termism, tyranny of small decisions, creeping normality, the price of anarchy, and moral hazard. Examining each problem offered us a fresh perspective and fruitful lessons. In addition, each problem provided us with an enlarged lexicon for our common language with business stakeholders and software development professionals.

This is perhaps the first time you have ever thought of technical debt, or indeed any software development problem, in terms of an economic problem. I hope that you have found it as enlightening as I do, and I hope that you will be motivated to explore other unresolved software development problems with the tools that economists have created.

A common theme within many of the economics problems we explored was that they have the characteristics of a **social trap** – where perverse incentives provide some individuals with a short-term gain but with an adverse outcome for all parties, as well as the system.

In the next chapter, we'll extend this theme of social traps, where we explore technical debt as a **wicked problem**. We'll learn what a wicked problem is and why it is so important that we treat technical debt as one, plus the consequences of trying to address technical debt while failing to recognize it as a wicked problem.

CHAPTER 8

Technical Debt As a Wicked Problem

In this chapter, we focus on the wicked problem layer of the technical debt onion model.

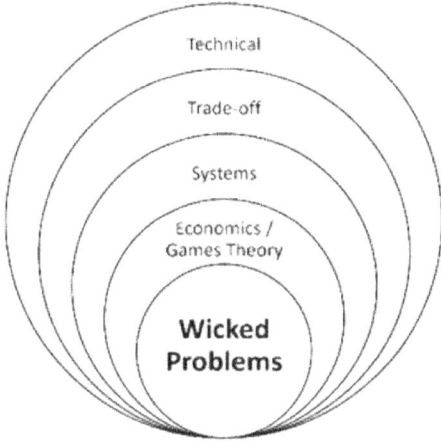

Figure 8-1. *The technical debt onion model*

In this chapter, we'll explore technical debt as a wicked problem driven by the social complexity of the systems we have created. We begin with Gerry Weinberg reminding us that every problem is always a people problem. Next, we ask why we need to study wicked problems and then briefly look at an example wicked problem – climate change. Next, we define wicked and tame problems. We then look at the characteristics of wicked problems and show how each characteristic impacts our technical debt problem. We then look at how wicked problems combine with social complexity to produce fragmentation within organizations. We finish by briefly outlining how we'll address wicked problems and fragmentation, by using dialogue mapping, a topic we'll cover in more depth in Part 3.

By the end of the chapter, you'll have a far better understanding of why problems like technical debt have persisted for so long and why addressing problems of fragmentation is so important, plus you'll have an important tool for addressing wicked problems.

Wanted: One-Handed Economist!

Give me a one-handed economist! All my economists say, "on the one hand… [and then] on the other…."

—US President Harry Truman

President Truman vented his frustration toward his advisers, complaining that they offered him discussions, rather than decisions. But were those advisers wrong? If they were offering the president their insights into a wicked problem, perhaps they were correct to offer the ambiguity of a tentative understanding, rather than the certainty of an oversimplified argument.

"It's Always a People Problem"

No matter how it looks at first, what the problem is, or what others tell you, it's always a people problem.

—Gerald M. Weinberg

This is a chapter about wicked problems. However, as we go through this chapter, always keep in mind this quote from Gerry Weinberg.

Later, we'll explore eight characteristics of wicked problems. These include, you cannot understand the problem until *after* you have a solution, you have no quick and easy test to check your solution worked, and every time you try a solution you also change the problem. Characteristics like these do make a problem truly difficult.

However, a problem with characteristics like these is still solvable. If you cannot understand the problem until after you have a solution, then you can keep trying solutions until you find one. If you have no quick and easy test to see if your solution worked, then you can keep monitoring the problem and make subsequent adjustments. If your solution attempt changes the problem, then you can address the new problem, which is hopefully smaller than the previous one.

Any problem with one of these characteristics is ultimately solvable, whether by brute force or elegant design. Even if you face a problem with a combination of these characteristics, it is probably still solvable. However, when people become involved, your problem may no longer be solvable. At the very least, it will become hugely more difficult.

In our chapter on technical debt as a systems problem, we identified a crucial difference between IT systems and social or biological systems. IT subsystems *lack the ability to determine and pursue their own goals*.

We saw that this was not true with biological or social systems, where subsystems can pursue their own goals. These goals are often in conflict with each other, as with the Y chromosome–placenta problem or with the prohibition legislators and the gangsters.

We in IT may not be a collection of prohibition legislators and gangsters, but we are distinct groups, with very different worldviews. Therefore, if one group enacts a change that improves something in their worldview, but which degrades something in another group's worldview, then the other group can and will react, possibly escalating the situation. This action–reaction leads to **fragmentation** within our organization. In a later section, we'll look at this fragmentation and how it arises from a combination of the wicked problem and the social complexity of our organization. When we try to address technical debt or any other wicked problem, we end up spending a lot of time dealing with this fragmentation.

Therefore, always remember that no matter how wicked your problem is, *it is still always a people problem*. And much of that people problem will involve addressing the fragmentation within your organization.

Why Study Wicked Problems?

In an ideal organization, one that followed the principles of our systems chapter, much of this chapter would be unnecessary. That organization would have a structure and system where all parties were aligned. This would mean that a major driver of the technical debt problem – organizational fragmentation due to various stakeholders being in conflict – would never exist.

However, there *is* conflict in our organizations. It occurs because different parties hold differing worldviews and frames for understanding the same problem. For example, the project sponsor may have a worldview that values first to market above all else, whereas the lead software architect may have a worldview that values a clean design highest. These conflicting worldviews cannot easily be resolved. Each party will carry out actions that conflict with the other's values. Where the parties must coordinate or cooperate, such cooperation will be minimal and grudging, and will tend to center around inefficient transactional exchanges or "horse trading."

As mentioned in this chapter's introduction, technical debt is a wicked problem, driven by the social complexity of the systems we have created. Therefore, to successfully address technical debt, you must understand what a wicked problem is and how it differs from a tame problem, plus how to address its wicked characteristics to achieve an enduring solution.

Next, let's look briefly at an example wicked problem – climate change.

Example Wicked Problems

Probably the most widely known example of a wicked problem is climate change. The world has recognized climate change as a problem since at least the 1980s. Yet 40 years later, we are still working toward a solution. We have had many rounds of talks, much genuine desire to solve the problem, as well as much posturing. All the while, levels of climate changing emissions continue to rise, as do global temperatures.

One possible reason for our limited progress so far is that different stakeholders hold diverging views. Some see the matter as urgent and potentially catastrophic. Others are far less concerned. A few deny that climate change even exists.

Another possible reason for our limited progress is that we have sometimes treated climate change as a collection of tame problems and attempted to apply a simplistic solution to each.

For example, the European Union imposed stringent emissions measures on manufacturing within the EU, with the intention of reducing CO_2 emissions from manufacturing. The result was that a lot of manufacturing shifted out from the EU to other countries, such as China. This allowed manufacturers to claim reduced emissions within the EU, despite net emissions increasing, due to manufacturing in a higher polluting country, plus additional transport pollution.

Other examples of wicked problems include how to prepare for natural disasters or respond afterward, overexploitation of natural resources, environmental pollution, health care funding, and poverty. None of these problems have been addressed satisfactorily. This is partly because they have not been addressed as wicked problems. Instead, when they have been addressed, it has been as a tame problem.

While we continue to treat technical debt not as a wicked problem but as a series of tame problems, we will continue to suffer the consequences of technical debt.

Next, let's look at wicked and tame problems.

Wicked and Tame Problems

Wicked problem: A problem that is impossible to fully solve due to its characteristics, which include incomplete, contradictory, and changing information, its interconnected nature, diverging viewpoints, and an absence of a true-or-false solution.

You will probably already be familiar with some wicked problems, even if you may not know them by that name. Often, these wicked problems will have been around for a long time and have proven resistant to attempts by many parties to solve them.

When we describe a problem as "wicked," we do not mean that the problem is evil or bad, but rather we're referring to the difficulty or impossibility of finding a problem resolution.

Consider a particularly difficult crossword puzzle. Perhaps, the clues are exceptionally cryptic or ambiguous, plus the words are obscure. However, no matter how difficult the puzzle is, there exists a unique solution that a sufficiently knowledgeable person could find, and which all reasonable and informed people would agree was the solution. Therefore, a crossword puzzle is always a tame problem. There is a solution out there, and if we don't get it, that's because either we're not smart enough or we lack specific knowledge.

If we contrast our problem of the crossword puzzle with problems like climate change, environmental pollution, or city congestion, we can see that they are fundamentally different. These latter problems may not have a universally accepted solution, no matter how smart or knowledgeable we are.

For a tame problem, our definition of the problem often reveals a solution. For example, the solution to a crossword puzzle is contained within the clues. In contrast, with a wicked problem we may not even understand the problem until we stumble upon a solution.

For a tame problem, the stakeholders are in agreement about the problem and its causes, whereas in a wicked problem the stakeholders are rarely in agreement about anything. Indeed, when you have a problem that involves stakeholders passionately holding differing perspectives, you'll generally have a wicked problem.

Finally, for a tame problem, the problem is complete when a solution is found, and a tame problem is like many other tame problems. For a wicked problem, this is not the case.

Characteristics of a Wicked Problem

How do we determine whether a problem is wicked or tame? Some problems, like a crossword puzzle, are obviously tame. Other problems, like climate change, are more clearly wicked. But what characteristics do wicked problems share?

Several groups have studied wicked problems, each coming up with their own criteria. Rittel and Webber (1973) listed 10 characteristics, while Conklin (2006) listed 6. We'll use the following characteristics, which are useful for software development problems:

1. You cannot understand the problem until *after* you have found a solution.
2. Stakeholders have radically different worldviews and different frames for understanding the problem.
3. How you currently understand the problem determines what you will try as a solution.
4. Solutions to wicked problems are not true or false, but better or worse.
5. You do not have an immediate and conclusive test to see if your solution has worked.
6. Every solution to a wicked problem is a "one-shot attempt."
7. Wicked problems are interconnected with other wicked problems.
8. You have no way of knowing when to stop.

Our technical debt problem matches most of these characteristics. Incidentally, software development itself has many characteristics of a wicked problem, especially point one.

We now explore each of these characteristics in turn.

1. You Cannot Understand the Problem Until *After* You Have Found a Solution

For a tame problem, you can create a list of all the information you need to understand and then solve the problem. However, you cannot do this with a wicked problem.

This is because the information you need to understand a wicked problem depends upon *how* you intend to solve it. In other words, to describe the problem in sufficient detail, you would need to create a complete list of all possible solutions ahead of time. Hence, to anticipate all the information you need to resolve the problem, you must know all the possible solutions in advance. If you cannot understand the problem until after the solution is found, then the solution *is* the definition of the problem, so you are trapped inside a circularity.

For example, in the case of our own technical debt problem – is it driven by decisions made on overdue projects, as discussed in the chapters on debt as trade-off problems and systems problems? Or is it because our affect heuristic causes us to make a poor trade-off, as discussed in that same trade-off chapter? Or is it because one party can impose an externality on another, as discussed in the chapter on debt as an economics problem? Or is it something entirely different, such as unstable requirements, which we haven't even talked about?

Think of the four chapters where we have discussed technical debt – the broken analogy, trade-offs, systems effects, and economics. Then think of the half-dozen or so possible causes of debt that we've explored in each of those chapters. That's an awful lot of possible causes, and it's not even a complete list. Nor have we considered combinations of causes in varying amounts.

Depending on what we have determined is the problem, our attempted solution will be different. If we believe our technical debt is primarily driven by decisions made on overdue projects, our solution is likely to involve improved estimation. However, if we believe our technical debt is driven by parties imposing externalities on others, then our solution is likely to involve reorganization of responsibilities.

We'll return to this circularity when we look at point three – how your understanding of the problem determines what solution you'll try. We'll also discuss it in the section on social complexity and fragmentation. Also, toward the end of the chapter, we'll revisit the connection between technical debt as a wicked problem and technical debt as a trade-off, systems, or economics problem.

2. Stakeholders Have Radically Different Worldviews

Most problems in IT involve multiple stakeholders with different worldviews. This characteristic of multiple stakeholders is central to our technical debt problem.

You can readily imagine product owners and senior management have their worldview shaped by facing constant demands from customers and end users, who are impatient to have their problems resolved. Meanwhile, their worldview is far less influenced by the relatively few demands from technical quarters.

In contrast, architects and developers have their worldview shaped by days filled with concerns about how to work around a limitation caused by a previous decision that led to a technical debt item, with demands from impatient customers a relevant but distant voice.

Later, we'll see how these radically different worldviews and frames for understanding the problem contribute to the intractability of wicked problems, through the process of **fragmentation**.

3. How You Understand the Problem Determines What Solution You Try

If our worldview frames how we understand the technical debt problem, then it will also frame how we try to solve it.

Each worldview offers a different direction to tackle the problem. But which one is right? In the next section, we learn that there is no true or false, but only better or worse. Hence, we have no way to determine the right explanation or combination of explanations, just better or worse ways. And our assessment of whether a way is better or worse will depend upon our worldview.

This reaches into the heart of not just our technical debt problem, but also into the heart of every wicked problem within IT, a topic we return to in our later section on social complexity and fragmentation.

Figure 8-2 shows a Venn diagram representing two groups within the organization: business and IT.

Figure 8-2. *Business and IT collaboration*

In the left-hand figure, there is no overlap between business and IT. Each group will view the technical debt problem entirely from their own point of view. Each will propose a solution from their own viewpoint. That solution will generally involve the other group changing their behavior to fit in with whatever their own group is already doing. This is a crucial point in the resolution of technical debt, one that we'll return to in the section on **Social Complexity and Fragmentation**.

In the left-hand figure, both parties – business and IT – work against each other. Much of what one party does will be undone by the other. Both parties will feel frustration and believe there must be a better way of working, if only the other party would see it their way!

For example, business may view the most important criteria as delivering functionality to customers. They will view their decisions that created technical debt as unavoidable, lying within the Deliberate and Prudent part of the technical debt quadrant. They will typically see a solution in terms of clearing up the technical debt afterward, or at least not slowing down their delivery pace.

In contrast, IT will view the problem entirely differently. Their preferred solution will involve addressing issues before they become technical debt and propagate further debt.

In the right-hand figure, there is some overlap between the business and IT. This indicates that both parties recognize and understand the problems of the other, so a workable solution becomes more likely.

The situation is not static, as there is a tendency for the groups to become polarized and move apart, as they each pursue their own objectives and encounter obstacles created by the other group pursuing their objectives. Later, we'll see that this polarization can be countered by working toward a **shared understanding** using workshops and appropriate tools.

4. Solutions Are Not True or False, but Better or Worse

In a tame problem, like a crossword puzzle, a solution is obviously true or false. However, for a wicked problem, there are no true-or-false solutions. You may feel qualified to judge a solution, but others are going to feel equally qualified to judge. Therefore, there can be no undisputable true or false, but merely better or worse. Importantly, that "better or worse" evaluation depends very much upon the viewpoint of the beholder.

For example, in technical debt, the product owner's preferred solution may be to enter it into the technical debt register and move on, as in their worldview the better solution is to deliver value through new functionality to the end users. This may contrast starkly with the development lead, who prefers to prioritize maintaining a clean code base. Neither solution is either correct or incorrect. And, depending upon your worldview, each solution could be considered better than the other.

At this juncture, the absence of a true-or-false solution combines with the three previous characteristics to bring progress to a halt:

1. You cannot understand the problem until after you have found a solution. At this point, you still don't have a solution, which means that neither you nor anybody else currently understand the problem. You are making judgments about something you do not understand.

2. Stakeholders have radically different worldviews and different frames for understanding the problem. So, everybody understands the problem differently. This is ironic, because at this point nobody understands the problem anyway.

3. How you understand the problem determines the solution you try.

Nobody can agree which solution is better, because everybody has a different worldview. This leads everybody to understand the problem differently. This means they each want to try different solutions. And in each person's worldview, their preferred solution is better than the preferred solution of other parties.

You cannot usually solve this conundrum by a bit of try-and-see, for two reasons. Firstly, results are neither immediate nor conclusive. Secondly, every attempt to solve the problem changes it. We'll examine these two characteristics in the following two sections.

5. You Do Not Have a Test of Your Solution

In our tame crossword puzzle or a chess game, we immediately know for certain if our solution worked.

However, with a wicked problem, we have no such test. Any implemented solution will subsequently generate a series of consequences that likely extend over a considerable period. Even if the immediate consequences are beneficial, you may find later undesirable consequences outweigh all previous benefits, as shown in Figure 8-3.

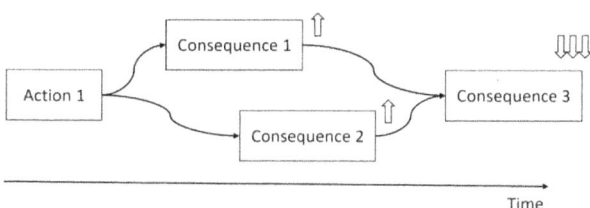

Figure 8-3. *Action 1 leads to Consequence 1 and then Consequence 2, which subsequently leads to Consequence 3. Consequences 2 and 1 are beneficial, but consequence 3 is highly undesirable*

In the example of technical debt, you may have decided that it was an utterly brilliant idea to discourage developers checking in code that broke the build. So, you make whoever broke the build responsible for all subsequent deployments, until the next unfortunate developer breaks it. You may see an immediate and gratifying reduction in build breakages and then declare your brilliant idea a resounding success.

However, you may later find out that coders now avoid working on the buggiest code areas, which might be the very areas they should be working on most. If so, you may want to rethink how successful your solution was, although you may be tempted to still declare it a resounding success to your boss.

Therefore, you should always regard your evaluation of any change as tentative – you may later discover something that causes you to re-evaluate your assessment. And remember, this is just your assessment. Others will have a different evaluation.

If your proposed change has some known delayed consequences, then you may be able to mitigate your risk by predicting the effect of your changes *before* they even occur by using **dynamic modeling software**. If you develop your model well, you can provide decision-makers with far better information for their decisions than they currently possess.

We cover models and simulation in a later chapter.

6. Every Solution Is a "One-Shot Attempt"

Back in our tame crossword puzzle, you can make as many solution attempts as you wish, provided you write in pencil and own an eraser. No solution attempt changes the problem.

In contrast, with wicked problems, *every* solution attempt may have irreversible consequences, leaving remnants that cannot be undone.

Remember your previously brilliant idea to make whoever broke the build responsible for subsequent deployments? You decide to revisit that decision, as nobody is touching those buggy areas. However, you may now find that those developers are not all that keen to revert to the previous way of working. (Apart from one poor sucker who is currently doing all the deployments and has been assigned the buggiest code areas, as he is the most junior developer and gets lumbered with all the crummiest jobs.)

Because every attempt counts significantly, you have little opportunity to learn by trial and error. Therefore, you must think through carefully every solution attempt.

7. Wicked Problems Are Interconnected with Other Wicked Problems

It would be nonsensical to consider your crossword problem as interconnected with your chess problem. However, most wicked problems are highly interconnected to other wicked problems, making it difficult to address one without influencing many others.

Let's consider technical debt. We know that it is driven, at least in part, by projects becoming overdue, which causes them to switch into irrational behavior that drives decisions that lead to technical debt. Therefore, you will find it difficult to reduce technical debt (as opposed to dealing with it afterward) without addressing the problem of overdue projects.

However, we also know that overdue projects are related to poor estimation, since underestimated projects inevitably become overdue.

We also know that poor estimation is related to technical debt, as high levels of technical debt make it difficult to accurately estimate a project.

Hence, we see not just interconnectedness but a **circularity of wicked problems**, with each problem feeding the next, as shown in Figure 8-4.

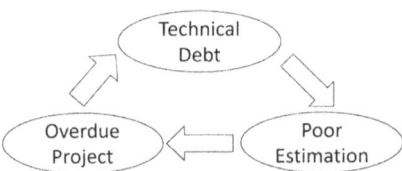

Figure 8-4. *Wicked problems are typically interconnected*

Wicked problems typically exhibit a high degree of interconnectedness. Either you cannot resolve one wicked problem while other connected wicked problems remain, or an attempt to improve one wicked problem will worsen another.

This interconnectedness means that attempts to solve a wicked problem through studying it risk descending into "analysis paralysis" and procrastination, as you uncover more information, which leads to more questions and then a need for more information.

8. You Have No Way of Knowing When to Stop

When solving a crossword puzzle or a chess game, you know when you are finished. You have criteria, like a captured king chess piece, that shows you have a solution.

However, if you cannot understand a wicked problem until *after* you have formulated a solution, then *you have no way of knowing if your understanding is sufficient* and you can now stop.

For technical debt, this means that the problem itself will never be completed. Therefore, you always end up stopping for other reasons, such as running out of time or budget, or receiving a higher priority task.

An important characteristic of any wicked problem is that stakeholders have radically different worldviews and different frames for understanding the problem. These differences lead to **social complexity**, which in turn leads to **fragmentation**. We'll cover these two topics next.

Social Complexity and Fragmentation

Social complexity: The number and diversity of players who are involved in a project. —Conklin, Jeff. Dialogue Mapping

Fragmentation = wickedness x social complexity.

—Conklin, Jeff. Dialogue Mapping

If you are facing a difficult problem as a lone individual, like Johannes Kepler faced the problem of planetary motion, then "not understanding the problem" manifests itself as an innocuous and thoughtful exploration into the problem's many mysteries.

However, if you are facing a wicked problem with multiple stakeholders, then "not understanding the problem" manifests itself in a very different way. This is because of another characteristic of wicked problems – stakeholders have radically different worldviews and different frames for understanding that problem. We can think of this characteristic as **social complexity** (Conklin 2006).

In Figure 8-5, we see two stakeholders, S1 and S2.

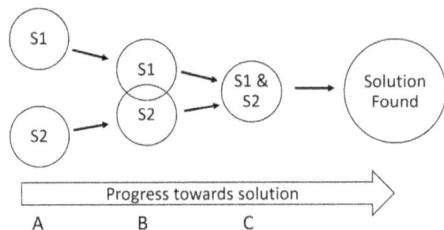

Figure 8-5. Stakeholders S1 and S2 start with radically different worldviews and then progress toward a shared understanding

At point A, stakeholders S1 and S2 hold radically different worldviews and understand the problem very differently. Remember, we *never* truly understand a wicked problem until after we have found a solution, so at this point neither stakeholder could have a correct understanding of the problem. However, each stakeholder believes they do have a correct understanding, or at least a better understanding than the other stakeholder. This is partially true, as each stakeholder will have a better understanding than the other *in their area of expertise*.

Therefore, instead of sharing an innocuous and thoughtful exploration into the problem's mysteries, like that 7-year exploration enjoyed by Johannes Kepler, each stakeholder heaps frustration and blame on other stakeholders and then attempts to persuade, cajole, or otherwise impose their beliefs of the problem and solution onto others. This may sound depressingly familiar to you.

Any attempt to resolve the different worldviews is made more difficult by two cognitive biases. Firstly, the *overconfidence effect* will cause each stakeholder to be more confident their position is correct than an impartial evaluation of the facts would warrant.

Secondly, *confirmation bias* will cause each stakeholder to search for and prefer information that confirms their preexisting beliefs, while ignoring or devaluing contradictory information. Thus, any effort by either party to investigate and resolve the issue is usually fruitless, as those efforts will be directed toward finding information to support *their* existing point of view. By doing this, they'll also try to refute any competing point of view.

A further complication is the political infighting that exists in all organizations. Each stakeholder is reluctant to accept the worldview of another stakeholder, for fear that acceptance means they will lose status or influence.

With stakeholders separated by their different understandings of the problem, and with each stakeholder unwilling and unable to understand the other's worldview, we have **fragmentation**. This makes collaboration difficult and undermines the organization's ability to work together on shared problems. You may notice it as people appearing more separated than united.

Fragmentation is most obvious when there are **visible differences**. For example, each stakeholder is convinced that their version of the problem is the only correct one. However, fragmentation can also be due to **hidden differences**. For example, each stakeholder possesses tacit assumptions that are incompatible with the tacit assumptions of other stakeholders, with each stakeholder unaware that their assumptions are not shared by all.

Fragmentation within your organization is now probably so endemic that you may accept it as inescapable, rather than try to do something about it. This is like the *learned helplessness* of the dogs we encounter in Chapter 8, who accepted the electric shocks, rather than attempted to escape them by jumping over the fence.

How can we jump over the fence, escape the shocks, and solve this dilemma?

We must start by creating a **shared understanding** of the problem, moving stakeholders in Figure 8-5 from point A to points B and then C.

Shared understanding does not necessarily mean that all stakeholders agree with each other on all material points. Instead, it means that stakeholders understand each other's positions well enough to *have an intelligent dialogue* about their different interpretations of the problem and exercise their collective intelligence to solve it.

Once we have gained a shared understanding, then we can move toward creating a **shared commitment** to possible solutions. We discuss both these processes further in Part 3, within the workshop chapters.

Dichotomy of Design

The problems of resolving technical debt, or indeed any wicked problem in IT, usually cause a dichotomy, shown in Figure 8-6.

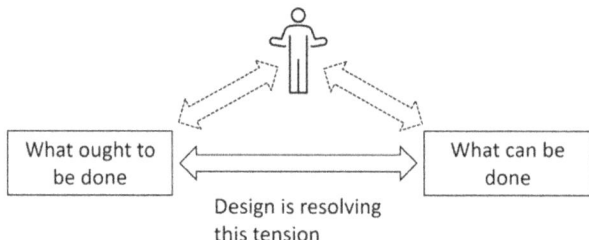

Figure 8-6. *The dichotomy of design – devising solutions that are feasible and cost effective*

On the left-hand side, you have the "what-ought-to-be." People working here are usually constrained by the demands from what ought to be possible in an ideal world.

On the right-hand side, you have the "what-can-be-done." People working here are usually constrained by the resources available to them.

When you try to solve a design problem, you are trying to resolve the tensions between the world of what ought to be and the world of what can be done. If the problem is small enough, so that you are a lone individual attempting to resolve it, like Johannes Kepler, then you will often eventually recognize the inherent dichotomy of the two sides and so come to some sort of resolution within yourself.

However, if the problem is sufficiently big that it requires several individuals to work on it, then those individuals tend to inhabit *one side or other of the dichotomy*. This means you now have a problem of resolving the two sides, as shown in Figure 8-7.

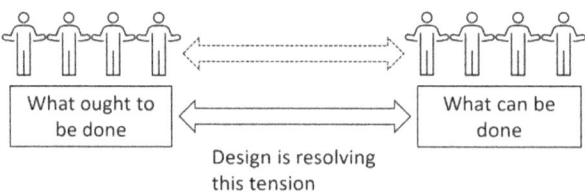

Figure 8-7. *Resolving this tension is more complex with groups*

This leads to the previously mentioned fragmentation. Those in the what-ought-to-be camp tend to be from marketing, sales, or senior management. Those in the what-can-be-done camp tend to be from IT and technical areas. Both camps tend to become an echo chamber of their own customs, values, and culture.

This dichotomy of design turns these two groups against each other in a cultural war that is expensive and fruitless. It only takes one intransigent actor from each side for fragmentation to occur and the whole process to become mired in deadlock.

This tension is caused not by incompetence, malice, nor any other human shortcoming, but instead it is caused by the nature of a wicked problem interacting with your organization's social complexity. Eventually, this tension becomes like a background pain or joint stiffness that we eventually come to accept and regard as normal.

There is one highly reliable indicator of fragmentation: blame. If your organization has a chronic blame culture, then it may well suffer from a high degree of fragmentation.

In the lead up to the *Challenger* launch disaster, some in NASA management blamed the Thiokol engineers for what they perceived as an overly conservative approach, saying, "When are those Thiokol engineers ever going to sign off the launch – sometime next year?"

At HMV we had a high degree of fragmentation. This was caused in part by the merger of HMV, the record shop, with Waterstones, the bookshop. Both HMV and Waterstones were themselves created from the merger of many record shops and bookshops – Tower Records, Zavvi, and others. Not only did we have a high degree of fragmentation, but oh boy did we have a chronic blame culture.

When we observe technical debt problems, instead of viewing the problem for what it is, an amalgam of trade-off problems, systems problems, and wicked problems, we see a big muddle and then blame each other for that muddle.

We blame senior management for sending mixed signals and offering a lack of direction. We blame HR for hiring decisions and company policies. We blame marketing and sales for making impossible promises. We blame IT for lack of reliability and problems with infrastructure. And of course, we love to blame the customers for never knowing what they want.

Ask yourself – how many conversations in your organization involve blame?

Much of our difficulty occurs because we believe we are working with a tame problem, so the wickedness of our problem sneaks up upon us. Because we do not understand we are dealing with a wicked problem, we tend to blame each other.

In the introduction, there was a story about an operation to relieve chronic migraine pain within your head, by drilling a series of small holes into your skull, to allow the evil spirit within it to escape. Although ineffective, it was a rational thing to do within that belief system.

Today, we attempt to address many of the problems that exist within organizations with solutions that are reminiscent of drilling holes into skulls to allow evil spirits to escape. And it is within our chapter on wicked problems that we most need to change our beliefs.

The good news is that once we recognize fragmentation for what it is, a whole new perspective opens up for us. Suddenly, our rivals and enemies become fellow sufferers – the only difference is that we suffer from a stiff knee whereas they have trouble with their elbow joint. In the workshop sections within Part 3 of this book, we'll explore how we can address this fragmentation, but we'll have a brief preview after the next section.

Let's now return to our earlier discussion of the connection between technical debt as a wicked problem and technical debt as a trade-off, systems, or economics problem.

Trade-Offs, Systems, Economics, and Wicked Problems

In an earlier section, we talked about not understanding a wicked problem until after we had found a solution. In it, we touched upon the connection between looking at technical debt as a wicked problem and looking at it in the ways we have previously looked at it. Here, we'll tie these connections together more explicitly.

In **Chapter** 4, we talked about the technical debt analogy being an oversimplification to financial debt, plus some flaws in the analogy. This oversimplification will lead to all factions in a wicked problem believing that they have a far better understanding of technical debt than they actually do. Those flaws in the analogy will lead different factions to understand the problem differently. Both lead to fragmentation.

In **Chapter** 5, we talked about how we make decisions using the affect heuristic, how our risk appetite switches when projects become overdue, and how hyperbolic discounting causes us to discount excessively the future cost of technical debt. These factors will affect stakeholders in different factions in different ways, again contributing toward that fragmentation.

In **Chapter** 6, we talked about how a decision that any agent makes is influenced by their role within a system. This concept is like a precursor to fragmentation and is central to wicked problems. In fact, much of the Systems chapter can be considered essentially a wicked problem description under another guise.

We can also see that the problem of policy resistance will often be the result of one faction imposing rules upon another faction, who then attempt to circumvent those rules in pursuit of their own goals.

In **Chapter** 7, we looked at eight problems:

- Principal-agent problem
- Tragedy of the commons
- Externalities
- Short-termism
- Tyranny of small decisions
- Creeping normality
- Price of anarchy
- Moral hazard

Many of these economics' problems are also wicked problems. Their presence in an organization's software development process increases the complexity of the problems which that organization faces, as well as increasing the fragmentation the organization experiences.

In conclusion, trade-offs, systems, economics, and wicked problems are all intimately related and are often simply a fresh view of the same technical debt problem, but offering different insights.

Addressing Technical Debt As a Wicked Problem

One of the more common approaches to addressing a wicked problem is to treat it as a collection of tame problems. This is done by repeatedly hacking off a piece of the problem that could be considered tame and then addressing that piece. This was the approach attempted in the earlier section on climate change, where the EU introduced CO_2 emission limits for manufacturing. However, the difficulty of this approach is, as the EU discovered, that the wicked problem often morphs around the tame solution. This often results in an outcome similar to before the intervention, but with an added complication that you generally cannot revert to the pre-intervention state.

Hacking off part of the problem and treating as tame is also a common approach with technical debt. The creation of a technical debt register, plus a team to work through the technical debt backlog, can be seen as an attempt to tame what is essentially a wicked problem. This approach may bring temporary relief, but, like the EU introducing CO_2 limits for manufacturing, it does not address the long-term problem. Also, this may lead to the wicked problem morphing around the tame solution. It may even exacerbate the problem, by encouraging the increased creation of debt, to be dumped into the register.

A more fruitful approach is to work toward addressing the organization's fragmentation problem, discussed in the earlier section on social complexity and fragmentation. This is a major source of the wickedness. For this approach, you need to take the organization on the journey depicted in Figure 8-5, beginning from their start point, through to shared understanding, and then eventually shared commitment.

To help with this, you can use tools such as facilitated discussions and dialogue mapping or argument mapping. Rationale is a software designed specifically for argument mapping. However, you can also use mind-mapping software, intended for creating and sharing ideas. Products include MindMeister, Lucidchart, XMind, Compendium, and Argunet.

A screenshot of an example argument map, displayed in the Rationale argument mapping software tool, is shown in Figure 8-8.

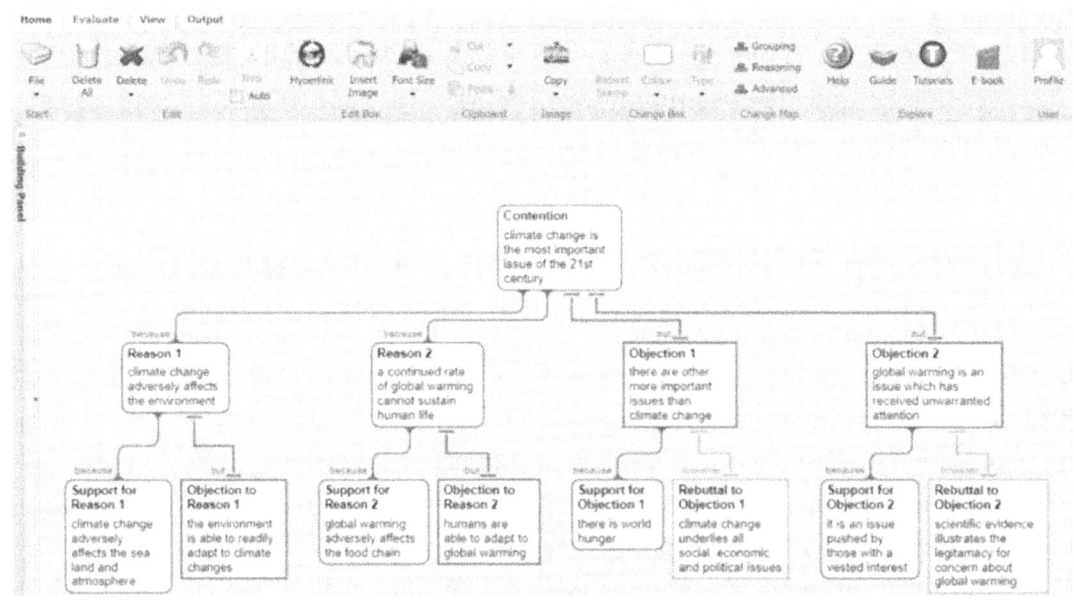

Figure 8-8. Argument mapping software, depicting a climate change argument map

Argument mapping is discussed further in the workshop chapters.

Further Reading

Rittel and Webber (1973) wrote the first paper that explicitly defined wicked problems. If you wish to master wicked problems, you should start by reading this paper. Other useful papers include *Wicked Problems in Design Thinking*, by Richard Buchanan, *Wicked Problems and Clumsy Solutions: The Role of Leadership*, by Keith Grint, and *Wicked Problems Modelling Social Messes with Morphological Analysis* by Tom Ritchey.

For an introduction to wicked problems, try *Wicked and Wise* by Watkins and Wilbur. You could also try *Exploring Wicked Problems* by Bentley and Toth.

If you want to learn how to use the techniques of dialogue mapping or argument mapping to build a shared understanding among stakeholders, I strongly recommend reading Jeff Conklin's *Dialogue Mapping: Building Shared Understanding of Wicked Problems*. You can download the first chapter from his Cognexus website.

Summary

In this chapter, we explored technical debt as a wicked problem. We started off with Gerry Weinberg reminding us that it's always a people problem. Next, we looked at what a wicked problem is and then compared it to a tame problem. We then explored eight common characteristics of a wicked problem. Next, we explored how wicked problems combine with social complexity to produce fragmentation in our organizations. We completed our exploration by briefly looking at ways to address this fragmentation.

It is this fragmentation of our organization into divergent factions that leads to so many difficulties in addressing technical debt. It is also why technical debt has been so resistant to a permanent solution.

The hard work of dealing with technical debt, or any other wicked problem, is usually managing this fragmentation aspect, shepherding diverging factions toward first a shared understanding and then a shared commitment.

Wicked problems and fragmentation lie at the heart of our technical debt problem. However, when we try to address technical debt, we usually don't address these aspects. The consequence is that the problem never really goes away. Therefore, we must address these aspects, and we'll look further into this in Part 3.

Although each organization is unique, your organization shares with other organizations many of the patterns and anti-patterns that lead to technical debt. In the next chapter, we'll look at some of these anti-patterns and how they lead to technical debt.

CHAPTER 9

Common Technical Debt Anti-patterns

In this chapter, we look at ten common anti-patterns that can lead to increased technical debt. For each anti-pattern, we'll use a causal loop diagram to show the process involved. We'll also explore potential leverage points, where making a relatively minor change could lead to a significantly different outcome.

You'll find anti-patterns and causal loop diagrams most effective when you use them as a *workshop facilitation tool*. When you run a workshop, you can use causal loop diagrams to help teams combat the growth of anti-patterns, through visualizing and socializing them.

You'll be most effective when you allow the workshop group *to build up their own* causal loop diagrams. Therefore, even though you could present a causal loop diagram much faster than the workshop group can build one, avoid the temptation to do so. Instead, allow the workshop group to build, make mistakes, argue, discuss, explore, learn, and then own their result.

We'll come back to causal loop diagrams in the workshop chapters.

Next, let's look at a well-known nursery rhyme.

There's a Hole in My Bucket!

There's a hole in my bucket, dear Liza, dear Liza,

There's a hole in my bucket, dear Liza, a hole.

Then mend it, dear Henry...

With what shall I mend it, dear Liza, dear Liza?

...

But there's a hole in my bucket, dear Liza.

CHAPTER 9   COMMON TECHNICAL DEBT ANTI-PATTERNS

Most of us are familiar with the nursery rhyme depicted above, having sung it countless times as a child, usually to the supreme irritation of any adult within earshot. The song begins with an identified problem – a hole in Henry's bucket – that he wishes to resolve. As the song progresses, we learn of a series of interconnected problems, where each problem cannot be tackled until the interconnected problem is resolved. Finally, we arrive back at the hole in a bucket problem, completing the problem's circularity.

The nursery rhyme reveals two important points relevant to our technical debt problem. Firstly, the interconnectedness and circularity of the problem, topics we explored in the chapters on systems thinking and wicked problems.

Secondly, the rhyme reveals the prohibitive cost of late intervention. By the time there is a hole in Henry's bucket, the other unresolved problems – of the uncut straw and un-sharpened knife – can no longer be resolved because Henry is unable to retrieve water.

Just like Henry's problem with his bucket, the anti-patterns we look at in this chapter typically have a high degree of interconnectedness and circularity. Also, like Henry's bucket, there is often a prohibitive cost of late intervention. Our problems are easier to fix before we get to the situation where we have a hole in our bucket, some uncut straw, and an un-sharpened knife.

Next, let's see how exploring anti-patterns helps us.

How Exploring Anti-patterns Helps Us

Pattern: A general, repeatable solution to a commonly occurring problem. Often used in software design.

Anti-pattern: A common response to a recurring problem that is usually ineffective and often highly counterproductive.

A chronic high level of technical debt within a system is rarely caused by a single isolated decision. More often, it is caused by a series of decisions, where those decisions have repeatedly resulted in increased technical debt.

If debt is caused by repeated decisions, then it is possible that many of these decisions will conform to sets of identifiable patterns. Or rather, sets of anti-patterns, as these repeated behaviors are ineffective and counterproductive. Therefore, if we can identify and understand these anti-patterns, plus why they occur, then we have an opportunity to intervene within them to achieve a different outcome.

Moreover, if we can identify leverage points within those anti-patterns, where a small investment of effort can bring about a substantial change, then we have another tool to help us in our journey to manage technical debt. These leverage points are like the "nudges" mentioned in the chapter on trade-off decisions, where behavioral scientists helped us choose an occasional salad, rather than eat a week's worth of burgers and fries.

There are three areas where exploring anti-patterns is helpful:

- **Understand the problem**: By mapping the anti-pattern as a causal loop diagram (covered next), we can easily visualize and hence more readily understand it.

- **Identify intervention points**: By examining an anti-pattern, we can identify points where we can intervene and hence "nudge" decisions in a better direction. In addition, if we can identify **leverage points**, then changes can be done more easily, with little resource expenditure. For example, if a person who wishes to stop smoking identifies that they only smoke while having a drink with fellow smokers down the pub, then this is an obvious leverage point to exploit.

- **Facilitate discussion to reach common understanding**: This is the most effective use of anti-patterns. In the chapter on Wicked Problems, we learned that a major difficulty of addressing technical debt was that different individuals had differing and often irreconcilable worldviews and frames of understanding. Exploring these anti-patterns as a facilitated group activity helps the group reach a common understanding.

Next, we look at causal loop diagrams.

Causal Loop Diagrams

A causal loop diagram, CLD, is a diagram that helps us visualize how different variables in the system are causally related. The diagram consists of variables, represented by words, and causal links, represented by arrows, as shown in Figure 9-1.

CHAPTER 9   COMMON TECHNICAL DEBT ANTI-PATTERNS

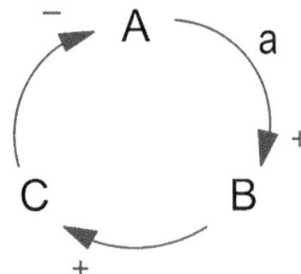

Figure 9-1. *A causal loop diagram*

The direction of the arrow indicates the causal relationship. The arrow labeled "a" goes from A to B. This indicates that A causes B, not the other way round.

A "+" sign at the arrowhead indicates that the relationship is positive. This means that an increase in A causes an increase in B. Conversely, a "-" sign indicates that the relationship is negative. An increase in C causes a decrease in A.

As mentioned in the chapter on technical debt as a systems problem, you can work out if a loop is reinforcing or balancing by counting the number of negative causal links. An odd number indicates a balancing loop, whereas an even number indicates a reinforcing loop.

You can build your own CLDs using a whiteboard or Post-It notes. I suggest you start with them. Alternatively, many mind-mapping tools and collaborative software have features you can use to build CLDs. Finally, you can use simulation or modeling software, which is the topic of our next chapter.

The diagrams you see in this chapter were drawn using the Vensim modeling tool, which we'll introduce in the next chapter. However, the same diagrams were originally drawn on a MIRO board.

The highly visual nature of a CLD enables individuals to readily grasp the essentials of the anti-pattern. However, keep in mind that CLDs are simply a convenient way of representing anti-patterns, and the two are different.

One of the most comprehensive attempts to map a problem with a CLD is the UK government obesity initiative. This initiative has produced an obesity atlas as a CLD. At the heart of this CLD are a series of energy balance loops. Surrounding this are loop clusters for major influence areas, including physiology, physical activity, psychology, food production, and food consumption.

The UK Health Authority uses this atlas to identify target interventions that can drive healthier behavior in the UK population. They also use it to model different policy options and outcomes, to help guide policy decisions.

We in software development can use CLDs for a similar purpose. Only, instead of driving healthier behavior in the human population, we can look to drive healthier behavior in our software development processes.

List of Anti-patterns

We'll explore the following anti-patterns in this chapter:

1. The estimation trap
2. Last race of the day
3. Moral credential effect
4. Broken windows theory and learned helplessness
5. Goal culture
6. Social loafing
7. OKRs and the surrogation effect
8. Descent into firefighting
9. Limited environments
10. Prototype into debt

This list is not exhaustive, and you can think up some anti-patterns of your own. Also, not all these anti-patterns directly cause technical debt. However, they will set up future conditions that lead to that debt.

We'll use the first anti-pattern to dive in a bit deeper. This is to show you how you can explore further into any CLD, to gain additional insights and identify potential intervention points. However, space dictates that we shall treat subsequent anti-patterns at a high level only.

Let's explore our first anti-pattern – the estimation trap.

CHAPTER 9 COMMON TECHNICAL DEBT ANTI-PATTERNS

Estimation Trap

The CLD for the estimation trap is shown in Figure 9-2 and works as described as follows.

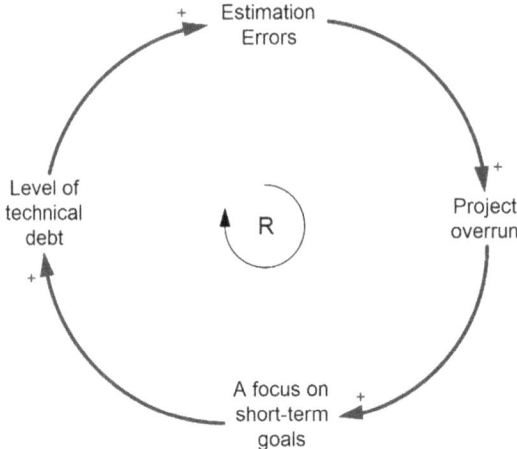

Figure 9-2. *The estimation trap. Causal links are indicated by the arrows. The circular arrow icon "R" indicates this is a reinforcing loop*

Project estimations are invariably wrong; we almost always underestimate both the time and resources required. This is represented by the item "Estimation Errors" at the top of the loop.

These estimation errors later cause the project to overrun, as represented by the arrow from "Estimation Errors" to "Project Overrun."

Once the project team recognize their project is behind schedule, they take steps to get back onto schedule. Typically, they do this by shifting their focus toward short-term goals. This is represented by the arrow from "Project Overrun" to "A focus on short-term goals."

One way the project team can recover lost schedule is by cutting corners. This leads to an increase in technical debt, represented by the arrow from "A focus on short-term goals" to "Level of technical debt."

Finally, an increase in technical debt leads to an increase in estimation errors, as explained later, thus completing the loop.

If we trace around the loop, we see that the causal links, represented by arrows, are all positive. This means that this loop is a **self-reinforcing loop**, as represented by the "R" clockwise arrow.

At HMV, we were frequently trapped in such a loop.

CHAPTER 9   COMMON TECHNICAL DEBT ANTI-PATTERNS

From Project Overrun to a Short-Term Focus

Figure 9-2 is a simple view of the estimation trap. While it is correct and informative, we cannot see where we could intervene to reduce the self-reinforcing effect. Hence, we must delve further to gain a deeper understanding. Therefore, we inserted additional steps between "Project overrun" and "A focus on short-term goals," to provide more details about how we move between the steps, as shown in Figure 9-3.

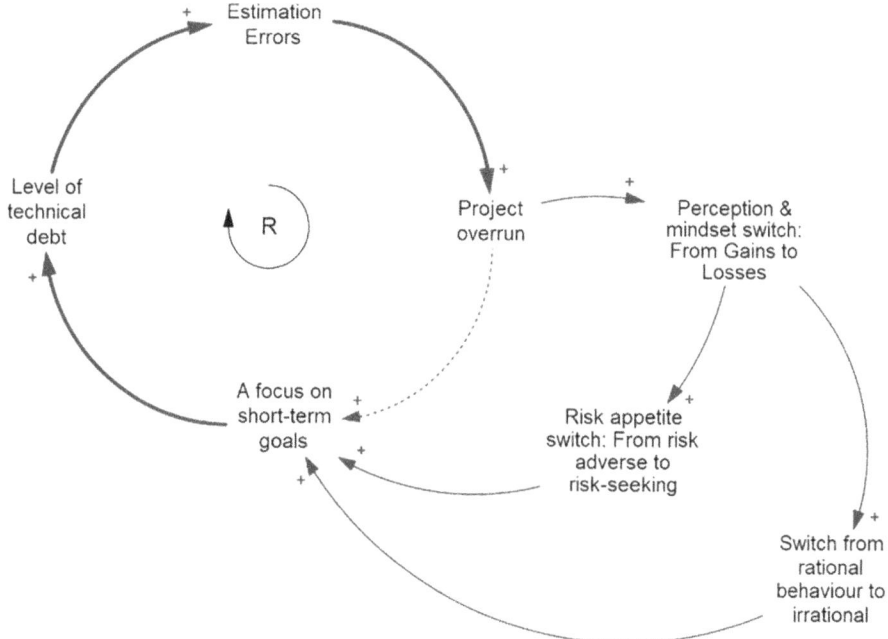

Figure 9-3. Estimation trap – from Project overrun to a focus on short-term goals

The causal behavior is now through the new links only, so we have represented the old direct link by a dashed arrow.

This new flow works as follows. After a project overruns, the mindset of the project team changes, from a mindset of gains to a one of losses. This change in mindset causes two profound changes in people's behavior, explained by the Nobel Prize–winning paper, *Prospect Theory*. Firstly, we **switch our risk appetite**, from risk-adverse to risk-seeking. Secondly, we increase our tendency toward **irrational behavior**.

The switch to risk-seeking behavior leads to overdue projects taking crazy risks. The increased tendency toward irrational behavior drives a focus toward short-term goals, or the **short-termism** discussed in our chapter on technical debt as an economics problem.

161

CHAPTER 9   COMMON TECHNICAL DEBT ANTI-PATTERNS

How does a focus on short-term goals lead to increased technical debt? To understand this, we must add other details into our diagram.

From Short-Term Focus to Technical Debt Levels

In Figure 9-4, we can see two items added – re-factoring and code reviews.

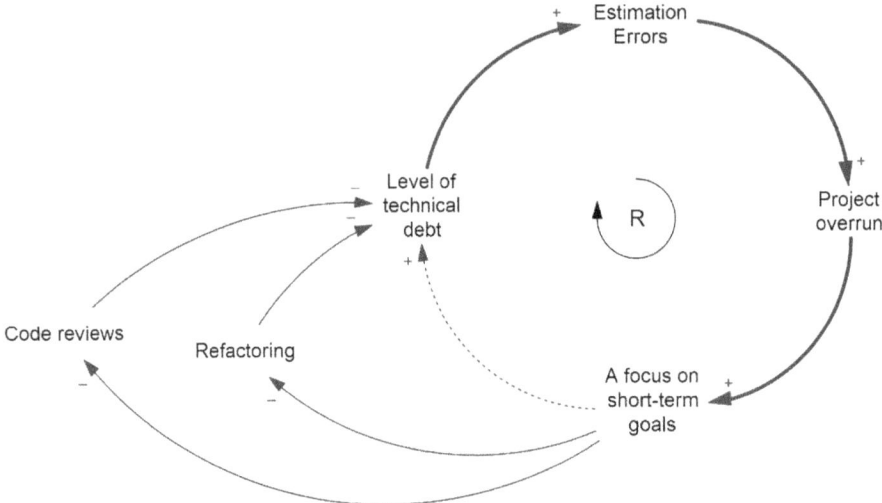

Figure 9-4. Estimation trap – from short-term focus to technical debt levels

Everybody on an overdue project is under tremendous pressure to recover lost schedule and budget in any way possible. Two common ways are to reduce or eliminate time spent on code reviews and re-factoring. Therefore, a focus on short-term goals will lead to a reduction in these activities.

The more we focus on short-term goals, the less re-factoring and code reviews we do. Therefore, both these causal arrows have a negative sign. Similarly, if we re-factor our code or do code reviews, then we will have less technical debt. Hence, the negative signs at these arrowheads.

Two successive negatives on each loop cancel out, leading them to be reinforcing loops.

We could find many other activities that would have led from short-term goals to technical debt, but for clarity we have included only these two.

Next, we look at the connection between technical debt and estimation errors.

CHAPTER 9   COMMON TECHNICAL DEBT ANTI-PATTERNS

From Level of Technical Debt to Estimation Errors

An increase in technical debt will lead to an increase in estimation errors on subsequent projects, through the following two routes, as shown in Figure 9-5.

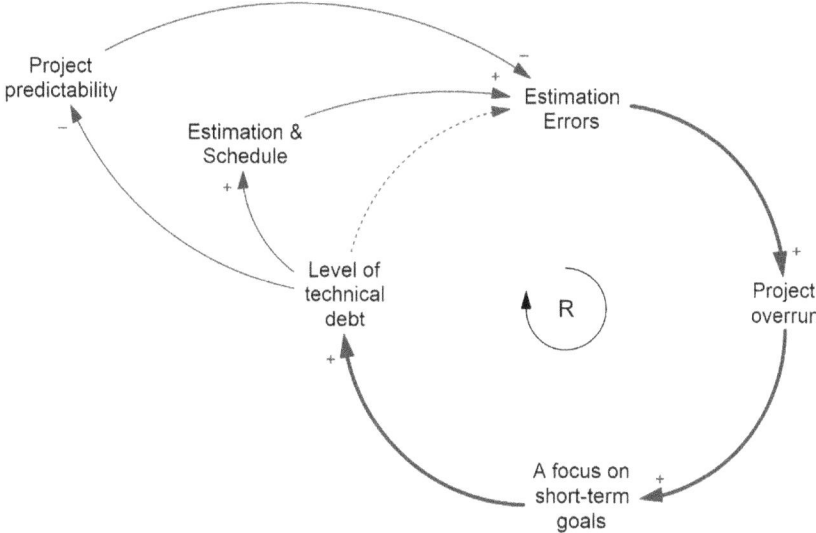

Figure 9-5. *Estimation trap – from technical debt to estimation errors*

In the first route, an increase in technical debt within the organization's estate makes projects *less* predictable. This is because when the project encounters technical debt that it must pay down, then the project will be delayed. However, the project cannot easily predict how much technical debt it will encounter, so it cannot allow for this in the estimate. Hence, an increase in technical debt reduces project predictability, which in turn increases estimation errors.

This is like the *focus factor* Henrik Kniberg talks about in *Scrum and XP from the Trenches*. It works as follows. Imagine someone with all the skills required to do a project working on it uninterrupted. How long will this job take? This gives the *ideal days*. Next, look at how long did it actually take? This gives the actual days.

> Focus factor = Ideal days/Actual days

Focus factor tells you what percentage of your team's time is taken up with non-productive activities, which includes tech debt.

In the second route, an increase in technical debt will increase the size of a project estimate. This will increase estimation errors through two mechanisms. Firstly, bigger projects have bigger estimation errors. Secondly, a project with a high estimation is unattractive. This leads to pressure from stakeholders to reduce that estimation, *even if that new estimation is known to be unrealistic*. We covered this second mechanism in the chapter on technical debt as a systems problem.

It is now time to put all these flows together.

Estimation Errors: A Complete Picture

In Figure 9-6, we can see the estimation errors CLD, with all flows included.

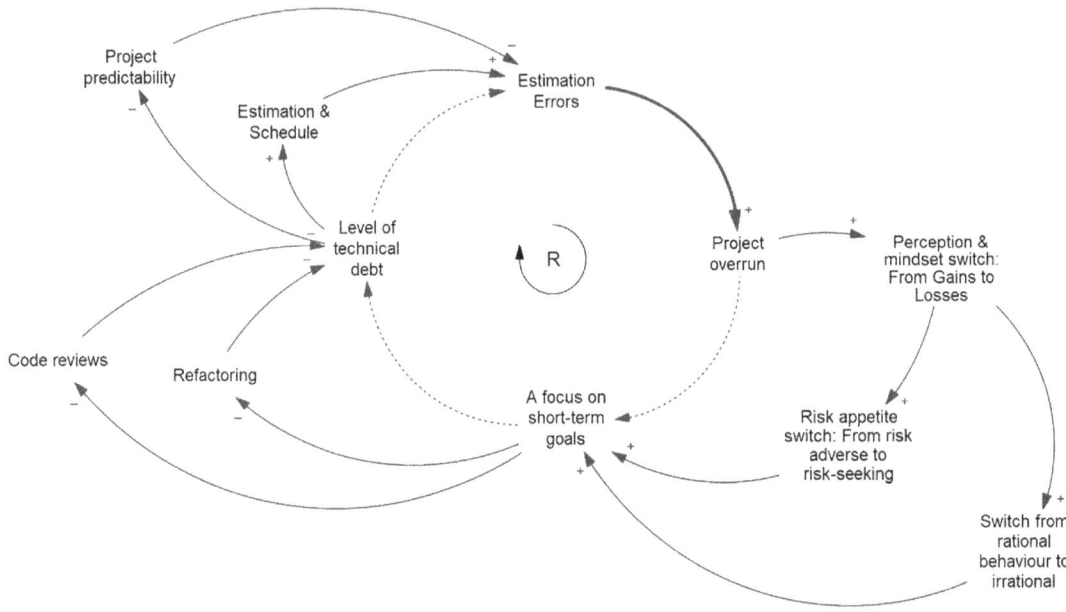

Figure 9-6. Estimation errors – a complete picture

By expanding the original causal links, we see a more comprehensive causal explanation for the anti-pattern. This more comprehensive explanation becomes useful when we switch from trying to understand to trying to intervene, since we are now looking for a leverage point, to apply a small change that will make a big difference.

Potential leverage points for estimation include

- **Estimation errors**: Reducing errors would reduce the effect of the self-reinforcing loop.

- **Project overrun**: Must a project overrun always lead to increased pressure and a focus on short-term goals? Could rescheduling be an option?

- **Level of technical debt**: Could any increased level of technical debt be tackled after project completion, through mechanisms like a Ulysses contract?

However, addressing any of these leverage points is not simple.

You can also see that there may be more than one causal factor driving an effect. Sometimes, different factors may work in opposition, with a reinforcing factor dominant in some circumstances and a balancing factor dominant in others. This may lead to complex behavior that is difficult to predict. We'll explore this further in the chapter on modeling with system modeling tools.

Finally, causal loop diagrams can rapidly become complex. While there is benefit in understanding these relationships in depth, this is a book about technical debt, not causal loop diagrams, so we'll tend toward simplicity, rather than comprehensiveness.

In the next section, we look at why project teams take gambles on options that have a low probability of succeeding, a phenomenon known as the "Last race of the day."

Last Race of the Day

The expression "Last race of the day" came from a study of horseracing gamblers, who sometimes make irrational choices on the final race of the day. See McGlothlin (1956) and Ali (1977). The effect works as follows.

Imagine you go for a day at the races with $100 in your pocket, intent on enjoying a gamble. There are ten races, and you have already decided the one horse in each race you will bet on, plus you have decided to gamble $10 each time. In the first scenario, each horse you bet on wins. This continues until, by the last race of the day, you are $200 up and feeling good with yourself. Therefore, you do not deviate from your original plan, so you put your $10 on the horse you fancied from the start of the day.

Now consider another scenario. You bet on the first race but lose. You bet on the second race, only to lose again. This goes on, until you end up at the last race with only $10 left. What you do in the last race?

You are now $90 down on the day. Horse A, the one you fancy is the hot favorite, so the odds are pretty crummy, at only 2 to 1. Therefore, if you bet on it and win, you will only end up with $30. This means that, even if you win this race, you will still be $70 down on the day.

However, there is another horse. You don't really fancy its chances, but it has fantastic odds of 10 to 1. This means that, if it wins, you will end your day not having lost any money.

The possible outcomes are shown in Table 9-1.

Table 9-1. *Possible outcomes for gambling $10 on horse A or B*

Outcome	Winnings for race	Gains (losses) for day
Horse A wins at 2 to 1	$30	($70 loss)
Horse B wins at 10 to 1	$110	**$10 gain**
Horse A loses	0	($100 loss)
Horse B loses	0	($100 loss)

The thought of going home with slightly more money than you started feels much better than returning home $70 out of pocket. Therefore, you decide to put your last $10 on the 10 to 1 longshot. As a long shot, it loses, and you watch the last of your money disappear.

Projects behind schedule often make similar decisions to those gamblers at the horse races, betting small amounts of project resource on longshots which, if successful, would return the project to its planned schedule.

The last race of the day effect works on a project as shown in Figure 9-7.

CHAPTER 9   COMMON TECHNICAL DEBT ANTI-PATTERNS

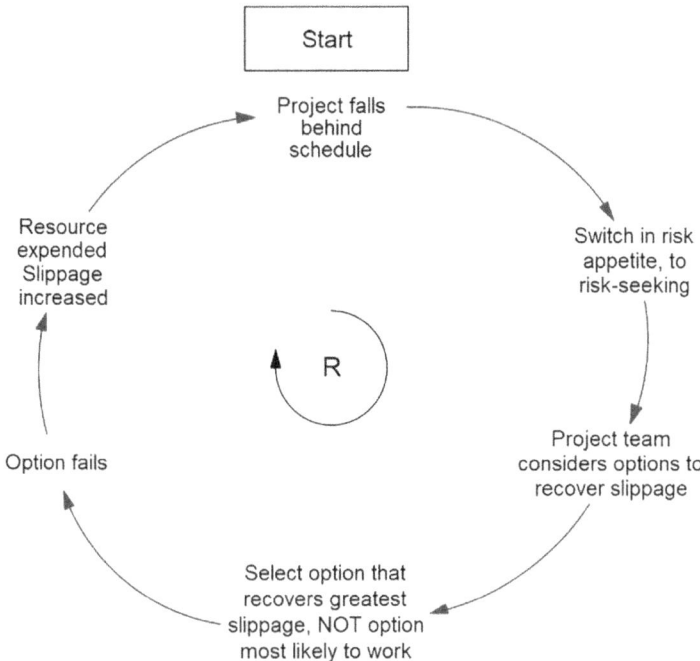

Figure 9-7. *Last race of the day on a software project*

After the project falls behind schedule, the project team switch their risk appetite into risk-seeking mode. They then consider available options to recover the slippage. Of the options available, the most attractive-looking option is the one that recovers the most project slippage. Ideally, it should offer the chance of recovering *all* the slippage. However, this option is unlikely to work.

This option is selected and subsequently fails. The project is now further behind schedule, has expended further project resource, and may be tempted to repeat the process.

Why might a project team select an option that has little chance of success? The reasoning is as follows. The project team want to avoid being blamed for late delivery. Therefore, they are most interested in options that recover *all* slippage. Hence, any option that still leaves the project behind schedule is of limited interest – your reasoning is that you will get criticized just as much if the project is 3 months late or 4 months late. Therefore, the project team plays last race of the day.

One possible leverage point is where the team selects the option with the potential to recover the most slippage, rather than the option most likely to succeed. At this point, you can aim to reduce the all-or-nothing incentive, by valuing *any* schedule recovery, rather than focusing on total recovery.

CHAPTER 9   COMMON TECHNICAL DEBT ANTI-PATTERNS

Moral Credential Effect

The moral credential effect anti-pattern is shown in Figure 9-8.

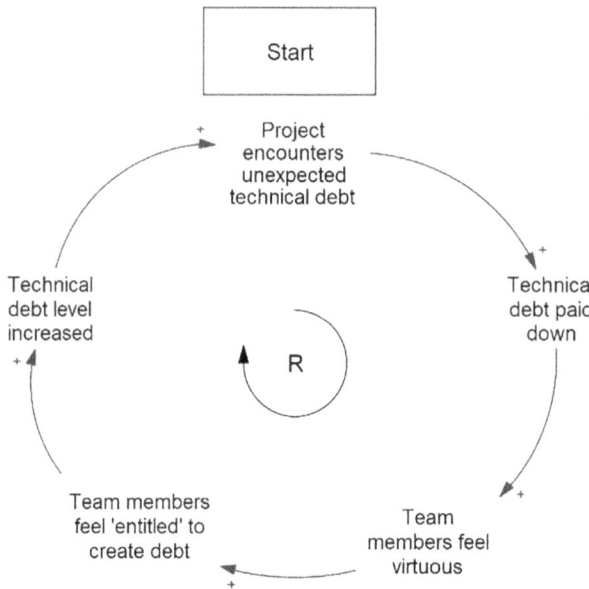

Figure 9-8. *Moral credential effect*

The moral credential effect is where someone who has previously done a good deed subconsciously gives themselves permission to be less good in the future. For example, someone who previously recruited a person from a minority group may later say in a different setting that a role is better suited to a white male.

Within the context of technical debt, the process works as follows. The project encounters some unexpected technical debt. The debt is paid down through additional effort by the project team. Consequently, the project team members feel virtuous and later feel entitled to create some technical debt to resolve a problem. This leads to an increased level of technical debt, thus forming a reinforcing loop.

CHAPTER 9 COMMON TECHNICAL DEBT ANTI-PATTERNS

Broken Windows Theory and Learned Helplessness

The learned helplessness anti-pattern is shown in Figure 9-9.

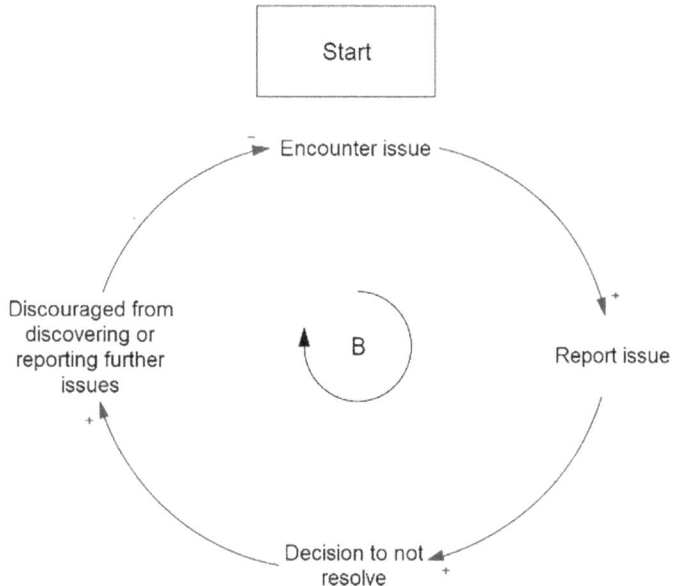

Figure 9-9. *Learned helplessness. Broken windows theory is a similar pattern*

The broken windows theory and learned helplessness are two distinct effects, although they follow a similar series of causal links.

The **broken windows theory** is where individuals notice a window that has been broken because of crime or antisocial behavior and are themselves encouraged to commit further crime and disorder. The broken windows theory is linked to social norms, which are shared standards of acceptable behavior within groups.

In the context of technical debt, this means that individuals who spot examples of debt or bad coding feel encouraged to do the same in pursuit of completing a task faster. Remember, technical debt is a trade-off decision. If you're surrounded by broken windows, and making a trade-off decision, you may be tempted to get your catapult out and aim for a personal goal in that trade-off, instead of deciding to avoid creating some technical debt.

In **learned helplessness**, individuals become conditioned to passive resignation and indifference following repeated exposure to negative events, such as reporting an issue that is not subsequently resolved.

CHAPTER 9   COMMON TECHNICAL DEBT ANTI-PATTERNS

Seligman (1972) demonstrated this effect, where he administered electric shocks to dogs, some of whom could stop the shocks by pressing a button. Later, he placed the dogs in an enclosure, where they received shocks that they could escape from by jumping over a low fence. Dogs who had learned to stop the shocks by pressing a button quickly learned to jump over the fence and escape the shocks. In contrast, dogs who could not escape the previous shocks did not attempt to jump over the fence.

If your bug tracker contains a long list of defects and those defects remain there unaddressed, then you should not expect project teams to maintain their enthusiasm for discovering bugs that are not deemed important enough to fix.

Learned helplessness also distorts information about your system quality, as the number of bugs is far higher than reported. Many individuals have simply stopped reporting defects that they believe will remain unfixed.

The consequences of broken windows theory and learned helplessness are likely to spill over into many different areas. Therefore, you should try to avoid setting up your organization in ways that allow them to proliferate.

A potential leverage point is to fix your broken windows.

Goal Culture

The goal culture anti-pattern is shown in Figure 9-10.

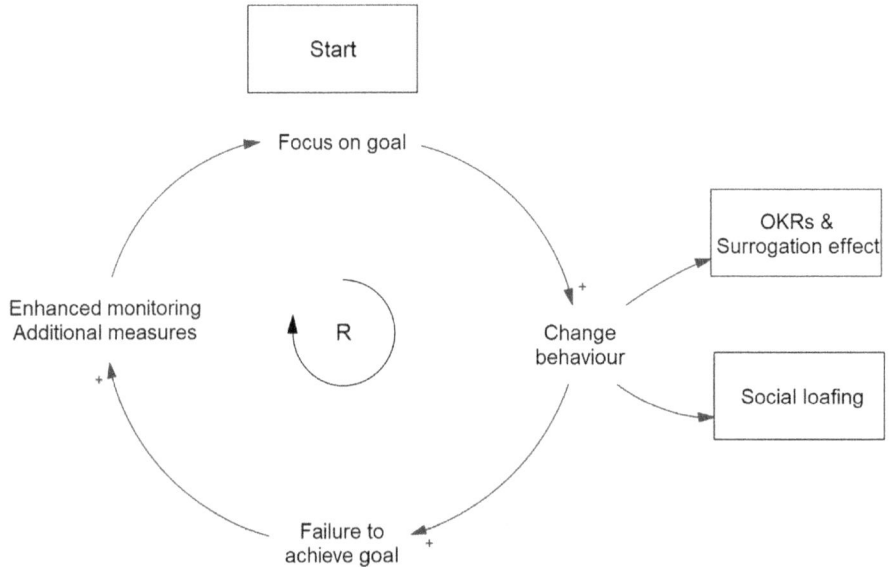

Figure 9-10. *Goal culture*

The effect of goal culture works as follows. The project team develops an increased focus upon its goal. This could be due to factors external to the team, such as stakeholders, or due to internal factors, like an influential team member, such as the project or program manager.

This increased focus on the goal leads to changes in behavior – OKRs and surrogation effect, and social loafing – which are dealt with in sections immediately following this.

However, these changes in behavior are counterproductive, so the team fail to achieve their goal. This leads to enhanced monitoring, the creation of additional measures, and an increased focus upon the goal.

One potential solution is to communicate that while a focus upon goals is useful, an excessive focus upon them will cause items that cannot easily be measured to become neglected, the problems we encounter in the change behavior step. You can incorporate this into a workshop discussion.

Social Loafing

Social loafing is where a person exerts less effort when part of a group than when alone. It goes under many names including skiving, free-riding, and slacking. Within software development, social loafing often takes the form of performing a task to the minimal standard you can get away with, or simply not doing the task, so you can conserve your resources for your personal goals.

It's important you realize that social loafing within a software development context *is not about laziness*. Social loafing does not mean that your software professionals are goofing off or shirking. Most software development professionals prefer to be busy. They often become quite problematic if there is no work for them. Social loafing in software development is about exerting less effort on group tasks or tasks that benefit others *because* you are already overloaded with numerous individual tasks that you cannot possibly complete within the allotted time.

When I joined an organization making mortgage software for banks, I experienced an extreme form of social loafing.

There was a contractor working on bug fixing, whose work usually failed even the most basic of tests. It was as if he hadn't coded any fix. I was new to the industry, so it was a useful experience to go to the various business analysts and verify exactly how it

CHAPTER 9   COMMON TECHNICAL DEBT ANTI-PATTERNS

should behave, then construct a series of tests to check this. Confident that I understood what was going on, I would then push the bug back, together with my tests and a detailed explanation of the expected behavior. Later, the bug would come back, usually fixed.

It was several weeks later that I discovered why his work always failed, as if he hadn't coded any changes. It was because he *hadn't* coded any changes. He didn't understand how the system was supposed to behave, and nobody had shown him. Therefore, rather than spend time learning, he simply set the item to "Ready for test" and hoped for the best. If the tester failed it, then he hoped to learn enough from the tester's comments to have a stab at coding it. If the tester passed it, so much the better, because then he didn't have to do *any* work.

Social loafing is especially prevalent on large waterfall projects that have been significantly underestimated. On such projects, all team members are seriously overworked and are looking for ways to reduce their own workload. In addition, because they are large projects, usually thrown together with external resource, there is a certain anonymity, so social norms are less binding.

Those on upstream tasks, like requirements and design, can reduce their workload by completing tasks to a minimal level and quality, as shown in Figure 9-11.

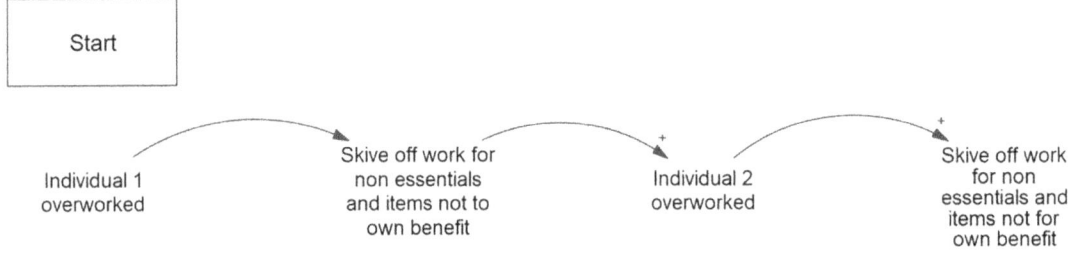

Figure 9-11. Social loafing, showing a cascade of overwork and skiving

However, completing the tasks only to a minimal standard creates additional work for those downstream, who are relying on that output. This is like the contractor at the mortgage software company, who set all his tasks to "Ready for test," causing me to spend time writing him a detailed explanation of the expected behavior. In turn, these downstream workers may behave in the same manner to others further downstream, leading to a cascade effect.

Because this social loafing involves one party imposing costs on another party, who has no say in the matter, this behavior is an *externality*, as discussed in the chapter on technical debt as an economics problem.

Examples of social loafing include

- Producing minimally complete requirements documents, so that developers and testers must expend additional effort to interpret, or place their own interpretations upon the requirements
- Skimping on unit tests or not building automated versions
- Business users not making themselves available to the project team for knowledge transfer

Social loafing is contagious, which can become a big problem. Therefore, you should try to avoid structuring organizations and work environments in ways that encourage it.

The ideal leverage point is to avoid underestimating the project, thus avoiding individuals becoming overworked. A second leverage point is to aim to reduce either the opportunity or incentive to complete work only to a minimal standard.

In the later chapter on modeling systems using simulation tools, we'll explore a model of social loafing and its effect on productivity.

We'll now look at a second consequence of having a goal culture – OKRs and the surrogation effect.

OKRs and the Surrogation Effect

What gets measured gets done.

—Peter Drucker

The above quote is commonly attributed to the management guru Peter Drucker. However, the quotation was originally from V. F. Ridgeway (1956) and was intended as a *criticism* of measurement. A more complete quotation is:

What gets measured gets managed – even when it's pointless to measure and manage it, and even if it harms the purpose of the organisation to do so.

OKRs stands for Objectives and Key Results. The danger of OKRs is that we can become so fixated upon achieving the key results that we lose sight of the objective. When this occurs, we are suffering from the **surrogation effect**. This is a bias whereby we lose sight of the strategic objective that a measure is intended to represent and instead act as if the measure was the objective. This is expressed in Goodhart's law.

CHAPTER 9   COMMON TECHNICAL DEBT ANTI-PATTERNS

> *Goodhart's law: When a measure becomes a target, it ceases to be a good measure.*

The surrogation effect is tragically illustrated in the following story.

PS General Slocum

At 09:30 AM on 15 June 1904, the passenger ship General Slocum departed on a trip from New York City to Locust Grove, a picnic site on Long Island. The ship had been chartered by St Mark's Evangelical Lutheran Church, Manhattan, for their annual trip to the picnic site. The 1,400 passengers were mostly women and children. As the ship passed East 90th Street, a fire started in the forward section.

As the fire spread, people, desperate to escape the flames, jumped into the water. Unfortunately, their heavy woollen clothes, widespread in 1904, weighed them down and many drowned. There were lifejackets on board, so mothers placed them onto their children and threw their children into the water. They watched horrified, as their children, clad in lifejackets, disappeared under the surface. Unfortunately, far from helping to save the children, the lifejackets contributed to additional deaths. How was this?

The lifejackets were manufactured to a standard that included a minimum weight requirement. The lifejacket manufacturer had met that requirement by filling the lifejackets with cheap, granulated cork, then bringing the lifejacket up to the required weight by placing **iron bars** inside the lifejackets. The lifejackets had been stored above deck, exposed to the elements for 13 years, during which time the canvas covers deteriorated, and the cork lost much of its buoyancy.

This is a tragic example of the consequences of surrogation. The purpose of a lifejacket is to provide buoyancy to a person in the water. The measure – the minimum weight requirement – had been intended to provide a minimum standard for buoyancy. Unfortunately, during the lifejacket manufacture, the original purpose of the measure was lost, and the lifejacket manufacturer acted as if the measure was the purpose. The lifejacket manufacturer added iron bars to the lifejacket, to meet the weight requirements, with tragic consequences.

Within software development, one way that the surrogation effect works is shown in Figure 9-12.

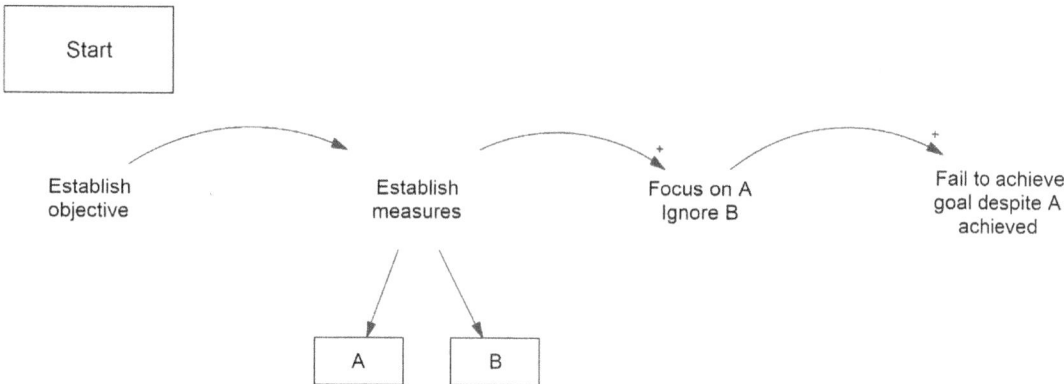

Figure 9-12. OKR and the surrogation effect

Imagine we establish an objective. We then establish some measures toward our objective. Suppose there are two important criteria – A and B. However, we can only measure A. The team progress their work, but since only A is measured, activities that would contribute to B tend to be ignored. The result is that we fail to achieve our goal, despite achieving success on measurement A.

Technical debt is an obvious victim in any OKR-surrogation effect anti-pattern. Technical debt is notoriously difficult to measure, so we rarely do so. Hence, it is the equivalent of criteria B, the ignored criteria, in this scenario.

Possible leverage points are to develop better, more balanced measures. If you cannot do this, then you should consider abandoning a focus on OKRs, as they may be doing more harm than good.

OKRs and the Social Contract

Another problem with focusing on OKRs is that excessive focus can cause us to neglect the social contract that is holding together all our relationships, including business relationships. Just as with the earlier example of the teachers and tardy parents at the children's daycare center, once you damage the social contract holding a relationship together, you end up experiencing all kinds of unexpected consequences.

In an almost comical example of this, I was once an engineer on assignment at a sister company, gaining some technical knowledge before I transferred to our Japanese agents. After I completed the training, I worked on the factory floor, to gain experience of the machines.

Now, the engineers who built the machines were diligent. They rarely stopped work at exactly 5:30, but instead would work anywhere between an extra five minutes and 45 minutes, finishing their current task. Also, they started their lunchbreak a bit late, after completing their current task.

Perhaps because they were giving a little extra at the end of the day, they were not always punctual returning after their lunchbreak. They weren't particularly tardy and would be between one and ten minutes late. The company was definitely getting the better end of the deal.

However, this late return from lunch bothered their manager. Either that, or it bothered someone higher up in the company, who in turn bothered their manager to do something.

Now the manager could have mentioned the issue in a low-key way at the regular engineers' meeting. However, he did something dramatically different.

One lunchtime, he waltzed into the engineers' break room and asked loudly, "Does anybody have the time?" Thinking that he did not have his watch and genuinely wanted to know the time, several of us engineers looked down at our watches. We all realized that it was three minutes past the end of our official lunchbreak, so, feeling slightly embarrassed, we quietly sloped back to work.

However, it was what happened later that afternoon that was fascinating.

At exactly 5:31, we heard a loud, anonymous voice on the shopfloor call out, "Does anybody have the time?" We all looked our watches, realized what the new game was, laughed, then immediately shut down our machines and trooped out.

That was the last time I saw an engineer on the factory floor after 5:30.

Descent into Firefighting

The descent into firefighting anti-pattern is shown in Figure 9-13.

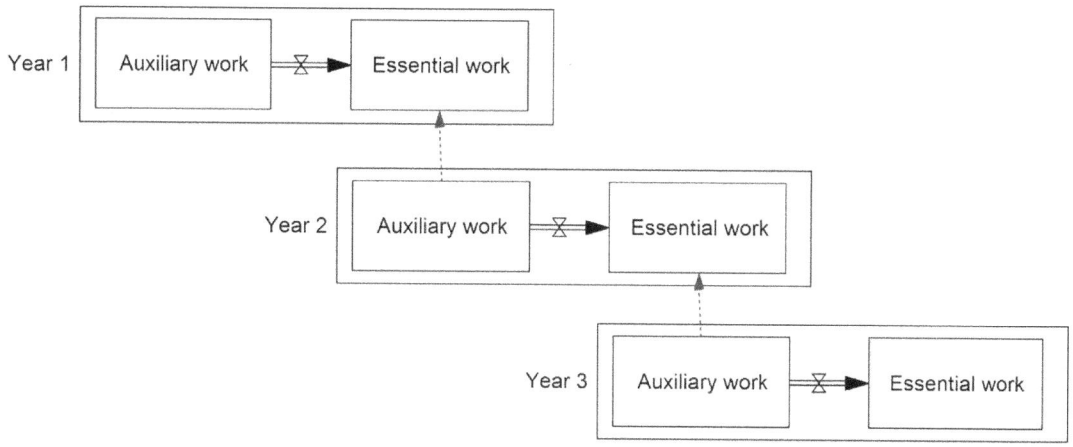

Figure 9-13. *Descent into firefighting, showing three projects, composed of auxiliary work plus essential work*

Nelson Repenning (2001) authored a thought-provoking paper on the descent into firefighting within new product development. He describes how an organization can slip from an efficient and effective mode into an ineffective one, *while consuming the same resources in both modes*. This anti-pattern has been adapted from that paper.

Consider an organization that can divide its software development work into two categories: auxiliary work, and essential work, with the auxiliary work completed first. The auxiliary work is activities like requirements gathering, design, and quality. While the auxiliary work is not essential for development, it enables the development work to be far more efficient and effective, so it is worthwhile doing.

This organization has multiple projects running in a staggered manner and can switch resources between projects and between tasks. If everything is running as planned, you will complete both the auxiliary and essential work on the project.

Now imagine the project in Year 1 gets a shock to its system and falls behind schedule when it gets to the essential work stage. What will you do?

Since the remaining work on the project is essential, you switch resource from the Year 2 auxiliary work, thus rescuing the Year 1 project. However, Year 2 now gets into trouble during its essential work phase, because the auxiliary work was not completed. Therefore, you switch resources from Year 3 auxiliary work into Year 2. And so on.

If the shock is small and your team has sufficient resilience or bandwidth, it can recover back into the efficient mode of operation. However, if the shock is sufficiently large, your team cannot recover. There is a tipping point, beyond which the development

CHAPTER 9 COMMON TECHNICAL DEBT ANTI-PATTERNS

process descends into an inefficient firefighting mode, from which it cannot easily recover. This descent into inefficient firefighting mode will eventually lead to a state of **collapse**, as discussed in the chapter on technical debt as a systems problem.

You often see teams stuck in inefficient modes. For example, test teams often get stuck in manual testing, not because they lack the skills or tools to create automated tests but because they never get sufficient free time to build an automated regression pack.

Development teams that are stuck in an inefficient mode of operation generate far more technical debt.

The primary leverage point is at the switching of resource from the auxiliary work in the future project to the essential work in the current project that is in trouble. You need to accept that switching resource will have a material impact upon the future project and persuade the business to replan accordingly.

Sometimes the system shock is self-imposed. For example, a project may have taken on additional functionality that it cannot deliver with the allocated resources. In this case, an alternative is to persuade the project or business to descope some functionality.

Limited Environments

The limited environments' anti-pattern is shown in Figure 9-14.

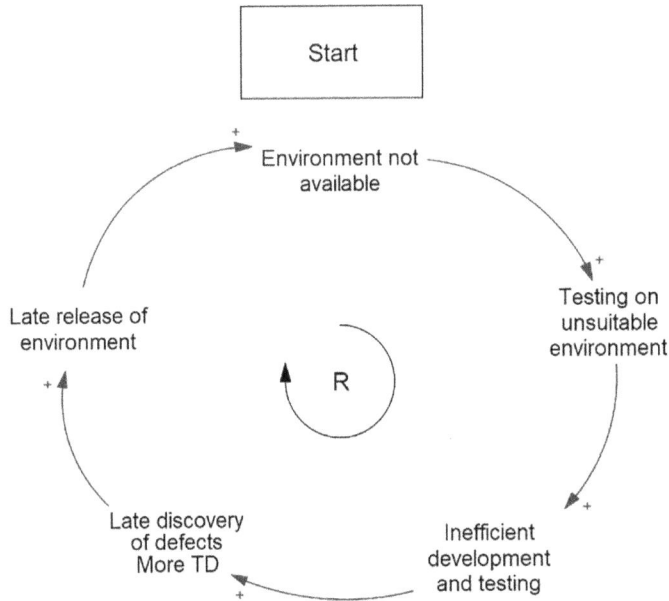

Figure 9-14. Limited environments' anti-pattern

CHAPTER 9 COMMON TECHNICAL DEBT ANTI-PATTERNS

This cycle works as follows. Several projects run in parallel. Each needs its own environment. There are insufficient environments for every project. This leads to an environment not being available when the project requires it. This causes work to be done on unsuitable environments. For example, work may be conducted locally on the developer or tester's machine, which is usually not representative of the production site.

Working on an unsuitable environment is inefficient. For example, developers and testers will be spending considerable time jury rigging a makeshift system together, nursing or cajoling the test scripts through the execution, and then spending considerable time interpreting the meaning of ambiguous results.

This leads to a late discovery of defects, plus an increase in technical debt, as project pressures compel the project to consign items to the technical debt register, rather than address them.

The project does finally get an environment but is then late in releasing it. This means that a subsequent project that is relying on that environment suffers the same cycle.

Leverage points include avoiding scheduling more projects than available environments, or developing capabilities in containerization, so that environments can be more easily generated.

Prototype into Debt

The prototype into debt anti-pattern is shown in Figure 9-15.

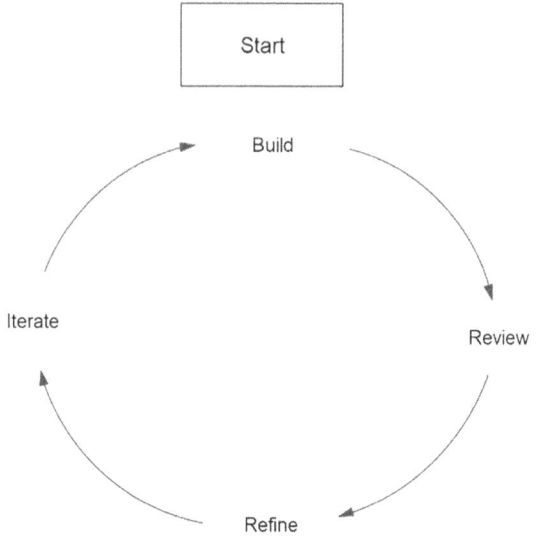

Figure 9-15. *Prototype into debt anti-pattern*

A prototype typically goes through multiple iterations. In each iteration, it inherits debt and builds up some more, plus pays some off. Because you are prototyping, the technical debt is high. However, this is not necessarily bad. In fact, mostly it's good, as your focus should be on prototyping to learn about what the product should be, not keeping debt low.

The problem comes when we need to produce a product. At this point, we should throw the prototype away as suggested in *The Mythical Man-Month*. At the very least, we should do some serious re-factoring.

However, at this point we are usually under schedule pressure. This is because either we underestimated how long it would take, were overconfident about our abilities to learn and refine quickly, or we succumbed to that temptation to build "just one more prototype."

Consequently, we often succumb to the temptation to use the final prototype as the initial version. Even if we don't succumb to that temptation, the business is likely to have been seduced by the prototype into thinking it is far more ready than it actually is, so it insists on using the prototype.

We may do some technical debt reduction, so that we feel less guilty. However, that reduction is often fig leaf sized, so our product begins its life with a pile of technical debt.

The leverage point is to follow the advice of a chapter in *The Mythical Man-Month* and "Plan to throw one away."

Further Reading

If you're interested in learning more about the tragic history of the General Slocum, then *Ship Ablaze* by Edward O'Donnell is an enjoyable read.

If you want to learn more about the surrogation effect, then *Supernormal Stimuli* by Deirdre Barrett explains the original sin of surrogation, where our primal instincts overran their evolutionary purpose.

If you want to find out how you organization may have descended into firefighting, then the paper *"Understanding Fire Fighting in New Product Development"* by Nelson Repenning is worthwhile studying and holds salient lessons.

If you want to see the large-scale use of a causal loop diagram, check out the UK government obesity map, listed in the references under "Obesity."

If you're serious about exploring your own anti-patterns through causal loop diagrams, I strongly recommend you study a book such as *Business Dynamics* by John Sterman. This will teach you everything you need to know about CLDs, stock and flow diagrams, and many other things. However, be prepared for a very involved read.

Summary

In this chapter, we looked at common anti-patterns that can lead to increased technical debt. When you address your organization's technical debt problems, you probably need to break one or more of these anti-patterns.

For each anti-pattern, we examined the causal loop diagram, CLD, that showed the process involved in the anti-pattern. We also explored potential leverage points for making relatively small changes that could make a significant difference. We saw in the estimation trap anti-pattern that we could often dig further into each causal linkage to reveal additional causal links, which may offer additional opportunities for leverage points.

One of the main benefits of looking at anti-patterns with a visual tool like a CLD is that it helps us better understand our problem and, hopefully, reveal fresh insights. As in Duncker's radiation problem, the more ways we have of thinking about the problem, the more likely we'll get an insight that will lead us to a good solution.

However, the greatest benefit of using a visual tool like a CLD is that it facilitates group discussions. This enables a group to move toward a shared understanding of the problem. In your workshop sessions, try facilitating the group to draw out a few of these anti-patterns, and then get them to brainstorm ways of breaking the anti-pattern.

Of the anti-patterns we examined, the most important one is the estimation trap. The problem of project underestimation is itself a wicked problem and deserving of its own book.

The causal loop diagrams we have used in this chapter are a useful tool for visualizing what is happening on a software development project as a result of anti-patterns developing. In addition, they are a stepping stone toward an even more useful tool: software simulations that model the dynamic behavior of our software development process.

One of the difficulties of any system is that you cannot easily predict its behavior simply by looking at its structure. Instead, you must examine the system behaving dynamically. Doing this in a live system can be expensive, problematic, or even impractical. In the next chapter, we look at how we can use dynamic modeling software to explore how our systems behave and build up technical debt.

CHAPTER 10

Modeling Technical Debt with System Modeling Tools

Technical debt builds up through dynamic processes. For example, a project becomes late. This causes people to become under pressure, which in turn causes people to make decisions that lead to technical debt. However, we cannot easily understand how this buildup occurs just by analyzing static diagrams like those in the previous chapter on anti-patterns.

In this chapter, we address this shortcoming. We'll run a simulation of a software development project using dynamic modeling software. Our aim is to better understand how project conditions and decisions, such as underestimation and attempts to recover schedule, affect both the current project and future projects.

This is a hands-on chapter. To get the most out of it, you should download the software and run the models. Also, watch the videos listed in the resources section at the end of this chapter. They'll save you a lot of time and confusion.

We begin by downloading the model reader tool, plus models. Next, we explore features of the model. The model extends across three screens – main workflow, workforce, and quality and productivity. As previously mentioned, this is a book on technical debt, not system dynamics or simulation models. Therefore, we'll avoid going into too much detail, except where it is most relevant to technical debt.

Next, we'll look at how to run simulations, including using controls, outputs, and dashboard.

We then discuss findings from running the model, including the effect of changing the scheduled completion date and the effect of technical debt creation upon subsequent projects.

We next briefly discuss a simulation model for social loafing, one of the anti-patterns in our earlier chapter.

We finish by discussing considerations you should make when developing a simulation model.

Part of the challenge in convincing an organization to address its technical debt is the difficulty in demonstrating how a decision to take on some technical debt to address an immediate problem may lead to severe problems on later projects. You can use the model from this chapter to help you in this task.

Software simulations can be difficult to understand from a static document like this. Therefore, you'll find some videos of the models and simulations on the Apress website. I recommend you start by watching the videos.

What You Gain from Dynamic Models

All models are wrong, but some are useful.

—George Box

The purpose of a model is not to accurately represent the world in every detail, becoming some sort of a huge prediction machine. To do this, a model would end up being as large and complex as the thing it was modeling, thus defeating the purpose.

Also, a model cannot *prove* a certain behavior or result, any more than a project estimation can prove that a project will deliver on the estimated time and cost. However, we still find estimates useful, even though we are aware of their inaccuracies.

So, what is a model most useful for? A model offers three useful purposes.

Firstly, a model enables you to **build a shared understanding** of a project's behavior and its impact, both upon itself and also upon future projects.

Secondly, a model enables you to **explore the potential consequences of decisions**, such as a shift left in testing, creation or avoidance of technical debt, or different levels of infrastructure investment. This is using a model for decision support.

Thirdly, and most importantly, **a model enhances your mental model of how a project is run**. Every individual within the project team and stakeholders has their own mental model of the project, the organization, and how they run. Everything those individuals do is based upon their mental model of the world. Things go wrong when those mental models do not match up to how the world actually works.

Manipulating these models is often a useful way of bringing considerations to the attention of senior management that they would not otherwise be aware of, prompting useful discussions regarding technical debt or other matters.

This is the WYSIATI, What You See Is All There Is, that Daniel Kahneman talks about in *Thinking, Fast and Slow*. By introducing everyone to a dynamic simulation model that shows project behavior, you are expanding the universe of understanding of all those involved in that project. In terms of WYSIATI, you are expanding what is seen and hence expanding what there is.

To enhance your models' usefulness, you should follow these three principles:

1. Build your model collaboratively and iteratively. Start simple and build complexity in only when needed. Demonstrate the model and gain continuous feedback. Five simple models demonstrating different aspects of project behavior are often better than one grand unified model.

2. Avoid the temptation to try and "prove" anything with the model. The model's findings can be consistent with or support a given assertion, but if you try to prove anything, it won't be long before someone is trying to disprove what you're doing, undermining the whole process.

3. Look out for heuristics and "rule of thumbs." For example, an equivalent rule of thumb in estimation may be that for everything we do, we find an extra 40% hidden there.

Modeling Tools

The tool I used to create these models is **Vensim**. The most basic version, Vensim PLE, is free for personal learning (PLE stands for Personal Learning Edition) and at the time of writing is only $50 for commercial use.

I currently use Vensim PLE Plus, for which I paid $169 for a commercial license. This seems pretty cheap to me. This version includes gaming and Monte Carlo simulation functionality. There are more expensive versions, with more functionality, but the PLE or PLE Plus editions will probably have all you need.

CHAPTER 10   MODELING TECHNICAL DEBT WITH SYSTEM MODELING TOOLS

In addition, there is a free read-only version, which allows you to distribute your models to others, who can then run the simulation, but not edit the model. You will use this when you run the models in this chapter.

I selected Vensim because a lot of the scientific papers I read identified it as the tool used. Alternative simulation tools include **Stella**, **iThink**, and **Powersim**, which other people seem equally happy with.

Getting Started

I have created some videos about how to run the simulations in the model reader. They are available on the Apress website. I recommend you start by watching those videos before moving to the next step.

Download the model reader tool from the download page on the Vensim website: `https://vensim.com/free-downloads/`

Select the "Model Reader" radio button, typing your email address, and then **click** the Download Software button.

Next, **install the software** in your preferred location and then launch it. You should see a screen like the one in Figure 10-1.

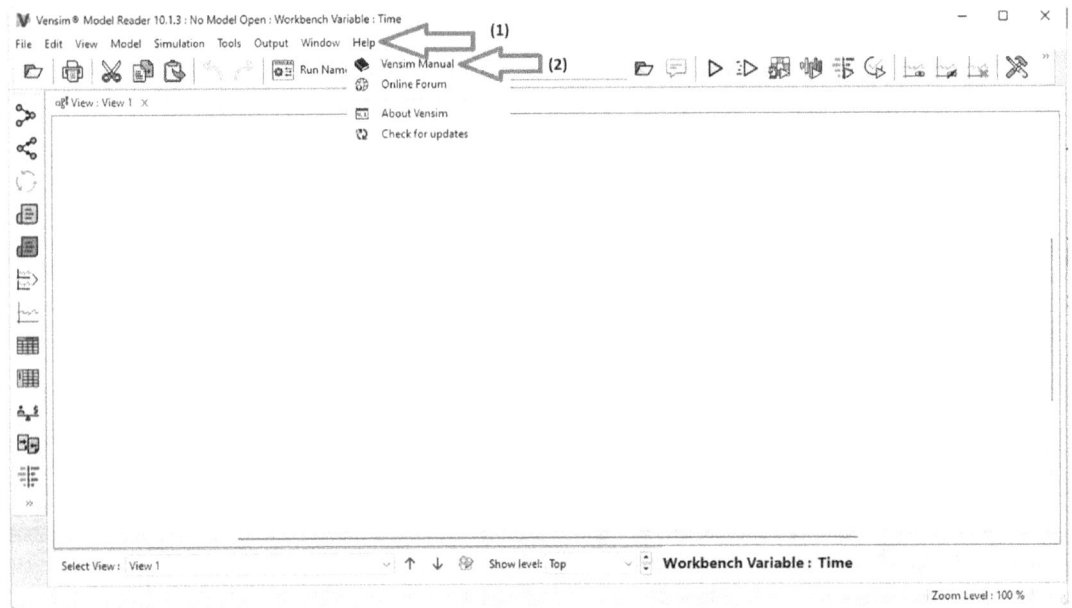

Figure 10-1. Vensim model reader screen. The modeling tool (PLE or PLE Plus) has a similar screen, but with additional functions

CHAPTER 10 MODELING TECHNICAL DEBT WITH SYSTEM MODELING TOOLS

In the menu bar at the top, **click** "Help" (1), and then **click** "Vensim Manual" (2). This will open the manual in a new window, as shown in Figure 10-2.

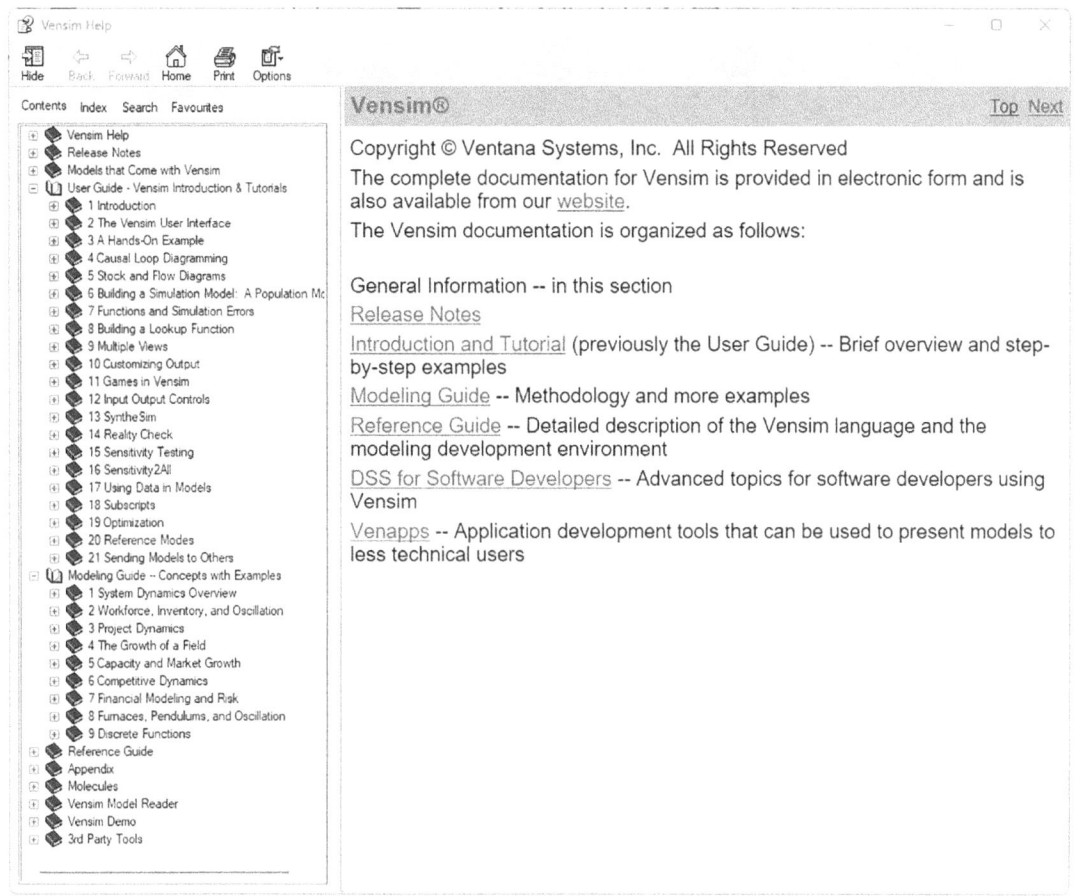

Figure 10-2. Help file, showing User Guide and Modeling Guide tutorials

If you want to create models with the tool (or another chosen tool), then I recommend you purchase the PLE or PLE Plus version, and then work your way through all the exercises within the user guide folder and modeling guide folder. This will take you a couple of weeks to work through all these exercises and begin to gain competence in the tool.

However, we are currently more interested in getting our hands on a model and playing with it to see what it can do.

Download the technical debt model named "Chapter 10 - Technical Debt.vpmx" from the Apress website. Place it in a folder that you can access from the model reader tool.

CHAPTER 10   MODELING TECHNICAL DEBT WITH SYSTEM MODELING TOOLS

Click the Open file icon (1), **navigate** to the file you just downloaded, and then click the "Open" button, as shown in Figure 10-3.

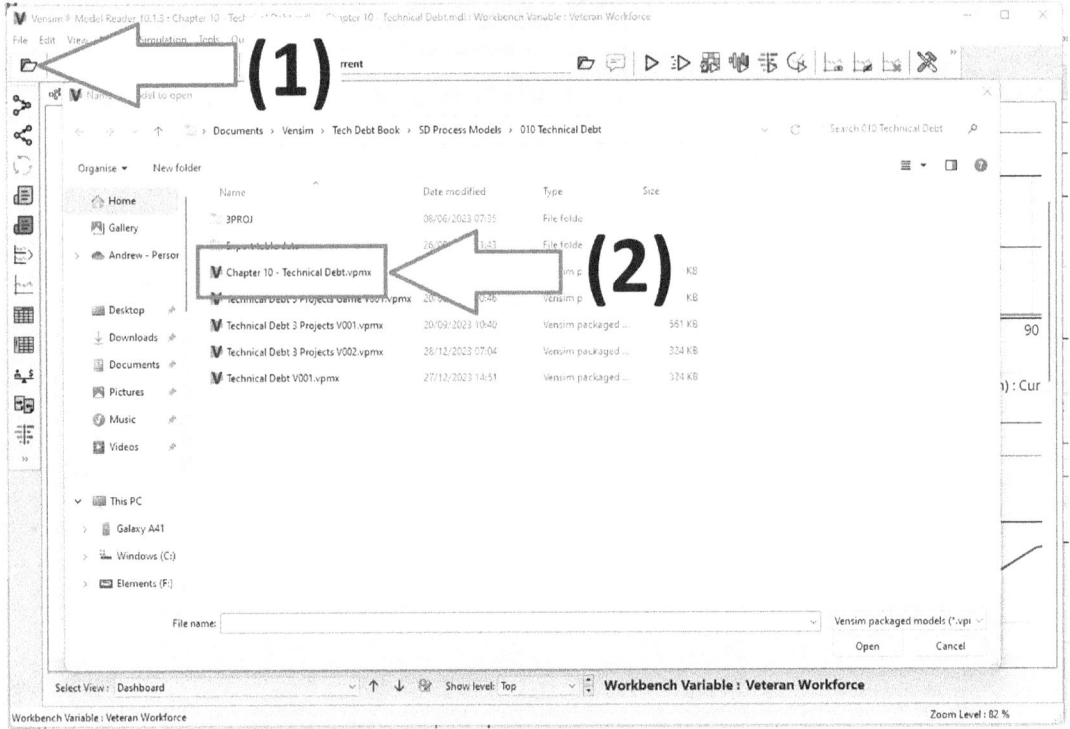

Figure 10-3. *Open the simulation model in the model reader*

The model should now open in the reader, as shown in Figure 10-4.

CHAPTER 10   MODELING TECHNICAL DEBT WITH SYSTEM MODELING TOOLS

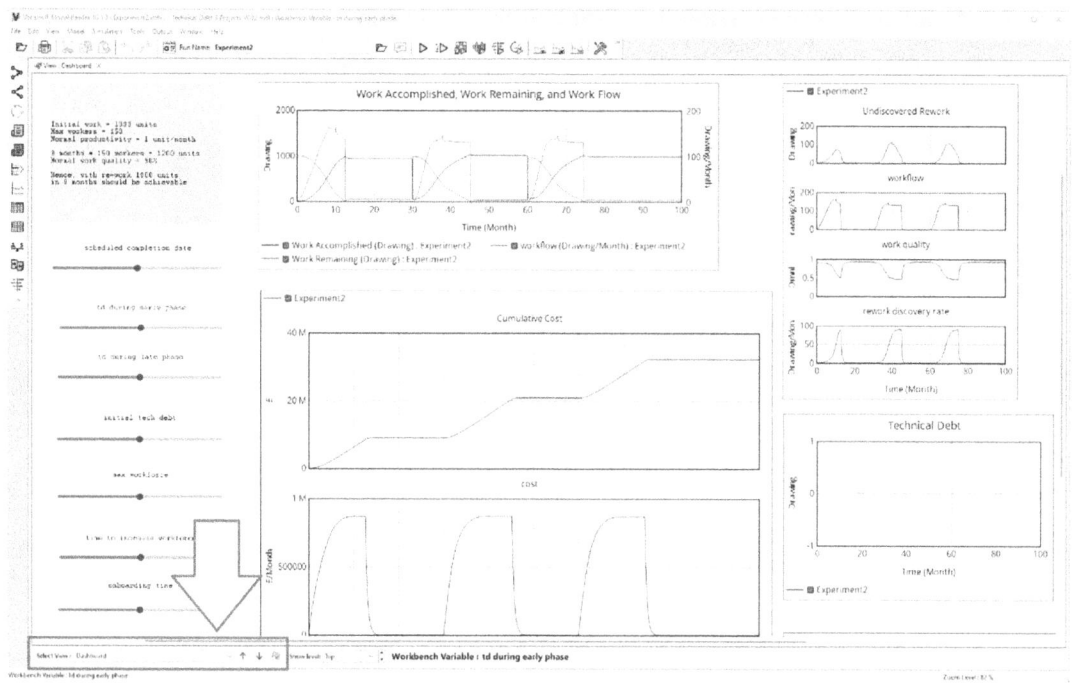

Figure 10-4. *Simulation model, opened in the model reader*

The model will open onto the screen that was last visible when the model was saved. In this case, it should be the "Dashboard" screen.

Navigate to the different screens, by using the Select View dropdown menu. **Explore** the screens for a few minutes, and then come back to the next section in this book.

Software Projects

You already have a good idea of what needs to happen on a software project. We need to do more things on larger, more complex projects than on simpler ones, but most projects will contain the following activities:

- We start with an objective.

- We break the objective down into a set of distinct activities.

- We onboard people onto the project to do the activities. There is usually a delay in onboarding. Once the work is complete, we release the people.

- People work on an activity until it is completed. Once completed, it goes to a "completed" area.

- Some work activities are done incorrectly and must be redone. We discover this later.

- Once we discover defective work, we assign somebody to rework that item.

- Sometimes, items are done in a way that is expedient, with the intention of completing them later. This is our "technical debt."

- The project eventually finishes.

To simulate a project, we need a model that simulates the above activities. In the next section, we look at details of our model. This model is an adaptation of a model from the tutorial section of the help file within the Vensim tool. It is in the section Modelling guide – concepts with examples/3. Project dynamics. If you want to understand in more detail how the model works, then go through the relevant sections of the help file. If you want to build your own model, then use this modeling guide as a basis.

Main Workflow

Navigate to the "Main workflow" view in the Vensim model reader.

You will now see the main workflow. A simplified view of that workflow, showing only the stocks (represented by text within boxes) and the flows (represented by pipes with arrows), is shown in Figure 10-5.

CHAPTER 10 MODELING TECHNICAL DEBT WITH SYSTEM MODELING TOOLS

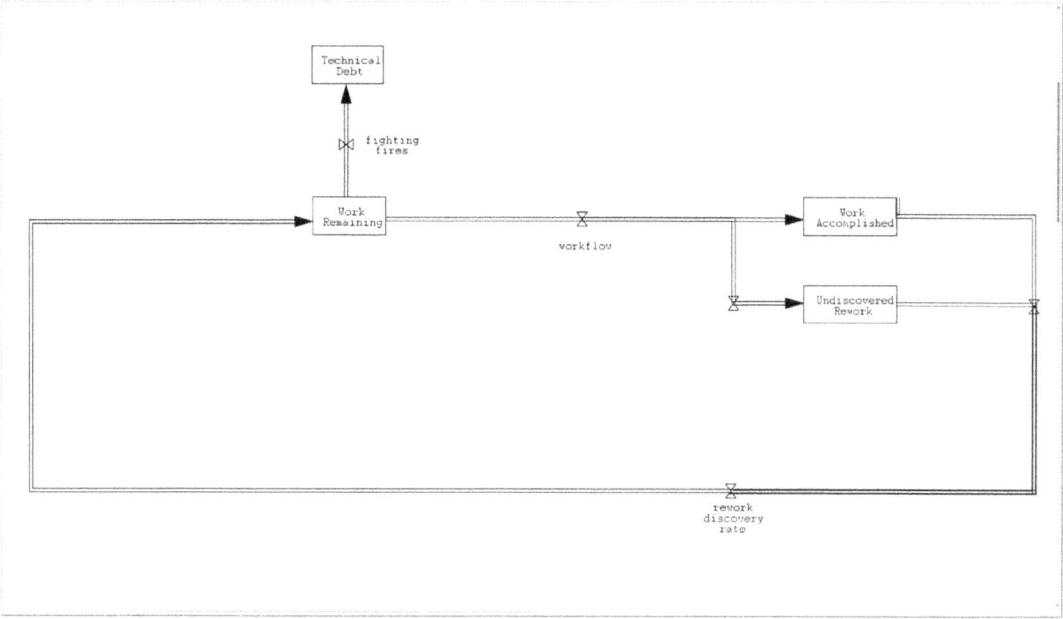

Figure 10-5. *Main workflow, showing stocks and flows only*

You'll see a lot more detail in your model, including causal links (blue arrows) and auxiliary variables (text only, without surrounding boxes). I have excluded them, so that you can concentrate on the main features.

The project work to do is represented by the box "**Work Remaining.**"

As the work is done, it flows through the pipe "**workflow.**"

After the work is done, it enters the "**Work Accomplished**" stock.

However, some work is not done correctly and will later need to be redone, once we have discovered the defect. This defective work goes into the "**Undiscovered Rework**" stock.

Once the defect has been discovered, it will flow out from the "**Undiscovered Rework**" stock, through the "**rework discovery rate**" pipeline, and then into the "**Work Remaining**" stock.

Under certain circumstances, for example, the project discovers it is behind schedule, the project team and stakeholders may attempt to accelerate work, for example, by cutting corners, leading to technical debt. This is represented in the diagram by the flow "**fighting fires,**" leading from "**Work Remaining**" to "**Technical Debt.**" We'll talk about this flow in the next section.

A reminder about notation: stocks are normally capitalized, while pipelines/workflows and auxiliaries are generally in lowercase.

CHAPTER 10 MODELING TECHNICAL DEBT WITH SYSTEM MODELING TOOLS

This is a simple model of a project. We are interested in technical debt, so we have added detail to represent that behavior, as described in a later section. If you are interested in a different aspect of project behavior, say the effect of adding additional scope, or "scope creep," then you would build detail around that area.

Figure 10-6 shows the main workflow view, with all the auxiliaries and causal linkages visible.

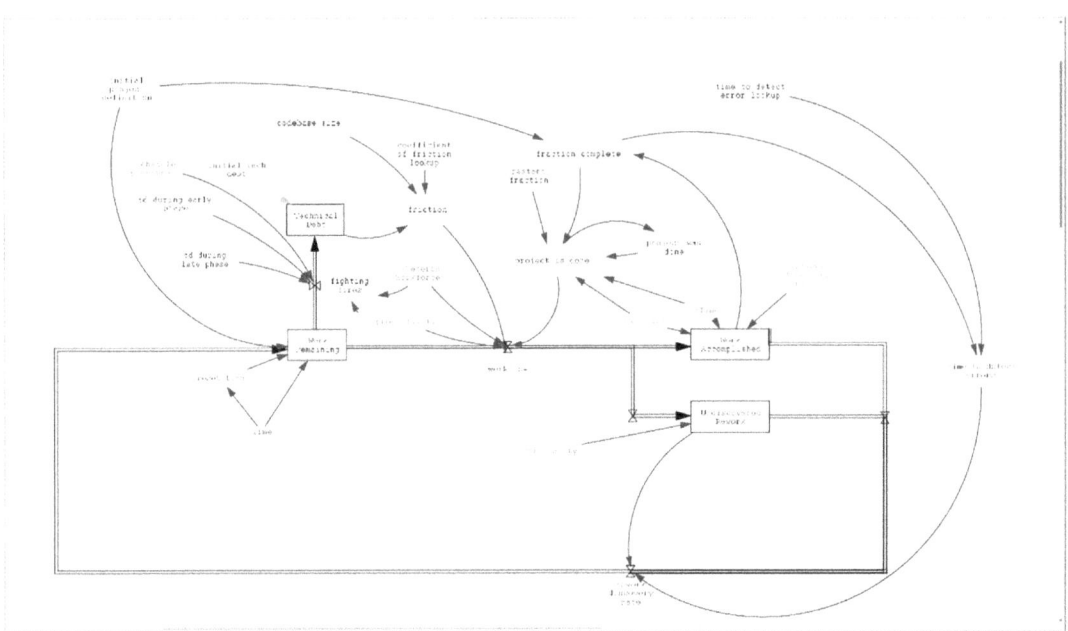

Figure 10-6. *Main workflow view, showing all variables*

The additional items in the above diagram control how the work items within the stocks flow around the pipelines. As previously mentioned, we will not go into details of how these work.

Modeling Technical Debt Creation

Most models built to study project dynamics usually place work items into one of three buckets or stocks: Work Remaining, Work Accomplished, and Undiscovered Rework.

However, this approach does not allow for work items to be completed to a minimal standard by creating technical debt items. Nor does it allow for such technical debt items to influence the productivity of subsequent development.

To model technical debt, I added two innovations to the model. The first innovation is the additional workflow, "fighting fires" that feeds into the stock "technical debt," as shown in Figure 10-7.

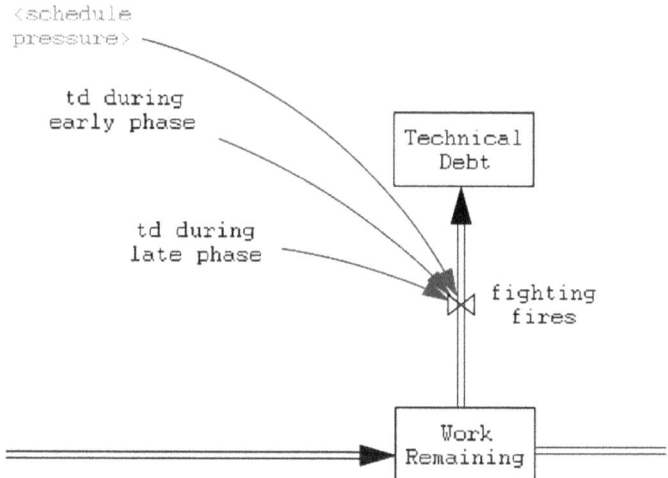

Figure 10-7. *Fighting fires workflow, leading to Technical Debt stock*

The workflow, "fighting fires," is controlled by three auxiliary variables of interest to us: "**<schedule pressure>**", "**td during early phase**", and "**td during late phase**". These auxiliaries influence the level of technical debt generated during the project.

Instead of requiring a project to complete all items, the project team can decide to not do certain items. This is an approximate model of technical debt that is sufficient for our purposes. In reality, debt represents items done to a minimal standard or done in a way that will not allow future development to build upon it.

Later, you will come to the sections where we are running the model. When running the model, if the technical debt sliders are set to zero, the model behaves the same as a model without the technical debt feature. If the sliders are above zero, the model will divert a proportion of the work items into the stock "Technical Debt." This will have two effects:

1. There is less work to do in the project.

2. Productivity is reduced, due to a "friction" effect.

CHAPTER 10   MODELING TECHNICAL DEBT WITH SYSTEM MODELING TOOLS

The second innovation of the model is as follows. Most models run for a single project. Consequently, you are unable to gauge the impact of past decisions about technical debt upon current or future projects. This model runs over three project cycles, so you can gauge the impact of technical debt decisions in the first project upon the two subsequent projects.

Workforce View

In the modeling tool, **navigate** to the Workforce view by using the Select View dropdown in the bottom left of the model reader tool. You should now see a view like the one shown in Figure 10-8.

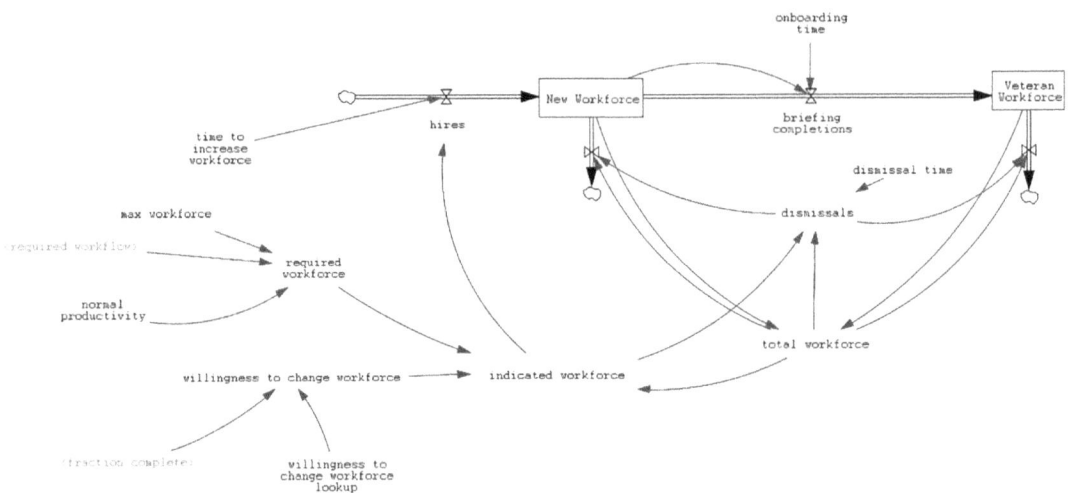

Figure 10-8. *Workforce view*

A project needs a workforce to carry out work. These activities are represented by the items in the Workforce view of the model. The workforce needs to be hired and trained. When the project is over, the workforce will be dismissed or reassigned. In addition, both new workers and veteran workers may choose to leave at various stages.

The model attempts to simulate a realistic workforce, so that workers cannot be hired and fired immediately, plus a portion of them naturally leave at a steady rate. Adjustments to the workforce are carried out by comparing the total current workforce against the indicated (needed) workforce, which is calculated from the expected work and productivity.

CHAPTER 10 MODELING TECHNICAL DEBT WITH SYSTEM MODELING TOOLS

Quality and Productivity View

In the modeling tool, **navigate** to the Quality and Productivity view by using the Select View dropdown in the bottom left of the model reader tool. You should see a view like the one shown in Figure 10-9.

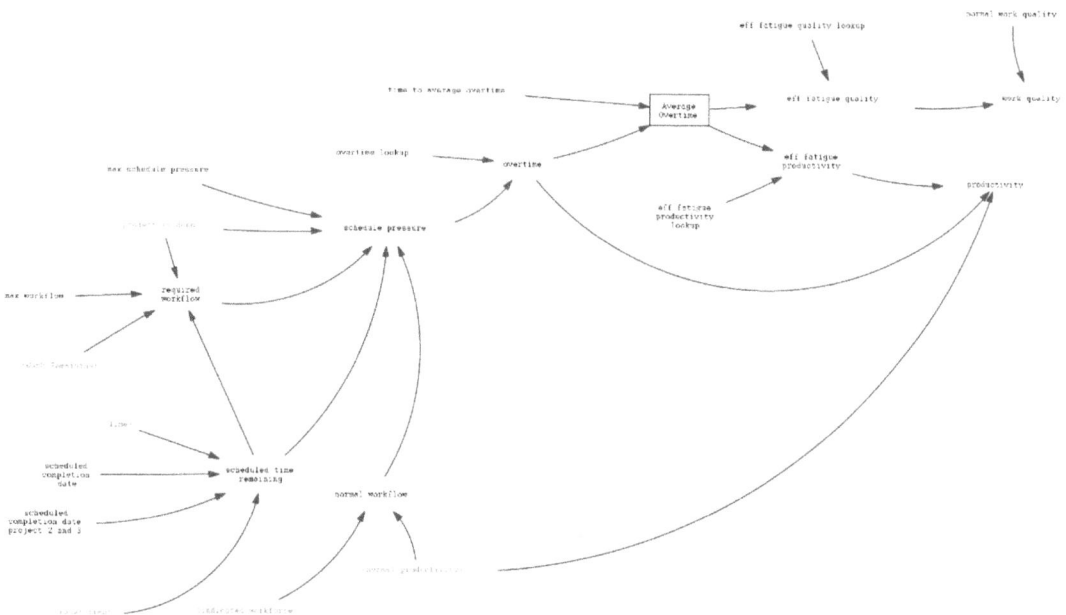

Figure 10-9. *Quality and productivity view*

The quality and productivity of the project is controlled on this view. There are two outputs from this view: **productivity** and **work quality**. These feed into the **Main Workflow** screen, where they are inputs to the **workflow** and **Undiscovered Rework,** respectively.

Dashboard View

In the modeling tool, **navigate** to the Dashboard view. You should see a view like the one shown in Figure 10-10.

CHAPTER 10 MODELING TECHNICAL DEBT WITH SYSTEM MODELING TOOLS

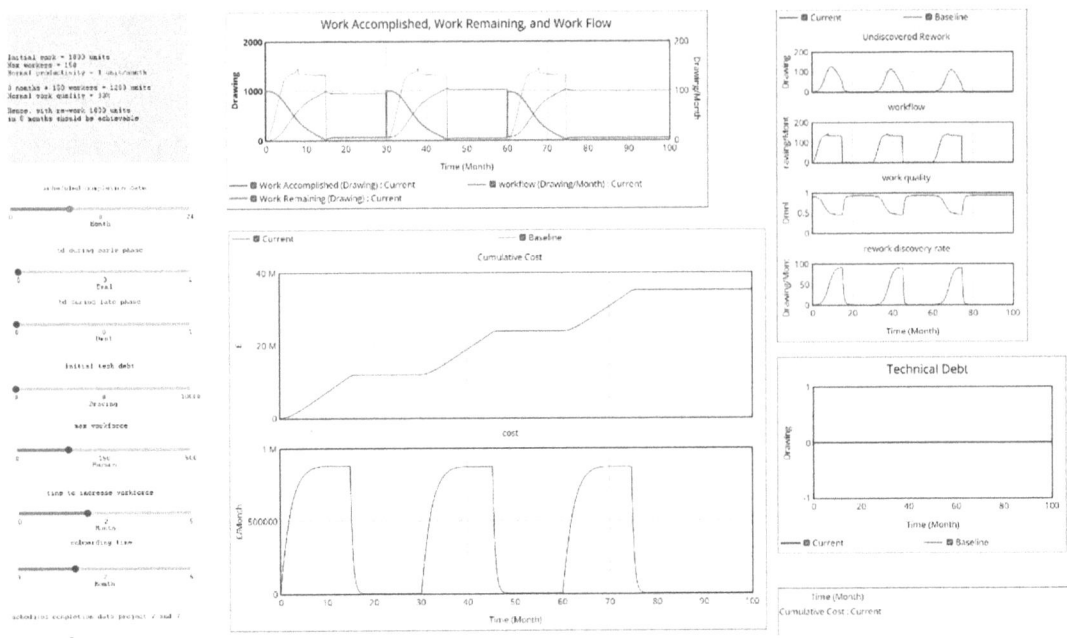

Figure 10-10. *Dashboard view*

Down the left-hand side of this view, we have some slider controls. We use these controls to change conditions when we run the model.

To the right of these slider controls, we have some output graphs. We use these to observe the effects of changing values in the controls on the left.

A dashboard screen is extremely useful in the following situations:

> **Explore and understand**: When you want to explore your model and understand its behavior, a dashboard view allows you to modify all variables influencing a given aspect of your model and observe the results.
>
> **What if?** Your ability to explore "What if?" scenarios is aided by a dashboard view.
>
> **Training**: You can train others in how a software project behaves, by taking them through various scenarios and changes. This allows them to see how changes to quality, technical debt, overtime levels, or other factors influence quality, cost, and other outputs.

We have now completed our exploration of the structure of the technical debt model. Next, we'll run a simulation.

CHAPTER 10   MODELING TECHNICAL DEBT WITH SYSTEM MODELING TOOLS

Run a Simulation

1. **Open** the model reader (if it is not already open).

2. **Open** the model (if it is not already open).

3. **Click** the multiple run button located in the toolbar, as shown in Figure 10-11.

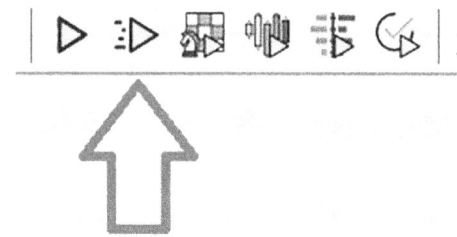

Figure 10-11.   Vensim menu, showing multiple run button

4. The model will begin running in dynamic update mode. You can check this, by observing that the toolbar has changed to the run mode, as shown in Figure 10-12.

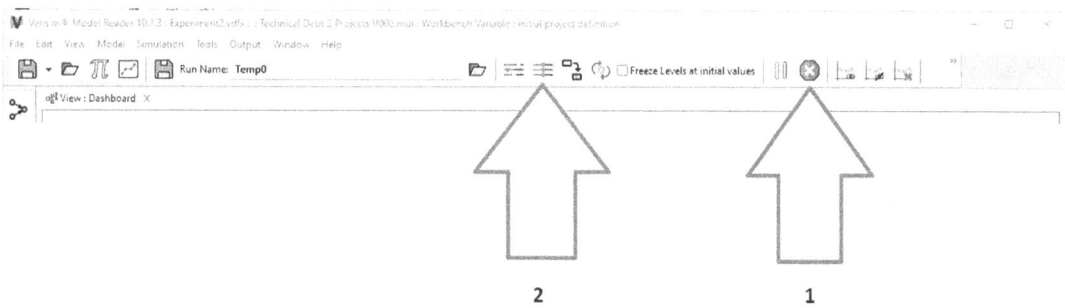

Figure 10-12.   Vensim toolbar, in run mode

The white "X" on a red hexagon is the "Stop current session" button (1). It indicates that the model is running in dynamic mode. Click here when you are finished running. To reset all slider controls to their original positions, click the reset button (2).

CHAPTER 10   MODELING TECHNICAL DEBT WITH SYSTEM MODELING TOOLS

5. **Navigate** to the Dashboard view.

6. **Move each of the slider controls** in turn, observing what happens in the output graphs as you do so. Once you are finished, **click** the "Reset All Sliders" button (2).

7. Next, **move** the "scheduled completion date" slider from its value of 8 months to 10 months, while observing the "Work Accomplished..." graph. What happens?

   You should see the first project completed faster – reducing from 15 months to 12.5 months. This is indicated by the change in the thick green workflow line shown in Figure 10-13.

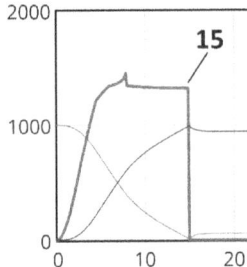 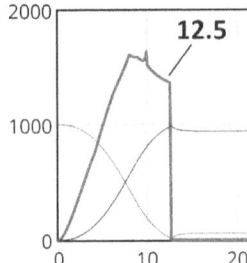

Figure 10-13. The left-hand project was scheduled to complete in 8 months, but completed in 15. The right-hand project was scheduled to complete in 10 months, but completed in 12.5.

We'll go through reasons why this occurs in the next section.

8. Now **adjust the slider** "scheduled completion date project 2 and 3" and observe what happens in the output graphs.

9. Try **adjusting the other slider** controls and observe what effect you have on project costs and completion dates. When you want to go back to where you started, click the "Reset All Sliders" button.

10. When you're finished, **click** the "stop current session" button.

This is a simple simulation model. It is not intended to be a comprehensive view of what occurs on a software development project. However, it does behave realistically to changes in completion date, plus decisions to change the levels of technical debt.

CHAPTER 10 MODELING TECHNICAL DEBT WITH SYSTEM MODELING TOOLS

When you want to build more refined models that more accurately reflect your organization, or models that enable you to gain insights into areas where you have specific "what-if" questions, then you can use the Vensim developer tool to do this.

Findings from the Model

As you were adjusting the slider controls while observing the effects on the output graphs, you should have noticed that when you increased the scheduled completion date, from 8 months to 10 months, the actual completion date *decreased*, from 15 to 12.5 months.

We'd like to understand why this counterintuitive effect occurs. Let's start by returning to the simulation model and running it again.

1. **Open** the model reader, then open the model, and then click the multiple run icon.

2. Next, **expand your screen**, so that you can see the "scheduled completion date" slider plus the graphs to its right.

3. **Move** the "scheduled completion date" slider between its extremes, and then observe and note down what happens in the "Work Accomplished..." graph.

   You should see the peak for the green workflow line initially decrease as you increase the slider. Try moving the slider with your mouse. Move it repeatedly, while observing the movement of the green workflow line. Eventually, you'll get a feel for its behavior.

4. Now **repeat**; only this time, observe the "Cumulative Cost" graph.

   As you move the slider, you should see the blue line for "Current" separate from the red line for "Baseline." By observing how the "Current" line moves relative to the "Baseline" line, you can see the effect that changing the scheduled completion date has upon costs. A screenshot of the effect is shown in Figure 10-14.

199

CHAPTER 10   MODELING TECHNICAL DEBT WITH SYSTEM MODELING TOOLS

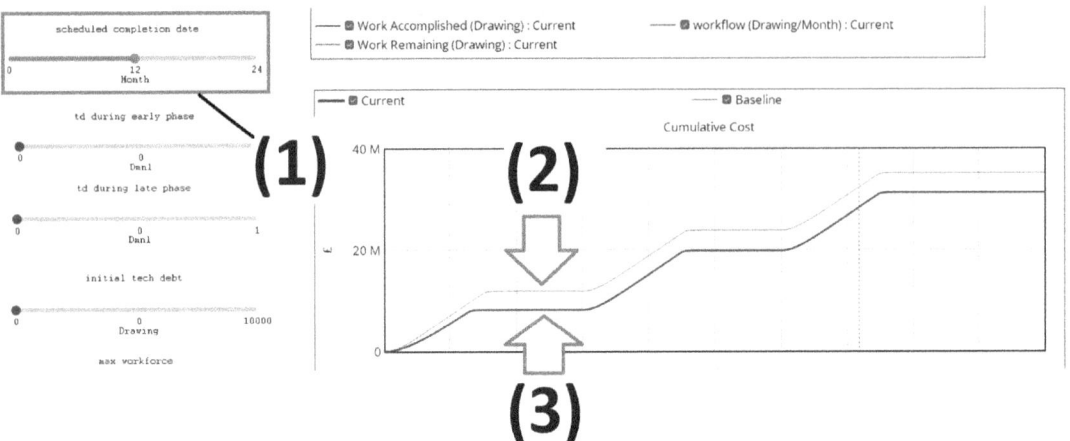

Figure 10-14. Cumulative Cost graph, with (1) scheduled completion date = 12 months. Note that the cumulative cost of the Baseline run (2) is about £12M, whereas extending the completion date by 4 months (3) has reduced this to about £8M.

5. Now **repeat**; only this time, observe the "cost" graph.

6. Now **repeat**; only this time, observe the four graphs inside the graph box, as shown in Figure 10-15.

CHAPTER 10   MODELING TECHNICAL DEBT WITH SYSTEM MODELING TOOLS

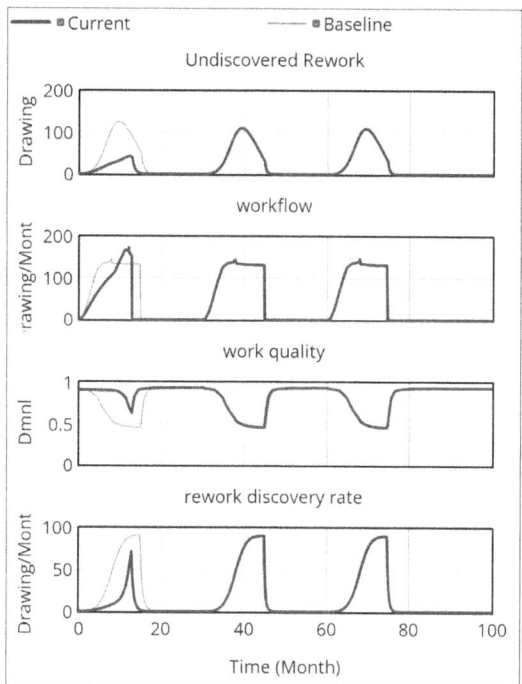

Figure 10-15. *Graphs for Undiscovered Rework. Scheduled completion date is 12 months for Current (thick blue line) and 8 months for Baseline (thin red line).*

Note that as we move the scheduled completion date out to 12 months, the work quality dip is minor (blue line, 3rd graph down), compared to 8 months (red line).

We'll return to these four graphs, particularly the "work quality" graph, to explore why the model behaves as it does.

7. **Stop** the run.

As you played around with the "scheduled completion date" slider and observed the various graphs, you should have spotted several noteworthy effects, listed in Table 10-1.

201

CHAPTER 10 MODELING TECHNICAL DEBT WITH SYSTEM MODELING TOOLS

Table 10-1. Observations of increasing scheduled completion date

Scheduled completion date range	Effect of *increasing* scheduled completion date			
	Actual completion date	Cost	Undiscovered rework	Work quality
Below 10 months	Decrease	Decrease	Decrease	Increase
10–12 months	Little effect	Decrease	Small decrease	Small increase
Above 12 months	Increase	Little effect	Little effect	Little effect

We find that if the scheduled completion date is below 10 months, then any increase leads to an earlier delivery and lower overall cost. If the scheduled completion date is between 10 and 12 months, then any increase reduces costs but has little effect on delivery date. Above 12 months, an increase in scheduled completion date has little beneficial effect.

Clearly, this project was never going to deliver in 8 months! We are reminded of another quote from Gerry Weinberg:

> *Managers often form a team which by any reasonable judgement cannot perform the designated task in the allotted time. Inevitably, the team is given an extension when the time limit is reached, and reality must be faced. Had it been faced earlier, the work could probably have been organised differently and thus produced more quickly.*
>
> —Gerald M. Weinberg

Why does increasing the scheduled completion date allow us to deliver faster and cheaper?

From Table 10-1 and Figure 10-15, we can see that as the scheduled completion date increases, the work quality improves. This means that there is less rework. This means that, with less rework, the project finishes earlier and for lower cost.

The reason for the work quality effect is as follows. When the scheduled completion date is unfeasibly early, there is a rapid increase in schedule pressure. This leads to increased overtime, which in turn leads to fatigue. This fatigue leads firstly to a drop in quality and an increase in rework and secondly to a reduction in productivity. The project costs more and takes longer because we do the work wrong, and then we must redo it. Plus, we do it slowly because we're fatigued.

Let's look at this drop in quality in more detail, as shown in Figure 10-16.

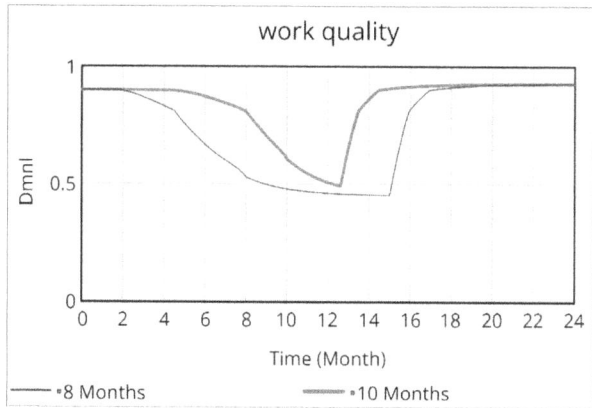

Figure 10-16. Work quality when scheduled completion date is 8 months (thin blue line) and 10 months (thick red line)

In the project scheduled to complete in 8 months, we see that work quality drops earlier in the project and then remains at a consistently low level for the remainder of the project.

In fact, work quality remains close to the value 0.5 for the period between 8 months and 15 months. This means that for almost half of the project duration, *approximately 50% of all work items have an error and must be reworked*. Things are worse than this, because those rework items then have a 50% chance of containing an error that must be worked upon.

Next, let's look at why the project was underestimated.

Why the Project Was Underestimated

In this project, there are 1000 units of work to do. With a maximum number of 150 workers and a normal productivity of 1 unit/month, a reasonable estimate is that in 8 months we should be able to complete 1200 units. Remember that we're keeping things as simple as possible. This means we're not considering specialist workers. In the later model on social loafing, we do differentiate between roles, as it is an important part of that model.

Under normal conditions, the work quality is 90% (i.e., 10% of units are defective and must be reworked). This would be 120 units, so the project was predicted that it could comfortably complete 1000 units in 8 months.

CHAPTER 10   MODELING TECHNICAL DEBT WITH SYSTEM MODELING TOOLS

However, we saw in Figure 10-13 that when we run our simulation, the project is not completed until 15 months. Why has the project taken so much longer than we anticipated? We find there are several reasons.

Firstly, the maximum workforce of 150 is not available and productive from day 1. The model has a delay in recruiting and training workers, so that it is a few months before they are fully productive.

Secondly, there is this issue of rework. We don't discover a lot of this rework until late in the project, delaying the eventual completion date. More importantly, we end up doing a lot more rework than we originally planned.

The reason we do more rework is because the assumption about a work quality value of 90% was incorrect when the project was under extended schedule pressure and workers became fatigued. Far from rework being a minor factor at 10%, rework became the dominating factor of the work.

Next, let's look at what happens when a project creates technical debt, a common response to schedule pressure.

Effect of Technical Debt on Current Project

How does altering the level of technical debt affect how long the project takes and how much it costs? We'll start by looking at the effect on the current project.

It's time to go back to the simulation model.

1. **Open** the model reader, then **open** the model, and then **click** the multiple run icon.

2. Next, **expand your screen**, so that you can see the "td during early/late phase" sliders plus the graphs to their right.

3. **Move these sliders** and observe what happens in the graphs.

4. As you move the sliders, you should see the green "workflow" line in the "Work Accomplished…" chart move, from its initial value of 15 for the first project, through a minimum value of 13.5, when the "td during early phase" slider has a value of 0.2.

5. Also, you should see in the cumulative cost graph that the line for "Current" separates from the line for "Baseline," moving from its initial value of £11.8 million, through a minimum value of £10.7 million, when the "td during early phase" slider has a value of 0.2.

204

The green "workflow" line in the "Work Accomplished, Work Remaining and Work Flow" can be seen in Figure 10-17.

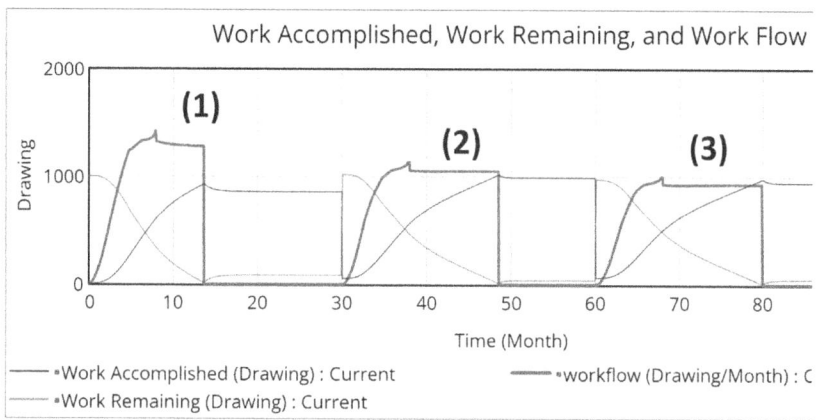

Figure 10-17. *The workflow line for the current project is indicated (1). The workflows for the subsequent two projects are also shown (2), (3).*

By adding technical debt, we have been able to shorten the project time by approximately 1.5 months, or 10%. We have also reduced costs by $1.2 million, a saving of 10%.

Therefore, if we make decisions that cause the accumulation of technical debt, we can deliver *our* project 10% earlier and cheaper.

Obviously, this is extremely good news for that project manager and the development team, plus any stakeholders being judged on the project deliverables. It will also benefit the organization, at least in the short term, as it will enjoy earlier delivery and lower cost.

But what are the longer-term effects, on subsequent projects? We explore those effects in the next section.

Effect of Technical Debt on Subsequent Projects

Once again, it's time for you to go back to the simulation model. You are doing the same as before, except that instead of focusing on the areas corresponding to the first project, you should focus upon the areas for the second and third projects (identified by (2) and (3) in Figure 10-17).

CHAPTER 10   MODELING TECHNICAL DEBT WITH SYSTEM MODELING TOOLS

1. **Open** the model reader, then open the model, and then click the multiple run icon.

2. Next, **expand your screen**, so that you can see the "td during early/late phase" sliders plus the graphs to its right.

3. **Move these sliders** and observe what happens in the graphs.

4. As you move the sliders, you should observe the green "workflow" line in the "Work Accomplished…" chart and the costs graph. The costs graph is shown in Figure 10-18.

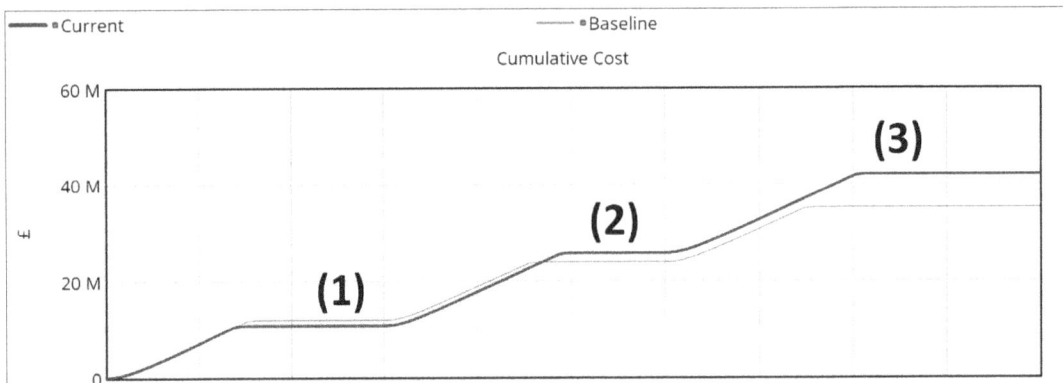

Figure 10-18. *The thick blue line represents the costs for a technical debt setting of 0.2: (1) first project costs, (2) second project costs, (3) third project costs. The thin red line is for a project that has not added technical debt*

The first project benefits by £1.2 million from the technical debt that it has added to the system. However, the subsequent projects are worse off. At project (3) the total additional costs are £7 million.

If you move your sliders further, you can add sufficient technical debt so that project 3 will never finish. At this point, the organization is probably suffering from a state of "collapse" discussed in the chapter on technical debt as a systems problem. This is the descent into firefighting that Nelson Repenning refers to in his paper.

Recall that the consequences of technical debt on the first project are positive – by creating technical debt, this project managed to finish 10% earlier and cheaper. However, the consequences of technical debt for each subsequent project are negative.

What is causing the rise in costs of subsequent projects in our model?

Friction

The growth in technical debt is linked to the variable – friction – created to model the effect on a project of the existence of technical debt from previous projects. This friction is analogous to the friction described by von Clausewitz in *On War* in the analogy chapter. Friction reduces the amount of work passing through the workflow pipeline. It is this reduction in work passing through the pipeline that causes the project to take longer and cost more.

To see the graphs representing technical debt and friction in the dashboard view of your model reader, you may need to zoom out a bit. Try running your model once more, and view these graphs while altering the technical debt control sliders.

Figure 10-19 shows the technical debt graph.

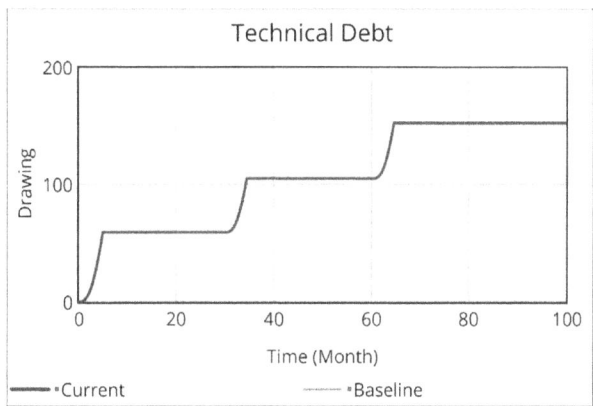

Figure 10-19. *Technical debt within the three system projects when zero technical debt is added (thin red line running along baseline) and when debt is added (thick blue line)*

We can see that the first project leads to a modest increase in technical debt, with further increases for the second and third projects.

This technical debt leads to an increase in the level of friction, as shown in Figure 10-20.

CHAPTER 10   MODELING TECHNICAL DEBT WITH SYSTEM MODELING TOOLS

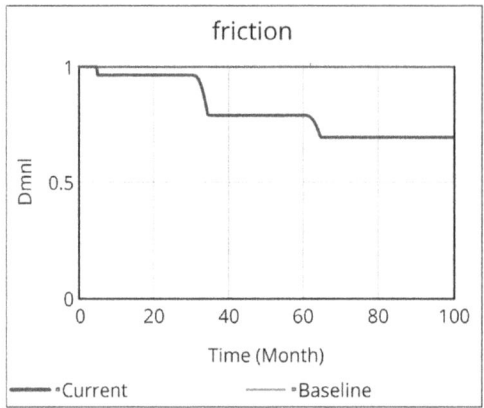

Figure 10-20. *Friction within the system for the three projects when some technical debt is added*

As technical debt increases, the effect of friction increases. By the time we get to project 3, beginning at month 60, the friction is such that a lot less useful work is being done by the project.

Like von Clausewitz's friction in *On War*, fiction in software development is likely to have a non-linear effect on an organization, so that at high levels of friction neither an army nor a software team can achieve much, no matter how much effort they expend.

Implications for Projects

Within project management, there is much talk of the "Iron Triangle," with the three key constraints of cost, scope, and time sitting at each of the corners, as shown in Figure 10-21.

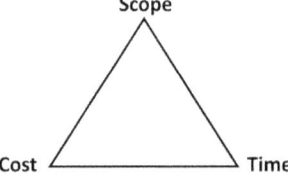

Figure 10-21. *The iron triangle*

It is known as the iron triangle because you cannot change one corner without impacting the others. That may be true, but a triangle has only two dimensions, and there are at least two additional dimensions that a project can change without impacting this iron triangle, at least for a while.

The first additional dimension is quality. You can skimp on quality to reduce cost or time. You cannot skimp forever on quality, because eventually it will come back and bite you, usually on cost and risk.

The second additional dimension is technical debt. You can reduce cost or time, or increase scope, all without impacting the other corners of your triangle, by increasing your technical debt. Someone might eventually need to pay down the technical debt, and it will cost them to do so, but it won't affect *your* triangle, at least for the moment.

You will recall the earlier quote, commonly misattributed to Peter Drucker, "What gets measured gets managed." When an organization measures a project, it measures those visible attributes of the triangle, things like the delivery date and functionality for users. And what gets measured gets managed, so these are closely managed by the project manager and project team.

What an organization is unlikely to measure, at least in any meaningful detail, is the technical debt created by that project. And what an organization most definitely does not measure, because it simply cannot measure it in a timeframe relevant to the project, is the impact of that technical debt upon the costs and schedules of future projects.

By building a dynamic model, you can, for the first time, begin to understand that impact, even if you cannot calibrate and quantitatively evaluate it. In addition, you can demonstrate it to stakeholders in a highly visual and easily understandable way.

If your demonstrations arouse sufficient interest, you can further enhance your model to give stakeholders additional insights. Example enhancements include

- **Opportunity cost**: Generally, you incur technical debt to achieve a goal, like additional features or earlier delivery. This goal has an opportunity cost, which you could build into the model, so that stakeholders can build up their understanding and mental model of whether it is worthwhile forgoing the opportunity cost.

- **Different interest rates**/consequences for different types of debt. As mentioned earlier, some types of technical debt, like architectural debt, will be more costly. This could be incorporated into the model to aid understanding and decision-making around the costs of different types of debt.

We shall now switch away from the technical debt model and look briefly at a different model.

CHAPTER 10   MODELING TECHNICAL DEBT WITH SYSTEM MODELING TOOLS

Social Loafing

This model is based upon the anti-pattern "Social Loafing" discussed in the anti-pattern chapter. You may find it useful to watch the video created for this model. Its location is described in the resources section of this chapter.

It's time to get hands-on once more.

1. **Download** the model "Chapter 10 - Social Loafing.vpmx", and **open it** in the Vensim model reader.

2. **Navigate** to the Workflow screen. Familiarize yourself with the model. In part of the screen, you should see the pipeline representing the software development process, shown in Figure 10-22.

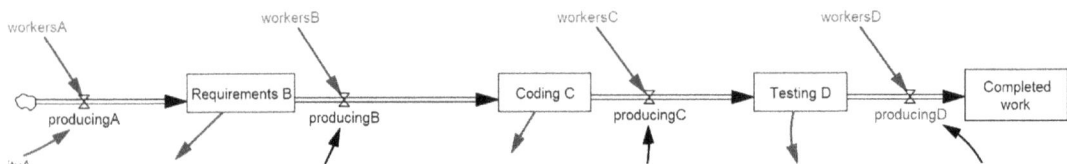

Figure 10-22. Software development pipeline

3. **Navigate** to the dashboard screen.

4. **Click** the multiple run icon to start the simulation.

5. **Adjust** the three sliders and observe the effects they have on the level of work produced and completed.

The dashboard should look like Figure 10-23.

CHAPTER 10 MODELING TECHNICAL DEBT WITH SYSTEM MODELING TOOLS

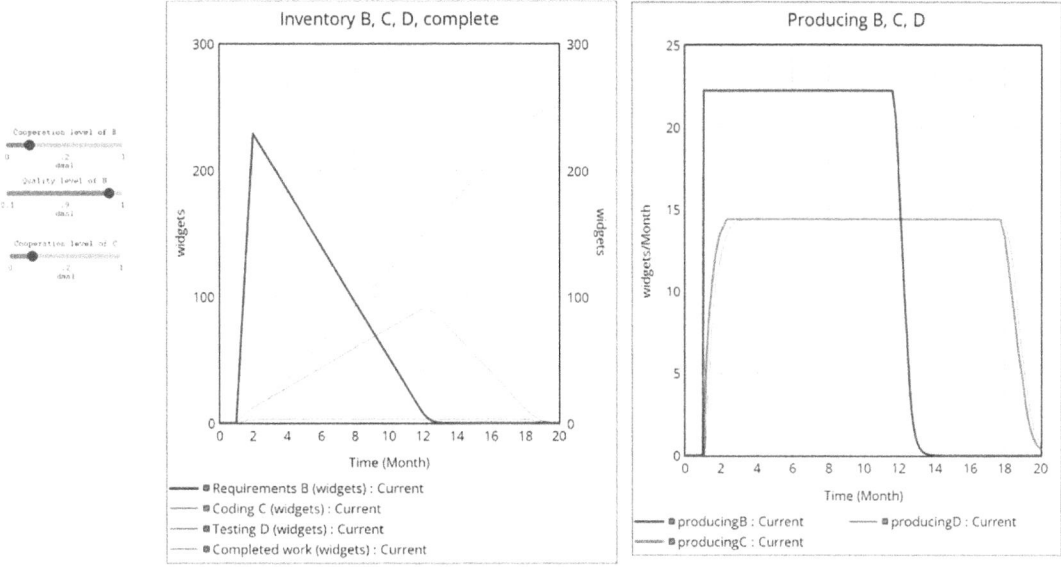

Figure 10-23. *Dashboard, showing controls on left, a graph showing inventory in the center, and a graph showing current production on the right*

The thick blue line represents the outstanding requirements work to be done by worker group B (left-hand graph) and their production rate (right-hand graph). The "Cooperation level of B" slider is set to .2. This means that individuals in that group spend 20% of their time in cooperation activities. The quality slider is set to .9, which means a 90% quality level or 10% defects.

This group can alter their production rate by altering their level of cooperation (topmost control slider) and the quality level (middle slider). Therefore, if this group is under pressure to increase production, they can do so by reducing quality and cooperation.

However, this has a knock-on effect to the work of the downstream groups C and D; the lower the cooperation and quality from B, the less work that C and D can complete.

Rerun your model and adjust the sliders once again, this time paying close attention to not just the line for requirements but also the other lines for downstream work.

What you'll find is that if group B optimize their cooperation and quality to get *their* work done quickly, which is probably what they are measured by, this will lead to a low level of completed work for the overall team.

If you model this as an agile process, instead of a waterfall-type, then you would expect to see less focus on local goals, more upon completed work, and fewer incentives for individuals to engage in this type of social loafing.

Considerations when Developing a Simulation Model

In the opening section of this chapter, we identified that a main purpose of developing a simulation model was to build a **shared understanding** among everybody in the organization. When you build a model, you should use it as an opportunity for also building shared understanding among everybody. Involve everybody in the building of the model. Seek out opinions and suggestions.

Approach model building like a business analyst would approach mapping a business process. Ask questions; get to understand how the organization, systems, and processes work. Then, build a small model, demonstrate it, and get some feedback, gradually adding in functionality that reflects how the organization runs its projects.

It is crucial to get these model behaviors and characteristics agreed. When you run the model as a dynamic simulation, you get all sorts of unexpected results, just like we did. This is, of course, the whole point of building a dynamic simulation model.

These stakeholders may dislike some of the results. They may want to disagree when the model produces unexpected or undesired behavior. However, if they have agreed behaviors and characteristics beforehand, it is much harder to reject the model's validity.

Further Reading

For an understanding of system dynamics and simulation, once again I recommend *Business Dynamics* by John Sterman.

A book specifically on modeling software projects is *Software Project Dynamics* by Tarek Abdel-Hamid and Stewart Madnick. It is quite dated and uses an old tool: Dynamo. However, the concepts are still relevant.

For learning to build and run models, I would recommend following the many good tutorial exercises within the help files of your chosen tool. You should run through all these exercises as your starting point before going deeper.

There are very few books that take you through hands-on exercises with the Vensim tool. However, I did find *Vensim Fast* gave me useful experience in building and debugging models.

In addition, you can find some useful videos on the tool vendor's site.

Also, I have produced some useful videos which are available on the Apress website and are listed in the Resources section of this chapter.

Resources

The following resources for this book are available on GitHub via the book's product page, located at www.apress.com/ISBN.

Models for Vensim model reader

Chapter 10 - Technical Debt.vpmx

Chapter 10 - Social Loafing.vpmx

These are the models I have built in the modeling tool and then published, so that they can be run in the free-to-use model reader. Use these models when you are doing the exercises in this chapter.

Models for Vensim modeling tool

Chapter 10 - Technical Debt.mdl

Chapter 10 - Social Loafing.mdl

These are the files I used to build and then publish the models for use in the modeling tool. You can use them to understand how the model works "under the hood."

Chapter 10 - Technical debt 01.mp4

Chapter 10 - Social Loafing 01.mp4

These are sample videos that I have created to help you understand how to use the models and interpret the results.

Vensim website URL

Here is the website of the Ventana/Vensim modeling tool. Download the free model reader or a trial version of the modeling tool from here:

https://vensim.com/free-downloads/

Summary

In this chapter, we have used a system modeling tool to demonstrate the usefulness of dynamic simulation to model the common software development problem of technical debt.

We started by downloading the model reader tool. Next, we saw how to open and download the model and then run simulations with that model to explore the dynamic behavior of a project and gain insights which are not possible from a simple static model.

We have seen how to get results by using outputs, such as graphs, plus how we can combine graphs and controls into a dashboard.

Through changing variables in our model while running simulations, we have confirmed that underestimation can adversely affect projects – something we already suspected.

In addition, we came across the counterintuitive insight that, under certain conditions, increasing the scheduled completion date leads to a *reduction* in the project length and cost, something you cannot learn simply by looking at that iron triangle.

By running the model over three project iterations, we learned that while technical debt usually benefits the project it is created upon, it will place a disproportionate burden on downstream projects.

However, we measure projects by visible measures, which means that we manage projects to maximize benefits for the *current* project, usually with little regard for damage to downstream projects.

Hopefully, you found that reading this chapter and running the models in the tool has convinced you of the value of building and running simulation models.

When you ran the technical debt model and adjusted the sliders, in the space of a few minutes you were able to try out a vast number of different variations of project scheduled end date. In addition, you were able to see the effect it had on not just the time and cost of the project, but other factors, such as the amount of rework, known and undiscovered, variations in work quality and productivity in response to schedule pressure, fatigue, and so on.

All this was discovered by adjusting only one variable – scheduled completion date – out of potentially dozens. To gain a similar level of insight into how your project will behave, you would need to invest months of analysis. It would then be difficult to communicate your understanding to others. However, by using a dynamic simulation tool, you can build a model as a shared, collaborative activity. In this way, you can gain the involvement, feedback, and agreement of all stakeholders. This in turn enables you to gain and share insights into project behavior that would not otherwise be visible.

Once again this is the WYSIATI of Daniel Kahneman in *Thinking, Fast and Slow*. By using dynamic modeling and simulation, you can expand the universe of understanding of all within that software development project.

This chapter has barely touched upon the potential of system dynamics and running simulation models to help stakeholders make informed decisions about complex problems. Through building simulation models, you can help your organization gain an insight into long-standing problems, like technical debt, project underestimation, depletion of shared resource, the effects of early testing, and so on.

We now move into Part 3 of the book – tackling technical debt – where we begin by looking at how we can safely convince others of the importance of tackling technical debt.

PART III

Tackling Technical Debt

CHAPTER 11

Safely Convincing Everyone

> *It ought to be remembered that there is nothing more difficult to take in hand, more perilous to conduct, or more uncertain in its success, than to take the lead in the introduction of a new order of things.*
>
> *Because the innovator has for enemies all those who have done well under the old conditions, and lukewarm defenders in those who may do well under the new.*
>
> *This coolness arises partly from fear of the opponents, who have the laws on their side, and partly from the incredulity of men, who do not readily believe in new things until they have had a long experience of them."*
>
> —Niccolò Machiavelli, The Prince

In this chapter, we look at one of our greatest challenges – safely convincing everyone to make changes in how they work. Or, in the words of Machiavelli, to take the lead in the introduction of a new order of things.

We begin with the cautionary tale of Dr Semmelweis, who pursued a groundbreaking idea that should have saved thousands of lives but was instead rejected by his colleagues. We take some lessons from Dr Semmelweis's experience, plus explore some more lessons of our own, including what we should do if our organization is not yet ready for change. We finish with a checklist of items to use when trying to convince everyone.

The purpose of this chapter is contained within its title – safely convincing everyone. Each word has significance.

CHAPTER 11   SAFELY CONVINCING EVERYONE

Safely. This endeavor is not without danger. Please go back and reread the quote from Machiavelli. As you do so, think of who in your organization is doing well under the current order of things and may oppose any attempts to change their behavior. Ask yourself – who may be happy to see this initiative fail, or you fail? Changing people can be dangerous, as we'll discover shortly.

Convince. We believe that we convince people by changing their minds. This is untrue. We convince people by *changing their hearts*. Hence, we need to address this subject emotionally, not logically. Remember those teenage smokers were left unmoved by appeals to logic but changed after appeals to emotions.

Everyone. Strictly speaking, it's *everyone who matters*, but since practically anyone in the organization can undermine efforts to reduce and manage technical debt, this means you need to convince everyone.

You now have a good understanding of what technical debt is. You understand that it is not so much a technical problem, but rather it is the result of a series of trade-off decisions made by individuals facing constraints from the system they work within. You also understand that it is a wicked problem, a type of problem that can never be permanently resolved, but instead must be managed.

Congratulations!

The problem is that few others in your organization currently share your understanding. This means that before you can address your technical debt problem, you need to convince others of the true nature of technical debt, as well as its importance. This is difficult and can be more dangerous than you first imagine, as we'll discover in the unfortunate case of Dr Semmelweis.

Dr Semmelweis

Dr Ignaz Semmelweis was a clinician at a maternity institute in nineteenth-century Vienna, Austria. At this time, infanticide of illegitimate children was an endemic problem throughout Europe. To help address this problem, many maternity institutions offered free health care.

There were two such maternity clinics in Vienna. However, a mothers' life expectancy was radically different at the two clinics. The first clinic had a mortality rate due to childbed fever of 10%, while the second clinic had a fatality rate of only 4%, as shown in Figure 11-1.

CHAPTER 11   SAFELY CONVINCING EVERYONE

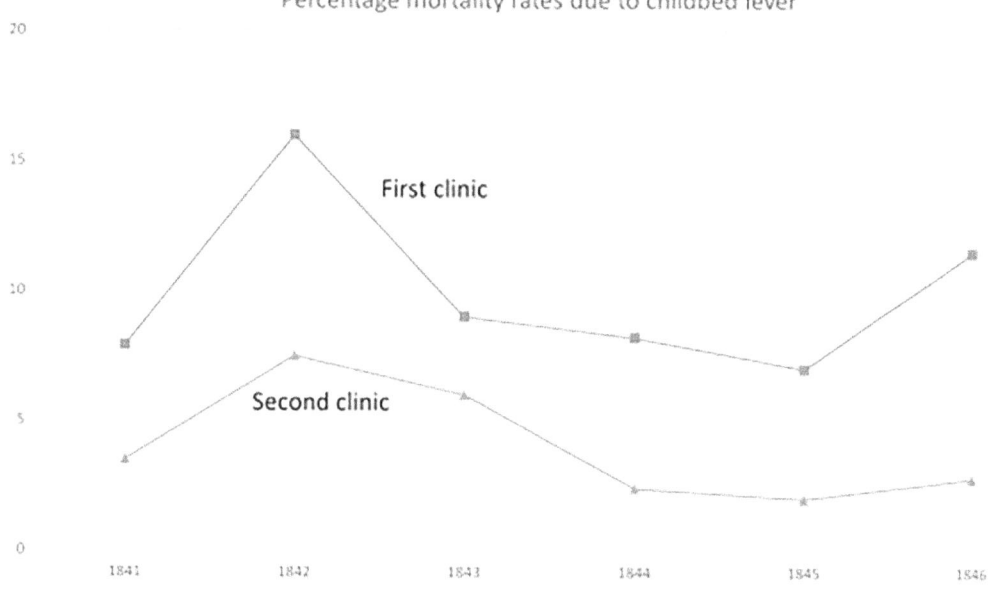

Figure 11-1. Mortality rates in two maternity clinics in Vienna. Source: Semmelweiss (1861)

Imagine yourself as an expectant mother stood on the entrance steps of the first clinic, looking inside. How would you feel, knowing that after you entered this building there was a 10% chance you would not come out alive?

Each clinic admitted patients on alternate days. Understandably, nobody wanted to enter the first clinic. Women would even give birth on the streets, pretending to be en-route to the first clinic, so they could avoid the clinic yet still qualify for free health care.

Surprisingly, childbed fever was low among those women who gave birth on the street, a fact that puzzled Semmelweis. He asked himself – what prevented women who delivered on the street from contracting childbed fever?

Dr Semmelweis searched extensively for an answer. He eliminated potential causes including differences in medical techniques, overcrowding, and so on. He achieved a lucky breakthrough following the death of a colleague (lucky, that is, for Dr Semmelweis, not his colleague), who was accidentally cut with a scalpel during an autopsy. His colleague's subsequent own autopsy showed a pathology similar to those mothers dying of childbed fever.

Semmelweis realized that in the first clinic the medical students performed autopsies and subsequently visited childcare patients. The second clinic was staffed by midwives, who did not perform autopsies. He speculated that contamination from

CHAPTER 11   SAFELY CONVINCING EVERYONE

contact with a dead body was transferred onto patients, causing childbed fever. (This might seem obvious to us, but don't forget we have the benefit of hindsight, plus one hundred and fifty years of medical advances).

Semmelweis also identified a remedy – washing your hands in a solution of chlorinated lime reduced mortality rates by 90%. Dr Semmelweis demonstrated this remarkable improvement in survival rates to his colleagues, shown in Figure 11-2.

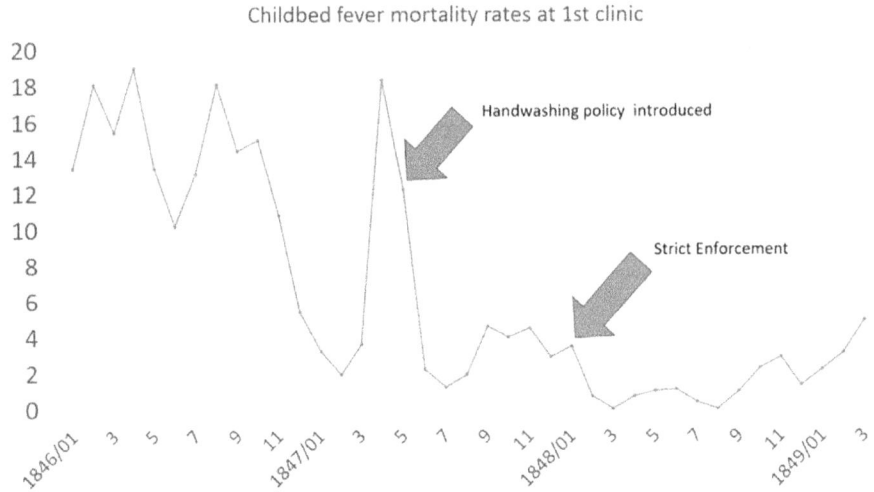

Figure 11-2. Mortality rates before and after introduction of chlorinated lime handwashing. Source: Semmelweiss (1861)

However, instead of Dr Semmelweis's colleagues congratulating him on his breakthrough that could save thousands of lives, he was met with fierce resistance.

Why was this?

The primary reason was that Dr Semmelweis's results conflicted with the existing belief system, which was that disease was caused by dycrasia, an imbalance of the body's four humors: phlegm, blood, yellow bile, and black bile. Furthermore, Dr Semmelweis was unable to offer a causal explanation of the disease or its transmission – remember Louis Pasteur's germ theory was still 20 years into the future. In addition, there were competing theories, such as childbed fever was due to uncleanliness of the bowel.

However, there were additional factors, entirely unrelated to medical considerations, that contributed toward Dr Semmelweis's colleagues rejecting his theory. Many doctors were outraged by his suggestion that a gentleman's hands could transmit disease. Also, Dr Semmelweis was not Austrian, but rather Hungarian – the poor relation in the Austro-Hungarian Habsburg Empire.

But perhaps the most important factor in preventing people changing their minds was that *Dr Semmelweis alienated important members of the medical establishment.* After his fellow doctors disregarded him, he wrote a barrage of letters, denouncing obstetricians as irresponsible murderers for ignoring his findings.

If you lived in nineteenth-century Europe, it wasn't a terribly smart idea to go around antagonizing a bunch of people who had the legal powers to get you banged up in a mental institution. Unfortunately for Dr Semmelweis, this is exactly what happened. He was lured under false pretenses into visiting an insane asylum. Once inside, the doors were locked behind him, he was committed to the asylum, beaten by the guards, and forced into a straitjacket. He died 2 weeks later.

Semmelweis's successor at the maternity clinic abandoned the cleanliness regime instituted by Semmelweis. Mortality rates increased sixfold, but nothing was said.

Lessons from Dr Semmelweis

Now, it is somewhat unlikely that your organization's stakeholders have the ability to lure you into an insane asylum, have you committed, and then force you into a straitjacket. (Although if you do spot a straitjacket lying around the HR section of your head office, then maybe it's prudent to work from home for a while). However, while those stakeholders may not be able to get you incarcerated, there are several reasons why you should take note of Dr Semmelweis's plight.

Like Dr Semmelweis, you are going up against an established paradigm or belief system – Semmelweis was up against the paradigm of dycrasia, whereas you are up against the paradigm of technical debt being a technical problem. Admittedly, our paradigm is less well-established than dycrasia was. Nevertheless, many people firmly believe it.

Also, just like Dr Semmelweis, we are rubbing up against some tender egos. For Dr Semmelweis, his physician colleagues were outraged at his suggestion that their gentlemen hands could possibly transmit disease. For us, we are firstly rubbing up against developers and techies, who can become defensive over any examination of the shortcomings of their creations. Secondly, many in business become defensive over suggestions that decisions they made had later negative impacts.

Dr Semmelweis's situation even had a couple of advantages over your own.

Firstly, he had incontrovertible proof of a remedy – that of washing your hands in a solution of chlorinated lime. You are unlikely to have such firm proof, since wicked problems, like technical debt, can never have an immediate and conclusive test that a solution has worked. We have no equivalent to the washing our hands in chlorinated lime solution.

Secondly, Dr Semmelweis clearly had lives at stake, which provided an added impetus to finding a solution. In contrast, few of our decisions around technical debt are likely to result in lives lost.

Hence, if Dr Semmelweis was unable to persuade fellow doctors, when mothers' lives were at stake, we should not be overly confident that we can easily persuade some software and business professionals, when the most that is usually at stake is some additional costs and slower delivery.

As we saw earlier with the sugar-fats debate in the obesity problem, a better explanation can be defeated by an incorrect but plausible explanation, promoted by an eloquent and less scrupulous advocate. This is especially likely if adopting the incorrect explanation benefits some influential parties.

The True Lesson from Dr Semmelweis

Many people are aware of the story of Dr Semmelweis, which has led to a cognitive bias being named after him:

> *The Semmelweis reflex: A tendency to reject new evidence that contradicts our current beliefs or paradigms. It also frequently results in an attack upon the person presenting the new evidence or advocating its acceptance.*

Most people who hear the story are puzzled by the behavior of Dr Semmelweis's colleagues. Many are outraged at the treatment meted out to him.

The more imaginative among us visualize ourselves as Dr Semmelweis, heroically battling to save lives against a callous and apathetic establishment. Or maybe we picture ourselves as the first brave soul to break ranks with our colleagues and support Dr Semmelweis. Try this yourself – spend a moment imagining yourself as either Dr Semmelweis or that first brave colleague.

It's very easy to do. You can imagine behaving in this way, holding within yourself a mixture of fortitude and moral outrage, as you battled for what is right.

However, you can also learn a different and far more important lesson from Dr Semmelweis. Try to imagine yourself as one of those colleagues who *rejected* Dr Semmelweis's findings. And as you do so, try to work out why you are feeling perfectly normal and justified in your behavior.

This is much more difficult, isn't it? We cannot easily imagine ourselves behaving like one of Dr Semmelweis's colleagues. Yet, the reality is that if we had been a doctor in nineteenth-century Vienna, then almost certainly we would have behaved in exactly the same way as those colleagues. It's difficult to stomach, isn't it?

One of the most important insights you can gain from this story is to not feel those predictable emotions – admiration and pity for Dr Semmelweis, plus outrage and disgust for his colleagues – but instead to put ourselves into the shoes of those colleagues and then identify the factors present that would have driven you to behave as those colleagues did. Next, try to work out what would have needed to change to make you and those other colleagues behave differently.

So, why might Dr Semmelweis's colleagues have behaved in the way that they did?

One reason that Dr Semmelweis's colleagues felt justified in rejecting his idea so forcefully was that his proposed causal mechanism – matter transferred from cadavers – appeared to be a retrograde step, rather than a medical advancement.

The idea that "corpse particles" could somehow turn a person into a corpse appeared reminiscent of magical or superstitious thinking. Any corpse particles must have been minuscule, as doctors could not see any contamination on their hands. Exactly how something so small as to be invisible could kill a human, millions of times larger, seemed like magical thinking? To some colleagues, Semmelweis appeared to be reverting to those speculative and unprovable theories of the past, which the scientific and medical communities were desperately trying to move forward from.

Next, let's look at what Dr Semmelweis could have done differently to increase his chances of success and reduce the likelihood of ending up in an insane asylum.

What Could Dr Semmelweis Have Done Differently?

How could Dr Semmelweis have convinced the medical establishment of the validity of his theory? This is an important question. If we understand what Dr Semmelweis could have done to convince his colleagues, then we have a better chance of applying lessons to win over any technical debt sceptics.

We can identify several actions that Dr Semmelweis could have taken to improve his chances of success:

1. Avoid alienating colleagues.
2. Better communications.
3. Recognize the sensitivity of gentlemen doctors' feelings regarding cleanliness.
4. Build a coalition of supporters.
5. Wait for an opportune moment.
6. Engage a different community.

Let's now look at each of these.

Avoid Alienating Colleagues

This ought to have been Dr Semmelweis's number one priority. No doctor thinks of themselves as a murderer. Unfortunately, in his frustration, Dr Semmelweis accused his colleagues of exactly this. In doing so, he antagonized and alienated his colleagues.

Similarly, no one in software development thinks of themselves as pursuing bad practices, like writing avoidably bad code, creating unnecessary debt, or making poor decisions.

If, like Dr Semmelweis, you feel that you are in the right about something, then it is all too easy to indulge in activities such as grandstanding, virtue signaling, or claiming the moral high ground. However, this usually does little to advance you toward your objective. Indeed, it often has an opposite effect.

Here, we should take a lesson from the accident investigation industry.

One of the most important breakthroughs that has led to enhanced safety is improved accident investigations. This was done by altering the mindset of the investigators. This mindset has moved away from searching for a mistake that has been made. Instead, it focuses upon exploring the point of view of the operators and making sense of the chain of events that led to the accident.

Today, enlightened accident investigators begin with the assumption that, until shown otherwise, *everybody involved was trying to work safely*. In addition, *everybody's behavior made sense from their viewpoint at the time*.

It is all too easy to find fault, especially with the benefit of hindsight. What is much harder is to step into the minds of the actors and understand why they acted as they did, plus why those actions made sense. Accident investigators must do this if they wish to prevent future accidents.

Instead of alienating his colleagues with accusations of murder, Dr Semmelweis should have focused upon why it made sense to his colleagues to reject his findings. If he had done this, he may have identified that it was the weakness of his causal mechanism explanation.

We must do similar if we wish to address our technical debt problem. All the actors within software development are trying to do the best they can with the tools they have, based upon *their* understanding of the situation. If they make a decision that results in technical debt, then they have usually done so believing this was the best outcome available. If they are rejecting our explanation of the reasons for or importance of technical debt, then we should first look toward any weakness in our own arguments or explanation.

Better Communications

To be successful, Dr Semmelweis needed to change the beliefs of a great many people. Unfortunately, he did not communicate well his ideas to a wider audience.

In this way, he was like John Yudkin, whose superior theory of the obesity link to sugar was defeated by Ancel Keys's superior advocacy for the role of saturated fats. One reason why we have spent several decades pursuing the reduction of saturated fats and largely ignoring the problems of sugar is that Ancel Keys was a far more effective communicator than John Yudkin.

Keys presented a logical and coherent flow to his clearly described arguments. He offered doctors, who were important stakeholders, the promise of a clear and simple route to reducing obesity. This was a problem that doctors were coming under increasing pressure to solve. And finally, Keys vigorously promoted his idea, helped by elements within the sugar industry.

In contrast, the explanations presented by John Yudkin were often highly technical, difficult for non-specialists to follow, and not vigorously promoted by elements within the food industry.

The lesson for technical debt is that any communications need to be adequate, clear, easy to follow, and vigorously promoted. In a later chapter, we'll hear from change management guru John Kotter, who identified that the most common problem with communicating a vision for change is under-communicating it, often by a factor of between 10 and 1,000.

Recognize the Sensitivity of Gentlemen Doctors

This would have been a difficult area for Dr Semmelweis. Even today, nursing staff commonly experience resistance if they highlight inadequate handwashing practices of doctors on wards. A surgeon's hands are reputed to be highly sensitive. But I'd wager they're nowhere near as sensitive as the ego of the surgeon they're attached to.

Dr Semmelweis may have had greater success if he had found an influencer to adopt his handwashing practices. However, he may have found this difficult, as senior members of the medical establishment in Vienna seemed against Semmelweis.

The lesson for technical debt is that you should be mindful of the sensitivities of your technical and businesspeople. You should avoid any suggestions that technical debt decisions are due to shortcomings such as incompetence or poor decision-making. Recall that we should begin with the assumption that everybody is trying the best they can, based upon *their* understanding of the situation.

Build a Coalition of Supporters

> *It is amazing what you can accomplish, if you do not care who gets the credit.*
>
> —President Harry Truman

Dr Semmelweis could have attempted to build up a coalition of supporters outside of the medical community, such as wealthy patrons interested in philanthropic work in return for recognition and approbation.

When you aim to address technical debt within your organization, you will need to build up a coalition of supporters, who may wish to take credit for any success.

Wait for an Opportune Moment

If your organization is not yet ready for change, then one option is to wait for a more opportune moment. However, to do this, you need to avoid burning your boats, for example, by alienating your colleagues. We'll discuss this further in a later section on the transtheoretical model.

Unfortunately for Dr Semmelweis, awaiting a more opportune moment was not realistic, possibly because he had already alienated his colleagues. His initial study in 1847 was roundly rejected by his colleagues, and then 14 years later his book, published in 1861, was still highly criticized.

Engage a Different Community

Dr Semmelweis could conceivably have found a community more receptive to his ideas, as several other communities in Germany, France, and Great Britain were advancing medicine during this period.

If your current organization is unreceptive to tackling technical debt, leaving you frustrated, then perhaps consider seeking out a more receptive organization.

We now understand what Dr Semmelweis could have done differently to achieve a better outcome. Many of these lessons are applicable to solutions within technical debt. In addition, there are some other techniques we could use to convince others.

We should begin by first seeking to understand before we seek to be understood.

First Seek to Understand, Then to Be Understood

In *The 7 Habits of Highly Effective People,* Stephen Covey talks about the principle – first seek to understand, then be understood. We should do the same.

If you want to reduce technical debt, then you must change the outcome of the decisions made that led to that technical debt. This means that you must understand why those individuals or teams made those decisions in the way they did, within the context that existed at the time. There will be good reasons why individuals acted as they did.

Recall the principle from accident investigation – everybody's behavior made sense from their viewpoint at the time.

So, it is with technical debt. Those individuals involved in a decision that created technical debt, did so believing that it offered the best outcome available, given the existing situation and constraints.

Therefore, much of your time during your interview and workshop sessions should be directed toward understanding and making sense of what individuals faced and why they made the decisions that they did.

Next, we consider how the problem of externalities may influence individuals.

The Problem of Externalities

A barrier to convincing everybody is the problem of externalities. This is one party's ability to unilaterally impose a cost on another, discussed in the chapter on economics. There are two parties to the externality: the beneficiary and the disadvantaged. Unsurprisingly, the beneficiary party is keen to continue imposing costs on the other, and often feels justified in imposing those externalities.

When working with these beneficiaries, you should bear in mind that their actions are often largely a result of their role. Even if that individual were replaced, their replacement would likely behave in the same way.

Somewhat counterintuitively, those disadvantaged by the externality are not always keen to have it removed. In a perverse case of co-dependency, those support teams suffering under the mountain of technical debt recognize that nobody can truly blame them for debt imposed upon them. Plus, with all that messy debt around, nobody can quite fathom out exactly what is happening, so it's safest to leave those support developers to their own devices.

Externalities are about people imposing costs on another, making it a people problem, a topic we cover in our next section.

It's a People Problem: Involve Everybody

You probably recall the quote from Gerry Weinberg in the previous chapter, about "it's always a people problem." Gerry gave us another quote that is highly relevant to solving our technical debt problem:

Unless and until all members of a team have a common understanding of the problem, all attempts to solve the problem are just so much wasted energy.

—Gerald M. Weinberg

This is why it is so important to hold workshops, plus ensure that everybody attends and actively engages in them.

Sometimes, you may find it difficult to arrange large workshops, with everyone in attendance. At HMV, we were geographically dispersed across several head offices, making it difficult to gather everyone into the same place. However, the most successful projects were those able to bring together all relevant stakeholders at critical project points.

Although nowadays you don't need to physically meet – after all, many people on great Open-Source projects *never* physically meet – it's a whole lot easier with everybody in the same room. The important thing is to develop a common, shared understanding of the problem.

If you cannot get important stakeholders to turn up to critical meetings, such as workshops, this is a warning flag that your initiative may not be workable, or your organization is not committed to addressing technical debt.

With people problems, start small, ideally with one person at a time.

Begin by Understanding One Person at a Time

Although you do need to involve everybody, and at some stage you will bring everybody together into a large workshop, when you are first trying to understand this problem, you can only step inside one person's shoes at a time. In addition, you'll receive more diverse views about the same issue when you interview people alone. You can then explore these viewpoints in depth without fear of interruption from a listener holding a contradictory viewpoint, plus you may receive franker views than the interviewee would express openly in a group.

Therefore, when you are gathering information, you're best to start with one-to-one meetings.

It is an obvious point, but do ensure you resist any temptation to join in agreement of any blaming that may be expressed in these meetings.

A further reason you should begin with individual meetings is that large groups have their own dangers. This is particularly true when addressing an unpopular topic, like technical debt. There will be large differences of opinion about the true cause of the problem, so avoid surfacing this prematurely and in an uncontrolled way. Therefore, you'll find it safer to delay bringing together large groups until you better understand the individuals involved.

Develop a Shared Commitment Among Stakeholders

Technical debt is a wicked problem that involves groups with widely diverging worldviews. Therefore, we should not be surprised when these different groups hold widely diverse beliefs about the problem, its causes, and potential solutions.

Through all of this, you need to develop a **shared commitment**, which is built on a **shared understanding**, as discussed in the chapter on wicked problems. As you recall, shared understanding does not mean that all stakeholders agree about everything. Instead, it means that stakeholders understand each other's positions well enough to have that *intelligent dialogue about their different interpretations of the problem.*

You can help build up shared understanding while you engage in your initial interviews and small group meetings. To do this, use visual collaboration tools, like Miro, Lucidchart, or Whiteboard. As you create notes and diagrams with one interviewee, you can record and upload appropriate items into your collaboration tool. These items can be subsequently modified and appended to, as additional information and points of view become available, or as your team's understanding of the problem changes.

An example process is shown in Figure 11-3.

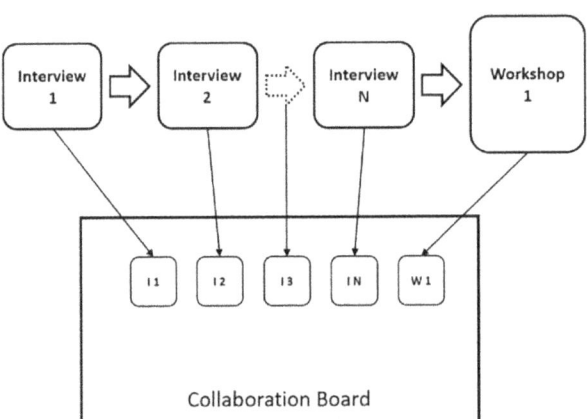

Figure 11-3. *Using your interview process with a visual collaboration tool to build up shared understanding*

If you are experiencing trouble in building up a shared commitment, do not rush through the problem identification stage of the workshops. A common pitfall is to rush into solution mode. If you do this, then any solution generated is likely to primarily benefit the dominant stakeholders and hence unlikely to lead to real shared commitment.

There are several useful tools for building shared commitment among diverse stakeholders. The first tool developed was Issue-Based Information System (**IBIS**), which is an argumentation-based approach for problem clarification. Other, similar tools include **issue mapping**, **dialogue mapping**, and **argument mapping**. We'll explore argument mapping in more detail in the relevant workshop chapter.

Sometimes, you cannot get sufficient shared commitment to proceed. At this point, you are probably better off disengaging gracefully, thus leaving the door open for a future engagement when the organization is more receptive. We briefly look at this option in the next section.

What If Your Organization Won't Change?

Technical debt has existed ever since that 1960s hippy developer with a flowery shirt, sideburns, and platform shoes decided it would be a super cool idea to solve the memory space problem by recording the year as a two-digit number, thereby storing up problems for all that Y2K tomfoolery.

Sometimes, organizations are simply not ready for change. Later, we discuss how to assess readiness, using the corporate marshmallow test. If you judge the time is not yet right, it is important you leave the door open for a future engagement. Had Dr Semmelweis done this, rather than alienate his colleagues, then thousands of mothers might otherwise have lived, and he may have enjoyed a far better outcome.

This idea of leaving the door open comes from the transtheoretical model of addiction treatment, developed by James Prochaska and Carlo di Clemente (1977). The model is intended to help therapists dealing with addictions and health-related behaviors, so it's obviously a bit heavyweight for us in software development, because we never become addicted to anything. Except perhaps technical debt, poor estimation, and death march projects, plus a whole bunch of other things.

The relevant part of the model for us is the initial stage – precontemplation. (The other five stages are contemplation, preparation, action, maintenance, and termination.)

CHAPTER 11   SAFELY CONVINCING EVERYONE

In the precontemplation stage, individuals (and organizations) are not thinking seriously about changing and are not interested in help. Individuals in this stage defend their current ways of working and do not feel it is a problem, or enough of a problem to justify a disruptive intervention. They often become defensive in the face of pressure to change, an effect linked to the *backfire effect*.

> *Backfire effect, a tendency to react to disconfirming evidence by strengthening one's previous beliefs. Also known as belief perseverance.*
>
> —Baumeister (2007)

If your organization is not yet ready for change, you are best avoiding premature efforts to force any major change, as such efforts tend to be counterproductive and hinder any future intervention. Instead, aim to limit your intervention to limited tactical improvements.

Safely Convincing Everyone Checklist

Here is a checklist to help you safely address your technical debt issues within your organization:

1. Have you avoided alienating colleagues?
2. Are your communications clear, easy to follow, and vigorously promoted?
3. Have you engaged with everyone?
4. Are you engaging with stakeholders individually, rather than in groups?
5. Have you built a coalition of supporters?
6. Is the present moment opportune?
7. If your organization is not ready for change, have you left the door open?

Further Reading

For an engaging account of Dr Semmelweis and his work, try *The Doctors' Plague*, by Sherwin Nuland. An English translation of Semmelweis's original book is available by Carter Codell.

For a deeper understanding of dialogue mapping, plus IBIS, read *Dialogue Mapping* by Jeff Conklin.

For an engaging read of an investigation trying to make sense of the chain of events that led to the accidental shoot down of two US Army Black Hawk helicopters by a US Air Force F-15 flight enforcing a no-fly zone over northern Iraq, try *Friendly Fire* by Scott Snook.

Suitable books on accident investigation include *Drift into Failure* by Sydney Dekker or *Human Error* by James Reason.

The original paper for the transtheoretical model by James Prochaska and Carlo di Clemente is available under the title, *The Transtheoretical Approach: Crossing Traditional Boundaries of Therapy*.

Summary

In this chapter, we explored how to safely convince everyone that technical debt should be addressed. We looked at the sad tale of Dr Semmelweis and took some lessons from his challenges, plus added some insights such as seeking to understand before being understood, the difficulty of externalities, and the importance of involving everyone. We concluded by considering what to do if our organization was not yet ready for change, the importance of leaving that door open for a future engagement.

Convincing everyone in your organization of the importance of tackling technical debt is an important stage on that route to a shared understanding and subsequently a shared commitment, both of which are necessary to tackle the wicked problem of technical debt.

In the next chapter we begin to put everything together, where we outline a program for an organization to address its technical debt problem.

CHAPTER 12

A Program to Address Technical Debt

Up until now, we've been mainly concerned with understanding what technical debt is and what drives its creation, plus what drives, or fails to drive, its reduction. We now move away from understanding the nature of technical debt and its drivers and move on to putting together an intervention aimed at addressing our technical debt problem on a sustainable basis.

In this chapter, we give a high-level overview of a technical debt reduction program, which is covered in more detail in the subsequent six chapters.

One difficulty of addressing technical debt is that while it is not primarily a technical problem, responsibility for addressing it is often delegated to highly technical people.

Addressing technical debt is less like a technical problem and more like a change management problem. You must get various diverse individuals and groups to change what they are doing, where many of these benefits will be felt by the greater organization, rather than themselves. In addition, the individual or team may be disadvantaged, both by the changes they must make, plus other teams' failure or refusal to make corresponding changes.

Technical Debt Reduction Program Framework

The framework for the technical debt reduction program is shown in Figure 12-1.

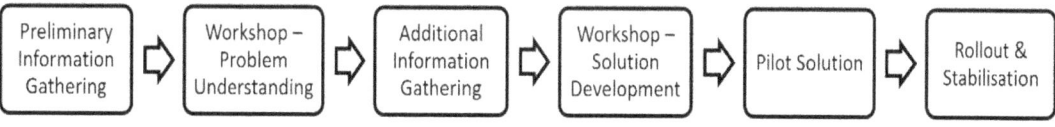

Figure 12-1. *The technical debt reduction program framework*

This framework has been adapted from a combination of frameworks, including the ADKAR model and Deming's Plan-Do-Check-Act cycle.

Next, we'll look at the first of these steps – preliminary information gathering.

Preliminary Information Gathering

There are four activities you need to carry out in any initial information gathering:

1. Gauge readiness.
2. Understand where you are now.
3. Determine how to go forward.
4. Prepare individuals for change.

An important task is to gauge the readiness of your organization for the necessary change. If your organization is not ready, you'll need to focus on helping it get ready for change. If after trying, you are unable to do this, you should consider whether you may be better off waiting for a more opportune time, rather than damage your credibility in an effort that risks failure.

As well as gauging organizational readiness, you need to understand where the organization is now and how it came to be there.

Once confident of where the organization is, you can begin to determine options for a way forward.

Finally, the preliminary information gathering provides you with a good opportunity to meet people on an individual or small team basis. In these sessions, you can begin to prepare individuals for the change likely to be coming.

Workshops for Problem Understanding

The goal of these workshops is to develop a shared, collective understanding about technical debt, the extent to which it is a problem, and the common causes of it.

There are two reasons you should involve all the stakeholders. Firstly, each stakeholder will bring different information about the problem. Secondly, if any stakeholder is absent, they will resent their exclusion and not cooperate later, causing your technical debt initiative to partially or completely unravel.

These workshops are also a good opportunity for individuals to meet people from different disciplines and explore alternative viewpoints. Therefore, it is a good idea to mix the groups up.

In this chapter we'll learn about some tools that have proved useful for problem understanding, particularly around exploratory analysis techniques, as well as critical thinking techniques.

Additional Information Gathering

Following your workshops for problem understanding, you may find you are missing critical pieces of information.

In this chapter, we look at how to carry out any supplementary investigations, plus analyze and understand the output from the first workshops.

Workshops for Solution Development

You are now ready to begin exploring potential solutions to your technical debt problem.

In this chapter, you learn how to organize workshops to develop a solution. You learn what inputs to bring into the sessions and some tools you can use, plus some tips on facilitation. Your output should be a set of pilot solutions to trial out.

Pilot Solutions

In this chapter you learn how to run your pilot solution and pitfalls to watch out for, plus how to keep the momentum going and why you must report back early wins to stakeholders.

Rollout and Stabilization

In this chapter you learn how to assess the success of each pilot, plus its suitability for rollout across the organization. You also learn ways to stabilize the new way of working and avoid regressing into previous ways of working that allowed a buildup of technical debt.

A More Complete Framework

You are unlikely to solve your technical debt problem in a single pass through the process. As you recall, technical debt is a wicked problem, and wicked problems can rarely be solved, but instead must be managed. One characteristic of a wicked problem is that if you attempt to solve it, you will change nature of the problem. Your intervention is likely to spark off consequences, which in turn will have their own consequences, and so on. You must manage these consequences, which means another cycle through the process.

A more complete framework for the technical debt reduction program is shown in Figure 12-2.

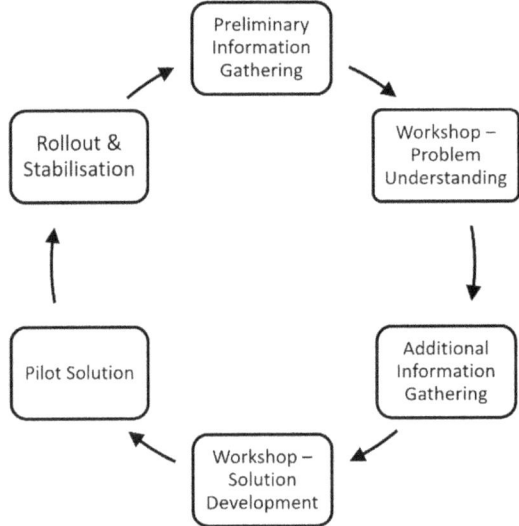

Figure 12-2. The technical debt reduction program framework

After you pass through a first time and get to rollout and stabilization, you will need to return to your start point, as your technical debt problem will have changed. Hopefully, your problem will be smaller than before. Nevertheless, it will have changed, so you must go round your loop once more.

You can cut out a lot of the activities in the problem understanding workshop – after all the group now knows enough about the technical debt onion – but the steps are likely still required.

Summary

In this chapter we moved away from understanding technical debt and its drivers, and onto putting together an intervention to address technical debt on a sustainable basis. We briefly explored a roadmap for a successful technical debt initiative, something we'll cover in more detail in the next six chapters.

In the next chapter, we'll begin the first stage of that initiative – preliminary information gathering.

CHAPTER 13

Preliminary Information Gathering

This chapter outlines the activities and processes involved in gathering information in preparation for the problem understanding workshops.

We begin with the corporate marshmallow test. This test determines how much your organization can delay gratification in pursuit of a long-term goal – an important ingredient of addressing technical debt. We then look at where we are now, how much debt we have, how and why we acquired it, and where our organization is feeling pain.

Next, we look at how much code-related and architecture-related debt we have. We then look at whether we are firefighting our way into debt, plus we look at if any anti-patterns are driving debt.

Next, we work out how to go forward, our trade-offs, and understanding our system and its leverage points. We finish by looking at how we can prepare individuals for any changes, plus introducing them to a simulation model.

Let's start by looking at the corporate marshmallow test.

The Corporate Marshmallow Test

You've probably heard about the marshmallow test. This is an experiment where children were offered a choice between one marshmallow immediately or two marshmallows if they waited for a while. The experiment is about the power of delayed gratification and showed that those children who were able to delay their gratification did better in later life.

Why is this relevant to technical debt? It's relevant because addressing technical debt is all about delayed gratification. It is about stakeholders and project team members choosing not to take a benefit now that will lead to a later debt that is bad value for the future organization. If stakeholders and teams are unwilling or unable to do this, then any technical debt reduction initiative becomes more difficult and limited, although still worthwhile.

The critical question you want answered is the following:

Is our organization capable of delayed gratification?

This is the marshmallow test for corporations.

The marshmallow test is not necessarily about measuring a child's innate capacity to delay gratification. For example, the child may live in a highly dysfunctional setting, where delayed gratification is impracticable. Any marshmallow or other goody left on the table would be immediately stolen and consumed by someone else.

Similarly, for the corporate marshmallow test, you're not measuring an individual, team, or organizational capacity to delay gratification. Rather, you are measuring a combination of their capacity to delay gratification, plus their belief of the likelihood that any delayed benefit will not be consumed by others, and hence actually will be available for their delayed benefit. This is the same dilemma faced by those fishing boat captains or the cattle herders in the tragedy of the commons problem in the economics chapter.

Unfortunately, if you asked this question, you are unlikely to receive an honest answer. So, you need to ask some different questions, in the hope that you can get an approximate answer to the question you really want to ask.

Examples of questions include the following:

How likely do you think it is that a project will decide to fully address its technical debt, adding 10% to the development time?

Definitely not	Highly unlikely	More unlikely than not	Equally likely and unlikely	More likely than not	Highly likely	Definitely
1	2	3	4	5	6	7

Additional questions are available for you in the appendix.

There are two things you can do if your organization fails the marshmallow test.

Highlight the results and discuss.

Highlight your findings back to the organization and arrange a workshop to explore why this is so, what organizational factors are driving the difficulty in achieving delayed gratification, and what can be done.

Focus on implementing solutions.

Focus upon implementing solutions that are not dependent upon delayed gratification as part of the solution.

You are unlikely to encounter an organization that is incapable of *any* delayed gratification. Therefore, try to work out where your organization has the capability to delay gratification, where it does not, and focus your efforts around the former areas.

The next thing you wish to know is where organization currently is regarding technical debt.

Understand Where You Are Now

Understanding where you are now means trying to answer questions such as

1. How much technical debt do we have?
2. How and why did we acquire it?
3. Where is the organization feeling pain?
4. What source code-related technical debt is there?
5. What architecture-related technical debt is there?

In addition to knowing where you currently are, you also want to get an idea of how much technical debt you currently have.

How Much Technical Debt Do We Have?

You will not be able to fully answer this question until after you have explored the other questions listed above. However, it is useful to start with this question, even if it is simply to remind yourself of your ultimate goal.

If your organization keeps a technical debt register, you can get some idea of the level of technical debt within the organization, provided the register is reasonably up-to-date. If the register is not kept up-to-date, well that tells you something about the organization, too.

Examples of questions include

1. Do you have a technical debt register?
2. Do you know if it is kept up-to-date?

Additional questions to help you with the technical debt register are available in the appendix.

You also want to know where this technical debt is coming from.

How and Why Did We Acquire It?

Although you may be tempted to focus on one group, for example, technical personnel, asking how and why your organization acquire this debt is equally relevant to others.

By enquiring across a diverse array of people, you will get very different viewpoints. For example, technical personnel may understand the details of the debt, plus the technical reasons it came about, while non-technical personnel may be able to give you insights into why the stakeholders, project, or organization chose a solution that created this debt (assuming that a conscious decision was involved).

Just like the dog that did not bark in Sherlock Holmes' story *The Adventure of Silver Blaze*, the absence of information can be equally telling. For example, if you find that several technical people discussed a particular item of technical debt at its creation, but that non-technical people were entirely unaware of it, this is telling you something about sharing of information.

Examples of questions include

1. Where do you feel technical debt is being created and destroyed?

2. What do you feel are the main drivers, causing technical debt in our organization?

Additional questions to help you with how and why the organization acquires technical debt are available in the appendix.

Other useful information includes where your organization is currently feeling pain from technical debt.

Where Is Your Organization Feeling Pain?

Technical debt is largely invisible to most non-technical people. However, the consequences are often visible, where they show themselves as symptoms. Therefore, many of the questions around pain points can be answered at least as well, if not better, by end users, customer support, and client facing personnel.

Examples of questions include

1. Do you feel the system is becoming more prone to defects?

2. Are you ever surprised at the estimated effort to implement what appears to be a small change or rectify an apparently small defect?

Additional questions to help you to understand where the organization is feeling pain are available in the appendix.

You'd also like to know how much of this debt is code-related.

What Code-Related Technical Debt Is Out There?

The technical debt that can be most easily addressed is code-related technical debt. In many organizations, a good portion of this will be created during the frantic portions of a project, when it is behind schedule.

Fortunately, code-related debt is generally easier to address than the architecture-related technical debt, discussed in the next section.

Examples of questions include

1. Do you use any static analysis tools, to check code quality (e.g., SonarQube)?

2. Do you routinely conduct code reviews?

Additional questions to help you to understand your code-related technical debt are available in the appendix.

You'd also like to know how much of this debt is architecture-related.

What Architecture-Related Technical Debt Is There?

The most expensive type of technical debt is usually architectural-related technical debt.

Architectural technical debt tends to be created in the earlier stages of a project, when the big decisions around architecture are being made. This means that if a project is seriously underestimated, so that the project team are aware from the start they are behind schedule, then decisions that result in architectural technical debt are far more likely to be made.

Examples of questions include

1. Are there many examples of where the system architecture suffers a lack of modularity?

2. Does the original design have lots of options and flexibility that were never exploited?

Additional questions to help you to understand what architecture-related technical debt you may have are available for you in the appendix.

A common cause of debt is firefighting.

Are We Firefighting Our Way into Debt?

Firefighting is a type of management that applies a reactive and corrective approach to every problem that occurs. It de-prioritizes or ignores the planning and priorities previously established because the management team have a feeling of urgency to react to problems as they arise.

Why does firefighting have its own section? The answer is that it's so common and so important that if you discover your organization has a firefighting habit, it is worthwhile highlighting and attempting to address it.

Firefighting can be seen as a style of individual management – many of us have worked for bosses who are incorrigible firefighters. Firefighting can also be an organizational culture, and it is in this form that it is at its most dangerous.

A firefighting culture is particularly damaging to technical debt. While the firefighters are heroically fighting fires, even the mere mention of the long-term debt consequences of their firefighting actions is considered heretical. Such a suggestion can even be used for grandstanding by the firefighter – "How can you even talk about possible future problems – if I don't fix this today, there won't be any future!" The people around firefighters soon learn not to even raise the issues of long-term consequences or technical debt when the firefighter is busy putting out today's fire.

A common cause of firefighting is giving a team or project an unrealistically overambitious target, one that is not achievable with the time and resources allocated.

Over-rewarding heroic firefighters is another major cause. Some individuals are not merely comfortable in the drama of but actually thrive in that environment. An organization that rewards such apparent heroism may have inadvertently locked itself into an undesirable reinforcement loop. These heroic firefighters not only extinguish the current fire but also tend to leave some fire accelerants and un-extinguished embers lying around, ready for the next conflagration that they can heroically extinguish.

Another cause is a failure to delegate and train subordinates. Firefighters often like to get involved as much as possible, and they are often quick to criticize or second-guess their subordinates' decisions. Consequently, staff learn to hand their problems upward, rather than learning to solve the problems themselves.

Inadvertent Descent into Firefighting

Organizations can inadvertently descend into a firefighting mode, one which they find difficult to retrieve themselves from. A project team that is set a series of increasingly ambitious targets may be able to cope with a small level of overextension, but once overextended too far, the team descends into firefighting mode, from which it is difficult to escape.

The most obvious symptom that you are in firefighting mode is that team members are unable to carry out non-essential tasks, because all time is spent on essential tasks or firefighting.

For example, an agile team that is stuck in endless cycles of manual testing each sprint, because the testers are too busy to create an automated test pack and framework. Alternatively, that same team may be stuck in endless cycles of manual testing because the development team is too busy to hand the completed stories over early enough for the testers to create automated tests.

Examples of questions include

1. What percentage of your time do you feel is spent on work that is reacting to events, rather than work that is preplanned?

2. Do you have time to carry out tasks that are deemed not essential but nevertheless useful for the organization?

Additional questions to help you to understand whether you have descended into a firefighting mode are available in the appendix.

Also, check out if technical debt is building up through any of the anti-patterns we explored earlier.

Questionnaires for Anti-patterns

In addition to the above major areas, you should try to establish the extent to which your organization may be engaging in any undesirable anti-patterns, listed in the anti-pattern chapter.

Examples of questions include

1. Do you routinely find that projects in your organization are routinely underestimated? (Estimation Trap.)

2. Have you found that projects that addressed items of technical debt in early project phases are feeling "virtuous" and justified to subsequently leave behind some technical debt? (Moral Credential Effect.)

Additional questions to help you to understand whether you have become vulnerable to other anti-patterns are available in the appendix.

Next, think about how you may go forward in the upcoming workshops.

Determine How to Go Forward

Now you understand more about the organization and its technical debt problems, you should start thinking about ideas of how the organization may best move forward.

You may recall President Harry Truman complaining of his economists telling him, "On the one hand… [and then] on the other…." At the risk of sounding like one of those two-handed economists, on the one hand you need to avoid jumping into solution mode and thereby blinding yourself to potential alternatives, but on the other hand if you have no idea of possible routes forward, you risk aimlessly wandering around, gathering information, to little purpose.

To balance these two needs, ensure you always walk into the workshop with at least two ideas for how to go forward, even if you hope you don't need to pull out those ideas.

Next, try to understand what trade-offs are being made that are leading to technical debt.

Understand Your Trade-Offs

Try to understand the trade-offs that people are facing when they are making their decisions. This may not be straightforward, as people are likely to be considering different trade-offs at different stages in the project. In addition, people on a project that is on schedule will be facing very different trade-offs from those that are on a project that is seriously behind schedule.

Also, try to imagine or understand the personal trade-offs that individuals may be making. Here, use your knowledge from the chapter on the economic aspects of the technical debt problem. For example, think of the principal-agent problem or the externality problem and how this may be influencing trade-offs.

Examples of questions include

1. Can you tell me about the trade-off you faced?

2. How did you evaluate the different possibilities?

Additional questions to help you understand about the trade-offs people are making in the minds available in the appendix.

Next, explore and understand your organizational system and how it may be contributing to technical debt.

Understand Your System

Your objective is to understand the organization's technical debt problem, not to understand the organization's system for creating and maintaining software. However, it is impossible to escape understanding at least parts of that system and how they relate to the creation of technical debt.

Ask for system, organizational, and process maps, if they exist. Once you have those maps, first study them to understand what is going on, or supposed to be going on, within them. Do this so that you don't ask questions that could easily have been answered from studying the maps.

Once you're familiar with the maps, get people from different areas to walk you through the maps and processes. If you do this one-to-one, you'll benefit from people speaking more openly. Conversely, if you do this in a group setting, you're more likely to catch something that an individual interview would have missed out.

Ask people to point out where they think the maps are inaccurate or problematic. Alternatively, start as a group activity without the maps and then introduce them.

While you're interviewing people, sketch out what they're telling you, ideally in a simplified diagram, and then feed your understanding back to them, to check if it is accurate and complete. Check if it's okay to show the map to others.

Also show individuals diagrams you have created in other interviews (providing you are not breaking any trust or confidentiality). You may get some additions or corrections, or you may get a look of surprise, as that individual may be unaware of what is happening in other parts of the organization.

Before you finish any interview, be sure to ask who else you should talk to, plus is there anything else you have missed.

Questions to help you understand about your system are available in the appendix.

At this point, you can explore possible leverage points, where a small change may make a large difference.

Understand Your Potential Leverage Points

Examine the maps and diagrams you have constructed during your interviews. As you look at them, try and understand if there are any places in the system where a small change could feed through into a big difference.

If you are building causal loop diagrams, you may be able to identify some reinforcing loops, where small changes may lead to a significant long-term difference in the level of technical debt.

Have a look at the diagrams in the anti-patterns chapter for examples.

If you can identify potential leverage points, aim to get them raised in the problem understanding workshops, which we'll come to in the next chapter. However, resist the temptation to raise them yourself, but instead try to get the workshop members to identify those potential leverage points. When workshop members identify items for themselves, they feel greater ownership and are often more pro-active in exploring them.

You can facilitate the workshop team toward identifying potential leverage points, plus, if all else fails, you can identify the potential leverage points yourself.

While you are interviewing people, it's worthwhile preparing them for the upcoming changes.

Prepare Individuals for Change

This preliminary information gathering provides you with a good opportunity to meet people on an individual or small team basis. In these sessions, you can begin to prepare individuals for the change likely to be coming.

Talk with individuals about how things would be different in an organization with a managed low level of technical debt. Talk about the benefits, such as more predictable and faster software development. Also, talk about the other factors, such as the greater discipline required, and that project should not look to recover schedule by creating technical debt.

When you're speaking to people, either individually or in small groups, you have an ideal opportunity to raise their awareness and interest in exploring the dynamic aspects of technical debt by using software simulation models.

Software Simulation Models

If you're planning to use a simulation tool and dynamic simulation models, now is a good opportunity to begin exposing individuals to the concepts of dynamic simulation.

Show individuals a model and how it works. Allow them to play around with it for a while. Next, ask them how its behavior resembles software development processes within the organization, plus how it differs.

If you gauge there is sufficient interest, try working with those individuals to modify the model, so that its behavior more closely resembles that of the organization.

Further Reading

If you want to learn more about how delayed gratification is related to success in life, then try reading *The Marshmallow Test* by Walter Mischel.

If you're looking for ways to introduce new ideas to an organization, then *Fearless Change* by Mary Lynn Manns and Linda Rising has lots of good suggestions within it.

Resources

You can find the interview questionnaires in the appendix of this book.

Summary

In this chapter, we have covered how you should go about your initial information gathering in preparation for your first workshop(s) for problem understanding.

Your primary tools are questionnaires and structured interviews based on the question set in the appendix.

Your expected outputs include

- Responses to questions
- Interview notes
- Tentative findings, constructed from your interviews

In addition to these outputs, you should be developing a feeling for the characteristics of technical debt at your organization and what is driving its creation, plus why it is at the level it currently is.

If you're planning to use a simulation tool, you may also have begun constructing some draft models that simulate some aspects of the debt creation.

By now, you should be ready for your first workshop, on problem understanding. This is the topic of the next chapter.

CHAPTER 14

Workshop for Problem Understanding

This chapter describes how to plan for and carry out a workshop, with the objective of enabling individuals within the organization to reach a common understanding over what technical debt is, plus the drivers causing it within this organization.

Armed with the results of your questionnaires and interviews from the previous chapter, plus your analysis of the organizational charts and processes, both official and unofficial, your idea of who are the key players and stakeholders, plus their viewpoints, you are now ready to begin work understanding the technical debt problem at your organization.

Hopefully, in the interviews outlined in the previous chapter, you managed to set reasonable expectations about anticipated progress and results.

We begin by looking at the agenda. Next, we explore each item on the agenda – trade-off decisions, systems effects, anti-patterns, economics, wicked problems, and putting it all together. We then look at workshop preparation, understanding your goal, who to invite, room setup, preparing attendees, and preparing your material, plus what to do afterward.

You need to be pragmatic. You need to balance your needs, of getting everyone to understand the nature of the technical debt problem and to explore solutions, against what your organization will realistically allocate in terms of time and resources.

As we mentioned earlier, this is a book about technical debt. It is not a book about workshop facilitation. If you need more information on setting up and facilitating workshops, there are some good books recommended in the Further Reading section.

I'm an experienced trainer. I've done training courses on most of this material, although I haven't done everything all together at once. This way of looking at technical debt is fresh, groundbreaking stuff, and, by definition, groundbreaking stuff has not been done before.

If you're an experienced workshop facilitator, there is enough in the following pages and slide deck to enable you to produce and run a 2-day workshop. If you're not an experienced facilitator, there's enough here for you to hand over to an experienced workshop facilitator to create a workshop.

If you've facilitated workshops before, you'll know many of the dos and don'ts, plus many of the pitfalls to avoid. Briefly, those dos are

- Prepare adequately
- Ensure a high level of engagement, through workshop design and good facilitation
- Ensure adequate follow-up

Note: This book assumes you are either familiar with the workshop techniques mentioned in the books *Liberating Structures* and *Red Teams*, or you have access to those materials. Therefore, if I mention something like "1-2-4-All in Liberating Structures," you'll know how to find out this information.

Let's start by looking at your workshop agenda.

Agenda

The following agenda is for a 2-day workshop. This is the minimum time you'll need to go through the materials and for the workshop attendees to gain sufficient understanding of technical debt to make informed contributions in a debt reduction program.

Distribute a copy of this agenda to each workshop attendee prior to them attending the session. A copy of this agenda is available on GitHub via the book's product page located at `www.apress.com/ISBN`.

Agenda: Workshop for problem understanding

Day 1

- Introduction (30 minutes)
- Understanding trade-offs: How we make decisions (90 minutes)
- Break (15 minutes)
- Understanding trade-offs: Mitigation approaches (90 minutes)
- Lunch (60 minutes)

- Understanding systems effects (90 minutes)
- Break (15 minutes)
- Anti-patterns (90 minutes)
- Summary of Day 1 (15 minutes)

Day 2

- Recap of Day 1 (15 minutes)
- Debt from an economics PoV (90 minutes)
- Break (15 minutes)
- Wicked problems, social complexity, and fragmentation (90 minutes)
- Lunch (60 minutes)
- Putting it all together: Exploration (90 minutes)
- Break (15 minutes)
- Putting it all together: Consolidation (90 minutes)
- Summary of Day 1 and 2 (30 minutes)

Day 1: Introduction

In this session, we introduce workshop attendees to the concepts of technical debt, including definition and causes. We conclude with an explanation of the technical debt onion model.

Understanding trade-off decisions

In this session, attendees learn the **role of trade-off decisions** in the creation of technical debt. In addition, attendees learn of the **affect heuristic**, the mechanism they use to make trade-off decisions, plus why using this mechanism leads us to build up too much technical debt. Attendees also learn mitigation techniques to reduce the influence of the affect heuristic.

Understanding systems effects

In this session, attendees learn **how systems influence the level of technical debt** within an organization. Attendees learn of the **prohibition problem** and how making a change to a system can lead to entirely unexpected consequences.

Attendees also experience a **simulation model** of software development, where they can change inputs, like scheduled completion date and levels of technical debt, to impact the costs and schedule of current and future projects.

Anti-patterns

In this session, attendees learn how **patterns of repeated behavior** can lead to self-reinforcing loops that influence the level of technical debt in an organization. Attendees create some simple anti-patterns and causal loop diagrams.

Day 2: Technical debt from an economics PoV

In this session, attendees learn some **economic problem concepts** and how they are relevant to technical debt. This learning is then reinforced by getting them to identify and discuss examples of where they have seen similar effects influence technical debt in this or other organizations.

Wicked problems, social complexity, and fragmentation

In this session, attendees learn what **wicked problems** are, plus how they influence technical debt. Attendees also learn of **social complexity**, plus how this leads to **fragmentation**.

Putting it all together

In this session, attendees combine their recently gained knowledge of trade-off decisions, systems effects, anti-patterns, and wicked problems to explore the technical debt problem, as experienced within this organization.

PowerPoint Slide Deck

There is a slide deck prepared, which you should adapt for your workshop. It contains over 100 slides and follows the agenda set out earlier in this chapter. **Save yourself hours of time and deliver a better workshop by taking this slide deck and adapting it for use in your workshop.**

This slide deck has sections for each of the areas listed in the agenda, beginning with the introduction at the start of Day 1 and finishing with the summary of Day 1 and 2. Within each section, you'll find slides for each of the main points you need to make. You need to modify each slide, so that it represents your own personal style of presentation.

Suggestions and instructions for how to modify/complete each slide, together with directions for what to speak about on the slide, are given in the notes section of each slide, as indicated in Figure 14-1.

CHAPTER 14   WORKSHOP FOR PROBLEM UNDERSTANDING

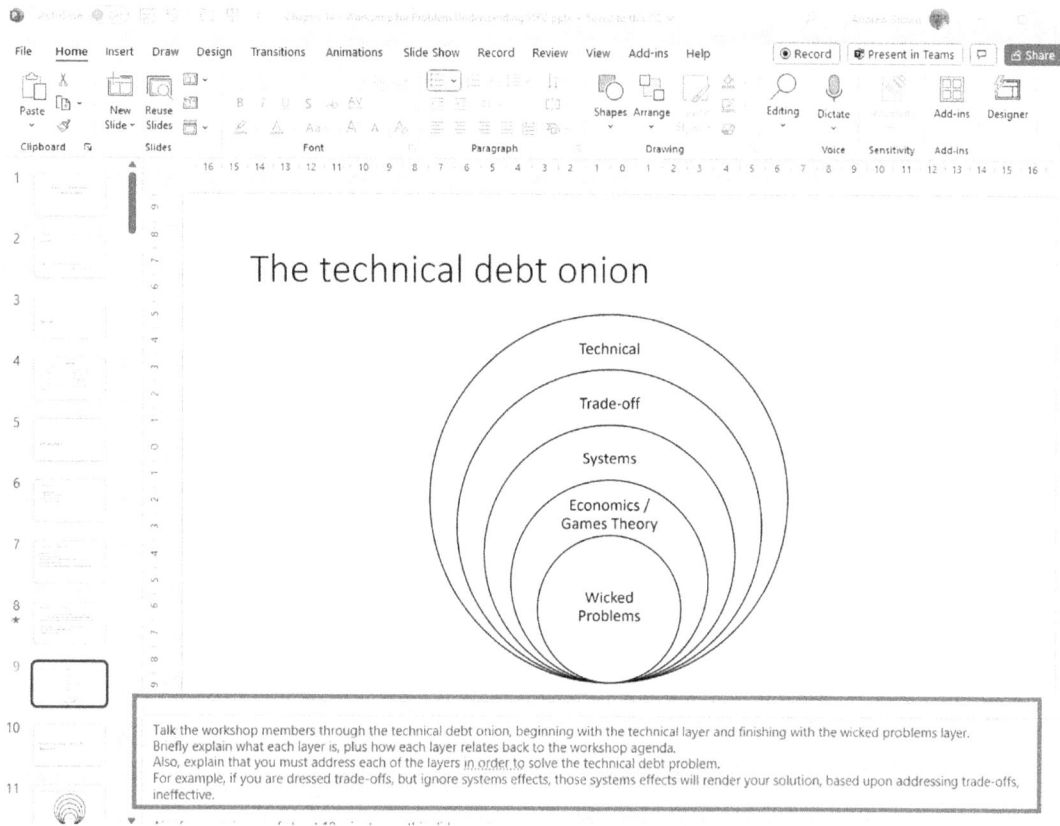

Figure 14-1. Example slide, showing directions to the presenter in the notes section (highlighted in red)

In addition to the suggestions and directions within the notes section of each slide, there are further instructions on the "READ ME!" slide, which is the second slide in the presentation.

Take this slide deck, create a copy, and then modify each slide until you are happy to deliver the workshop from the deck. You may also wish to add additional slides, to emphasize areas of particular interest or relevance to you or your organization.

This slide deck represents only a subset of the material available in this book. Therefore, when looking to enhance or supplement your slides, this book is the first place to look for material.

A copy of this slide deck is available on GitHub via the book's product page located at www.apress.com/ISBN.

Workshop Details

The following sections describe what you are seeking to deliver within each workshop section. Remember, the slide deck available with this book already contains a lot of the material you need to deliver this workshop. You should use that as your oracle as you read through this section.

Introduction

Workshops are more effective if participants get to know each other and come out of their normal working persona into their workshop persona. Try starting by breaking into small groups and getting each workshop member to give a brief introduction to that group. Because you have many small groups talking in parallel, everybody gets to speak but it shouldn't take too long. If workshop members already know each other, try getting each member to briefly speak on a subject, such as a hobby or little-known fact about themselves.

The important thing is to *get everyone to speak at the beginning of the workshop*. If you do this, you'll find participation and engagement much higher. If you run a workshop and a person does not speak in the first 30 minutes, then you have given them implicit permission to remain silent for the remainder of that workshop.

After the attendee introductions, introduce the concept of technical debt, based around the **technical debt onion model**. Elaborate on how technical debt is a layered combination of technical, trade-off, systems, economic, and wicked problems.

Understanding Trade-Off Decisions

In this session, you aim to get workshop members to understand how each of them makes trade-off decisions, which is using the **affect heuristic**. You also want members to understand why using this heuristic leads them to make decisions that favor increasing the level of technical debt, plus show them some techniques they can use to reduce their vulnerability to making poor trade-off decisions.

In addition, you should make people aware that they make quite different decisions when a project is doing well, or a project is going badly.

Begin by letting people have the chance to be hands-on in an exercise, as described on the slide "Which dictionary is more valuable?" Recreate these experiments of Christopher Hsee for music dictionary/ice cream/crockery. The music dictionary experiment was described in the trade-off chapter, while the other experiments are described in his papers listed in the references.

Next, explain how we make decisions, which is using the affect heuristic. Later, you'll use this to account for the findings of the Christopher Hsee exercises.

Next, explain how our decision-making ability evolved and the requirements of such a system, plus how this led to us using our emotions, or the affect heuristic, to guide our decision-making.

Explain the benefits and disadvantages of using the affect heuristic for decision-making and then relate it back to the technical debt trade-off decision.

Next, get the workshop to explore why the health warning messages on cigarette packets were initially ineffective; how the tobacco manufacturers appealed to potential smokers, despite widely available health information; and how the health authorities in most countries eventually addressed this.

Next, highlight the similarities between the problem health authorities faced in addressing smoking prevention in teenagers and the problem we face of addressing technical debt. See trade-off chapter for details. Use 1-2-4-All from *Liberating Structures*, as follows:

> 1: Ask attendees to self-reflect upon the similarities between smoking prevention in teenagers and our technical debt problem. Spend 1–3 minutes.
>
> 2: Ask attendees to find a partner to discuss their thoughts and generate ideas in pairs. Spend 1–3 minutes.
>
> 4: Combine pairs into foursomes to discuss and generate ideas. Spend 3–5 minutes.
>
> All: Each group now shares their best idea with the whole group.

If time permits, facilitate a discussion on why a second-hand car dealer always ensures his vehicles are valeted to a high standard. (The answer is that the dimensions the customer is interested in – condition of the engine, transmission, running gear, and so on – are not easily evaluable. However, the cleanliness of the car is, so potential customers use this as a proxy. Dealers know this, so they valet their cars.) Ask the group for other examples. Use 1-2-4-All.

Next, engage the workshop in an exercise to show how you can appeal to emotions, and hence engage the affect heuristic, through use of a story.

After a short break, return to the experiments of Christopher Hsee. Explain how we use both **valence and precision** to value an item, plus why this causes us to value the smaller but undamaged dictionary more highly than the larger but slightly damaged one. Follow this with an exercise, where the workshop discusses how we can use precision to influence our decisions around technical debt.

Next, explain the concept of **Ulysses contracts**, then take the workshop through an exercise where they think of ways they could apply a Ulysses contract to address their technical debt problem.

Next, use the example of making a series of unhealthy meal choices in the company canteen, as discussed in Chapter 5, to illustrate how we can sometimes improve our decision-making through making several decisions simultaneously, rather than sequentially. Follow this with a workshop exercise on **simultaneous versus sequential decisions**.

If time permits, explain the **premortem technique**. In this technique, we try to spot unanticipated risks through imagining ourselves in a future scenario where the problem has materialized. Run an exercise, where the workshop uses this technique to identify technical debt problems that may materialize in the future.

Next, discuss in what ways people may make different decisions when a **project is going well versus going badly**. If time permits, get the group to explore the evolutionary reasons why we may switch our decision-making in this way.

Next, explore the **effect of time constraints** on making decisions, plus the effects of hyperbolic discounting.

Close this session with a brainstorming session or discussion around how to change decision-makers' perception of technical debt, so that they can make decisions that are more closely aligned to the long-term interests of the organization.

Augment your slide deck based upon the material in the chapter on trade-off decisions.

Understanding Systems Effects

In this session, you aim to get workshop members to understand how **system effects influence the level of technical debt** the organization experiences. You can make this session more enjoyable and engaging for workshop members through interactive games.

Begin with explaining what is meant by a system, including a system definition, as illustrated by the first slide in this section.

Follow this with the famous "slinky demo," used by Donella Meadows to show how the patterns of behavior of a system are primarily linked to the internal structure of that system, rather than the external influences upon that system.

Next, use an analogy to an ERP or other IT system to show that while we think of IT systems or other inanimate objects as systems, we neglect to consider our software development team as a system.

Highlight the crucial difference between IT systems and social systems – within social systems, subsystems can determine and pursue their own personal goals. Use the example of the **Y-chromosome–placenta problem** to illustrate this.

If time permits, get attendees to do an exercise to try and predict the outcome of crossing mice from the monogamous and promiscuous strains. This will become useful later, as you demonstrate the difficulty of predicting how systems behave without considering their dynamic behavior.

Next, use **the prohibition problem** to explain how making changes within a system may result in unexpected effects.

Next, take the workshop through some common system dynamic behaviors – **exponential growth, balancing behavior, growth then leveling off,** and **overshoot and collapse**.

Next, look at some ways in which individuals pursuing their own goals while working within a system can drive technical debt:

1. Individuals constrained by role
2. Overdue projects and schedule recovery
3. Project underestimation
4. Overshoot and collapse
5. Policy resistance

Next, explore some patterns of system behavior using the **Vensim model reader** to run the example technical debt simulation model.

As you show the model, gauge the participants' interest. If the room is interested in exploring models more, take down some names and plan to do this during the period between the problem understanding and the solution development workshops.

Ensure that you are familiar with the model before demonstrating it to your audience. If you intend workshop participants to use the model themselves, ensure that they bring laptops to the session and have downloaded and installed the software and model beforehand.

If workshop participants cannot install software on their machines, you can get them to run an online game, such as a variation of **the beer distribution game**. A link is provided in the Resources section.

Next, break out into small groups and brainstorm ways in which system effects may be adversely affecting technical debt. Get the groups to put the ideas onto post-its, in the usual way and then assemble for a larger discussion.

Anti-patterns

Most people are quick to grasp the idea of **anti-patterns** and **causal loop diagrams (CLDs)**. Depending on how you arrange your workshop agenda, attendees may already have seen a CLD during the discussion of understanding systems.

Begin by briefly discussing what a pattern and anti-pattern are. Next, identify to attendees three reasons why exploring anti-patterns is helpful:

1. Help understand the problem.
2. Identify intervention and leverage points.
3. Facilitate discussion to reach common understanding.

Next, show a simple CLD and explain its features.

Next, get the workshop attendees to do an exercise by posing the question – "How could estimation errors lead to technical debt?" Facilitate the group through building an example of **the estimation trap** CLD. Don't begin with the finished product on a slide, but instead get them to work through it in small groups on a whiteboard or with post-it notes.

Next, get the workshop groups to compare their estimation trap CLDs and invite discussion.

Next, run an exercise to get the workshop attendees to expand deeper into the estimation trap CLD, by providing additional detail within each of the existing causal links. Finish the exercise by showing attendees a completed CLD of the estimation errors and technical debt.

Next, run exercises to get the workshop attendees to create a causal loop diagram for **social loafing** and then for a **descent into firefighting**.

Finish the session by listing other anti-patterns that can lead to technical debt, like "last race of the day" or "broken window effect." Make suggestions of possible anti-patterns they may find relevant to technical debt or allow individuals to use ideas they think of themselves.

Technical Debt from an Economics PoV

The great advantage of economics is that a brief explanation of each problem is sufficient for most people to immediately understand it and figure out situations where it may apply to them.

For myself, the mere description of the term "Externality" was sufficient for me to immediately recognize the problem that we had all experienced with one project manager at HMV, whose response to costs that he had imposed on others was invariably, "That's not my problem!"

Start by identifying the three benefits you get from exploring the technical debt problem from an economics point of view:

1. Fresh perspectives offer new insights, plus potential solutions.

2. Economics offers many fruitful lessons.

3. Economics offers us a common language.

Next, list and then briefly define the eight problems that the workshop attendees will explore within this session.

Next, describe the **principal-agent problem** in more depth. Get the workshop to break into small groups and discuss where they may encounter the principal agent problem in their software development processes, plus to think about potential mitigation factors. Get each group to briefly discuss their main findings to the rest of the workshop, while inviting comment from other teams. Be mindful of the time and aim to limit this to 15 to 20 minutes.

Next, describe **the tragedy of the commons**, and then repeat the process of getting the workshop to break into small groups and discuss.

Next, repeat this process for the **externalities** problem.

Given the limited time available, you will need to restrict your exploration of the remaining items to a description and brief discussion (without the workshop breaking into small groups).

The one possible exception is "**creeping normality**," which, if you have time, you should treat in more depth by breaking into small teams and discussing, like you did with the first three economics problems.

Finish with a summary and, if time permits, a discussion on each of the economic problems identified.

CHAPTER 14 WORKSHOP FOR PROBLEM UNDERSTANDING

Wicked Problems, Social Complexity, and Fragmentation

Unless and until all members of a team have a common understanding of the problem, attempts to solve the problem are just so much wasted energy.

—Gerald M. Weinberg, Becoming a Technical Leader

A wicked problem goes to the very heart of technical debt. Therefore, you need to ensure that all attendees have a complete and accurate understanding of what a wicked problem is.

Most people are unfamiliar with the concept of wicked problems, often treating wicked problems as if they were tame. Even seasoned executives, who typically spend a great deal of their professional lives working on wicked problems, are often unaware of their nature, typically treating wicked problems as if they were tame ones.

Those often quickest to grasp the concept of wicked problems are designers and technical architects, who frequently need to wrestle with explicit wickedness in their design problems.

As with other areas, try to get workshop participants hands-on for as much time as possible. Begin by explaining what a wicked problem is. Next, list out the characteristics of a wicked problem, perhaps displaying the list on A4 sheets for workshop members to refer to.

Next, divide the workshop into small groups to work upon the example wicked problem of a fictitious country introducing legislation regarding carbon reduction targets.

Next, get attendees to return to their small groups and get each group to discuss the technical debt problem. Identify how closely the wicked problem matches the list of characteristics. Then, get each of these smaller groups to share their results back to the whole group.

Next, work through the slides that describe social complexity and fragmentation. Discuss what **social complexity** is, plus how it combines with wickedness to produce **fragmentation**.

Many people who have worked in an organization are already intuitively aware of social complexity and fragmentation. If so, you need to just give words and meaning to that intuition. Start off with the slides that highlight what these concepts are and the problems they bring, and then move swiftly into small group discussions.

Discuss how different specialisms within an organization need to come to a **shared understanding** of the problem. Discuss the **dichotomy of design**, plus how organizations are typically structured so that individuals perform distinct roles, which leads to individuals standing on one side or the other of the dichotomy. This leads to the fragmentation.

Next, get the workshop to break into small groups. You may wish to consider the composition of those groups, as people tend to sit within their own specialisms. You'll find that the developers tend to sit together, the testers together and the businesspeople together. You may wish to mix up the composition. Pose questions to the workshop. For example,

- Is fragmentation contributing toward our technical debt problem?
- If so, what things could we try to address it?

Periodically pull the small groups together for an all-workshop update on their findings, which, as always, you should be aiming to capture on post-its and putting onto a board.

You are now trying to transform your workshop away from teaching the attendees about different aspects of the technical debt problem, moving it toward the workshop attendees exploring for themselves the technical debt problem, using the tools and understanding they have acquired over the past day and a half.

If you find **argument mapping** techniques useful, now is an appropriate time to introduce attendees to such tools.

Putting It All Together

Now that the workshop group have a more complete understanding of what technical debt is, plus why it is impossible to solve and difficult to manage, it is now time to start exploring what are the specific drivers causing technical debt problems at your organization.

Break into small groups and discuss ways in which technical debt is a problem, for example, in its unmanaged generation or in its consequences. Use the example questions on the relevant slide as an inspiration for brainstorming and **facilitated discussion** of the topic.

1. What do we now understand about our technical debt problem?
2. What are the factors driving our technical debt creation?

3. What are the factors making our technical debt unnecessarily worse?

4. What is mitigating our technical debt? Something we don't want to lose?

5. How is the way that we make trade-off decisions, that is, using the affect heuristic, influencing our levels of technical debt?

6. How are project factors, such as schedule overrun, influencing our mindset and hence our decision-making?

7. How are the systems factors and our organizational setup influencing the creation of technical debt?

8. How are the economists' problems influencing the creation of technical debt?

9. How are the wickedness aspects of technical debt influencing its creation?

10. How might social complexity and fragmentation inhibit us getting to a solution?

11. Where are we missing information that we need to get?

In this session, you will find your facilitation skills most useful. Alternatively, bring in the services of an experienced facilitator.

Get the workshop to frequently break into small groups or use the 1-2-4-All or other techniques to discuss a selected question. Periodically bring the workshop back together to share and discuss their findings so far, plus get those findings onto post-it notes and onto that shared board.

If the attendees' energy is flagging or losing interest, look to regain it, for example, with one of the following options:

- Select a new question for the attendees to consider.

- Rearrange the groups into new compositions.

- Try out one of the many techniques available from Liberating Structures or Red Teams.

If one group is following a particularly fruitful line of enquiry, allow them to share it with the other groups.

Remember, what you are trying to achieve is a **new and enhanced understanding** of the technical debt problem that is shared by all the relevant stakeholders within the organization.

Try to avoid the workshop rushing into **solution mode**, as once attendees start considering possible solutions, they tend to stop exploring the problem. If this occurs, remind people that you'll be having a separate workshop on solution development soon, so they should be focusing on problem understanding at this point.

This is the final item on the workshop agenda. Next, we look at workshop preparation.

Workshop Preparation

To maximize your chances of success, you must adequately prepare for your workshops. For many people, this will be the first time they meet you and this program. Do not delude yourself that everyone will be just as enthusiastic as you about the idea. While many will be positive, others will be less so.

Some will be apprehensive, and others resigned to more tasks piling up on their desk while they spend time away in a workshop. Others may be planning to bring their own agenda in. For example, the technical people may see this as a chance to rein in some of the more outrageous demands placed upon them, while others may seek to undermine the whole process, viewing it as a threat to their ability to get stuff done.

If you don't adequately prepare for your workshop, you run the risk of it being hijacked and veering off in an undesirable direction. Worse, you may end up looking unprofessional, with your credibility undermined. One of the bigger components to prepare is your presentation. The previous sections have covered the content that you need to include. Later, we'll say a bit more about preparing your material and yourself.

You'll find a workshop checklist, to use before running your workshop, in the appendix of this book.

Understand Your Workshop Goal

Although the goal may seem self-evident – understanding technical debt at your organization – you may find it helpful to also think in terms of subgoals. Each session should have a clear, specific goal that will be different from the overall goal.

By the end of the workshop(s), you should have achieved the following:

- Attendees understand what technical debt is and what it is not.
- Attendees understand the **technical debt onion**.
- Attendees understand how they make decisions, using the **affect heuristic**.
- Attendees understand how an **organizational system influences their decisions**.
- Attendees understand **anti-patterns** and **causal loop diagrams**.
- Attendees understand that problems can arise out of the **dynamic behavior** within organizations, and this behavior can be modeled using **simulation tools**.
- Attendees understand some common **economic problems** and how they relate to technical debt.
- Attendees understand **wicked problems, social complexity**, and how this leads to **fragmentation**.

Decide Who to Invite

Aim to invite everyone who is relevant to the problem. This may be a big list of people, so consider how to address that. Options include

- Each area sends a representative to the workshop
- Break into smaller, more manageable-sized workshops

Each approach has its advantages and disadvantages.

The advantage of the send a rep approach is reduced cost. However, this is normally more than offset by the disadvantages of lack of knowledge sharing and buy-in. Since our purposes are to achieve a common understanding and win hearts and minds, this option should be avoided if possible.

Having several manageable-sized workshops is an attractive option, particularly since you can learn from your mistakes in the earlier sessions. In addition, small sessions are easier to control, especially if there is a risk of disruptive elements or individual agendas causing the workshop to veer off course. The disadvantage is that everybody does not hear everybody else's viewpoint, so reaching a common understanding is more difficult.

You may be considering running one super-sized workshop, Big Room Planning style. However, *I would recommend against this approach*. Such workshops are complex and difficult to run successfully. Also, you cannot test things out in a small workshop and then apply the lesson to later sessions. I have never attempted this, and I have run lots of workshops.

You're bringing in large numbers of people to these workshops, so be prepared to justify the expense, plus anticipate and prepare for any objections. When I was at HMV, my attempts to introduce software requirements inspections failed at the first meeting, when barely 2 minutes into the meeting, someone raised the objection that, "What on earth are we doing with twelve people sitting here around a table looking at one document? What is the cost of this, and what will the benefit be?"

I hadn't anticipated that someone would come into the room with the sole intention of sabotaging the whole process (the person objecting could have raised the objection with me beforehand or not attended, but chose to do neither).

Room and Setup

Try to get a room that has sufficient space to mingle and interact. Avoid a lecture theater style room. Try to get tables arranged **cabaret style**, so that attendees can cluster around in a group facing each other.

Ensure the room has the facilities you need, which will include a large TV or projector, whiteboards (ideally one for each group), an ample supply of post-it notes, and breakout areas for any activities that require minimized interaction between groups.

If some team members are geographically distributed, consider how you'll engage with them. Aim to get them to travel to the workshop. In fact, if those remote team members rarely meet the rest of the team, it is even more important for them to attend, as it gives them a rare opportunity to interact with their co-workers.

If remote team members cannot attend the session, then the best option is a separate session for them. Avoid a hybrid session, with some attendees in person and some online.

Preparing Your Attendees

Preparing your attendees can make a big difference to the success of your workshop.

In your mail to each attendee, thank them for attending, even if they had no choice in the matter. Attach the agenda to the mail, so they know what to expect. Also, inject some participation and enthusiasm into your mail.

Behavioral scientists have found that if you need to ask individuals to do something big for you, like turn up to a workshop and contribute, then getting them to do a small ask first increases the likelihood they will do the big ask.

Therefore, *include a small ask* in your workshop invitation mail. For example, ask them to read Chapter 1 of this book, or think about examples of technical debt, overrunning projects, or another relevant item.

If your organization's budget allows it, provide copies of this book to everyone.

Prepare Your Material

Prepare your material, based upon your agenda and the relevant chapters of this book.

Your biggest task is to get your presentation prepared, plus to familiarize yourself with your presentation so that you are comfortable with delivering it. Preparing a presentation is much more than simply creating or modifying your slides. You need to be thoroughly familiar with the message that you want to get over to your audience, and then create your presentation to support that goal. This means that you should be thoroughly familiar with all the concepts within this book.

If you need more detailed help on preparing your material, then *The Workshop Survival Guide* by Rob Fitzpatrick and Devin Hunt is very helpful.

As you are preparing your slides for each session, you should be trying them out. When I prepare workshop or presentation material, I am constantly trying it out, mostly to myself, to check that it works.

Alternatively, if you're not confident to deliver the workshop, arrange for consultants who have previously delivered these types of workshops to deliver a training intervention for you.

Dry Run Your Material

Workshops can be uncertain events. Lots of things happen that you cannot anticipate. Therefore, reduce uncertainty by having a dry run of as much of your material as you can. Do this in front of someone who is sufficiently comfortable to give you honest feedback and sufficiently well informed to give you useful feedback.

As a rule of thumb, you should spend somewhere between 3x and 10x as much time preparing for a presentation or workshop as you spend delivering it.

At this stage, you should now be thoroughly prepared and ready to begin. *Go for it and best of luck!*

After the Session

Ensure that any gains and lessons from the workshop are captured before they are lost. Capture everything from the boards during the session, of example by taking frequent photos.

Shortly after the session is completed, send an email around to every participant, with the following content.

1. Thank them for their contributions.
2. Say how much you enjoyed the session and hope they did too.
3. Summarize the main findings from the session.
4. Summarize any missing information that needs to be gathered.
5. Ask if anything has been missed.
6. Outline the next steps, which will be additional information gathering and then the workshop for solution development.

Further Reading

Useful books for preparing and running workshops are as follows. My favorite is *The Workshop Survival Guide* by Rob Fitzpatrick and Devin Hunt. Also good are *The Workshop Book* by Pamela Hamilton and *How to Run a Great Workshop* by Nicky Highmore Sims.

If you are looking for help around facilitating the workshop sessions, then try *The Skilled Facilitator* by Roger Schwarz.

I assume that you already have some experience of workshop activities and have in your personal toolkit a variety of useful techniques for workshop tasks and objectives, like encouraging open discussion or thinking creatively. If you want additional techniques to add to your toolkit, I suggest the following two books:

The Surprising Power of Liberating Structures, by Henri Lipmanowicz and Keith McCandless. This is a wonderful book, stuffed full of useful techniques for workshops. This book belongs on every workshop facilitator's bookshelf. The Liberating Structures website is also a source of useful information and contains explanations of many of the liberating techniques.

Red Team Handbook, by the US Army. This booklet is used by the US military and others for red team activities. It has many useful techniques for workshops, albeit with a slightly different goal from us. Currently, it is freely available from the US Army website, listed in the references under "R."

The premortem technique was originally developed by Gary Klein. A description of it plus how to use it is available on the Harvard Business Review website.

The slinky demo is mentioned in Donella Meadow's book, *Thinking in Systems*. Alternatively, look up the YouTube vintage video of Donella performing the demo.

Resources

You can find workshop resources in the appendix of this book.

A copy of this agenda is available on GitHub via the book's product page located at www.apress.com/ISBN.

A copy of the slide deck is available on GitHub via the book's product page located at www.apress.com/ISBN.

If you want to get attendees to try out argument mapping, they can try the free limited edition of Rationale here: www.rationaleonline.com/.

If you want to play a variation of the beer distribution game with your team, an online version is freely available from The Open University at this URL: www2.open.ac.uk/openlearn/supply-chain/index.html.

Summary

In this chapter we have learned how to plan and conduct a workshop to enable an organization to explore and understand its technical debt problem.

We began by looking at an agenda, then stepped through the major items in that agenda including trade-off decisions, systems effects, anti-patterns, economics, and wicked problems. We then looked at how to put it all together in a facilitated workshop discussion.

Next, we looked at how to prepare for your workshop, including understanding your goals, who to invite, room and set up considerations, preparing your attendees, and preparing and dry-running your material, plus what to do after your session.

Workshop participants now have a far better understanding of what technical debt is, its causes, and the difficulties it leads to. In addition, in our workshop, we will have generated a list of things that we do not yet know and must find out before we begin to develop a better way to manage debt than we are currently doing. This is the subject of our next chapter – additional information gathering.

CHAPTER 15

Additional Information Gathering and Sensemaking

In this chapter, we go through the additional information gathering and workshop preparation that we must do before the solution development workshops, as shown in Figure 15-1.

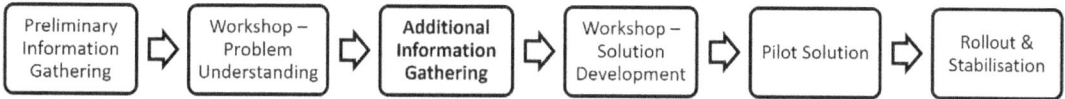

Figure 15-1. Technical debt reduction program, with additional information gathering step highlighted

We begin by trying to understand the political landscape, then addressing the missing information from the first workshop. Next, we try to make sense of all the information we now have. We then look at how to shape ideas for potential solutions and preparing for the next workshop. We finish by briefly exploring dynamic simulation models.

Remember, this way of looking at technical debt is fresh, groundbreaking stuff, and, by definition, groundbreaking stuff is new. I have done many of the things in this chapter, but not all possible combinations of things.

But first, let's have a brief recap of where we are now.

CHAPTER 15   ADDITIONAL INFORMATION GATHERING AND SENSEMAKING

Recap

By the end of the first workshop, you and the workshop participants should have achieved the following:

1. Have a better understanding of technical debt and its complexities.

2. Enthusiasm about the possibility of making a real difference to levels of technical debt, and hence the working experience.

3. An understanding of the likely main drivers of technical debt.

You will also have come out from the workshop with some tasks you need to do:

1. Address the information identified as missing or unknown by the workshop.

2. Attempt to make sense of the information you now have.

3. Begin to shape ideas for potential solutions or interventions.

However, before you go charging out to get that additional information, don't forget our discussions in Chapter 11. Make no mistake; what you're doing is difficult and, if handled clumsily, could be damaging to your career. Even if you don't end up in a straitjacket, like Dr Semmelweis, you don't want to end up on the wrong end of a political spat involving senior stakeholders.

Therefore, before looking for any missing information, let's first try to understand the political and stakeholder landscape. Remember Gerry Weinberg's advice – "It's always a people problem."

Understanding the Political Landscape

Often in organizations, information that appears missing may instead be hidden or disguised. Moreover, attempting to unearth that information may threaten those who hid or disguised it, which may become dangerous for you.

I had an experience of hidden or disguised information while I was at HMV. Fortunately, it was not dangerous. As head of testing, I wanted each of the testers to have a second screen. This was the early 2000s and screen prices were coming down, so that the extra productivity would easily pay for a second screen in only a week or two.

However, this was fiercely resisted, which I found puzzling. As this didn't make sense to me, I kept pushing, but getting nowhere. Eventually, I cornered the development manager, who told me the reason.

"Unfortunately, testers can't have a second screen," he stated. "Due to screen envy."

"*Screen envy*?" I asked. "What on earth's that?"

"Look, the Java developers are top of the pile here," he said. "We're having trouble keeping them, so we've given them an extra screen, so they feel special."

"But with an extra screen, we'll be so much more productive and –"

"It doesn't matter," he interrupted. "Besides, the mainframe developers only have one screen."

"The mainframe developers only *need* one screen," I countered. "Besides, if they need two, then they can have extra as well."

He shook his head. "Sorry. We need to keep the Java developers happy. Which means they get two screens and everyone else gets one. Besides, mainframe developers are higher than testers, so they'll get any second screens before you."

I had finally discovered the reasoning behind the decision. It was nothing to do with efficiency, effectiveness, or lack of budget, but rather to maintain a status hierarchy as rigidly enforced as anything in *Downton Abbey* or a Jane Austen novel. You can also understand why this reasoning was never made explicit to any of the teams.

During the workshop(s), you have had many opportunities to observe individuals and groups within the organization. This should have enabled you to develop an understanding of the individuals, the various political factions, and where both are likely to stand on any proposed technical debt solution.

Try building a mind map, to capture these different factions, their likely objectives, and their relationships to each other. Try to think through the political landscape, and who may help or hinder you in your objectives. For obvious reasons, do not put this mapping function in a shared or accessible place.

As you read through this and subsequent chapters, I'm not going to repeatedly caveat each suggestion with a warning, but whenever you are interacting with workshop attendees, stakeholders, or project team members, always remember Dr Semmelweis and keep in the back of your mind the question, "*Is it safe to do or say this*?"

Now that we understand the political landscape and its dangers, let's look at the first of those tasks – addressing missing information.

CHAPTER 15 ADDITIONAL INFORMATION GATHERING AND SENSEMAKING

Addressing Missing Information

During the workshop, participants may have raised questions that could not be answered at the time. In addition, you will also be forming ideas in your mind, for which you have further questions or missing information. You should now work on these items.

Aim to get answers to what you can. However, also remember that many things may be hidden, disguised or politically sensitive, so accept that you may not get all the answers, plus ensure you tread carefully.

Aim to map out where you think the biggest holes are, and then focus your efforts there. Arrange your questions into a prioritized list. Go through each item, beginning with the highest priority, and try to get an answer. If you cannot get an answer, jot down a note of what you tried, as it may later prompt someone to suggest a next step.

Try mailing the list around. Ask people if they have any information on the items, or know someone who may do. This activity requires little effort but may get you answers to some questions and leads to others.

Work through the remaining items, getting the best answers you can. You'll usually find this an iterative operation. When you discover information, it may lead you to realize that there are other things missing or that you need to reinvestigate.

You'll find it impossible to obtain all missing information. You may need to live with this, as with technical debt there is always some information that is forgotten, cannot be known, or has been hidden. Don't forget, if it's okay for our president or prime minister to invade another country without all the evidence of WMDs, then it should be okay for us to go into a workshop without all the information about technical debt.

Once you've got as much information as you can, aim to put closure to the missing information. Send an email with all the known information, plus comments against any item you have been unable to get information for.

Now we have that information, let's try to make sense of it.

Sensemaking: What Does It All Mean?

You should begin formulating ideas in your mind around the following areas:

- What is it that's happening?
- What is causing technical debt to build up?

CHAPTER 15   ADDITIONAL INFORMATION GATHERING AND SENSEMAKING

- Is it the usual suspects – projects behind schedule, one party imposing externalities on another, or something else?
- Who is suffering from this technical debt?
- Who is doing quite well out of all this technical debt?

Try to build up in your mind a picture of what is happening. You don't want to go into the next workshop with a confused mind. If you do, you risk your workshop veering off in a direction preferred by one or other vested interest.

Use the output from the workshop and your interview feedback, plus your own experiences to sketch out what you think are the main drivers of technical debt. An example is shown in Figure 15-2.

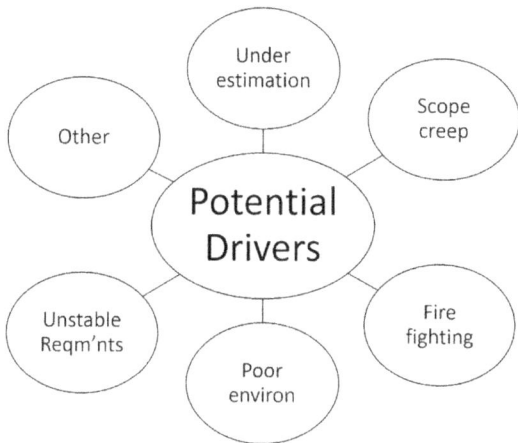

Figure 15-2. Example potential drivers for technical debt creation

Review the workshop output material you captured. If your workshop built any mind maps, study them. If you built causal loop diagrams, trace them through, looking for consistency, missing items, and things that should not be there or should be elsewhere.

If you have not already done so, arrange for a commonly accessible place where you can share all material generated as part of the technical debt initiative. Use whatever collaboration tool the organization has adopted, whether it is Miro, Mural, Jamboard, or another one.

Apply your critical thinking and creativity tools to making sense of this technical debt problem. Useful tools can be found in the books listed in the Further Reading section of this chapter. Ones I have used include

- Simple and cluster brainstorming
- Key assumptions check
- Causal loop diagrams
- Mind maps

Other techniques I've found useful include repeatedly returning to the problem and ruminating upon it, sleeping on the problem, rubber ducking (which we'll cover later in this section), and boredom.

Yes, I've found boredom a useful technique. You need to think about something so much, until eventually you get thoroughly bored with it. Once bored, forget it, do something entirely different, and then sleep on it. When you come back, you may have an insight or inspiration.

Once you begin to form an idea of what is happening in a particular area, try to develop it into a more formal statement or hypothesis. Spend some time looking at your hypothesis. List data that support your hypothesis. Next, and this is most important, spend some time thinking of things that would *reveal your hypothesis to be false*. For this activity, the Devil's Advocate technique in *Red Teams* and *Intelligence Analysis* is useful.

For example, if you are building up a hypothesis that technical debt is primarily created when a project is behind schedule, look for examples of where debt was created by a project that was not behind schedule at the time the debt was created.

Bounce your ideas off others, to check their validity and relevance. Also, consider bouncing your ideas off someone who is outside of the technical debt initiative. They have no axe to grind and can offer a fresh perspective, plus it doesn't matter if you influence their perspective of the issue with your notions. A disadvantage of using a complete outsider is that they will lack context and so are less able to give key insights.

If you truly have no one else to bounce ideas off, try rubber ducking. This is where you try to solve a problem by explaining the problem aloud. The process of articulating the problem often leads you to a solution, even if the other person offers you no helpful suggestions, as would be the case if you were talking the problem through with a rubber duck.

Next, let's look at shaping potential solutions.

Shaping Potential Solutions

To successfully shape a potential solution, we need to know two things:

1. What is driving technical debt in our organization?
2. What can we do about it, such as potential solutions?

You should already have answers, or partial answers, to the first question from your work in the sensemaking section. Next, we need to work out potential solutions. These can be broken down into two main categories – reducing existing debt and avoiding creating debt – as shown in Figure 15-3.

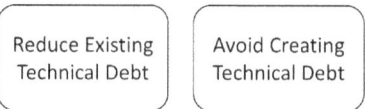

Figure 15-3. *The two primary avenues for addressing technical debt*

You must do both. The best long-term solution is to control and reduce the amount of technical debt that the organization is creating through its development processes. However, you cannot avoid placing some focus on initiatives that reduce the amount of existing technical debt. You need to secure continued stakeholder support, which means you must demonstrate early progress to those stakeholders funding this initiative.

However, avoid getting sucked into becoming no more than a series of activities to address existing technical debt issues. This can occur because, as well as the pressure to show immediate results by addressing existing issues, to reduce technical debt creation your organization must change some of the ways it develops software. This means that individuals must do things differently, plus they may not experience benefits they previously enjoyed. Neither of these things is popular.

We previously encountered an example of a scenario that could have addressed both existing debt and avoiding creating new debt. This occurred in Chapter 2, where we discussed the HMV Jukebox.

As you recall, this project was a response to Apple's iTunes, which the HMV directors desperately wanted to respond to. The project was conducted by an outside consultancy using the Microsoft C# technology stack. The project excluded the in-house development team, which used the IBM Java technology stack. This project left behind a huge gaping hole of technical debt that required constant maintenance and workarounds.

Two years later, this technical debt was resolved by discarding the entire Microsoft C# solution and rewriting it in Java. This addressed the left-hand side of our diagram, as that existing debt was not merely reduced but eliminated.

Unfortunately, the right-hand side – avoid creating future debt – was never addressed. HMV directors and senior managers continued to begin strategic initiatives without fully including input from IT, with predictable results.

Therefore, you should avoid the problem we suffered at HMV and identify a mixture of potential solutions, some focused on addressing existing technical debt items and others focused on creating conditions that will lead to a reduced creation of technical debt.

Next, you should prioritize those solutions. Possible prioritization criteria include

- Size of initiative (effort, plus payback)
- Timescale of effort and payback
- Likelihood of success/adoption

Next, take these potential solutions, show them around your stakeholders, and then solicit feedback. By doing this, you are seeking buy-in from the stakeholders and preparing the ground for any changes. In addition, their feedback will suggest improvements.

This process of sensemaking, then shaping potential solutions, is not a simple linear process. Rather, you should aim for it to be iterative, as shown in Figure 15-4.

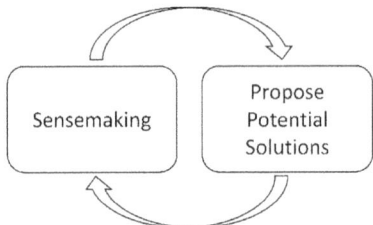

Figure 15-4. *The sensemaking–shaping potential solution process*

Each time you go around this loop, highlight to the relevant stakeholder(s) that you incorporated their previous suggestions into the solution. Then get feedback that you have understood correctly what they wanted. By doing this, you'll find your buy-in is significantly increased.

Your output at the end of this process is a list of candidate solutions of how the organization could reduce and manage its technical debt, plus some ideas of how to go about doing this. You should use these candidate solutions in the solution development workshop as **guidelines to your facilitation of the workshop**. Avoid going into the workshop and presenting these as the finished solutions, as that will undermine everybody's initiative and enthusiasm.

Next, let's look at preparing for your next workshop.

Preparation for Your Next Workshop

You should also use this period before the second workshop to prepare for it. We'll talk about your slide deck in the next chapter. However, one thing you'll need to do is plan a lot more flexibility into your second workshop. In the first workshop, you spent a lot of time getting everyone to the same level of understanding about technical debt. It was only in the last session that there was much flexibility in what the workshop explored.

Because your solution will be unique to your organization, and you cannot determine it before the workshop, you must be prepared to be flexible. Hopefully, your multiple iterations through the cycle of sensemaking–shaping potential solutions will have shaped up the general direction(s) where you and the senior stakeholders expect any solution to develop. However, anticipate that you will have some surprises in the session.

To enhance buy-in, consider either involving or handing over responsibility of some workshop activities to some of the attendees. This may offer you two advantages:

1. Increased ownership, felt by those attendees

2. Improved solution, based on the greater contextual understanding of those attendees

If you choose to do this, there is always the risk that the attendees will go off onto their own agenda. You can minimize this risk by insisting that they rehearse their material with you before the workshop session.

As a final act of preparation, give your slides a dry run through, to ensure that they make sense, and the timings are correct.

Dynamic Simulation Models

If you demonstrated dynamic simulation models in your previous workshop and participants showed interest in developing those models further, then use this time between workshops to develop simple simulation models of the behavior and situations described in the previous workshop.

As you build the models, engage those interested workshop participants in a consultation process. Try to ensure that as many participants as possible have an opportunity to engage in the model building and exploration. Don't wait until you're in the workshop before sharing the models; otherwise, you'll miss an important opportunity to improve your models and increase engagement.

Select an appropriate moment during the next workshop to show the models, putting an appropriate slide in your deck. Avoid choosing a moment where it can distract from the main purpose and suck up time. Many people find playing with models intensely interesting, and you risk the focus of the workshop diverting into playing with models. Choose a moment that is either immediately before a break or toward the end of the workshop.

If you are building a model to test out a hypothesis, as mentioned earlier, then involve those relevant workshop participants in the building of that model. Run your model with those participants and see if its behavior is consistent with your hypothesis. If so, then use this simulation as supporting evidence of your hypothesis. If it is inconsistent in some places, then investigate why that is – is your model wrong and requires adjustment, or is your hypothesis wrong?

Next, explore the limits and extreme conditions of your model, to see if it makes any novel predictions.

Further Reading

If you are looking for analysis and sensemaking techniques, then *Structured Analytical Techniques for Intelligence Analysis* by Pherson and Heuer is a highly relevant, if somewhat expensive, book. It's brimmed of useful techniques, even if you're not a CIA analyst trying to search out Soviet spies.

Another source of useful techniques is *The Thinker's Toolkit* by Morgan D. Jones, who is also a former CIA analyst.

However, remember that these are CIA analysis techniques, for an organization with the Pentagon budget behind them. If your budget is more skunkworks than Pentagon, then other useful books are *Red Teams* and *Liberating Structures*, both of which have some simpler, less involved analysis techniques.

Summary

In this chapter, we have looked at the activities we must carry out after the workshop for problem understanding has completed and before the workshop for solution development has begun.

We began by trying to understand the political landscape and then seeking out additional information that we uncovered in the workshop. Next, we tried to make sense of the information we now have. We then looked to shape those ideas into potential solutions and ran those candidate solutions past senior stakeholders. Next, we looked at preparing for our next workshop and then finished by briefly exploring dynamic simulation models.

We are now ready to begin the next step, our solution development workshop.

This workshop can be challenging. Difficult choices and sacrifices must be made. Also, different people will still have a different viewpoint of the nature and causes of the problem, together with what is an appropriate solution. We're back to those wicked problems.

CHAPTER 16

Workshops for Solution Development

In this chapter, we go through how to conduct a workshop for developing solutions to your technical debt problem, as shown in Figure 16-1.

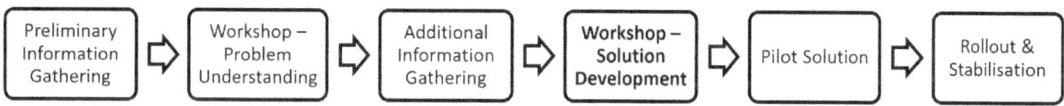

Figure 16-1. Technical debt reduction program, with Workshop for Solution Development step highlighted

Armed with the findings from your first workshop, the information you have gathered, plus your analysis and sensemaking, you should now have a good understanding of the major causes of technical debt within your organization. In addition, everybody in your organization should have attended the problem understanding workshop and therefore understand about technical debt and its drivers.

The format for this chapter is similar to Chapter 14. We begin by asking – why are we running this workshop? Next, we look at our agenda. Next, we explore each item on the agenda. We start with a recap and update, recalling the causes of technical debt and the findings from the first workshop, plus a summary of the analysis we have conducted. Next, we look at addressing existing technical debt versus avoiding new debt creation and then conclude we must do both. We finish the recap by presenting any new results from the software simulation models.

Next, we explore our first candidate intervention for addressing technical debt, using a mixture of facilitated discussions, plus other tools and techniques. We then repeat this process for the second and third candidate interventions. We conclude the workshop with a summary of our new understanding, followed by our proposed next steps.

We then briefly explore some workshop techniques you may find useful in the solution development workshop.

Next, we look at what you should do after the workshop session, and then we list the outputs you should have produced by the end of the workshop session.

Let's start by looking at the purpose of this workshop.

Workshop Purpose

You should always be clear in your mind why you are running this workshop. This is a workshop for solution development. Therefore, *your purpose is to end the workshop with some potential solutions to take into the pilot project stage.*

At the start of the workshop, remind yourself and others of this purpose. In addition, periodically remind participants of this purpose, plus aim to keep the workshop momentum heading in the direction of developing potential solutions for the pilot stage.

Let's now look at the workshop agenda.

Agenda

The following is the agenda sessions list for this 1-day workshop. A copy of the full agenda is available on GitHub via the book's product page located at www.apress.com/ISBN. Distribute a copy of this full agenda to each workshop attendee prior to them attending the session.

If you need to do subsequent workshops, you can reduce or eliminate the time spent on recap and update, especially if the subsequent workshop is only a short time after the first solution development workshop.

Agenda: Workshop for solution development

- Recap and update (105 minutes)
  - Causes of technical debt (30 minutes)
  - Findings from first workshop and further investigations (30 minutes)
  - Summary of analysis (15 minutes)

- Addressing existing debt vs avoiding new debt (15 minutes)
  - Simulation update, if applicable (15 minutes)
- Break (15 minutes)
- Explore first candidate intervention (90 minutes)
  - Select candidate intervention (15 minutes)
  - Facilitated discussion and activities (60 minutes)
  - Useful workshop techniques (15 minutes)
- Lunch (60 minutes)
- Explore second candidate intervention (90 minutes)
- Break (15 minutes)
- Explore third candidate intervention (90 minutes)
- Summary and next steps (15 minutes)

Your presentation should closely follow your agenda. We'll look at the presentation slide deck next.

PowerPoint Slide Deck

There is a slide deck prepared, which you should adapt for your workshop. It contains over 50 slides and follows the agenda we have just covered in the previous section. **Save yourself hours of time and deliver a better workshop by taking this slide deck and adapting it for use in your workshop.**

This slide deck has sections for each of the areas listed in the agenda, beginning with the recap and finishing with the summary and next steps. Within each section you'll find slides for each of the main points you need to make. You need to modify each slide, so that it represents your own personal style of presentation.

Just like the slide deck for the previous workshop, suggestions and instructions for how to modify/complete each slide are given in the notes section of each slide.

In addition to the suggestions and directions within the notes section of each slide, there are further instructions on the "READ ME!" slide, which is the second slide in the presentation.

Take this slide deck, create a copy, and then modify each slide until you are happy to deliver the workshop from the deck. You may also wish to add slides, to emphasize areas of relevance to your organization.

A copy of this slide deck is available on GitHub via the book's product page located at `www.apress.com/ISBN`.

Workshop Details

The following sections describe what you should deliver within each workshop section. Remember, the slide deck available with this book already contains a lot of the material you need for this workshop. You should use that as your oracle as you read through this section.

Recap and Update

The purpose of the recap is to refresh everyone's memories as to the nature and causes of technical debt. The purpose of the update is to share with participants the findings from the first workshop and any further investigations. In the summary of analysis, you are looking to share your analysis findings, as well as beginning to shape the direction of the interventions.

If many of the participants have not met each other before, or if it is a while since participants met at the previous workshop, consider starting with an icebreaker activity to get everyone loosened up.

Causes of Technical Debt

You may not have time to go through every item on the slides provided in the time allocated, so you'll need to be selective in your material and focus around where participants' recall appears weakest.

Aim to make this session as interesting and engaging as possible. Try organizing it like a quiz. Get individuals to break out into small groups, say four people, and then pose the points as a series of questions. If you're feeling truly organized, try creating some answer sheets.

Begin by asking the question, "Is technical debt a technical problem?" Hopefully, the entire workshop should answer, "No!" Next, display the **technical debt onion** and ask workshop participants if they can recall each of the layers.

Next, work through the questions on **trade-off decisions.** There are a lot more questions on the slides than you need – so be selective. Don't forget, the goal is to stimulate participants' memories, so that these concepts are fresh in their mind, rather than grill them on their knowledge.

Next, work through some questions on **systems**. Begin by asking questions around what is meant by a system. Try to tease out that a crucial characteristic of a system is the characteristic set of behaviors or patterns that it produces.

Next, work through **anti-patterns** and **causal loop diagrams**. Get attendees to identify relevant parts of a causal loop diagram, and then get attendees to use a causal loop diagram to explain how estimation errors can lead to a self-reinforcing loop of increased technical debt.

Next, work through technical debt as an **economics problem**. Show the eight economics problems we studied (principal-agent problem, tragedy of the commons, and so on), and ask attendees to explain the meaning of each.

Next, move to the topics of **wicked problems, social complexity**, and **fragmentation**. Ask attendees to recall as many as possible of the eight characteristics of a wicked problem. Alternatively, if they cannot recall any of the characteristics, display a list of those characteristics, and ask them to briefly explain the meaning of each item.

Next, ask attendees what is social complexity, plus what is fragmentation. Also, ask them what is shared understanding and why it is so important. Finish by talking about the dichotomy of design.

Findings from the First Workshop and Further Investigations

Create slides to display the tentative results from that first workshop. You are best off putting each result/finding on a separate slide.

As you display your slides, ask participants to think about which topics they consider would be most important/fruitful in the later sessions, where you explore candidate interventions.

In this and the subsequent slides, you are doing more than simply presenting those findings. This is an opportunity to shape the direction of this workshop. Emphasize the areas that you think are more important or fruitful and give less emphasis on other areas.

To enhance engagement from workshop attendees, consider allowing part of the results/presentation to be delivered by team members relevant for that area. However, bear in mind time constraints and the risk of wandering in undesirable directions.

Summary of Analysis

Prepare a summary of your own analysis, which should also include the analysis and summary from talking to the stakeholders during your investigations.

This summary should include tentative identifications of the major drivers of technical debt, plus where the workshop should consider focusing its efforts to be most fruitful. This is another opportunity to shape the direction of this workshop.

However, be prepared to modify this summary if the discussion from the findings of the first workshop and further investigations (that you have just conducted) revealed a more fruitful direction.

Addressing Existing Debt vs Avoiding New Debt

Identify to attendees that there are two approaches to reducing technical debt. The first, and most common, approach is to identify existing technical debt items and then tackle them. Point out the benefits and limitations of this approach.

Explain why you need to address both the reduction of existing technical debt and also avoiding the creation of future technical debt. Addressing existing debt allows you to demonstrate early progress, which may be important to stakeholders. However, if you do not address future debt creation, then any improvement will be only temporary.

Simulation Update, If Applicable

I find simulation models extremely useful. The act of building them helps everyone involved think more clearly about what is causing a certain behavior. Running dynamic models helps everyone think in ways they would not otherwise have done. However, model building skills are not commonplace. If you have access to them, use them. However, you can still tackle technical debt without building dynamic simulation models.

If you have done any work on dynamic simulation models since the previous workshop, now is a good time to demo it.

You should enhance the credibility of your models by involving relevant team members in building those models, before the workshop, and then getting them to walk other participants through the models. Don't forget to rehearse this walk-through with them.

Encourage a discussion of the models' findings, plus invite ideas for further enhancements, or additional models to test some other aspect of the organization's development process.

Dynamic modeling gives you insights you cannot get by just looking at static diagrams. Be sure to exploit this by exploring the behavior and outputs over a wide range of inputs. If somebody asks, "What about...?" manipulate the model into those conditions and see what happens.

Capture all insights and comments onto your recording medium, whether that is a whiteboard, post-it notes, within the model, or other.

It is easy to get carried away and spend too much time in dynamic modeling. I often do. This is why this session has been scheduled just before a break, to provide an enforced stop.

Explore First Candidate Intervention

In this session, we are looking to explore the most promising candidate intervention for managing technical debt. Remember, you'll probably end up running several interventions, some aimed at reducing existing debt, while others are aimed at avoiding debt creation.

This session consists of three activities:

1. **Select candidate intervention**, based upon agreed criteria
2. **Facilitated discussion and activities**
3. Learning **useful workshop techniques**

Let's look at selecting the candidate intervention.

Select Candidate Intervention

By this stage of the workshop, you should have a list of candidate interventions to investigate further. Some will come from the output of the first workshop session or subsequent additional information gathering. Since these both occurred some time ago, you can have already prepared these items, plus relevant/salient information and can therefore create slide material.

Other candidate items may have come out from the earlier discussions in this workshop session – either while discussing the findings from the workshop and investigation or in the summary of analysis. You can either quickly add these to the list on this slide, or if you are working from a whiteboard, then add to the whiteboard.

Go through each of the candidate intervention items, and ensure that workshop attendees understand each item.

Now, you want to get workshop attendees to decide which candidate intervention they would like to work on first. The simplest way is to use "dot voting," where each attendee is assigned a given number of votes or dots, and they assign those to their preferred candidate item(s). If you're not familiar with dot voting, you can find out more, either in *Red Teams*, *Liberating Structures*, or similar sources.

Once everyone has voted, count the votes, work out the item with the highest number of votes, and then take that into the facilitated discussion.

Facilitated Discussion and Activities

This session will require all your facilitation skills, or the skills of whoever is facilitating. If you're not confident you can facilitate this session effectively, then consider other options:

1. A skilled and well-briefed facilitator.
2. Practice with a small, friendly group beforehand.
3. Get one of the senior stakeholders to support you or lead the facilitation.

At this point, the workshop attendees have selected the candidate intervention, so you are exploring what that intervention may look like.

Start by getting the workshop to create a statement of the intervention, and then get agreement on it. For example, if the workshop has deemed that the biggest problem is caused by project underestimation, then your problem statement may be something along the lines of "*Project underestimation leads to project overrun, which then leads to the creation of technical debt. This organisation will improve project estimation, until it is no longer a factor in technical debt creation.*"

Once you have a problem/intervention statement, next generate a list of potential approaches to a solution.

Combine the technique of 1-2-4-All with brainstorming to generate ideas. First, get participants to spend a couple of minutes thinking of potential solution approaches. Next, combine into pairs and discuss. Next, combine the pairs into fours and discuss the ideas. As individuals are discussing, additional ideas should come out, which they should record down. Finally, combine the workshop together, and record down on a whiteboard or other common area all the ideas the individuals and groups have generated. Do not reject any ideas at this stage.

Take a brief break, and then use dot voting to vote for the most promising idea to take further.

Use whatever techniques you find useful or comfortable to explore this idea. Potentially useful techniques include those listed in the **"Useful Workshop Techniques"** section of this chapter.

You'll find it most useful to go through several iterations of breaking into small groups discussing an issue and then reforming as the whole workshop. In this way, you can get the benefit of multiple fresh ideas while ensuring that the most relevant or important ideas are shared with all.

Useful Workshop Techniques

This section of the slide deck is a placeholder for you to create slides for workshop techniques that you find useful and wish to introduce to the workshop attendees. Useful techniques include

- Wicked questions
- TRIZ
- PMI, Plus, Minus, Interesting
- Chesterton's fence
- Imagine an alternative
- 9 Whys
- Dialogue mapping/argument mapping

The above list is merely an example list. You should add or remove from that list, according to your own preferences.

These techniques are in one place in the slide deck for convenience. However, do not have a dedicated session, where you go through all these techniques. This will take you too long, plus attendees will lose focus on the primary goal, of developing an intervention. Instead, introduce the attendees to these techniques as a "drip feed" approach, when you judge that conditions within the workshop are appropriate for using that technique.

These techniques are discussed in more detail in a later section of this chapter.

Explore Second and Third Interventions

Repeat the same process you used for the first candidate intervention. You do not need to spend as much time selecting your second or third candidate intervention, as everyone is now familiar with the interventions and do not need to spend so much time comparing and evaluating them.

Alternatively, if your first intervention is proving fruitful and still has plenty to discuss, then you can use these subsequent interventions to go into greater depth. Remember, the whole purpose of this workshop is to get a candidate intervention that you can do a pilot on.

Summary and Next Steps

Summarize the main points of this workshop. Identify the main points from each of the three candidate interventions.

Remember the purpose of this workshop – to create some potential solutions to take into the pilot project stage. Therefore, if possible, **seek to get agreement on the next step, which should be to run one of the interventions as a pilot solution**. If that is not possible, or is not agreed, then keep pressing the workshop attendees until you *do* get a next step, even if it is to do further investigation. If you close this workshop without a clearly defined next step, you run the very real risk that the technical debt initiative will peter out.

You may need to run additional solution development workshops. They do not need to take a whole day, but if appropriately focused they could be as short as 90 minutes.

We've now come to the end of the agenda items. Next, we'll dive a little deeper into those workshop techniques we mentioned earlier.

Useful Workshop Techniques

You'll find the following techniques useful during your sessions to develop solutions and candidate interventions. Practice first in a safe environment before attempting to use in an important workshop setting.

A good place to start is with wicked questions, which is described in detail in *Liberating Structures*.

Wicked Questions

Wicked questions aim to engage everyone to think more incisively, by revealing entangled complexities and paradoxical challenges. A wicked question consists of two parts, where both parts consist of an undeniable reality. For example, "How can we be dedicated to our work and at the same time be fully present for our families?"

Warm participants up with a practice run.

1. Pose a sample wicked question, like "Why is the unemployment rate high while employers cannot find talent?"

2. Get participants to turn to their neighbor, and briefly discuss the question for 2 minutes.

3. Afterward, get participants to call out any particularly salient insights.

Now, get participants to do it for real.

1. Display to the participants your previously prepared warm-up question on technical debt. For example, "How can we reduce our technical debt, while at the same time maintaining our velocity?"

2. Ask participants if this qualifies as a wicked question and, if so, why?

3. Now get the workshop to develop their own wicked questions around the technical debt intervention you are working on.

    - Get everyone to spend 1 minute in silent self-reflection, aiming to generate a good, wicked question.

    - Next, spend 2 minutes generating ideas in pairs, building upon their ideas from self-reflection.

- Next, generate ideas in foursomes.
- Finally, get each group to share their most wicked question.

4. Post the wicked questions on a board.
5. Use dot voting to decide the best wicked question.
6. Next, the whole group should spend 5 minutes refining the question.
7. Next, the whole group should spend 5 to 10 minutes reflecting upon the implications of that question.

Ensure you capture the outputs from this session. Specifically, aim to capture

- A list of wicked questions, each of which reveals one aspect of the tension between reducing technical debt and some other important but conflicting goal.
- Insights and possibilities that are not immediately obvious but have revealed themselves through the paradoxical nature of the wicked questions.

Use the insights and possibilities in later workshops, placing the questions in a commonly accessible area.

TRIZ

A useful technique to follow up your wicked question is to use the TRIZ technique from *Liberating Structures*. TRIZ is the Russian acronym for theory of inventive problem-solving. If participants are not familiar with the technique, briefly explain it, and then walk through an example.

1. Explain that we want to identify all the things we must **stop doing** to make progress on technical debt.
2. We do this by identifying all the things that we could do to ensure **the worst possible outcome**.

3. Give participants a potentially humorous example. For myself, I might suggest – "How could I absolutely guarantee that my two daughters will one day dump me in a horrible old people's home and never come visit me?" Suggestions could be items such as

    - Always forget their birthdays.
    - Mix their names up.
    - Get really cranky as you get older.
    - Let them know that you plan to leave all your money to a cat rescue center.
    - And so on.

4. If you feel the workshop participants need a warm-up, get them to divide into pairs, and work on a non-threatening example for 2 minutes.

5. Now, do this for real. Get the workshop to break into groups of 4–7. Set the workshop participants the following question, or a similar, more focused one:

    How can we make sure we build an IT system that is so full of technical debt that we cannot make any modifications without doing major rework?

    If you want the workshop to come up with their own question, let them brainstorm for a few minutes then choose their preferred question.

6. Get each group to use the 1-2-4-All technique to create a list of all the things it could do to ensure that it achieves this unwanted result. (5 minutes)

7. Now get each group to use the 1-2-4-All technique to create a second list, this one of items they are currently doing that resemble items in the first list. (5 minutes)

8. Next, get each group to look at each item on the second list and determine what steps they can take that will help stop this unwanted activity.

9. Finally, get each group to showcase their results to the rest of the workshop.

Be prepared for some controversy when the groups discuss their results. For example, if one group has produced a list result like, "Never fund a project unless it is badly underestimated," individuals associated with the estimation may respond with comments about how difficult it is to correctly estimate a project.

Just how far you allow these discussions to go is very much a judgment call. You do want to surface these contradictions. However, once surfaced and captured, avoid spending too much time, energy, and goodwill endlessly circling around the issue.

PMI, Plus, Minus, Interesting

PMI is from Edward de Bono. PMI means Plus, Minus, Interesting.

You take an idea or suggestion, and then consider the positive aspects of it, the negative aspects of it, and then the interesting aspects. When we consider an idea, we rapidly decide whether we like it or not. If we like it, then we tend not to consider any of the minus points. Conversely, if we dislike it, we ignore the positives. Either way, we neglect to consider the interesting aspects of the idea.

Demonstrate the technique by asking participants to consider an example such as "windows should be made of transparent plastic, rather than glass," then get participants to consider the plus, minus, and interesting aspects of this.

Next, try it out on an idea relevant to technical debt such as, "projects should not have estimates."

Chesterton's Fence

Before everybody in your workshop gets too carried away about removing or changing things, you should offer a word of caution. Two words, actually: Chesterton's fence.

Chesterton's fence is the principle that changes to a setup should not be made until the reasoning for the current setup is fully understood.

I experienced Chesterton's fence on my very first proper software project at a software house. We were doing some work for a Swiss pharmaceutical company, moving a system from a mainframe to a client-server. As part of the upgrade, were told to also "tidy up" the code and not port over anything that was no longer needed. This code had been written years earlier, by programmers who had since left, so nobody really knew what the system was doing or what other systems were connected to it.

As part of this tidying up, we identified a whole bunch of interfaces that were never used. Or so we thought.

We investigated a couple of these interfaces – we asked around and then commented out the code to see if anybody complained. Nobody did. Convinced that they weren't being used, the program manager directed us not to port them over.

We went live one morning in September 1999. Over the next few hours, we received a series of increasingly frantic phone calls from production plants all across Europe. Each plant manager was pleading, "My plant's stopped. Where's my data gone?" We were receiving phone calls from places we hadn't heard of and couldn't even find on a map!

To explain Chesterton's fence, show workshop participants a slide depicting a fence that cuts across a road for no obvious reason, and then use it to explain the concept of Chesterton's fence. Follow this with a slide containing Chesterton's quotation:

> *In the matter of reforming things, as distinct from deforming them, there is one plain and simple principle... Let us say, for the sake of simplicity a fence or gate is directed across a road.*
>
> *The more modern type of reformer goes gaily up to it and says, "I don't see the use of this; let us clear it away." To which the more intelligent type of reformer will do well to answer: "if you don't see the use of it, I certainly won't let you clear it away. Go away and think. Then, when you come back and tell me that you do see the use of it, I may allow you to destroy it".*
>
> —G. K. Chesterton

Next, caveat the above sentiment by pointing out that within IT there are lots of things that are there for reasons that no one in the organization can remember. However, unlike Chesterton's fence, there are often no longer any good reasons for having the fence present.

Get the team to spend 10 minutes in a 1-2-4-All to discuss this conundrum and potential ways to address it. Capture these potential solutions on a whiteboard or post-it notes.

CHAPTER 16 WORKSHOPS FOR SOLUTION DEVELOPMENT

Imagining an Alternative

The only thing harder than getting a new idea into the military mind is getting an old one out.

—Basil Liddell Hart, Thoughts on war, 1944

Your workshop now has the following outputs:

- Your list of wicked questions, plus any insights and possibilities that have revealed themselves through the question exploration

- Your TRIZ list, of ways to achieve the unwanted result, plus list, of activities the organization does that resemble the first list

- Insights and comments from demonstrating the dynamic models, if used

Your workshop is now ready to begin imagining ways of working that will result in less technical debt.

Use the output from the earlier sessions to construct a whiteboard list of candidate solutions. Remember, technical debt is a wicked problem that has built up within your organization over a long period of time. Moreover, its buildup has enabled individuals in the organization to benefit, including some of those in the room now. Therefore, you are looking for new ways of working, rather than apportioning blame.

Also, you are not going to solve all the organization's technical debt problems either instantly or painlessly. What you can do though is take a step toward reduced technical debt, even if it is a small step.

Once you have created the list of candidate solutions, ask the workshop members to evaluate the solutions against a set of criteria. You can create your own, or use a list like the one below:

- Impact
- Ease of doing
- Coordination with others required
- Risk
- Budget required

- Long-term/short-term
- Existing debt reduction/future debt avoidance

If you're at an early stage of your technical debt journey, you are probably trying to create some momentum that will enable the organization to see some benefits and justify further work on technical debt reduction and management.

Therefore, get the workshop group to focus on items that are within their discretion to do, not things they cannot change. You are aiming to embody participants with a **sense of agency** that they are capable of changing things. You wish to avoid feelings of helplessness or powerlessness.

Next, ask the workshop, "Is there anything else we can do? Something that doesn't require permission of anyone?" Wait in silence for several seconds before moving on. Most people are uncomfortable in a silence, so there will be strong pressure to think of *something* that can be done. When that happens, thank the person for the contribution, write it down, and then look expectantly and ask, "And what else?"

If you are fortunate, you will end up with a list of small things that can be done to reduce technical debt, preferably with names against them.

This technique is similar to the "15% solution" in *Liberating Structures*.

9 Whys

This technique is used to make the purpose of your work together clear.

Begin in pairs, then groups of four, and then the entire workshop. After you have paired up, ask your partner, "when working on <item> what do you do?" Ask "why" questions until you make a discovery about your partner's most basic purpose.

Switch roles and then repeat.

Move to a group of four, discussing similarities and differences.

Return to the whole group and share your discoveries. Make a note if a group purpose becomes clear.

For more details, refer to the book, *Liberating Structures*, or the website.

Dialogue Mapping/Argument Mapping

You can use dialogue mapping or argument mapping tools to aid in facilitated discussions. Rationale is software designed specifically for argument mapping. However, you can also use mind-mapping software, intended for creating and sharing ideas.

If the workshop discussion has moved into the area where you would benefit from tools for argument mapping, then you should probably stand back and take stock of the situation.

If you do decide you want to use an argument mapping approach, then trial out whatever tool you plan to use with a friendly audience first.

We are now finished our section on useful workshop techniques. Next, we look at preparing for that workshop.

Workshop Preparation

To maximize your chances of success, you must adequately prepare for this workshop. You'll have a lot of information from the output of the first workshop and your additional information gathering, plus your discussions with stakeholders and your sensemaking. It would be a waste if you didn't make the most of these assets, by creating comprehensive and informative presentation material for this workshop. Therefore, follow the suggestions in the workshop details section of this chapter, and ensure your presentation material is completed.

Also, ensure that you have covered off everything on the **workshop checklist**, which you can find in the appendix.

After the Session

After the workshop for solution development, you should follow up on any small improvements that the workshop participants identified were within their gift to change.

To use the misquote of Peter Drucker, "What gets measured gets managed," ensure that the participants know that you, or someone else, will be following up on the identified small improvements.

If further workshop sessions are needed, aim to get dates for those sessions pencilled in.

In addition, commence preparation for the pilot project (if you already have approval), or prepare the business case for the desired pilot project.

Outputs

By the end of the workshop session, you should have the following outputs:

- Between 1 and 3 interventions to pilot or take higher up for approval, plus any agreed actions on those interventions
- List of further candidate interventions, for future workshops
- List of small items that the workshop participants have the power to do
- List of wicked questions, plus any insights and possibilities
- List of TRIZ items to stop doing
- Observations and insights from a demo of any dynamic models

Further Reading

For running workshops, use the same books suggested in the chapter for the problem understanding workshop.

For ideas for techniques to use in interactive and creative workshop sessions, try *Liberating Structures*, or *Red Team Handbook*.

For an explanation of dialogue mapping, try *Dialogue Mapping: Building Shared Understanding of Wicked Problems* by Jeffrey Conklin.

For more information on the Plus, Minus, Interesting technique, plus many other useful thinking techniques, try *De Bono's Thinking Course: Powerful Tools to Transform Your Thinking*.

Summary

In this chapter, we learned how to plan and conduct a workshop to enable us to begin developing solutions to our organization's technical debt problems.

We began by asking the purpose of the workshop. Next, we looked at the workshop agenda and then each agenda item. We gave a recap of the first workshop and then looked at additional information gathered since the workshop and a summary of our analysis.

Next, we explored three candidate interventions, using a mixture of facilitated discussions, plus other workshop tools and techniques. We concluded with a summary of our understanding and our proposed next steps.

Workshop participants now have a list of activities they can now do that will either reduce technical debt or avoid its creation. We also used intervention sessions to work upon developing bigger improvements to the technical debt situation.

We'll need to trial out these bigger improvements in a pilot program. This is the subject of the next chapter.

CHAPTER 17

Pilot Solutions

In this chapter we go through how to put together a pilot solution, as shown in Figure 17-1.

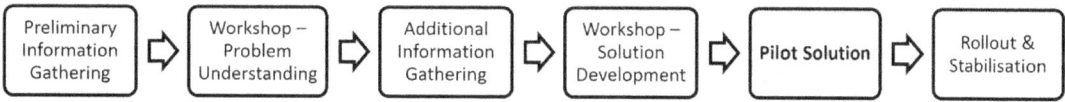

Figure 17-1. Technical debt reduction program, with Pilot Solution highlighted

We begin by reminding ourselves of the dangers in trying to introduce change, including running a pilot project. Next, we explore whether we need to run a pilot project and then conclude that we probably do. Next, we go through each of the steps in one approach to running a pilot project. Those steps are

1. Agree/reiterate goals and set expectations.

2. Select your pilot project.

3. Set a timeline.

4. Run pilot and gather information.

5. Analyze results and create report.

6. Capture lessons learned and identify next steps.

To give us something concrete to hang our ideas on, let's suppose that your organization has agreed to trial out the use of **Ulysses contracts** on a project.

As you recall, a Ulysses contract is an agreement we voluntarily enter into, but which binds us under certain future conditions. Your organization will allow the trial project to create pieces of technical debt, to solve tactical project problems, but has a mechanism for reserving time and funds to subsequently pay off that debt.

Let's now go through each of the above steps, beginning with the dangers within pilot projects.

CHAPTER 17   PILOT SOLUTIONS

Dangers of Pilot Projects

> *... there is nothing more difficult, more perilous, or more uncertain, than the introduction of new things... Because the innovator has for enemies all those who have done well under the old conditions....*
>
> —Niccolò Machiavelli

We should remind ourselves of Machiavelli's quote regarding introducing change. There are some within your organization who are doing quite well under the current setup and may like to see your pilot project fail.

There are others who, while they want your pilot to succeed, want its success to prove *their* interpretation of the problem. Remember that with a wicked problem like technical debt, stakeholders have radically different worldviews and different frames for understanding the problem.

Hence, as you run any pilot project, be aware that there will be some seeking to ensure your project fails, plus others intent upon interpreting the results in support of their own self interests.

Is there a limit to how far people will go to use an event to further their own self-interest? Sadly, no.

When I was a PhD student at Imperial College, London, I also served as a sub-warden in a student hall of residence. At end of the academic year, students let off steam and indulged in a lot of noisy horseplay. Sadly, during this horseplay, one student fell to his death from a ninth-floor window.

Shortly afterward, the hall management team were requested to a meeting with the Chancellor of the University. He had received a suggestion from a nearby resident that, to prevent further deaths, the windows in the hall of residence should be permanently screwed shut.

This nearby resident was notorious for his frequent complaints about student noise. His suggestion, apart from being completely impracticable, was little more than a self-interested attempt to use the tragic event of a student death to further his own interests.

If someone will seek to use a tragedy to further their own self-interest, be under no illusion that someone within your organization will seek to use, or trash, your pilot project for their own interests.

We have repeatedly talked about technical debt as a wicked problem. This is useful, as understanding wicked problems, social complexity, and fragmentation helps us recognize the challenges we need to overcome to find a solution.

However, an alternative way of looking at the problem is using the Cynefin framework, shown in Figure 17-2.

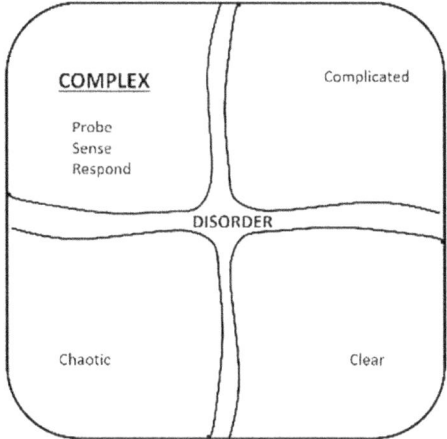

Figure 17-2. *The Cynefin framework. Technical debt within an organization usually sits within the COMPLEX system phase or environment.*

Within this framework, our technical debt problem normally lies within the COMPLEX environment. Science and engineering struggle to run controlled experiments within a complex environment. This is because there are simply too many variables, most of which cannot be controlled. In addition, any intervention will likely change the nature of the problem. We're back to characteristics of wicked problems again.

However, we're not running pharmaceutical drug trials, where the outcome may put lives in danger and a high degree of proof is needed. We're running trials on ways of building software, and in any case those existing ways haven't exactly been proven in a strict, double-blind scientific experiment.

Therefore, we should be satisfied if we can show that our intervention is *more likely to have improved rather than worsened* the outcome. This is a similar level of proof suggested by Rory Sutherland in *Alchemy,* his fascinating book on behavioral insights interventions.

If we don't need the same level of proof as we would in a clinical drug trial, are there other things we can do to get our answers quicker? You can take more of a lean approach, when appropriate. Look for opportunities where you can make a small change on an existing project, inspect, and then adapt. This is the approach advocated by Eric Ries in *Lean Startup*.

However, if there are dangers in running pilot projects, must we even run one? Let's look at that next.

CHAPTER 17   PILOT SOLUTIONS

Must We Run a Pilot Project?

There are two, very limited, circumstances where you could manage technical debt without running a pilot project:

1. Limit yourself to addressing only the list of small items that the solution development workshop participants identified were within their power to do.

2. Restrict yourself to using past project data.

(There is a third way, which is to only address existing technical debt. This is not really a solution, as new debt continues to arrive at the same rate as before. Indeed, your actions of addressing debt may even encourage an increased rate of creation!)

Both the above approaches are likely to take you only so far. Once you have applied all the small fixes that individuals can do, you are likely to find the remaining items require a large investment, for which a pilot is required before organization-wide rollout could be approved.

For example, the problem of preventing overdue projects generating technical debt is a large investment. You could address it by avoiding projects becoming overdue, which in turn means improving estimation. Alternatively, you could create a mechanism to allow projects that have become overdue to address technical debt generation, say through a Ulysses contract approach.

Neither addressing estimation nor creating Ulysses contracts can be done as a small-scale intervention, so they require a pilot project.

Next, let's look at the second point: using past project data.

Using Past Project Data

Many organizations have lots of data on many aspects of their business and software development process. This amount of data will only increase.

You may be able to use this data to answer some questions without even running an expensive and time-consuming trial intervention, one that risks being manipulated by self-interested parties.

The example data we examine below was taken from a program I once worked on that was unrelated to technical debt. I subsequently realized it could be adapted to explore the question of whether overdue projects are responsible for creating a disproportionate amount of technical debt.

The data related to two projects. Project 1 was 20% late (not unusual at this organization), whereas Project 2 delivered 60% late. Notice the change in gradient for Project 2 before and after the original deadline, as shown in Figure 17-3.

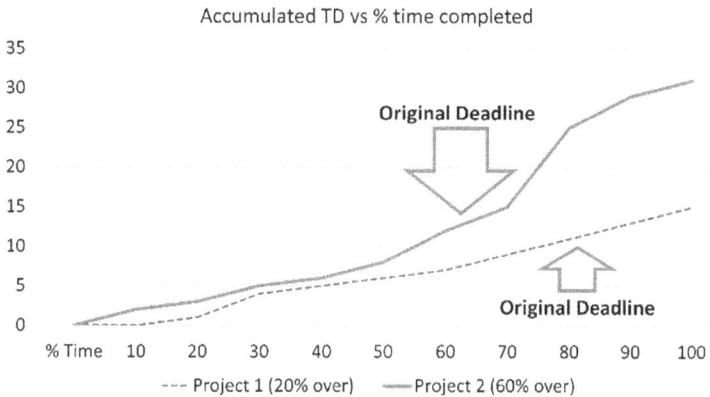

Figure 17-3. Technical debt items entered into register for an accurately estimated project (Project 1) and an inaccurate one (Project 2)

For project 1, the technical debt was evenly accumulated throughout the project lifetime. In contrast, in project 2, you can see that after the project became behind schedule, there was a marked increase in the rate at which technical debt items were added.

The following interpretation was confirmed in interviews with development team members. After the project fell behind schedule, the team found themselves under considerable pressure to recover that lost schedule. This led them to make decisions that increased the number of technical debt items, which were simply put into the register. There was some intention to address these items later, but that never occurred.

Let's continue with the Ulysses contract example to look at our goals, plan our intervention, and consider our metrics.

CHAPTER 17   PILOT SOLUTIONS

Agree Goals and Plan Intervention and Metrics

Your goal would be something like – **determine whether using a Ulysses contract within a project reduced the gradient of the technical debt slope or had other beneficial effects**.

You will determine this by the following items:

1. Set up/agree a Ulysses contract for the creation of technical debt within the project.

2. Measure the count of technical debt items added to the technical debt register.

3. Your hypothesis is that by doing this you can reduce the gradient of the technical debt line.

How might that Ulysses contract look like? You'd like that contract to do the following:

- Encourage desirable project behaviors.
- Discourage undesirable behaviors.

Desirable behaviors would include high transparency, avoid creating high-cost debt, and only taking on debt when it is advantageous to the organization (not just the project).

The most common undesirable behavior that you'll need to discourage is the temptation to use the existence of the Ulysses contract to solve all manner of problems that the project could or should have resolved itself.

Other undesirable behaviors will likely stem from the list of problems identified in the economics chapter, such as the principal-agent problem, externalities, and so on.

Your Ulysses contract would likely include the following items:

- Budget for addressing technical debt items.
- Rules for adding technical debt to the register. For example:
  - Proportion of cost paid by project versus proportion paid by organization.
  - When to be paid down and with what resources.

The structure of your contract should reflect what you are trying to do, which is get the project finished in a timely manner and avoid creating expensive technical debt and increasing transparency (so debt is not merely hidden). Therefore, you need to spend some time thinking about how individuals may decide to behave in response to your rule structures.

For example, you may decide at all costs would be picked up by the organization, rather than the project. This is likely to result in everything, including the kitchen sink, getting assigned to the technical debt register. You may counter this, for example, by measuring how much the project assigns to the register under a Ulysses contract.

Conversely, you may decide that all costs should be borne by the project. This will likely result in the project hiding most technical debt items, leading to a loss of transparency of what is really happening on a project.

Now that you have your goal and set up your Ulysses contract, you now need to decide your metrics. In simplest form, your metrics would simply consist of your technical debt register, with tags for items created by this project.

Other potential metrics include

- Length of time debt item is in register
- Effort required to resolve debt item
- Number of bugs, changes, releases

Metrics will give you a lot of information, but you should also interview project team members to gauge how effective your Ulysses intervention was and how it can be improved, plus other aspects or problems that are visible to them but not you.

Now you are ready to start the next stage – selecting your pilot project.

Select Your Pilot Project

You already have your pilot project idea – Ulysses contracts. What you are now looking for is a candidate project to trial out that idea. Set yourself some criteria for the candidate project. Example criteria include

- **Timely:** The project should be at a suitable stage for your trial.
- **Amenable:** How supportive are the project team likely to be?
- **Not too big**: where any perceived failure becomes highly visible.

- **Not too urgent:** If the project falls behind schedule, the experiment will be forgotten. Worse, it may be used to deflect blame from the schedule overrun.
- **Not too long:** If the pilot takes too long, you risk losing momentum.

Once you have selected your pilot project, you are ready to start the next stage – setting a timeline.

Set Timeline

Once you know the project and its scheduled plan, you can then determine how long it should take to get an answer to the questions.

Remember, after you have gathered the information from the project, you will still need to analyze it, so ensure this is included in your timeline.

Now it's time to run your pilot.

Run Pilot and Gather Information

Remember, you're running a pilot to gather information about how that technical debt buildup is changed by your pilot intervention, a Ulysses contract. You're not running the project itself, so avoid getting drawn into doing that.

If the project team have not been involved in the workshops (although they should have been), then spend time taking them through what you're trying to do and why.

Work with your project team to think of ways to best achieve your goal, which is to determine whether a Ulysses contract is a useful tool for helping manage technical debt. The team will be knowledgeable and, hopefully, interested in helping.

During your interactions with the team, try and gain ideas about other potential improvements. They have insights and values quite different from yours, so they may see something that is either invisible to you or that you see but fail to grasp its significance.

Next, let's briefly look at analyzing the results.

Analyze Results and Create Report

You need to try and answer the following two questions:

1. Was this step in the right direction?
2. Did it help more than it cost?

Your report should strive toward being simple in its message – key stakeholders are busy people, often with short attention spans. They do not usually invest large swaths of time interpreting overly lengthy reports. Therefore, ensure your main message is in the initial summary and is clear.

People love numbers. Be sure to include your numbers and graphs.

People also love a story. Put a story to those numbers.

Next, we look at capturing lessons learned.

Capture Lessons Learned and Identify Next Steps

Aim to capture lessons learned at two levels. First, capture answers to the questions posed by the pilot – was our hypothesis correct or not? Second, are there any lessons to improve your next pilot?

Two ways to capture lessons for your next pilot are firstly to capture any learnings down as they occur, ideally in a shared location, like Miro or Mural. A second way to capture your learnings, as well as share them, is to run a **retrospective** at the end of the pilot project.

Further Reading

To learn more about a lean approach to running pilot projects, *The Lean Startup* by Eric Ries is an excellent guide. Although he is talking about an entrepreneurial start-up, the concepts are the same – you have critical questions you need answers to, so your focus should be on quick and cheap experiments to get answers as quickly as possible, rather than conducting elegant trials.

If you're looking for how to gather momentum for an initiative, *Fearless Change* by Mary Lynn Manns and Linda Rising is a good read.

CHAPTER 17   PILOT SOLUTIONS

For a good account of why we shouldn't get too hung up on high levels of proof, try reading the chapter, "Why It's Better to Be Vaguely Right and Precisely Wrong," in *Alchemy: The Surprising Power of Ideas That Don't Make Sense* by Rory Sutherland.

To learn more about the Cynefin framework, try, *Cynefin - Weaving Sense-Making into the Fabric of Our World* by David Snowdon, or visit the Cynefin website.

Summary

In this chapter, we used the example of a Ulysses contract to walk through the steps to pilot a trial change and then collect and analyze the information needed by stakeholders. Those steps were

1. Agree/reiterate goals and set expectations
2. Select your pilot project
3. Set a timeline
4. Run pilot and gather information
5. Analyze results and create report
6. Capture lessons learned and identify next steps

Thinking beyond this immediate pilot project, you could envision that embedded within the above steps is the kernel of a process. For example, if you

1. Create a technical debt register
2. Create a Ulysses contract
3. Analyze and discuss what the contract has done to the gradient of the register

This could be a simple methodology to help control your technical debt. This could be bolted onto another methodology, like scrum.

Once you have an improved way of working, whether it is from a successful pilot project or from that list of small items workshop participants identified they had the power to do, you'll want to roll it out to the rest of the organization. In the next chapter, we'll look at what you can do for a successful rollout and stabilization.

CHAPTER 18

Rollout and Stabilization

In this chapter we look at how you can roll out to the whole organization your lessons from the pilot projects and workshops, as shown in Figure 18-1. This will help ensure technical debt remains at manageable levels while still allowing a high tempo of software development.

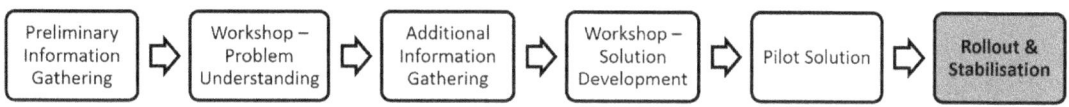

Figure 18-1. Technical debt reduction program, with rollout and stabilization highlighted

We begin by reminding ourselves of the perils of change. Next, we briefly look at different change management models, before exploring in depth John Kotter's eight-step transformation process model. We conclude by briefly exploring critical success factors to a change management program.

Let's now look at the perils of change.

The Perils of Change

It ought to be remembered that there is nothing more difficult to take in hand, more perilous to conduct, or more uncertain in its success, than to take the lead in the introduction of a new order of things.

—Niccolò Machiavelli, The Prince

Remember Machiavelli? Of course, you remember him. Even if you had managed to forget him for a while, you found yourself repeatedly reminded of his quotation, as we went through Part 3 of this book and learned of the difficulties and dangers you face in trying to address technical debt.

Note that these dangers occur not because you seek to reduce existing technical debt with a code change or other technical means – few people are against that – but rather because you seek to reduce the creation of technical debt *by getting people to change the way they work*.

The most difficult and dangerous part of addressing technical debt is getting people to change. Hence, you should consider your technical debt initiative as a **change management initiative**. And now I have some bad news.

Most change programs fail.

IT change is not immune to this, as change programs that have a significant IT input fare no better than other change programs.

In Chapter 3, we explored why technical debt has proven so resistant to solutions. We came up with several factors, including

- **Misunderstood**: Most people believe technical debt is a technical problem, not realizing it is fundamentally a trade-off problem.

- **Wrong place**: We only deal with debt when it is visible and has become a problem, rather than preventing its creation.

- **Rarely urgent**: There is always something more urgent than addressing technical debt.

- **Not sexy**: Nobody ever impressed their boss by avoiding creating technical debt.

- **No silver bullets**.

As a result, even if an organization does fund a technical debt program, it is invariably aimed at addressing existing debt and ignores the problem of new debt creation.

It seems puzzling that organizations will do the expensive stuff, like replacing their debt-laden legacy system with a brand-new one, but those same organizations cannot successfully implement a change management process needed to stabilize their expensive gains.

This is not simply because of short-term constraints. Indeed, if you ask anybody who has been involved in a major upgrade to a system, where that upgrade mostly consisted of paying down technical debt, that expensive stuff is not a short-term thing.

Therefore, if you wish to roll out and stabilize the gains from your technical debt program, you need to take change management seriously.

Change Management Models

Although there are many models available for managing change within an organization, we'll use **John Kotter's eight-step transformation process**. We'll select this because it is a well proven, widely used framework, with ample literature and resources available, plus change management professionals with relevant experience are readily obtainable.

Other change models include as follows:

The **McKinsey 7-S framework**, which is based around seven key elements: structure, strategy, system, shared values, skills, style, and staff.

The **ADKAR change management model**, which is based upon the belief that organizational change can only happen when individuals change. The ADKAR elements are awareness, desire, knowledge, ability, and reinforcement.

Lean change, which is an amalgam of change management ideas, with an emphasis on Lean Startup and Agile. Principles include

1. Creating shared purpose, rather than creating a false sense of urgency
2. Dialogue, rather than one-way communications
3. Experimentation and adaptation, rather than following a plan
4. Understanding resistance to change, rather than enforcement or blame
5. Cooperation, rather than achieving buy-in

For the remainder of this chapter, we'll use Kotter's eight-step transformation process, as it consists of clear steps that you can readily follow. However, if your organization is familiar with agile processes and mindset, you should consider blending in elements of Lean Change.

Let's now look at Kotter's eight-step transformation process.

Kotter's Eight-Step Transformation Process

This model places great emphasis on communication and obtaining buy-in. Advantages of this model include

1. **Simple to implement**: The eight steps are clear and have voluminous documentation available to help you.

2. **Focus on stakeholder buy-in**: The model places a big emphasis on involvement and getting acceptance of stakeholders and other employees, a critical success factor in any change program.

3. **Emphasizes action through creating a sense of urgency**: This addresses a major problem that all change programs face – the urgent business problems displace the important need for change.

Disadvantages of this model include

1. **Urgency**: Creating a false sense of urgency can backfire.

2. **Sequential, time-consuming, resource heavy**: This process can require significant investment of resource.

3. **Top-down approach:** This can limit the level of participation, engagement, and can backfire. A top-down approach could be considered an anti-pattern for many agile practices that organizations now pursue.

The eight steps of the transformation process are

1. Establish a sense of urgency
2. Form a powerful guiding coalition
3. Create a vision
4. Communicate the vision
5. Empower others to act on the vision
6. Create short-term wins
7. Consolidate improvements
8. Institutionalize new approaches

Let's now look at each of the steps in turn.

Establish a Sense of Urgency

Establishing a sense of urgency is often a challenge with technical debt. We can recall President Eisenhower with his problems that were urgent but not important and problems that were important but not urgent.

Technical debt is not naturally an urgent problem. Indeed, much of it is generated because of attending to other, more urgent, problems. Nevertheless, to succeed in addressing technical debt, you must instill a sense of urgency in individuals. Aim to convince three quarters of the managers that doing nothing about technical debt is more dangerous than doing something.

Actions you could do to establish this sense of urgency include

1. **Estimate the cost** of technical debt to the organization. Better still, try and identify a trend – you should expect a self-reinforcing loop, with the more technical debt you have the more expensive to fix each item becomes.

2. **Create a narrative**. As discussed in Chapter 5, tell a story of an item of technical debt and its consequences to the organization.

3. Use **dynamic simulation models** to show the effect of different levels of technical debt on development costs.

Avoid establishing a false sense of urgency, with exaggeratedly urgent problems. While you may be able to convince people initially, you risk encountering **organizational change fatigue**, which is a sense of apathy toward change when too much change takes place.

I once worked as an engineer at an organization that seemed to exist in a constant state of change. We engineers used a secret acronym for this change, borrowed from the military – BOHICA. We pretended to management that the acronym stood for, Business Oriented HIgh level Change Amendment, but to us engineers it stood for "Bend Over, Here It Comes Again."

Because change was always present and always depicted as urgent (although never quite as urgent as shipping product), we became fatigued, merely going through the motions while we awaited the next change initiative.

Form a Powerful Guiding Coalition

The three important words are powerful, guiding, and coalition.

Powerful: To make change happen, you need individuals with sufficient power to get things done. A common problem with our IT change initiatives at HMV was that the assembled team often did not include a senior line manager from the London head office.

Guiding: This coalition needs to guide the rest of the organization.

Coalition: You need to assemble or self-form a group of individuals with a shared commitment to the objective of addressing and managing technical debt.

Encourage this coalition to work as a team outside of their normal hierarchy, meeting regularly. A common challenge is that these individuals are often already overstretched.

In the initial phase, a successful guiding team may consist of only two to four people. However, when you come to be rolling out big changes in areas important to technical debt, like changing how projects are estimated, then your guiding coalition must be influential enough to ensure change.

Create a Vision

You need to create a **vision that is clear, attractive, and believable**. From this vision, your organization can develop strategies to achieve that vision.

The most important thing is that the vision is sufficiently clear and simple to be easily communicated. The most common pitfall is to create a vision that is too complex or vague to be communicated to others in only 5 minutes. You may also need a different message for different groups.

For technical people, this vision may be that they can focus on how to deliver the desired capability, instead of spending time shoehorning in code to give the minimal viable product within the constraints of a heavy burden of code debt.

For the users and stakeholders, the vision may be that they enjoy predictability, where the functionality they desire is delivered when they were expecting.

Communicate the Vision

The most common problem with communicating the vision is **under-communicating** it, often by a factor of ten or more. Some organizations may decide upon a major change, but then communicate that change in a single meeting or communication, not referring to it again. Unsurprisingly, change rarely occurs in these organizations.

You should use every vehicle possible to communicate the new vision to individuals within the organization. We all have many opportunities to communicate change, in meetings, or incorporating the message into our normal activities. In a routine discussion about a development or project activity, you can incorporate a message about how the proposed solution fits, or doesn't fit, into the technical debt vision.

You should also ensure that you and senior stakeholders **display those behaviors by example**. One of the more damaging ways to undermine a change initiative is for senior stakeholders to behave in ways that are antithetical to the vision. Employees will not make sacrifices if they see senior stakeholders openly behaving in ways incompatible to that vision.

For example, I once worked on an agile project at an insurance company. We were under a lot of pressure from stakeholders, so we habitually put too many stories into the sprint, causing carryover. Stakeholders eventually agreed to restrict the story points to the number we could sustainably address. This worked fine for a couple of sprints. However, we then received a directive from the board to implement a big government-led initiative for flood reinsurance.

Even if we had done only flood reinsurance stories, we would still have struggled. However, no stakeholder was willing to upset their director boss by delaying their story for a couple of sprints. So once again we squeezed too much in. However, we did have a solemn promise that this would never happen again.

Shortly after we had digested flood reinsurance lump, the board of directors passed another emergency onto us. A few months later, we had fully regressed back into our old firefighting mode. I believe a large part of the reason for our regression was the directors behaving in ways antithetical to their own vision.

The corollary of this is also true. If people in an organization see supportive behavior demonstrated by senior leaders, that is a powerful signal that they are behind the change. The most memorable demonstration of this that I have ever seen was not within IT. It wasn't even in my country, but occurred when I lived in Japan.

CHAPTER 18   ROLLOUT AND STABILIZATION

While I was waiting to transfer to our Japanese partners, Harima san, my new boss and head of engineering support came to the UK. He gave a factory-wide talk about the importance of quality for customers in Japan. I didn't really pay too much attention, as I'd heard plenty of similar talks from our own management, usually followed shortly afterward by an instruction to "just ship it, they'll sort it out on site," directed toward a particularly troublesome machine.

After a few months in Japan, I was asked for my input to a problem. One model took two and a half days to service. As the distance between customers meant that engineers could usually only visit one site per day, the company was keen to avoid this wasted half day.

I looked at the maintenance schedule and identified what we could cut out to avoid that wasted half day. For example, we could stagger certain items that only needed to be changed every two or three visits. Eventually, I worked out a schedule and then showed it to my boss.

"I've managed to save you that wasted half day, Harima san," I said, feeling pleased.

There was a long silence, as Harima san tried to put into words something he didn't quite know how to tell me, then translate those words into English. Eventually, he found the words.

"Andy san, well done! But that is not the wasted half day."

"What you mean?" I asked, puzzled.

"Service take two and half days, but engineer is on site for three days."

"Yes, I know," I said, still puzzled. "This way the engineer is on site for only two days."

Harima san shook his head, stubbed out his habitual cigarette, and then drew a diagram of the schedule, as shown in Figure 18-2.

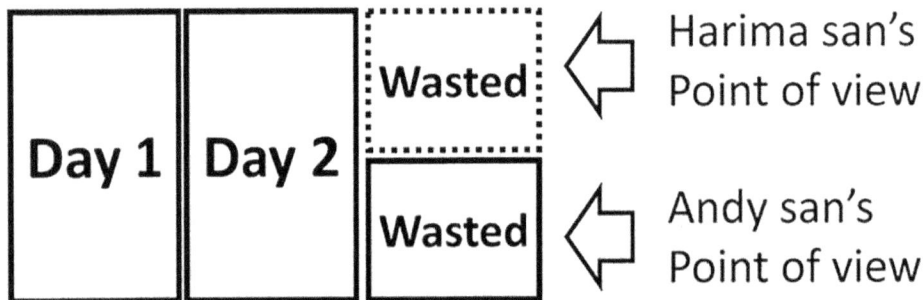

Figure 18-2. Service schedule, showing wasted half day, from Western viewpoint and Japanese viewpoint

Harima san and I were thinking in totally opposite ways. For me, the waste was from being on site for a half day, which could be addressed by somehow cutting down the service. For Harima san, the waste was from leaving the site after only a half day, when we could use that extra time to improve quality.

Harima san demonstrated to me his commitment to his vision by his actions. He chose to use efficiency savings to improve quality, rather than degrading quality in the name of efficiency.

Empower Others to Act on the Vision

To empower others, **you need to remove or alter structures that undermine progress toward the vision**. You also need to encourage risk-taking and the trialling of non-traditional ideas, activities, and actions. This means creating a safe environment, where failed experiments are not punished.

The biggest barrier to empowerment of others is failing to remove or change powerful individuals who are resisting the change effort. Recall Machiavelli's quote, that resistance to change came from those who were currently doing well under the present regime, and the lukewarm support was due in part to fear of reprisals from those resisting change. Five hundred years later, this quote is still valid.

Usually, those resisting change are persons who believe they are doing quite well out of the status quo situation. For example:

- Product managers, who squeeze one or two more stories out of each sprint, or who browbeat the team into adding in their pet functionality.

- Bidding teams who accept a quote they know is unrealistic, in the belief that they will be seen as having got the organisation "a really good deal"

- On overdue projects, stakeholders insisting that features that are not minimally necessary are retained, to the detriment of quality and technical debt

- Firefighting heroes, who wage constant battles to douse the fires, but in the process undermine their colleagues' efforts to create a future landscape with fire breaks

Create Short-Term Wins

You must show some early visible improvements. Stakeholders will not continue on a path of sacrifice unless they can see evidence of gains within a reasonable time span.

Therefore, include in your technical debt reduction program some initiatives that let you demonstrate early wins. Also, reward team members who contributed to those improvements, thereby encouraging others.

Do not leave the achievement of an early success up to chance. If you're not in control, then fate is in control, and fate has a nasty habit of letting you down.

Therefore, include into your workshop some activities aimed at identifying areas for early gains. Use the workshop activity "Imagining an alternative" in Chapter 16 to enable participants to capture opportunities for improvement that are within their control. Follow up, to ensure they are done. Celebrate their successes, plus ensure those improvements are rolled-out to others.

Consolidate Improvements

Leverage your increased credibility from the early wins to argue for changes to the systems, structures, and policies that are undermining the vision.

In terms of a technical debt initiative, this is often arguing for changes to estimation processes that lead to significant project underestimation, and hence under-resourcing and insufficient timelines.

Also, look to reinvigorate the change process with new projects, either aimed at reducing particularly painful examples of technical debt, or projects aimed at reducing its accumulation.

Use **retrospectives** to review what technical debt has been generated, plus what led to it.

Institutionalize New Approaches

Finally, identify connections between the new behaviors and improved software development, leading to enhanced business success.

Aim to get these new approaches embedded in a permanent process or methodology. It is all too easy, and indeed tempting, to revert to the old way of doing things in an emergency.

One of the difficulties we experienced at HMV with improvements IT made during the post-Christmas quiet period was that we were separated from the London head office by a 90-minute rail journey. This meant that we rarely met with the primary stakeholders to consolidate and institutionalize our improvements. This led to us reverting to our customary ways of working during the April–November project season.

Critical Success Factors

The following are common critical factors in successful change projects:

- Define measurable stakeholder aims.
- Effective communication to all stakeholders.
- Create an effective training program. This is the workshop program.
- Be vigilant for resistance and address it.
- Monitor and fine tune your progress.

Further Reading

Leading Change by Philip Kotter is the go-to text on the eight-step change program. Even if you adopt a different process, this is still a worthwhile read.

For an overall view of change management, then *HBR's 10 Must Reads on Change Management*, from Harvard Business Review, is a useful collection of papers on the subject.

If you want to learn more about the ADKAR model, then *ADKAR: A Model for Change in Business, Government and Our Community* by Jeff Hiatt is a useful start.

If you want a more lean or agile approach, then you'll find Jason Little's *Lean Change Management* insightful.

Peter Senge's *The Fifth Discipline* is good background to change, plus it goes into depth in many other areas.

If you're looking to supplement your change process with additional activities, then *Leading Change* by Mary Lynn Manns and Linda Rising contains plenty of highly useful ideas.

CHAPTER 18 ROLLOUT AND STABILIZATION

Summary

In this chapter, we tackled what Machiavelli described as the most difficult and perilous endeavor, that of introducing a new order of things.

We began by reminding ourselves of the perils of change. We then briefly looked at different change management models, before exploring John Kotter's eight-step transformation process and then concluded by briefly exploring critical success factors.

In the final chapter, we draw some conclusions and explore what the next steps may be for organizations looking to address their technical debt problems.

CHAPTER 19

Conclusion

If you had a magic button you could press to extend your life, you'd have no hesitation in pressing it.

Similarly, if you had a button to extend not your life but the life of your software systems, you'd have no hesitation in pressing that button, too.

Unfortunately, neither button exists. Nor are they ever likely to.

However, while there is no button to extend your life, lose weight, become a black belt in a martial art, or to banish that debilitating chronic migraine you learned of in the introduction, that does not stop some people seeking it. Nor does it stop unscrupulous vendors attempting to sell a solution to the desperate or gullible.

Meanwhile, others accept that no such button exists and instead follow a healthy lifestyle, embark upon a weight loss program, or engage with a martial arts instructor.

A few more visionary individuals seek to banish that chronic migraine, not by drilling crude holes in skulls to allow evil spirits to escape, but by changing our understanding of the world. They learn to treat migraine not with holes in skulls but with a combination of diet, lifestyle, and preventative medication.

We face similar choices in software. That magic button to extend the life of our software systems does not exist, or rather it only exists in the hands of unscrupulous vendors.

However, you *can* extend the life of your software systems, perhaps by 50% or more, by preventing its arteries clogging up with technical debt. What's more, life is a whole lot better in a system that does not have clogged up arteries. You can run further in your sprint, bench press more story points, and react faster to unexpected events. This journey requires effort and delayed satisfaction, but it does exist.

Like the treatment of migraine, this journey also requires us to change our understanding of our world. We must stop drilling holes in skulls and instead address our problem by understanding its causes, then treating it with the software equivalent of diet and lifestyle changes, coupled with preventative medication.

CHAPTER 19 CONCLUSION

The place to start is with our understanding of the technical debt world, which is based partly upon a **broken analogy**. The analogy to financial debt has mostly served us well. It has enabled technical people to engage with business stakeholders, who often have limited technical knowledge, and it has allowed those stakeholders to understand a complex issue sufficiently well to make reasoned decisions. However, the analogy has served us less well in areas where it breaks down, or where we have extended the analogy too far.

The technical debt analogy lulls us into thinking of it as a mainly technical problem. However, it is primarily a **trade-off problem**, where we trade taking on debt in return for new features, earlier delivery, or lower immediate cost.

If we want to address the problem of too much debt, then we need to begin by understanding how we make trade-off decisions and how this leads to decisions sometimes being suboptimal. After reading this book, you know that we make decisions using the affect heuristic. Unfortunately, this heuristic works entirely in our subconscious, so there are ample opportunities for it to be distorted, without us ever realizing those distortions even happened.

Technical debt is also a **systems problem**. Those individuals making trade-off decisions do not make them within a vacuum. Rather, they make them within a system, which we usually term an organization. They occupy a role within that system, and the demands of that role also cause distortions to that trade-off decision.

Individuals occupying a role may well know that their decision will result in some very expensive debt that will be bad for the organization. However, they also know that they are being judged to deliver a project by a certain date with limited resources, so they will trade debt in pursuit of what they are being judged by.

One of the reasons our technical debt problem has proved so intractable is that it is a **wicked problem**, which combines with the social complexity of our organizations to produce fragmented groups that battle with each other.

However, despite all these complications, we *can* put together a program to manage our technical debt and thereby extend the life of our very expensive software systems. We can raise understanding of the nature of technical debt and its causes. We can educate people on how to make better decisions, plus we can change their decision landscape, so that they are nudged toward those better decisions. And we can restructure our organizations and processes, so that people are less inclined to create technical debt that is difficult and expensive to pay down.

These changes are neither easy nor assured. Remember, that many change initiatives fail to achieve all intended goals. This is because, in the words of Machiavelli, "There is nothing more difficult, perilous, or uncertain than to introduce change." Hence, we should take advantage of all that we know about managing change, plus use a recognized change management process.

However, while managing technical debt is not easy, it is both possible and desirable. *You should do it*. You should put together a program to reduce and then control your technical debt. By doing this, you can extend the life of your systems by 50% or even more, plus get a whole lot more out of those systems during their lifetime.

You'll gain enormous benefit from this. Firstly, you'll gain significant savings from those lifetime extensions. IT development already consumes a large proportion of your organization's budget. As software becomes ever more ubiquitous, with technologies like AI reaching into areas we have not previously imagined, that proportion will only increase.

Secondly, you'll benefit by focusing more on your business, since you'll face less disruption from major IT projects.

Thirdly, you'll benefit from reduced risk. IT and software projects are *risky*. Many projects fail. If you have a system that's working and you can keep it working and extend its life by managing the debt, you should do so – it's *far* less risky for you.

Taming the dragon of technical debt will provide you with enormous advantages that you can leverage to do all those exciting things your organization wants.

In the introduction, I wished you the best of luck in your journey.

Now, I shall wish you courage in that journey!

Afterword by Mark Stringer

I have greatly enjoyed reading Andrew's book on technical debt. I have spent the last 15 years or so trying to manage software development projects. I've seen legacy projects become unmaintainable and unmodifiable because of technical debt. And for most of that time, I've agreed that technical debt is a bad thing, and we should definitely do something about it. However, until I'd read this book, I'd been mostly at a loss to know exactly what it is that I, my team, or senior management could do.

Now, I have a much better idea of what I can do about technical debt, and that partly comes from a better understanding what kind of thing that debt is and where it comes from.

One thing that Andrew does beautifully in this book is to take the metaphor that is being used frequently in business discussions, as if everybody knew what it meant and how it worked, then pointing out its problems. That metaphor is financial debt. Yes, we might think of the work that's needed to be done to tidy our code as being like money we owe. But if we're to take that metaphor to its full extreme, it's money we owe that we might never have to pay back, or we might have to pay back with brutally high interest rates. Or suddenly, without warning, technical debt can just put us out of business altogether.

By talking through technical debt in terms of systems thinking and modeling, he gives us an account of how technical debt works, why that metaphor of debt is only a partially helpful description, and why, if we continue to crank the technical debt creating handle, it can become so unpredictable and destructive. By offering us models that we can actually look at in modeling software, he actually gives us a chance to watch technical debt increase to the point where it passes the point of no return.

But for me, as a project manager who expects to have further projects to manage in my future, it's two other aspects of this book which are the most useful. Firstly, the account of technical debt in terms of the affect heuristic. This makes it clear that, although technical debt has technical symptoms and potentially catastrophic technical consequences, its causes are human and psychological. What aspects of software get developed and get the most resources and the most attention? It's aspects of software that stakeholders respond to most emotionally that get built. They are the ones than attract the most resources. It's the aspects that have the most "affect" – that produce the most emotion.

And of course, the corollary of this is that, if we want technical debt to be attended to, we need to manage affect as much as we can throughout the whole software development life cycle. From the point of view of project management, I can see that initial estimates of how long software is going to take, and also behavior around deadlines, particularly heroics around deadlines are danger points of high affect. These are dangerous technical debt creation opportunities. If we can manage them out of the process of software development, we can have less technical debt and fewer of the problems that it brings with it.

The second thing of keen interest to any working project manager is Andrew's account of what a practical attempt to reduce existing technical debt, on any software development project, in any organization, would look like. It's one thing to establish that you're an authority on the cause of a problem, and I have no doubt that Andrew achieves that in this book. It's quite another to persuade the reader that you are any kind of authority on the solution. And I think he achieves this by being measured about his claims for authority. For me, what makes this more persuasive is that he's very clear that we must do this safely. He recommends a full program of change, and he walks us step by step through how that would work. He's clear that this is what's required if we are to have any chance of reversing the level of technical debt.

Appendix

This appendix contains details of activities and techniques used by a programmer to tackle technical debt. Some items in the appendix may be included as downloadable assets in GitHub.

Chapter 13 Resources

The following are the resources referred to in Chapter 13.

The Corporate Marshmallow Test

1. Imagine that one of the projects in your organization faces the following conundrum.

A developer on the project has encountered an unexpected piece of technical debt. This debt was not anticipated in the original project plans and estimation. It would be a significant effort to correct it, adding perhaps 10% to the development time. The project is currently on schedule but with little slack in the plan.

The developer indicated there is a workaround, which will be much quicker, perhaps adding less than 1% to development time. However, this approach will not only leave the existing debt, but will add to it.

How likely do you think it is that the project will decide to fully address the technical debt, adding 10% to the development time?

Definitely not	Highly unlikely	More unlikely than not	Equally likely and unlikely	More likely than not	Highly likely	Definitely
1	2	3	4	5	6	7

2. You now have some more information about that debt.

The developer tells you it is obvious that the code has been problematic for some time. Source control records show that it has been picked up and modified by previous projects, who have left the problem for a later project to address.

Given this new information, how likely do you think it is that the project will decide to fully address the technical debt, adding 10% to the development time?

APPENDIX

Definitely not	Highly unlikely	More unlikely than not	Equally likely and unlikely	More likely than not	Highly likely	Definitely
1	2	3	4	5	6	7

3. Imagine that, instead of the project being approximately on schedule, it is significantly behind schedule, partly because the project has encountered several similar technical debt issues that it has invested time fixing.

Given this new information, how likely do you think it is that the project will decide to fully address the technical debt, adding 10% to the development time?

Definitely not	Highly unlikely	More unlikely than not	Equally likely and unlikely	More likely than not	Highly likely	Definitely
1	2	3	4	5	6	7

Technical Debt Register Questionnaire

1. Do you have a technical debt register?
2. Do you know if it is kept up-to-date?
3. Do you know if it is accurate?
4. Do you know if items in the register are worked upon?
5. What do you think is the purpose of the technical debt register?
6. In what ways is it helpful for the organization to have a technical debt register?
7. In what ways is it unhelpful?

How and Why Did We Acquire This Debt?

Remember: this questionnaire is equally relevant to technical personnel, such as developers and architects, as well as non-technical personnel, such as stakeholders. Therefore, if someone raises what you think is a particularly interesting story, do check with others, particularly those from a different discipline, about the item in that story.

Please, could you imagine for me an item of technical debt in your system? Something that is representative/interesting/large/involved many others.

1. Can you describe to me that debt?
2. How did it come about?
3. What were the circumstances of its creation?
4. Were other options considered?
   - If so, what options?
   - If not, what was the reason other options were not considered?
5. Was the issue discussed with others?
   - If so, who?
   - Was the disagreement about the course of action?
   - How was consensus reached?

Moving on,

1. Where do you feel technical debt is being created and destroyed?
2. What do you feel are the main drivers, causing technical debt in our organization?
3. Is there anything that could be done that would be easy to implement and would lead to a reduction in technical debt?

Organizational Pain Points

1. Do you feel the system is becoming more prone to defects?
2. Do you feel your system is becoming prone to *certain types* of defects?
3. If so, what type of defects?
4. Are customers making more change requests?
5. Does it appear to take longer for development to implement changes or make fixes?

APPENDIX

6. Are you ever surprised at the estimated effort to implement what appears to be a small change or rectify an apparently small defect?

7. Do changes seem to go through several cycles of testing and bug fixing before they are released?

What Code-Related Technical Debt Is Out There?

1. Do you use any static analysis tools, to check code quality? (e.g., SonarQube)

2. To what extent would you say that within the code base there are portions of unnecessarily complex code?

3. Do you routinely conduct code reviews?

4. If so, can you describe the process to me?

5. Are there some areas of the code base that are particularly difficult to maintain?

6. How are defects related to different areas of the code base?

    - Are there some areas that are particularly buggy?
    - If so, why? For example, are they particularly complex areas, areas with lots of interconnections, or some other reason?

7. Are particular areas of the system targeted by developers?

8. If you need to implement a small change, how many locations in the code would you be likely to have to touch?

9. In which area do developers spend most of their time working?

What Architecture-Related Technical Debt Is There?

Architecture-related questions are, somewhat unsurprisingly, most fruitfully directed toward the system architects or senior developers. Non-technical people are generally unlikely to have been present in the types of meetings or conversations where architectural decisions were discussed or made.

1. Are there many examples of where the system architecture suffers a lack of modularity?
2. Does the original design have lots of options and flexibility that were never exploited?
3. Does the original design lack options and flexibility that would have been useful?
4. Looking at the present system design, are there any decisions that you or others made that you would have made differently today?
5. If so, what aspects of those decisions?
6. How much time was spent exploring alternate architectures?
7. When exploring or examining a potential architecture choice, do you have a set of checklist questions to guide exploration?

Are We Firefighting Our Way into Debt?

Begin by describing what firefighting is. For example:

Firefighting is a type of management that applies a reactive and corrective approach to every problem that occurs. It de-prioritizes or ignores the planning and priorities previously established because the management team have a feeling of urgency to react to problems as they arise.

Now ask suitable questions from the list below:

1. What percentage of your time do you feel is spent on work that is reacting to events, rather than work that is preplanned?
2. Do you have time to carry out tasks that are deemed not essential but nevertheless useful for the organization?
3. How is firefighting viewed within your organization? For example, is it admired, normalized, discouraged, investigated, and remedied, or something else?
4. How are firefighters viewed in your organization?
5. Is the cause of the need to firefight ever investigated?

APPENDIX

6. If so, how often is that cause found to be actions taken in a previous firefighting event?

7. Is the development team unable to carry out work not deemed essential for code delivery, for example, creation of unit tests?

8. Is the test team unable to create an automation suite, because they are too busy testing each release as it comes?

9. Does your management team regularly engage in firefighting, thereby depriving junior team members of the opportunity to develop skills and experience in difficult situations?

10. When recruiting for a role, does your organization often need to recruit externally, because internal candidates lack skills, experience, or aptitude?

Questions to Identify Anti-patterns

Listed as follows are the common anti-patterns identified earlier, together with example questions.

Anti-pattern	Question
Estimation trap	Do you routinely find that projects in your organization are routinely underestimated? If so, by how much?
Last race of the day	<Describe the "last race of the day effect" to the interviewee, then ask, "Does this occur in your organization?">
Moral credential effect	Have you found that projects that addressed items of technical debt in early project phases are feeling "virtuous" and justified to subsequently leave behind some technical debt?
Broken window effect and learned helplessness	Do you feel that visible examples of technical debt or bad coding in the system have encouraged others to do the same? Do you feel that a failure to fix issues that have been reported has later led to passive resignation by some team members?

(*continued*)

Anti-pattern	Question
Goal culture	Do you feel that the organization has an excessive focus upon measurable goals?
Social loafing	Do you feel that some individuals exert less effort toward group goals or helping other team members, so that they can conserve effort and resource for their own personal goals? How common is this?
OKR and the surrogation effect	Do you believe that there is an excessive focus on Objectives and Key Results? Has this led to a focus on measured objectives, to the detriment of items that are less easy to measure? Has any excessive focus on OKRs lead to any adverse consequences? If so, can you give an example?
Descent into firefighting	(Already covered)
Limited environments	Are there generally sufficient environments for the organization's development program? If not, what consequences has this led to?
Prototype into debt	Does your organization tend to produce prototypes? If so, is the prototype thrown away at the end of the prototyping process, so that an entirely new version is created for production or release? If the prototype is not thrown away but instead it is used, does technical debt in the prototype often get into the production or release version?

Understanding Trade-Offs

Before any discussion about trade-offs, start with an explanation such as:

"For most people when they are making decisions, they are usually making some sort of trade-off decision, whether they are trading off the benefits and disadvantages of one option against other options, often in a situation of uncertainty, where they might not know all relevant details about the situation, or indeed the options."

APPENDIX

"I'm trying to understand what trade-offs you may have faced and how you decided them."

"Think about a specific piece of work that involved some kind of trade-off."

1. Can you tell me about the trade-off you faced?
2. How did you evaluate the different possibilities?
3. What caused you to decide in the way that you did?
4. What would have caused you to decide differently?

You are also interested in trade-offs that people may make between benefits for the organization overall, the team they are in, and personal benefits. However, most of us find this difficult to answer truthfully.

One solution is to ask people to answer not for themselves, but what they have observed others do in the organization. This leverages, to a certain extent, a bias that is known as the bias blind spot, which is where we can clearly see a bias or shortcoming in others but are blind to that bias or shortcoming in ourselves.

1. Tell me about decisions made within the organization in general. I'm interested to learn how individuals balance organizational needs, those of the team, and themselves. Can you give me an example of a decision where others have had to make those balances, and what they did about it?

Understanding Your System

Sketch out your understanding of the system/organizational chart/process. Show it to the interviewee and then get their feedback. Use the following questions as prompts:

1. In what way is this sketch correct?
2. In what way is it wrong?
3. What have I missed out? Anything else?
4. Can you walk me through what happens here?
5. Where do the problems occur?

6. What are the most complicated parts of this process?

7. Is there anyone else I should speak to?

8. Is anything you think I may have missed?

Chapter 14 Resources

The following are the resources referred to in Chapter 14.

Workshop Checklist

Use this checklist **before** running your workshop:

1. Goal: Have you communicated a clear goal for this workshop? (See "Agenda" section, Chapter 14.)

2. Attendees:

    - Have you identified and invited all attendees?

    - Have you received a reply or commitment from each person to attend?

    - Have you considered possible factions and political camps of attendees?

3. Is the room(s) booked for the date/time required?

4. Is the room(s) appropriate for your needs?

5. Have you ensured the room will have the necessary facilities and materials (projector and connections, whiteboards and pens, post-its)?

6. Have you prepared and distributed an agenda?

7. Have you checked or tested that agenda for approximate timings?

8. If the workshop will be breaking into small groups, have you considered the composition of those groups, so that it will support your goal?

APPENDIX

9. Do you require a co-facilitator or assistant? Are they booked?
10. Do you have your presentation material ready?
11. Do you have any handouts ready?
12. Have you had a dry run through of all material that can be trialled?

Additional Useful Techniques

Note that many of the liberating structures are also available on their website: www.liberatingstructures.com/.

You may find the following techniques useful in this workshop:

- TRIZ (Liberating Structures, Red Teams)
- User experience fishbowl. Useful for getting different specialisms to share their experiences and worldviews with other specialisms. (Liberating Structures)
- Devil's advocacy (Red Teams)
- Key assumptions check (Red Teams)

Chapter 16 Resources

The following are the resources referred to in Chapter 16.

Workshop Checklist

Use this checklist **before** running your workshop:

1. Have you identified and invited all attendees?
2. Have you received a reply or commitment from each person to attend?
3. Is the room(s) booked for the date/time required?
4. Is the room(s) appropriate for your needs?

5. Have you ensured the room will have the necessary facilities and materials (projector and connections, whiteboards and pens, post-its)?

6. Have you prepared and distributed your agenda?

7. Have you checked or tested that agenda for approximate timings?

8. Do you require a co-facilitator or assistant? Are they booked?

9. Are you using any workshop team members to deliver relevant parts of the workshop/presentation? If so, are they prepared and have you had a dry run with them?

10. Do you have your presentation material ready?

    - Outputs from previous workshop? (to Recap and Update)
    - Findings from further investigations (to Recap and Update)
    - Summary of analysis work, including stakeholder feedback (to Recap and Update)
    - All other slides

11. Have you had a dry run through of all material that can be trialled?

References

Ackoff, R (1974). "Redefining the Future." Wiley: London.

Ali, M. (1977). "Probability and utility estimates for racetrack bettors." Journal of Political Economy. 85 (4): 803–815.

Ariely, D. (2009). "Predictably Irrational: The Hidden Forces that Shape Our Decisions." HarperCollins.

Banja, J. (2010) "The normalization of deviance in healthcare delivery." Business Horizons, 53 (2).

Barrett, D. (2010). "Supernormal Stimuli." W. W. Norton & Company.

Barrett, L., Dunbar, R., Lycett, J. (2002). "Human evolutionary psychology.. Palgrave.

Baumeister, R. F., et al., eds. (2007). "Encyclopaedia of Social Psychology." Thousand Oaks, CA: Sage.

Bentley, J., Toth, M. (2020) "Exploring Wicked Problems: What They Are and Why They Are Important." Archway Publishing.

de Bono, E. (2006). "De Bono's Thinking Course: Powerful Tools to Transform Your Thinking." BBC Active.

Brooks, F. P. (1965) "The Mythical Man Month." Addison-Wesley.

Brown, G., McLean, I., McMillan. A. (2018). "The Concise Oxford Dictionary of Politics and International Relations (Oxford Quick Reference)."

Buchanan, R. (1992). "Wicked Problems in Design Thinking." Design Issues, 8 (2). MIT Press.

Buss, D. (2017). "Evolutionary Psychology: The New Science of the Mind." Psychology Press; 5th edition.

REFERENCES

Chesterton, G. K. (1929). "The Thing: Why I am a Catholic." Sheed & Ward; Reprint edition (1 Jan. 1957).

Coase, R. (1960). "The Problem of Social Cost." Journal of Law and Economics. 3 (1): 1–44.

Conklin, J. (2006). "Dialogue mapping: building shared understanding of wicked problems." Wiley.

Conklin, J. (2001). "Wicked problems & social complexity." From https://cognexus.org/wpf/wickedproblems.pdf

Coram, R. (2002). "Boyd: The Fighter Pilot Who Changed the Art of War." New York: Little, Brown.

Covey, S. (2020). "The 7 Habits of Highly Effective People." Simon & Schuster UK; Reissue edition.

Cunningham, W. (1992). "The WyCash Portfolio Management System." Presented at OOPSLA 1992, Vancouver.

Dagstuhl seminar 16162 (2016). Avgeriou, P., Kruchten, P., Ozkaya, I., Seaman, C. "Managing technical debt in software engineering."

Damasio, A. (2006). "Descartes' Error: Emotion, Reason and the Human Brain." Vintage.

Dekker, S. (2011). "Drift into Failure: From Hunting Broken Components to Understanding Complex Systems." CRC Press.

Diamond, J. (2004). "Collapse: How Societies Choose to Fail or Succeed." Viking Pr.

Duncker, K. (1945). "On problem-solving." (L. S. Lees, Trans.). Psychological Monographs, 58 (5), i–113.

Eisenhardt, K. (1989), "Agency Theory: An Assessment and Review." The Academy of Management Review, 14 (1): 57–74.

Epstein, S. (1994). "Integration of the cognitive and the psychodynamic unconscious." American Psychologist, 49, 709–724.

Fitzpatrick, R., Hunt, D. (2019). "The Workshop Survival Guide: How to design and teach educational workshops that work every time." Independently published.

Fowler, M. "Technical debt quadrant." www.martinfowler.com/bliki/TechnicalDebt.html

Frank, R. (2008) "The Economic Naturalist: Why Economics Explains Almost Everything." Virgin Books.

Gaulin, S., DcBurney, D. (2003). "Evolutionary Psychology." Pearson; 2nd edition.

Gentner, D. (2002). "Analogy in Scientific Discovery: The Case of Johannes Kepler." In "Model-Based Reasoning: Science, Technology, Values." L. Magnani (Editor), N.J. Nersessian. Springer.

Gentner, D., Bren, S., Ferguson, R., Markman, A., Levidow, B., Wolff, P., Forbus, K. (1997). "Analogical Reasoning and Conceptual Change: A Case Study of Johannes Kepler." The Journal of the Learning Sciences, 6 (1): 3–40.

Gick, M., Holyoak, K. (1980) "Analogical Problem Solving." Cognitive Psychology 12, 306–355.

Grint, K. (2008). "Wicked Problems and Clumsy Solutions: The Role of Leadership." Clinical Leader, Volume I, Number II. BAMM Publications.

Hamilton, P. (2016). "The Workshop Book: How to design and lead successful workshops." Pearson Business.

Hardin, G. (1968). "The Tragedy of the Commons." Science. 162 (3859).

Harvard Business Review. (2011). "HBR's 10 Must Reads on Change Management." Harvard Business Review Press.

Hiatt, J. (2006). "ADKAR: A Model for Change in Business, Government and our Community." Prosci Learning Center Publications.

Highmore Sims, H. (2006). "How to Run a Great Workshop: The Complete Guide to Designing and Running Brilliant Workshops and Meetings." Pearson Business.

Horn, R (2001). "Knowledge Mapping for Complex Social Messes." Presentation to the "Foundations in the Knowledge Economy," David and Lucile Packard Foundation.

Hsee, C. "The Evaluability Hypothesis: An Explanation for Preference Reversals between Joint and Separate Evaluations of Alternatives." Organizational behavior and human decision processes, 67 (3), September 1996, pp. 247–257.

Hsee, C., Loewenstein, G. F., Blount, S., Bazerman, M. H. (1999). "Preference Reversals Between Joint and Separate Evaluations of Options: A Review and Theoretical Analysis." Psychological Bulletin 1999, 125 (5), 576–590.

REFERENCES

Johnson, D., Blumstein, D., Fowler, J., Haselton, M. (2013). "The evolution of error: error management, cognitive constraints, and adaptive decision-making biases." Trends in Ecology & Evolution August 2013, 28 (8).

Jones, M. (1998). "The Thinker's Toolkit: 14 Powerful Techniques for Problem Solving." Three Rivers Press (CA).

Kahn, A. (1966). "The Tyranny of Small Decisions: Market Failures, Imperfections, and the Limits of Economics." Kyklos. 19: 23–47.

Kahneman, D. (2011). "Thinking, Fast and Slow." Farrar, Straus and Giroux.

Kahneman, D., Tversky, A. (1979). "Prospect Theory: An Analysis of Decision under Risk." Econometrica. 47 (2): 263–291.

Klein, G. (2007). "Performing a Project Premortem." Harvard Business Review.

Kniberg, H. (2015). "Scrum and XP from the Trenches – 2nd Edition." `https://lulu.com`

Koller, T., Manyika, J., Ramaswamy, S. "The Case Against Corporate Short-Termism." Milken Institute Review. `www.milkenreview.org/articles/the-case-against-corporate-short-termism`

Kopelman, S., Weber, M., Messick, D. (2002). "Factors Influencing Cooperation in Commons Dilemmas: A Review of Experimental Psychological Research." In Ostrom, E., et al. (eds.). The Drama of the Commons. Washington, D.C. National Academy Press. Ch. 4., 113–156.

Kotter, J. (2012). "Leading Change." Harvard Business Review Press.

Kravitz, D., Barbara, M. (1986). "Ringelmann rediscovered: The original article." Journal of personality and social psychology. 50 (5): 936–9441.

Kreuter MW, De Rosa C, Howze EH, Baldwin GT (2004). "Understanding wicked problems: a key to advancing environmental health promotion." Health Educ Behav.; 31 (4): 441–454.

Kruchten, P., Nord, R., Ozkaya, I. (2019). "Managing technical debt." Addison-Wesley.

Kunz, W., Rittel, H. (1970). "Issues as elements of information systems." Institute of Urban and Regional Development, University of California, Berkeley.

Landsberg, S. (2012). "The Armchair Economist: Economics & Everyday Life." Simon & Schuster UK.

Levitt, S., Dubner, S. (2006). "Freakonomics: A Rogue Economist Explores the Hidden Side of Everything." Penguin.

Liddell Hart, B. (1944). "Thoughts on war." Faber and Faber.

Lipmanowicz, H., McCandless, K. (2014). "The Surprising Power of Liberating Structures: Simple Rules to Unleash a Culture of Innovation." Liberating Structures Press.

Little, J. (2014). "Lean Change Management: Innovative practices for managing organizational change." Happy Melly Express.

Lloyd, W. (1833). "Two lectures on the checks to population." Available at JSTOR.

Lustig, R. (2009). "Sugar: The Bitter Truth". University of California Television, May 26, 2009; July 20, 2009. www.uctv.tv/shows/Sugar-The-Bitter-Truth-16717

Manns, M. L., Rising, L. (2005). "Fearless Change." Pearson.

Mainelli, M., Harris, I. (2014). "The Price of Fish: A New Approach to Wicked Economics and Better Decisions." Nicholas Brealey Publishing.

McDonald, A. (2012). "Truths, Lies and O-Rings: Inside the Space Shuttle Challenger Disaster." University Press of Florida.

McGlothlin, W. (1956). "Stability of choices among uncertain alternatives." American Journal of Psychology. 69 (4): 604-615.

Meadows, D. (2008). Thinking in Systems: A primer. Chelsea Green Publishing.

Miller, G. (2000). "The Mating Mind." Vintage Books.

Mischel, W. (2015). "The Marshmallow Test." Corgi.

Moore, G (2014). Crossing the chasm. Harper Business; 3rd edition.

Nesse, R., Williams, G. (1996). "Why We Get Sick: The New Science of Darwinian Medicine." Vintage Books.

Nuland, S. (2004). "The Doctors' Plague: Germs, Childbed Fever, and the Strange Story of Ignac Semmelweis (Great Discoveries)." W. W. Norton & Company.

Norris, P., Epstein, S. (2014). "An Experiential Thinking Style: Its Facets and Relations with Objective and Subjective Criterion Measures." Journal of Personality 79 (5), October 2011.

O'Donnell, E. (2003). "Ship Ablaze: The Tragedy of the Steamboat General Slocum." Crown; Reprint edition.

REFERENCES

Obesity systems map. www.gov.uk/government/publications/reducing-obesity-obesity-system-map

Odum, W., E. (1982). "Environmental degradation and the tyranny of small decisions." BioScience, 32 (9); October 1982; pp. 728–729.

Ohno, T. (1988). "Toyota production system: Beyond large-scale production." Productivity press.

Okrent, D. (2010). "Last Call: The Rise and Fall of Prohibition." Scribner.

Oxford Quick Reference: "The Concise Oxford Dictionary of Politics and International Relations." See Brown, G. (2018).

Perrow, C. (1999). "Normal Accidents – Living with High Risk Technologies – Updated Edition (Princeton Paperbacks)." Princeton University Press.

Pherson, R. H., Heuer, R. J. (2020). "Structured Analytic Techniques for Intelligence Analysis." CQ Press; Third edition.

Prochaska, J. O., DiClemente, C. C. (1984). "The transtheoretical approach: crossing traditional boundaries of therapy." Dow Jones-Irwin.

Pusey, A., Packer, C. (1994). "Infanticide in lions." In Parmigiani, S. vom Saal, F.S. (eds.). Infanticide and Parental Care. Harwood Academic Press, Chur, Switzerland.

Read, D., Antonides, G., van den Ouden, L. and Trienekens, H. (2001) "Which is better: simultaneous or sequential choice?" Organizational Behavior and Human Decision Processes, 84 (1). pp. 54–70.

Reason, J. (1991). "Human Error." Cambridge University Press.

Red Team Handbook (2019). UFMCS, University of Foreign Military and Cultural Studies. At time of printing, it was available at this URL: https://usacac.army.mil/sites/default/files/documents/ufmcs/The_Red_Team_Handbook.pdf

Repenning, N. (2001). "Understanding firefighting in new product development." Journal of Product Innovation Management, 18 (5).

Repenning, N., P., Sterman, J. (2001) "Nobody ever gets credit for fixing problems that never happened." California Management Review, 43 (4).

Ridgway V.F. (1956). "Dysfunctional consequences of performance measurements." Administrative Science Quarterly, 1 (2) (Sep., 1956), pp. 240–247.

Ridley, M. (1994). "The Red Queen." Penguin Books.

Ridley, M. (1999). "Genome." Harper Perennial.

Ries, E. (2011). "Lean Startup." Portfolio Penguin; 1st edition.

Ritchey, T. (2013). "Wicked Problems: Modelling Social Messes with Morphological Analysis." Swedish Morphological Society. AMG 2 (1).

Rittel, H., Webber, M. (1973). "Dilemmas in a General Theory of Planning." Policy Sciences. 4 (2): 155–169.

Spaniel, W. (2011). "Game Theory 101: The Complete Textbook." CreateSpace Independent Publishing Platform.

Sapolsky, R. (2017). "Behave." Vintage Digital; 1st edition.

Seligman M. E. (1972). "Learned helplessness." Annual Review of Medicine. 23 (1): 407–412.

Semmelweis, Ignaz (1983) [1861]. "Etiology, Concept and Prophylaxis of Childbed Fever." Translated by Carter, K. Codell. University of Wisconsin Press.

Senge, P. (2006 2nd ed). "The Fifth Discipline: The art and practice of the learning organization." Random House Business.

Slovic, P., Finucane, M., Peters, E., MacGregor, P. (2007). "The affect heuristic." European Journal of Operational Research 177, 1333–1352.

Snook, S. (2002). "Friendly Fire – The Accidental Shootdown of U.S. Black Hawks over Northern Iraq." Princeton University Press; Revised edition.

Snowdon, D., Blignaut, S., Goh, Z., Greenberg, R., Bertsch, B., Borchardt, S. (2022). "Cynefin – Weaving Sense-Making into the Fabric of Our World." Cognitive Edge – The Cynefin Co.

Spolsky, J. (2004). "Joel on Software: And on Diverse and Occasionally Related Matters That Will Prove of Interest to Software Developers, Designers, and Managers, and to ... or Ill Luck, Work with Them in Some Capacity." Apress.

Sterman, J. (2000). "Business dynamics." Irwin McGraw-Hill.

Sutherland, R. (2019). "Alchemy: The Surprising Power of Ideas That Don't Make Sense." WH Allen.

REFERENCES

Technopedia: www.techopedia.com/definition/27913/technical-debt

Thaler, R. (2009). "Nudge: Improving Decisions About Health, Wealth and Happiness." Penguin; 1st edition.

Thaler, R. (1981). "Some Empirical Evidence on Dynamic Inconsistency." Economics Letters. 8 (3): 201–207.

Truman, H. https://quotefancy.com/harry-s-truman-quotes (One handed economist quote).

UK government Treasury Green book. www.gov.uk/government/publications/the-green-book-appraisal-and-evaluation-in-central-government/the-green-book-2020

Vaughn, D. (2016). "The Challenger Launch Decision: Risky Technology, Culture, and Deviance at NASA, Enlarged Edition." University of Chicago Press.

von Clausewitz, C. (1832). "On War."

Watkins, A., Wilbur, K. (2021). "Wicked & Wise: How to Solve the World's Toughest Problems (Wicked & Wise Series)." Complete Coherence Ltd.

Weinberg G., M. (1986). "Becoming a Technical Leader." Dorset House Publishing.

Wilson, J., Kelling, G. (1982). "Broken Windows." www.theatlantic.com.

World Health Authority (2023). "WHO acceleration plan to stop obesity." ISBN: 978-92-4-007563-4. www.who.int/publications/i/item/9789240075634

Yudkin, J. (1972). "Pure, white and deadly." Penguin Books.

Index

A

Accident investigation, 26, 27, 226, 229, 235
Addiction, 47–53
Additional cost, 20
Affect heuristic, 4, 55, 58, 257, 260, 270
    affective impression, 58, 68
    affective system, 59
    characteristics, 58, 59
    dimension, 68
    precision and valence, 68–71
    rational system, 58, 59
Alchemy, 311, 318
Ali, M., 165
Analogy, 36
    alternative, 44
        addiction, 47–50
        environmental pollution, 46
        friction, 50
        obesity, 44–46
    characteristics, 39, 40
        familiarity, 39
        representativeness, 39
    explanatory power, 40
    familiarity/accuracy quadrant, 40
    power of analogy, 37–39
    predictive power, 40
    quadrant analysis, 51, 52
    rethinking, 42, 43
    suitability analysis tool, 41, 52, 53
    why we use them, 36, 37
Ancestral past, 57–59, 78

Anti-patterns, 155, 156, 243, 250, 258, 264, 270, 293
    broken windows theory, 169, 170
    definition, 156
    descent into firefighting, 176–178
    estimation trap, 160–165, 181
    goal culture, 170, 171
    intervention point, 157, 159
    last race of the day, 165–167
    learned helplessness, 169, 170
    leverage point, 157, 252
    limited environment, 178, 179
    moral credential effect, 168
    OKRs and the surrogation effect, 173–176
    prototype into debt, 179, 180
    social loafing, 171–173
Argument mapping, 152, 233, 267, 274, 305, 306
Ariely, D., 128
Astronomical clock, 35
Auxiliary activities (auxiliary work), 81, 102–104, 177, 178
Auxiliary work, *see* Auxiliary activities (auxiliary work)

B

Backfire effect, 234
Beer distribution game, 264, 274
Bergman, I., 70, 76
Bid process, 99
Bogart, H., 70, 76

BOHICA, 323
Bounded rationality, 111
Box, G., 184
Brittle software, 37, 42, 43
Broken analogy, 5, 6, 10, 31, 35–54, 111, 139, 150, 332
Broken windows theory, 22, 159, 169–170
Brooks, F., 28

C

Casablanca, 70
Cattle herders, 117, 124, 244
    See also Tragedy of the commons
Causal loop diagrams (CLD), 155, 157–159, 165, 264, 270, 281, 293
Challenger launch decision, 70–71, 77, 125, 126, 131, 149
Change management, 29–30, 228, 320, 321, 333
Change management models, 321
    ADKAR Change Management Model, 321
    Kotter's eight step transformation process model, 321
    Lean change, 321
    McKinsey 7-S Framework, 321
Chesterton's fence, 24, 297, 302, 303
Childbed fever, 220–222
Child day care center, 128, 129
CLD, *see* Causal loop diagrams (CLD)
Climate change, 136, 151
Coase, R., 120
Coase theorem, 121, 122
Collapse (overshoot and collapse), 82, 124, 125, 178, 206
    See also Overshoot and collapse
Confidence limit, 21

Confirmation bias, 146
Conklin, J., 138, 145
Corporate marshmallow test (Marshmallow test), 243–245, 337, 338
Corpse particles, 225
Covey, S., 229
Crazy risk taking, 74, 75
Creeping normality, 112, 123, 125, 126, 131, 132, 151, 265
Cunningham, W., 3
Cynefin framework, 311, 318

D

de Bono, E., 302
Decision-making capability
    origins, 56
    subconscious, 57, 58
Delayed gratification, 243–245, 253
Descent into firefighting, 176–178, 264
Design problem, 148
Devil's Advocate, 282
Dialogue mapping, 133, 152, 153, 233, 235, 305–306
Diamond, J., 100, 125
Dichotomy of design, 147–150, 267
    what-can-be-done, 148
    what-ought-to-be, 148
Diversification bias, *see* Simultaneous *vs.* sequential decisions
DNA, 87
Drucker, P., 173, 209
Duncker, K., 37, 39, 54
Dycrasia, 222, 223
Dynamic model, 184, 185, 209
    See also System modeling tools
Dynamic modeling software, 143, 181, 183

E

Easter Island, 100, 125
Eat-your-own-dogfood, 114
Economic problems, 5, 110–133, 258, 270, 293
Economics/games theory layer, 8, 151
Eight step transformation process model, *see* Kotter's eight step transformation process model
Eisenhardt, K., 113
Eisenhower, D., 27
Environmental pollution, 44, 46, 47, 51, 52, 136, 137
Essential work, 177, 178
    See also Auxiliary work
Estimations, 21, 144, 160, 163
    error, 99
    trap, 160–165, 181, 264
Evil spirits, 149, 331
Evolutionary fitness, 56
Externalities, 46, 47, 98, 111, 112, 119, 130, 172, 230, 235, 265

F

Facilitated discussion, 152, 267, 289, 291, 296–297, 305, 308
Financial debt, 15, 24, 37, 39, 40, 42, 52, 54
Firefighting, 103–105, 124
    culture, 248
    definition, 248
    descend into, 249
    management style, 248
Fish in water parable, 96
Five whys technique, 26
Focus factor, 163
Fowler, M., 9, 24
Fragmentation, 135, 139–141, 147–149, 258, 266, 270, 293
    definition, 145
    hidden differences, 147
    visible differences, 147
Friction, 50–53, 193, 207, 208
Fundamental attribution error, 96

G

Gaze heuristic, 58, 59
General Slocum, 174, 180
Germ theory, 222
Gick, M., 41, 54
Goal culture, 170, 171
Goodhart's law, 173, 174
Gut feel, *see* Affect heuristic

H

Handwashing practice, 228
HMV, 18–20, 65, 120, 149, 160, 231, 278, 283, 284, 324
HMV Jukebox, 115, 283
Hsee, C., 67, 260, 262
Hyperbolic discounting, 76–78, 98, 103, 122, 150, 262

I

Imagine an alternative, 297, 328
Individuals constrained by role, 95–98, 263
Interest rate, 10, 11, 43
Iron Triangle, 208, 214
Irrational behavior, 74, 75, 116, 123, 130, 144, 161
iTunes, 19, 20

J

Joint and separate evaluation, 68
　　See also Precision and Valence

K

Kahn, A.E., 123
Kahneman, D., 74, 77, 185, 214
Kepler, J., 35–37, 44, 53, 146, 148
Keys, A., 227
Kniberg, H., 163
Kotter, J., 228, 319, 321, 330
Kotter's eight step transformation process model, 321
　　communicate the vision, 322, 325–327
　　consolidate improvements, 322, 328
　　create a vision, 322, 324
　　create short-term wins, 322, 328
　　empower others to act on the vision, 322, 327
　　establish a sense of urgency, 322, 323
　　form a powerful guiding coalition, 322, 324
　　institutionalize new approaches, 322, 329, 330
Krugman, P., 128

L

Last race of the day, 165–167, 264
Laws of planetary motion, 35, 36
Lean Startup, 311, 317
Learned helplessness, 147, 169–170
Liberating structures (book), 256, 261, 274, 296, 299, 300, 305
Liddell Hart, B, 304
Limited environments, 159, 178–179
Lloyd, W., 117

Loss leader, 100
Lowballing, 100

M

Machiavelli, N., 219, 220, 310, 319, 327, 330
Management by example, 323, 326
Marshmallow test, 233, 243–245, 253
　　See also Corporate marshmallow test (Marshmallow test)
Maternity clinic, 220, 221, 223
McGlothlin, W., 165
Meadows, D., 54, 83, 91, 101, 105, 263
Migraine, chronic, 149, 331
Mind map, 279, 281, 282
Missing information, 277–280
Monkey on your back (Passing the monkey), 111, 119, 131
Moral credential effect, 46, 168
Moral hazard, 112, 128, 129, 132, 151
Mortality rate, 220–223
Music dictionary, 67, 68, 70, 260

N

NASA, 16, 17, 71, 77, 126, 149
Netscape Navigator, 17–19
Newton, I., 36
9 Whys, 305
Non-linearities, 22
Normalization of deviance, 125
Nudge, 56, 60, 73, 77, 157

O

Obesity, 44–46, 51–53, 158, 180, 224, 227
OKRs and the surrogation effect, 173–176

One-handed economist, 134, 250
1-2-4-All technique, 261, 268, 297, 301, 303
On War, 50, 53, 207, 208
Organizational change fatigue, 323
O-ring failure, 71, 125
    See also Challenger launch decision
Overconfidence effect, 23, 146
Overdue projects, 74–77, 98, 99, 144
Overshoot and collapse, 81, 94, 95
    See also Collapse

P

Parent-offspring conflict, 86
Pareto efficient, 119
Passing the monkey, see Monkey on your back
Pasteur, L., 222
Past project data, 312–313
People problem, 230, 231
Perils of change, 319, 320
Pilot projects (Pilot solutions)
    agree goals, 314, 315
    analyze results & create report, 317
    dangers, 310, 311
    lessons learned, 317
    must we run one?, 312
    run pilot & gather information, 316
    select project, 315
    set timeline, 316
Pilot solution, see Pilot projects
Placenta, 86
    See also System, prohibition problem
Plus, Minus, Interesting (PMI), 302
Policy resistance, 104, 105
Political landscape, 277, 279, 287

Pollution, see Environmental pollution (Pollution)
PowerPoint, 258, 259, 291, 292
Precision and valence, 78–80, 262
    See also Affect heuristic, precision and valence
Predictability, 21
Predictably irrational, 128
Preference reversal, 68
    See also Precision and valence
Preliminary information gathering, 238
Pre-mortem technique, 262, 274
Price of anarchy, 112, 127
Principal-agent problem, 111, 112, 116, 265
    alignment of interests, 117
    asymmetric information, 113, 116
    collective action problem, 114, 116
    discrepancy of interests, 113
Prohibition problem, 89, 90, 95, 106, 135, 257, 263
Projections, 21
Project delivery, 21
Project tempo, 20, 21
Project underestimation, 49, 95, 97, 99, 100, 104, 181, 215, 263, 296
Prospect Theory, 74, 77, 161
Prototype into debt, 179, 180
Proximate cause, 25–27
    See also Ultimate cause

Q

Questionnaires, 253
    anti-patterns, 342, 343
    architecture-related debt, 340, 341
    code-related debt, 340
    corporate marshmallow test, 337, 338

Questionnaires (*cont.*)
    firefighting into debt, 341, 342
    how & why did we acquire?, 338, 339
    organizational pain points, 339, 340
    technical debt register, 338
    trade-offs, 343, 344
    understanding your system, 344, 345

R

Radiation problem, 38, 41, 54
Red Teams (book), 256, 268, 282, 287
Retrospectives, 317, 328
Ridgeway, V.F., 173
Risk appetite switch, 75, 77, 98, 161, 167
    See also Prospect theory
Rittel, H., 138
Rollout and stabilization, 239, 319–330
Rubber ducking, 282

S

Schedule recovery, 98–100
Schedules, 21
Screen envy, 279
Self-reinforcing loops, 22
Seligman, M.E., 170
Semmelweis, I., 220–226, 228, 229, 235, 278, 279
Semmelweis reflex, 224
Sensemaking, 283–286
Shakespeare, W., 95
Shared commitment, 147, 232, 233, 235
Shared understanding, 141, 147, 184, 212, 231, 232, 235, 238, 267
Sherlock Holmes, 246
Short-termism, 112, 121, 122, 130, 161
    infanticide within lions, 122

Silver bullet, 28, 29
Simulation models, 184, 188, 189, 199, 212, 253, 258, 277, 286, 287
    See also System modeling tools
Simultaneous *vs.* sequential decisions, 80, 118
    See also Tragedy of the commons
Simultaneous *vs.* sequential decisions, 73, 74, 262
Skull, drilling holes, 149, 331
Smith, A., 110
Smoking prevention programs, 62–64, 261
Social complexity, 136, 139, 141, 145–147, 149, 258, 266, 270, 293
Social contract, 128, 175
    pro-social activities, 129
    social norm, 129
Social dilemma, *see* Social trap
Social loafing, 171–173, 203, 210, 211, 264
Social trap (social dilemma), 112, 132
Software development lifecycle (SDLC), 11, 12
Space shuttle, 16
Space shuttle challenger, *see* Challenger launch decision
Stalin, J., 65
Surrogation effect, 173–175, 180
Survivorship bias, 129
Sutherland, Rory, 311, 318
System, 150, 262, 263, 293
    collapse, 94, 95
    definition, 83
    introducing change, 89, 90
    layer, 8
    overshoot, 94, 95
    patterns, 83, 84, 91
    placenta-Y chromosome conflict, 86–88, 263

problem, 5, 6, 332
prohibition problem, 89, 90
subsystem conflict, 86
subsystem goal pursuit, 85, 135
systems dynamics (*see* Systems dynamics)
understand, 251, 252
System modeling tools, 213–217
Systems dynamics, 263
    balancing behavior, 92, 93
    causal links, 91
    exponential growth, 92
    feedback loop, 91
    flows, 90
    goal-seeking, 93
    overshoot and collapse, 94, 95 (*see also* Overshoot and collapse)
    runaway system effect, 92
    stocks, 90
    variables, 91

T

Tame problem, 135–139, 141, 149, 151, 153
Technical debt
    architectural-related, 247, 248
    code-related, 247
    firefighting, 248, 249
    how acquired?, 246
    how much?, 245, 246
    pain points, 246, 247
Technical debt onion, 6, 260, 293
Technical debt quadrant, 9, 10, 24, 141
Technical debt register, 129, 130, 245, 246
    legitimised debt creation, 130
Technical layer, 7

Tempo, 20, 21
Thaler, R., 60, 76, 77
The Mythical Man Month, 28, 30, 180
Theory of gravitation, 36
The Prince, 219
The Seven Habits of Highly Effective People, 229
The Workshop Survival Guide, 272, 273
Thinking, Fast and Slow, 185, 214
Thinking in Systems, 54, 101, 105
Time constraints, 75
Tipping point, 22
Trade-off, 4, 150, 243, 251, 256
    decisions, 293
    layer, 7
    problem, 332
Tragedy of the commons, 112, 117, 118, 244, 265
Transtheoretical model of addiction treatment, 233
TRIZ, 297, 300, 304, 307
Truman, H., 134, 228, 250
Tyranny of small decisions, 112, 124

U

Ultimate cause, 25–27
    See also Proximate cause
Ulysses contracts, 72, 78, 80, 99, 118, 165, 262, 309
Underestimation, 25, 49, 183, 214, 215
    current project, 183
    subsequent projects, 183
Urgent
    and the important, 27
    urgency of technical debt, 27, 28

V

Valence, 66, 68–71
    See also Affect heuristic, precision and valence
Vaughan, D., 125
Vensim, 185, 186, 190, 197, 212, 263
Volkswagen, 126
    emissions scandal, 125
von Clausewitz, C., 50, 52, 53, 207, 208

W, X

Wallace, D.F., 96
Wealth of Nations, 110
Webber, M., 138
Weinberg, Gerald M., 278
Weinberg, G.M., 133, 134, 202, 231, 266
    people problem, 133, 134
What You See Is All There Is (WYSIATI), 185, 214
Wicked problem, 5, 129, 131, 240, 258, 266, 270, 293, 310, 311, 332
    characteristics
        circularity, wicked problems, 144
        interconnected problems, 144, 145
        no stopping rule, 145
        no test for solution, 142, 143
        no true-or-false, 141, 142
        one-shot attempt, 143, 144
        radically different worldviews, 140, 142
        solution, 139–142
    definition, 137
    dichotomy of design, 147–150
    economics, 150–151
    vs. evil, 137
    fragmentation, 145–147
    layer, 8
    social complexity, 145–147
    systems, 150–151
    vs. tame, 138
    technical debt, 151–152
    trade-offs, 150–151
Wicked questions, 297, 299, 300
Workshops
    agenda, 264, 269, 290, 307
    checklist, 345–347
    problem understanding, 238, 240, 256–276
    preparation, 269, 277, 306
    solution development, 239, 289
Workshop techniques, 297
    argument mapping, 306
    Chesterton's fence, 303
    imagine an alternative, 297
    Plus, Minus, Interesting (PMI), 302
    TRIZ, 300
    9 whys, 305
    wicked questions, 299
Worldview, 135

Y, Z

Y chromosome, 86, 87, 97
Yudkin, J., 227

GPSR Compliance

The European Union's (EU) General Product Safety Regulation (GPSR) is a set of rules that requires consumer products to be safe and our obligations to ensure this.

If you have any concerns about our products, you can contact us on

ProductSafety@springernature.com

In case Publisher is established outside the EU, the EU authorized representative is:

Springer Nature Customer Service Center GmbH
Europaplatz 3
69115 Heidelberg, Germany

www.ingramcontent.com/pod-product-compliance
Lightning Source LLC
LaVergne TN
LVHW080310260326
834688LV00038B/1043